RICHARD III.

VOL. II.

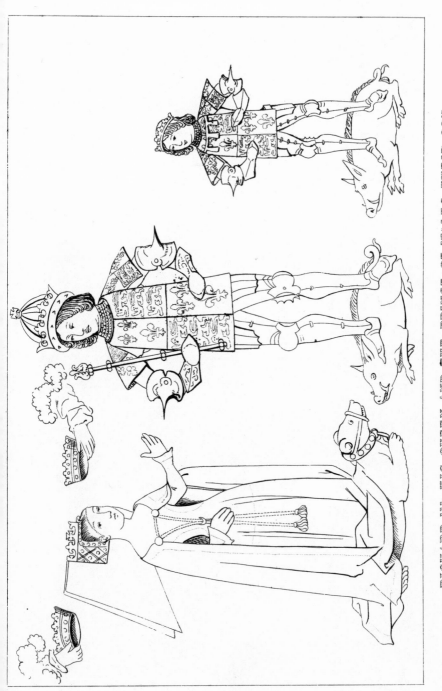

RICHARD III, HIS QUEEN AND THE PRINCE OF WALES THEIR SON.

RICHARD III.

AS

DUKE OF GLOUCESTER AND KING OF ENGLAND.

BY CAROLINE A. HALSTED,

AUTHOR OF THE "LIFE OF MARGARET BEAUFORT," AND "OBLIGATIONS OF LITERATURE
TO THE MOTHERS OF ENGLAND."

IN TWO VOLUMES.

VOL. II.

LONDON:

LONGMAN, BROWN, GREEN, AND LONGMANS,
PATERNOSTER-ROW.

Copyright © in reprint Alan Sutton 1977
First published 1844, this edition published
by Alan Sutton, Dursley, Gloucestershire

ISBN 0 904387 14 3

This edition contains a new index prepared
by Linda Miller

Printed in Great Britain by
REDWOOD BURN LIMITED
Trowbridge & Esher

Bound by Cedric Chivers Limited
Bath

CONTENTS

OF

THE SECOND VOLUME.

CHAPTER XI.

CHAP. XII.

CHAP. XIII.

CHAP. XIV.

CHAP. XV.

CHAP. XVI.

CHAP. XVII.

CHAP. XVIII.

CHAP. XIX.

CONTENTS

RICHARD THE THIRD,

AS DUKE OF GLOUCESTER, AND
KING OF ENGLAND.

CHAPTER XI.

The Duke of Gloucester in the north at the period of his brother's decease. — Edward V. proclaimed king. — State of affairs at the accession of the young monarch. — Gloucester takes the oath of allegiance, and exacts the same from all under his jurisdiction. — Divisions in the council. — Effect of these divisions on the conduct of Gloucester. — He hastens southward. — Seizes the person of the young king. — Imprisons the Lords Rivers and Grey. — Escorts Edward V. in state to London. — The Queen and her family take sanctuary at Westminster. — The Duke of Gloucester chosen "protector and defender of the realm" by the unanimous voice of the council and the senate.

RICHARD of Gloucester was with the army in the marches of Scotland, adjusting finally the differences in that district, previous to removing the soldiery for the contemplated invasion of France, when intelligence of King Edward's death was forwarded to him. Although that event so unforeseen, and in the ordinary course of things so little to have been anticipated, considering the age of the deceased monarch, was likely to produce a vast change in Gloucester's political position and future personal career, yet there is no reason to doubt

that the sorrow which he evinced at the announcement of the mournful occurrence, was otherwise
than genuine; for it was altogether consistent with
the affection and fidelity which he had, under adverse as well as prosperous circumstances, invariably testified for his royal brother.[1]

But, not only has the sincerity of his feelings on
this occasion been called in question, and the
respect which he immediately showed for the memory of the deceased monarch, in the strict observance of the religious offices enjoined by the
church, been imputed to hypocrisy and the most
hateful deception; but as if no death could occur
from natural causes during the reign of Edward IV.,
or be otherwise than hastened by the murderous
hands of Richard Duke of Gloucester[2], even that
of his royal brother, whom he had loved and served
with a devotion altogether remarkable, has been
attributed to poison administered by him. " They
who ascribe it to poison," observes King Edward's
biographer, " are the passionate enemies of Richard
Duke of Gloucester, who permit not nature at
that time to have been obnoxious to decay, but
make the death of every prince an act of violence
or practice ; and in regard this cruel lord was
guilty of much blood, without any other argument
condemn him for those crimes for which he was
actually most innocent." From this iniquitous
deed, the which has not however been generally
enumerated among the list of enormities laid to
Gloucester's charge, he is fully exculpated ; not

[1] Buck, lib. iii. p. 83.   [2] Habington, p. 222.

alone from his absence in the north during the
period of the late king's illness and death, and
from the true cause of his dissolution being clearly
established, but because unusual pains were taken
to prove to the civic authorities and the lords spiritual and temporal, that neither violence nor
unlawful means had accelerated their sovereign's
unlooked-for decease. Immediately after his death
he was placed on a board, naked from the waist
upwards; and partially unrobed, was so exposed
to the view both of friendly and of suspicious eyes
for the space of twelve hours[1]—a precaution rendered the more imperative from his demise occurring in the prime of life, and likewise from the
charge of poisoning being so common in those evil
and turbulent times.

The funeral of the deceased monarch was most
sumptuous, and befitting in all respects the splendour and magnificence which had characterised his
proceedings during life. He was interred at Windsor, in a chapel which he had there erected[2] ; and
his eldest son, aged twelve years and six months[3],
was forthwith proclaimed his successor by the
name and title of King Edward V.

Almost the last act performed by the deceased
king had been to assure to Gloucester, " to him

[1] Sandford, book v. p. 391.
[2] The full particulars of this imposing ceremony, together with a
description of the royal chapel at Windsor, are given by Sandford,—
copied from the original document preserved in the College of Arms,
—in his Geneal. Hist., book v. p. 392.—See also *Archæologia*, vol. i.
p. 348.
[3] Edward Prince of Wales was born in the Sanctuary at Westminster, 4th Nov., 1470 ; proclaimed king, April, 1483.

and the heirs of his body," by the authority of
parliament[1], the wardenship of the west marches
of England[2], together with the castle, city, town,
and lordship of Carlisle[3], 10,000 marks in ready
money, and such an extent of territory, and consequent increase of authority, in the north, where
he was already so popular, that this fact evinces,
far beyond any mere allegation or surmise, the absence of all jealousy on the king's part, and the
deserts of a prince who could be thus fearlessly
entrusted with almost unlimited power.

The amicable terms on which the two brothers
had ever continued may, in great measure, be attributed to the pacific conduct which Gloucester
observed towards the queen and her relatives.

A keen discernment of character, with the talent
of adapting that faculty to his own particular circumstances, as well as those of the times, was a
leading feature in Richard of Gloucester. It was,
indeed, the union of those valuable qualities, foresight and prudence, that preserved this prince in
all likelihood from the violent death of Clarence
and the untimely fate of Warwick; for Gloucester
possessed, in a remarkable degree, the power of
suppressing a display of hostile feelings in matters
where opposition would.have been futile.   Nevertheless, he had been no unobservant spectator of
the undue influence exercised by the royal Eliza-

---

[1] Rol. Parl., vi. p. 204.   [2] See Appendix A.

[3] Sir George Buck states, on the authority of an old MS. in the
possession of Sir Robert Cotton, that Gloucester had the "earldom
of Carlisle." "But whether he were Comes thereof, after the ancient
Roman understanding, that is, governor; or Comes, or count, after
the common taking it by us English, or others ; that is, for a special
titular lord,.I will not take upon me to determine, but affirm I have
read him *Come Carliolensis.—Buck,* lib. i. p. 8.

beth and the house of Wydville over the council and actions of the king. He participated in the indignation felt by the ancient nobility at the elevation of a race who, having no claims for preferment but that of consanguinity to the queen, had been raised to the highest offices in the state, and permitted to occupy the chief seat in the council chamber. He viewed too, with distrust and misgiving, the blind policy of his royal brother, who had removed the heir apparent from all intercourse with the proud and noble kindred of their illustrious line, and placed him under the direct tuition and immediate influence of his mother's family, in a remote part of the kingdom.[1] These feelings, which had been wisely concealed during the lifetime and reign of Edward IV., wore a far different aspect when the unlooked-for death of that sovereign, and the minority of his successor tended in all probability to place Richard in the identical position which he had grieved to see so neglected and abused by the deceased monarch. As the sole surviving brother of Edward IV., and first prince of the house of York—with the exception of the youthful offspring of that king—his situation became one replete with difficulty; and judging from the fate of the princes who had been similarly placed, one beset with danger also. But Gloucester's mind was not constituted to shrink from difficulties however great ; rather was he fitted to shine when energy and promptitude were requisite. Abandoning, therefore, the furtherance of his personal interests, and relinquishing his ardour for

[1] More, p. 19.

military fame in the plains of France, he hastily
prepared to quit the north, and assume that lead
in the direction of public affairs which the minority
of his nephew had imposed upon him.

Meanwhile he wrote most soothing letters to the
queen: he promised " advent, homage, fealty, and
all devoir, to the king and his lord, eldest son of
his deceased brother and of the said queen." [1] Proceeding to York with a retinue of 600 knights and
esquires, " all attired in deep mourning[2]," he commanded the obsequies of the deceased king to be
performed at the cathedral with the splendour due
to his regal station, and the solemnity befitting the
mournful occasion, assisting himself at the ceremony " with tears[3]," and every apparent demonstration of sorrow. He then constrained all the
nobility of that district, as the late king's viceroy
in the north, " to take the oath of fealty to the
king's son, he himself setting them the example by
swearing the first of all." [4]

The youthful monarch was residing at Ludlow
when his father expired, under the immediate
charge and tutelage of his maternal uncle, the
Lord Rivers, and his half-brother, the Lord
Richard Grey[5]; to whom intelligence was forth-

---

[1] Chron. Croy., p. 565.   [2] Ibid.   [3] Ibid.
[4] Ibid., and Drake's Ebor., p. 111.

[5] The widowed queen of Edward IV., by her first husband, Sir
John Grey of Groby, had two sons, viz. Sir Thomas Grey, created
by her royal consort, in the eleventh year of his reign, earl of
Huntingdon, and four years after marquis of Dorset ; and the Lord
Richard Grey, an appointed counsellor of the young Prince of
Wales, and associated with the Lord Rivers in the important charge
of his personal safety. Of the queen's brothers two only survived
at the death of Edward IV., viz. Anthony Earl Rivers, governor of
Prince Edward's household, and Lionel Wydville, bishop of Salisbury.—See *Dugdale's Bar.*, 719. vol. ii. ; *Cal. Rot.*, 313.

with sent of the demise of Edward IV., accompanied by letters from the queen to her son, urging his immediate return to London.[1]

To make somewhat more clear the very startling circumstances that occurred after the young king's departure from Ludlow, and before his arrival in the metropolis, it becomes necessary to explain, that, during the late king's life, the court was divided into two distinct parties—the queen's relatives and supporters, together with those who coveted honour and official distinction without claim of high birth or lineage; and the ancient nobility and proud kindred of the house of York, attached either to the king's household or his administration. A perpetual rivalry and constant collision of interests existed between parties so jealously opposed to each other; and the king on his death-bed, foreseeing the disastrous consequences which were likely to arise from his son's minority, and the prospect of a regency—that fruitful source of intrigue and evil ambition—used his expiring efforts to effect a reconciliation between the factious opponents.[2] He is even alleged to have nominated the Duke of Gloucester as protector[3] and guardian[4] during the young Edward's nonage; and considering the high esteem with which he had ever distinguished his

---

[1] More, p. 23.   [2] Ibid. p. 13.

[3] Drake's Ebor., p. 111.

[4] " The nobles at London and in the south parts speedily call the duke home by their private letters and free approbation, to assume the protection of the kingdom and two princes committed unto him by the king. ' Rex Edwardus IV. filios suos Richardo Duci Glocestriæ, in tutelam moriens tradidit ; ' as Polydor testifieth."—*Buck*, lib. i. p. 11.

brother, and the neutral conduct observed by that
prince, such a recommendation to his council in
his dying hours, at least appears far, from improbable.   One thing at all events is most certain,
viz. that the two dissentient parties who were
present at their monarch's dissolution, united in
testifying their affection and respect for his memory,
by co-operating at the solemnisation of the last sad
rites[1]—his funeral being attended by the Lord
Hastings, the Lord Stanley, the Lord Howard, and
other leaders of the ancient nobility; and by the
Marquis of Dorset, the Lord Lyle, and other near
relatives and warm supporters of the queen's
authority.[2]

Very brief, however, was the unanimity thus
formally displayed.   Immediately after the funeral
the council assembled to fix a day whereon Prince
Edward should receive the ensigns of his coronation; and the queen's ambitious views are made
known, not merely by her desire that the young

---

[1] Harl. MSS., No. 6. fo. 111.

[2] William Lord Hastings was chamberlain of King Edward's
household, and so great a favourite with his royal master, that he
was styled by him his "beloved servant, William Hastings."—
Dug. Bar., vol. i. p. 580.   Thomas Lord Stanley was high-steward, and
was another of the deceased king's chief and most esteemed counsellors. — *Ibid.*, vol. ii. p. 248.   John Lord Howard was high in the
confidence of Edward IV. : he bore the royal banneret at the king's
funeral. — *Fœdera*, xii. p. 50.   Thomas Lord Grey, Earl Huntingdon, Marquis Dorset, was the queen's eldest son by her first husband.
He had been appointed governor of the Tower with extensive privileges by Edward IV., who had bestowed upon him the marriage and
wardship of Edward Earl of Warwick, son of the late Duke of
Clarence.— *Dug. Bar.*, vol. i. p. 719. ; *More*, p. 169. ; *Cal. Rot.*,
325.   The Lord Lyle, so created by Edward IV., was a brother
of Sir John Grey of Groby, the queen's first husband. — *Dug. Bar.*,
vol. i. p. 179.

king should be conducted to London with a powerful army, commanded by her brother and son, but
yet more from information supplied by the annalist
of that period [1], who states that, though all parties
united in wishing due regal state should be observed
in the progress of the young monarch to the capital
of his kingdom, yet that the more prudent of the
council thought that the custody of the king's person, until he became of age, ought not to be entrusted " to the uncles and brothers on the mother's
side; which they considered could not be prevented if they were permitted to attend the
coronation otherwise than with a moderate number
of followers."[2] —The very expression " moderate
number " displays, in a remarkable manner,
the spirit of the times and the character of the
people. Little knowledge, indeed, of the condition of England at the accession of Edward V.
is necessary to perceive that physical strength was
the chief agent employed to acquire and maintain
authority ; that justice was measured out in proportion to the force which could command it ; and
that the most clear and legitimate claims were
sacrificed to the bad passions of such as could oppose
the decision of the sword to the legislative enactments of the realm. The 4th of May was the
day fixed upon by the council for the coronation of
the young king[3]; and after much consideration,
bestowed by the assembled lords, relating to the
peculiar position of Edward V.,—" every one as
he was nearest of kin unto the queen, so was he

---

[1] Chron. Croy., p. 564.   [2] Ibid.   [3] Ibid.

planted next about the prince "[1]—and due attention having been given to the suggestion, that he
should enter the metropolis with an armed force,
" in manner of open war[2]," the result of this latter
question, upon which the council had met more
especially to determine[3], confirms the opinion generally entertained, that his royal parent aspired to
be regent, and to govern in concert with her own
family during the minority.[4]

It also pourtrays the evil which was anticipated
by the counsellors of the late king, should the
Wydville family continue to exercise over the
actions of Edward V. the unpopular influence
which they had exerted over the mind of his deceased parent. But the wisdom of their decision
in limiting the retinue of the young prince to 2000
horsemen, can only be comprehended by taking
into consideration the fact, that the Lord Rivers
was possessed of almost unlimited power at the
critical period of the death of Edward IV. The
youthful monarch was in his hands, and under his
entire control as governor of is household. Invested too as was this nobleman with the supreme
command of South Wales, and of the royal forces
in the surrounding district[5], he had only to sum-
mon the army in the king's name, and forthwith
march in triumph to the metropolis; the military
command of which he knew to be already in the
hands of his kinsman, from his nephew the Marquis
Dorset being governor of the Tower.

[1] More, p. 19.   [2] Ibid. p. 22.
[3] Chron. Croy., p. 564.   [4] Hist. Doubts, p. 22.
[5] Cott. MS., Vitel. C. fol. 1.

With access to the royal treasury there deposited, and with the entire command of the soldiery connected with this important strong-hold, there was nothing wanting to complete the aspiring views of Elizabeth and the Wydville family than possession of the young king's person, and effecting a junction with Earl Rivers and the overwhelming force, which was available by him in the west country. This dangerous collision was defeated by the far-seeing sagacity of those prudent counsellors who aimed at limiting the authority of the queen without an open and positive rupture. By indirectly diminishing the power of the Wydvilles and the Greys, it gave time also for communication with a third party in the state, on whom the attention of the great mass of the people, but above all the ancient nobility, were intently fixed[1] as likely to secure their young sovereign and his administration from the factious spirit which had so long agitated the council, and embittered the last days of King Edward IV.

This third party consisted of the surviving members of the Plantagenet race and the powerful kindred of Cecily Duchess of York; the latter of which, although disgusted at the preference given by their late sovereign to his newly created nobles, were firmly attached to the House of York, with which through her they were so closely allied.

The persons who may be designated as the

---

[1] A retinue not exceeding two thousand, which number was satisfactory to Lord Hastings, because he calculated that the Dukes of Gloucester and Buckingham, on whom he chiefly confided, would not bring with them a less number." — *Chron. Croy.*, 565.

heads of this illustrious and influential party were Richard Duke of Gloucester, Henry Duke of Buckingham, and Cecily, the widowed parent of Edward IV.

As first prince of the blood royal, the laws and usages of the time pointed out the Duke of Gloucester as most fit for the responsible situation of regent during the minority of his nephew; and the amicable terms on which he had invariably lived with the late monarch, his shining abilities, his talent for ruling, and his invaluable services in the council as well as in the state, rendered him eminently qualified to guide the youthful king, and preserve undisputed his lawful succession to the throne.

Henry Duke of Buckingham, although possessing no claim to be associated in the guardianship of Edward V. by reason of near consanguinity, was nevertheless a member of the royal house of Plantagenet, being the lineal descendant of Thomas of Woodstock, the youngest son of King Edward III., and consequently one in a direct line of succession to the crown, although at the present time far removed from it by nearer and legitimate heirs belonging to the elder branch. He however, as thus allied to their royal ancestor, made common cause with Richard Duke of Gloucester, whom he felt to be the representative of the Plantagenet interests during the minority of Edward V.

Cecily Duchess of York had retired altogether from public life after the decease of her illustrious consort; but although refraining from political interference, and resisting the temptation afforded by means of her powerful kindred to balance the intolerable power which was exercised by Elizabeth Wydville over her late son, was yet keenly alive to every species of danger that threatened the stability of a race of which she was the common parent, although by an unlooked-for calamity she had never been "queen by right" of the Yorkist dynasty. Her anxious wishes for the aggrandisement of her sons had been early crushed by King Edward's marriage, in direct opposition to her remonstrance[1], and likewise by the preference which he immediately and invariably gave to his new relations over the interests and claims of his own family.[2] All her hopes had long centered in her youngest son, Richard of Gloucester, whose enlarged and statesman-like views, together with his courage and zeal, had mainly contributed for some years to uphold his brother's authority, and to keep the country well ordered and in obedience.

---

[1] " The Duchess of York, his mother, was so sore moved therewith, that she dissuaded the marriage as much as she possibly might, alleging that it was his honour, profit, and surety also to marry out of his realms, whereupon depended great strength to his estate by the affinity and great possibility of increase of his possessions."— *More*, p. 93.

[2] In addition to the chagrin felt by the Duchess of York, when King Edward bestowed her grand-daughter on his son-in-law, Sir Thomas Grey, contracted as she had long been to a member of the house of Neville, he greatly offended his mother by uniting the heiress of the Lord Scales to Anthony Wydville, afterwards Earl Rivers, the Lady Cecily having wished to promote a union between her and Prince George of Clarence, then just entering into life. The young Duke of Buckingham, too, and the old Duchess of Norfolk, the one matched with the queen's sister, the other married to her young brother, were both nearly connected with the house of Neville, which increased the indignation felt by that haughty race at the Wydvilles being so closely allied to them.

Both herself, therefore, and her connections are found, as might be expected, supporting this prince in his just pretensions to the protectorate, and in firmly opposing the rapacity and inordinate ambition of the young sovereign's maternal relatives.

Such was the state of affairs when Edward V., after waiting at Ludlow to celebrate St. George's Day [1], quitted that ancient abode of his ancestors for the capital of his kingdom on the 24th of April, 1483 — just a fortnight after the dissolution of his royal parent. Richard Duke of Gloucester, it must be here observed, had been in no position to take any part either in the resistance made to the queen's assumed authority, or to the decisive measures adopted by the council as regards the mode and means of conducting the young monarch to the metropolis.

The interval thus occupied in dissensions at court, and by divisions in the cabinet [2], had been passed by this prince in travelling from the Scottish borders to York, in commanding requiems to be solemnised there and in other large towns [3] for the repose of the soul of Edward IV., and in exacting allegiance from all under his

---

[1] Rymer's Fœdera, vol. xii. p. 179. The first instrument in this collection, which issued in the name of King Edward V., is tested on the 23d of April, 1483.

[2] " Hastings, captain of Calais, declared that he would betake himself thither rather than await the coming of the new king, if he came not with a moderate number; for he feared that if the supreme power fell into the hands of those of the queen's blood, they would avenge upon him the injuries which they had received." — *Chron. Croy.*, p. 564.

[3] Harl. MSS., 433. fol. 176.

dominion towards his brother's youthful successor.

Gloucester's conduct was open and honourable throughout, consistent in every respect with the deference which he had invariably paid to his sovereign, and the love he had shown him as his brother, and such too as was best calculated to insure the peaceful succession of his nephew to the throne.

There was no undue assumption of power ; no assembling of the army, of which he had the entire control, to enforce his authority as nearest of kin to the royal minor ; no tarrying in his viceregal territories to ascertain the feeling of the populace, or to induce the most remote suspicion that he contemplated usurpation of the sceptre. He had long possessed the sole command of one half of the kingdom, and had been the means of dissipating in the north many of the factions which had disturbed the peace of the realm. He was lord high-admiral and chief constable of England, and lieutenant-general of the land forces; and his administration in these different capacities, maritime, civil, and military, were allowed by all to have been just, equitable, and prudent.

So long as Gloucester pursued the dictates of his own unbiassed feelings his conduct was irreproachable : his progress through his district being characterised only by affectionate respect for the memory of the deceased monarch, by setting an example of fealty and loyalty to the young king [1], and by the

---

[1] Chron. Croy., 565.

most temperate use of his own unlimited authority and elevated station.

At York, however, the aspect of affairs assumed
a very different hue [1] ; and Richard found himself
called upon to assume the lead, and forcibly to
seize that authority [2], which his behaviour up to
this time would seem to imply he hoped to have
entered upon in tranquillity, and maintained without opposition.

Throughout his remarkable career, this prince,
it cannot be denied, was the victim of unhappy
consequences induced by the bad passions of
weaker minds and of ill-concerted designs ; but in
no one instance was the path he pursued more
decidedly forced upon him than at this great crisis
of his fate, when the exigencies of the case and
the deep-laid schemes of his opponents compelled
him to act with the promptitude and determination
which was inherent in his nature.

A private messenger from Henry Duke of Buckingham appears to have placed before Richard,
during his stay at York [3], full particulars of the
aspiring views of the queen and her family ; and
farther communication from the Lord Hastings [4]

[1] " It was here," observes Drake, " that the Duke of Buckingham
sent a trusty servant, one Percivall says Hall, to instil those notions
of ambition into him which afterwards proved of such dire effect to
his nephews as well as himself."—*Drake's Ebor.*, p. 111.

[2] Buck, lib. i. p. 11.

[3] Drake's Ebor., p. 111., and More, p. 135.

[4] " The Lord Hastings, whose trouth toward the king no man
doubted nor needed to doubt, persuaded the lords to believe that the
Duke of Gloucester was sure, and fastly faithful to his prince ; and
the Lord Rivers and Lord Richard, with the other knights, were,
for matters attempted by them against the Duke of Gloucester and
Buckingham, put under arrest for their surety, not for the king's
jeopardy."—*More,* p. 32.

—such, at least, may be surmised from his conduct in the metropolis—unveiled to the pene-
trating Gloucester the deep plot formed by the
Wydvilles, and the total overthrow designed by
them of his claims to the regency, provided strong
measures were not immediately undertaken for securing the person of Edward V., and crushing the
designs of his mother, his uncles, and his step-
brothers, to obtain possession of him.

Impressed with these ideas, he quitted York for
Northampton, so as to intercept the royal progress;
and that he must have been possessed of some authority to act, either derived from the expressed
wishes of the deceased monarch, as asserted by
Polydore Virgil[1], or arising from the guardianship
being actually conferred upon him in King Edward's will[2], and communicated possibly to Richard

---

[1] Poly. Virg., lib. iv.

[2] From certain documents published in Nichol's valuable collection of Royal Wills, p. 345., and communicated by Dr. Ducarel
from the registers at Lambeth, it appears that Edward IV. left a will
that is not now known to be extant, and which, it has been conjectured, was intentionally destroyed. A will of Edward IV., transcribed by Rymer from the Rolls' Chapel, and dated at Sandwich,
20th June, 1475, was printed in the " Excerpta Hist.," p. 366.; but
as the executors therein named differ from those enumerated by
Dr. Ducarel, it may justly be concluded that the published will was
not the last will, although where this latter document is now deposited is unknown. In the will dated at Sandwich, " Elizabeth the
Quene" is the first executor named ; in the Lambeth registers her
name is altogether omitted ; and four only of the executors associated
with her in the published will are contained in the list there recorded.
From motives which remain unexplained, the executors of the last will
refused to act ; consequently the nature and contents of King Edward's
final testament have never been divulged. But that such an instrument was executed is indisputable, from the fact of the executors
who are enumerated in the Lambeth registers having placed the
royal property under ecclesiastical sequestration within a few weeks

by the executors at York, seems certain from a passage contained in the Croyland Chronicle, to the effect, "that, when the Duke of Gloucester reached Northampton, there came there, *to do him reverence*, Anthony Earl Rivers, the king's uncle, and Sir Richard Grey, the king's uterine brother, and others sent by the king his nephew, that they might submit *all things to be done to his decision.*" [1]

The Lords Rivers and Grey were of no temperament to make this submission to Richard of Gloucester, unless necessitated so to do; neither was that prince likely to have received them "at their first coming," as the annalist proceeds to state, "with a pleasant and joyful countenance, and sitting at supper, at table, to have passed the time in agreeable conversation," [2] unless each party had been mutually satisfied with the performance of duties required from the one, and the deference due to the other: for although Gloucester was endowed with an insinuating address and great flexibility of manners, that proud asperity of look so peculiarly his own when thwarted or displeased, could scarcely have softened into a "joyful countenance," had indignation characterised his first meeting with the obsequious lords. A vast change, however, appears to have occurred before the close of this eventful day.

In the evening Richard and his associates were joined by Henry Duke of Buckingham, ac-

---

of the monarch's decease ; and it is by extracts from these registers that the important information is furnished of there having been a second will.

[1] Chron. Croy., p. 565.   [2] Ibid.

companied by 300 horsemen [1]; "and because it was late, they went to their several abodes," Rivers and Grey well pleased with their reception, and the success which had attended designs they believed to be unsuspected; for only four days intervened between the time appointed by the council for the coronation of Edward V., and he was already some miles advanced towards the metropolis, whither they intended " on the morrow to follow the kyng, and bee with hym early ere hee departed."[2] Gloucester and Buckingham to assemble a few of their most chosen friends in council, where they spent a great part of the night, revolving, as proved by the result, the extraordinary proceedings of the queen's family in the metropolis, and the sinister conduct of Earl Rivers and the Lord Grey, in greeting the Duke of Gloucester, unaccompanied by the young king, to whom, as his paternal uncle, HE was the natural, if not the appointed guardian[3], and from whom THEY, as his delegated counsellors, and governors of his household, were bound not to have separated. Momentous indeed was the intelligence received from the capital, and made known, as it would appear, by Buckingham, or by some of the secret messengers, who had communicated with Gloucester on his progress to Northampton[4]; for the Marquis Dorset had taken possession of the king's treasure[5],

[1] Chron. Croy., p. 565.   [2] More, p. 28.
[3] If the duke aspired to nothing more than the protectorate, his ambition was not to be blamed. It was a dignity which the precedents of the two last minorities seemed to have attached to the king's uncle.—*Lingard*, vol. v. p. 241.
[4] More, p. 135.   [5] Ibid. p. 27.

and had already commenced equipping a naval
force; thus usurping a power altogether unpre-
cedented as regards the appropriation of the royal
funds, and personally offensive to Richard of
Gloucester as relates to the mode of its expenditure, that prince having the entire control, as
admiral of England, over the maritime affairs of
the country. The subtle part acted by Lord Rivers
in sending the young king to Stoney Stratford, a
day's journey in advance of his illustrious uncle,
although the duke[1] was hourly expected at Northampton, and thus withdrawing him on the very
verge of his coronation from all intercourse or
interview with his father's brother, was by this
information explained; and the intolerable and
premeditated usurpation of authority thus early
exercised by the young king's maternal relatives,
so fully confirmed the suspicions entertained by
the late king's advisers as to the Wydvilles' aspiring to the regency, and their resolution of de-
taining in their own hands the person of the young
monarch, until he was irrevocably invested with the
symbols of royalty[2], that it roused every indignant
feeling in Richard, and induced measures which
but for these crafty proceedings might never have

---

[1] "Now was the king in his way gone from Northampton, when
these Dukes of Gloucester and Buckingham came thither : where
remayned behynd the Lord Rivers, the king's uncle, intending on
the morrow to follow the king, and be wi'h him at Stony Stratford."
—*More*, p. 23.

[2] One important fact appears always to have been overlooked, viz.
that after the coronation, however young the sovereign, there could
no longer be a protectorate, that office being expressly instituted to
protect and defend the realm until such time as the minor was
solemnly anointed king.—See *Turner, Middle Ages*, vol. iii. p. 2.

been resorted to, either in his own mind or that of the nobles attached to his party. Their little council sat in deliberation until near the dawn of day, and the nature of their conference may be judged from the exigency of the occasion, and the strong measures which resulted from it; before entering upon which it is fitting, however, to observe, that these measures, harsh as they may appear, and attributed as they have been by most historians solely to the ambition, tyranny, and individual act of Gloucester alone, were, in effect, the result of a general council. Small, it is true, and not legally constituted as such, but fully justified in their deliberations and the degree of responsibility which they assumed, considering that they were assembled under the auspices of the late king's only brother, in a city especially under his jurisdiction as seneschal of the duchy of Lancaster, and driven to adopt hasty but firm resolutions, in consequence of the artifice exhibited in removing the young monarch, under a flimsy pretext, to an unimportant town, incapable of accommodating, in addition to the royal suite, the duke and his retinue [1], and altogether unsuited for the kingly progress. The town of Northampton, from whence Edward V. was hurried, was but thirteen miles from Stoney Stratford, and the castle in the former place where parliaments had been heretofore held, appertained by virtue of his office to his uncle, who was hastening thither expressly to meet, and receive with all loyalty and affection, his youthful

---

[1] " It was too streighte for both companies." — *More*, p. 26.

and illustrious kinsman, when he found him clandestinely removed to favour designs which it required but little penetration to fathom.

Richard of Gloucester was as firm in purpose as
he was resolute in action. Discerning in the estimation of character, and master of the politics of
the times — if mere political expediency and selfish
ambition may deserve such a name — his experience
and judgment were all-sufficient for the difficult
part which he was called upon to sustain; and
before the day had dawned, or his rivals were
stirring, every avenue of the city was guarded, and
horsemen stationed on the high road to intercept
all communication with the king and his escort.[1]

Astonished at their rising to find the gates
closed, and " the wayes on every side besette,"
and satisfied that proceedings which offered so remarkable a contrast to the courtesy of the Duke
on the preceding day were not " begun for nought,"
and most probably foreboded evil to himself and
his companion, the Lord Rivers resolved on neither offering opposition nor expressing surprise,
lest, by betraying suspicion, " he should seem to
hyde himselfe for some secret feare of his own
faulte."[2] The uncle and nephew were in fact
caught in their own net ; but having brought
themselves into this difficulty by proceedings
equally disingenuous as that now practised upon
themselves, the Lord Rivers farther determined,
" sithe hee could not get awaye, to keep himself
close;" and when opportunity offered, " to goe

---

[1] More, p. 24.   [2] Ibid.

boldly" to his detainers, and "enquire what thys matter myghte mean."[1] Accordingly, all the lords departed together, and in seeming amity, to present themselves to the new king[2]; but when they had nearly approached the entrance of the little town where he was sojourning, Earl Rivers and Richard his nephew, with certain others who came with them, were suddenly arrested, by command of the Duke of Gloucester. Continuing their route, Richard, Buckingham, and their companions proceeded with all speed to Stoney Stratford, where the wily scheme concerted by the young king's attendants for hurrying him to the metropolis, and separating him from his uncle of Gloucester, became still more evident; for "they founde the kinge with his companie readye to leape on horse-backe;"[3] and this, too, be it remembered, at a very early hour, the lords having quitted Northampton at dawn of day, so as to frustrate designs which Richard's sagacity had penetrated, and for whose promptitude his adversaries were unprepared, " many of Lorde Rivers' servantes being unreadye."[4]

Entering Prince Edward's abode, to whom the apprehension of his maternal relations was as yet unknown, the Duke of Gloucester arrested Sir Thomas Vaughan, his chamberlain ; Dr. Alcock, Bishop of Worcester, his chief preceptor ; and other of his personal advisers.[5] For it was the duke's conviction that the young monarch was a

---

[1] More, p. 25. [2] Chron. Croy., p. 565.
[3] More, p. 26. [4] Ibid. p. 24.
[5] Rous, p. 212.

party to the deception sought to be practised upon him ; and his indignation at the insincere part which he had acted, in sending the Lord Rivers to Northampton ostensibly to submit " all things to his decision," but in reality to gain time, and to blind Richard to the scheme at which his royal nephew seems to have connived, is made apparent by the following remarkable passage, with which the Croyland historian terminates his brief account of these most singular proceedings : — " The Duke of Gloucester, who was the chief of this faction," (herein he plainly intimates that the duke did not act merely on his own responsibility,) "made no obeisance to the prince, by uncovering, bowing, or otherwise. He merely said that he would take heed for his safety, since he knew that those who were about him conspired against his honour and his life. This done, he caused proclamation to be made, that all the king's servants should forthwith withdraw themselves from the town, and not approach those places whereunto the king should remove, under pain of death.—These things were done at Stoney Stratford the 31st April, 1483." [1]

This chronicler and Rous, the antiquary of Warwick, are the only two contemporary writers of this period, although Sir Thomas More's history, as before explained, is considered to have been derived, also, from co-existent authority. The diffuse narrative of More, despite of the romance with which it is tinctured, helps frequently to explain many facts which the Croyland annalist

[1] Chron. Croy., p. 565.

leaves obscure by his conciseness; and when More's explanations are confirmed by the testimony of Rous, the evidence of the three writers forms a clear and connected chain in the confused and disjointed accounts, which have so long been received as the history of one of the most momentous epochs in English annals.

The whole of these authors agree upon the leading facts of Richard's junction with Edward V. at Stratford, the arrest of the royal attendants, and the possession taken of the young king's person by the Duke of Gloucester. But here " Rous " becomes invaluable ; for he states in addition the cause of the duke's so acting, " and being by his own authority made protector of Edward, as protector he took the new king, his nephew, into his own keeping;"[1] thus clearly implying that he was possessed of some power to act definitively and upon his own judgment. In this step he was borne out by ancient usage, being first prince of the blood royal, and the only member of the house of York capable by age, or entitled by near affinity, to be guardian to his brother's heir. But Rous follows up his account by explaining farther the *cause* of Gloucester's assuming the protectorate on his own authority, and the reason for his removing the queen's kindred from their abuse of that ascendancy which they had acquired over the prince, and had cunningly devised to appropriate to their own purposes. " They were accused of having compassed the death of the protector," he says; and

[1] Rous, p. 212.

this, not on the uncertain medium of public report, not from the casual hints of mercenary informers or nameless eavesdroppers, but, as positively asserted by Rous[1], on no less authority than that of the " Earl of Northumberland !"[2]   He was "their chief accuser."[3] This coeval testimony of an historian so bitterly opposed to Richard of Gloucester is most important, as it fully justifies that prince in his proceedings, and exonerates him from premeditated tyranny.   He was possessed of the affection of the army, and was by royal appointment their chief commander; yet he proceeded southward accompanied merely by 600 of his own retainers.   With the small addition of 300 horsemen, added to this little band the day previously by Buckingham, he nevertheless boldly seized upon the person of the young king; no opposition being made to his will, no attempt at rescue from the 2000 horsemen appointed to guard their prince, and who, as picked men, can scarcely be imagined so pusillanimous as to have tamely abandoned their trust, if unprovoked insult or unlawful violence

[1] Rous, p. 213.

[2] By indenture, dated 1st May, 1483, Henry Earl of Northumberland was appointed warden of the east and middle marches, towards Scotland.—*Harl. MSS.*, 433. fol. 228.   This was the second instrument issued by Edward V., and the first after Richard had so abruptly assumed the protectorate ; and its occurring the very day following the seizure of the young king's person, would certainly imply that it was under the duke's auspices that a power corresponding with the last conferred upon him by his deceased brother, Edward IV., was bestowed in reward on a nobleman who was the means of divulging a plot, which, if credit is to be attached to the unanimous testimony of each contemporary writer, had been formed, and was ripening, for destroying Gloucester and the leading members of his race.

[3] Rous, p. 214.

had been exercised against their royal charge ; considering, too, that their force was double that which arrested their progress, and under the influence of which they were commanded to disperse on pain of death.

Power is seldom attained by violence. Much as it may be misused when possessed, yet it is almost always voluntarily yielded. When, therefore, the startling events of the brief fortnight following the death of King Edward are dispassionately considered, and the whole tenor of the conduct pursued by the rival parties impartially compared, it cannot but favour the surmise, that Gloucester, acting under such disadvantages as arose from inadequate force, and from his ignorance of much that had occurred, in consequence of his absence from the conflicting scenes which led to such stern measures when they were fully made known to him, would never have so immediately attained the mastery, had not a sense of right given nerve to his actions, and a consciousness of error and duplicity awed and enfeebled his opponents.

Sir Thomas More's account corroborates the statement both of Rous and of the Croyland writer; but he narrates in addition, that the rival lords began to quarrel on the road, when Rivers was accused by Gloucester and Buckingham of intending "to sette distance between the kynge and them;"[1] and that when that nobleman " beganne in goodly wise to excuse himself, they taryed not the end of his answer, but shortly tooke hym and put hym in warde;"[2] that on entering the king's presence,

---

[1] More, p. 25.   [2] Ibid.

before whom the Duke of Buckingham and his attendants prostrated themselves with respectful homage, they communicated to Edward the arrest of the Lords Rivers and Grey, accusing them of conspiring, with the Marquis of Dorset, "to rule the kynge and the realm, to sette variance among the states, and to subdue and destroy the noble blood of the realm,"[1] informing him likewise that the marquis " hadde entered into the Tower of London, and thence taken out the kynge's treasure, and sent menne to sea."[2]

The astonished prince expressed his ignorance of the part pursued by the Lord Dorset, but sought to establish his conviction of the innocence of Lords Rivers and Grey. The Duke of Buckingham, however, assuring him that his kindred " had kepte their dealings from the knowledge of his grace,"[3] the remainder of the retinue, supposed to have been leagued with Rivers and Grey, were seized in the royal presence, and the king himself taken " back unto Northampton," where Gloucester and the nobles by whom he. was supported " took again further counsyle."[4] And truly they had need so to do; for although the day approached in which Edward V. was to be solemnly invested with the insignia of royalty, no regency had been nomi-

---

[1] More, p. 26.　　　　　　[2] Ibid.

[3] This assertion goes far to prove that Buckingham was the agent who infused into Gloucester's mind the conviction he entertained respecting the insincerity of the Lord Rivers ; neither must it be forgotten, that Buckingham having married the sister of this latter nobleman (and of the royal Elizabeth also), may have had substantial grounds for making this accusation against the Wydville family.

[4] More, p. 26.

nated to guide the helm of state; no protectorate
appointed to watch over the interests and aid the
inexperience of the royal minor; no measures
taken to provide for his safety, to guard the capital
from insurrection, or to secure the co-operation and
attendance at the approaching ceremony of those
lordly barons whose support and allegiance could
alone insure stability to his throne; but a self-
constituted council, at variance among themselves,
and possessing in reality no legitimate authority to
act after the decease of the monarch to whose administration they had belonged—a sovereign un-
fettered in his minority by restraining enactments—
a faction long hated and jealously viewed by the
ancient nobility, who, having obtained possession of
their young prince, sought to retain it, and to exclude the surviving members of the house of York
from all intervention or communion with their
future ruler, until Edward should be irrevocably
anointed king; these were the discordant materials, these the unpromising auspices, with which,
on the approaching 4th of May, the acts of Edward V. would have been ushered in, had not his
royal uncle, with the firmness and decision which
the occasion justified and his own position rendered imperative, changed the whole face of affairs,
and delegated to himself the office of protector,
until the three estates of the realm could meet to
legislate at so important a crisis. Time was requisite to mature further proceedings; but a state
of things like that above described was not tolerable to a mind constituted like Richard of Gloucester when the end of April had arrived, and four

days only intervened before that appointed for the coronation. With the fixed resolution, then, and the self-possession which so peculiarly characterised this prince's actions, he hesitated not, in this case of direful emergency, to act as became the brother of Edward IV., and as befitted the natural protector of Edward V.

On their return to Northampton, he despatched a messenger to the assembled lords in the metropolis, informing them, through the Lord Chamberlain Hastings, of the decisive measures he had taken, the which were fully approved by that most devoted partizan of the late king.[1] He likewise wrote to the leading nobles of the realm, explaining the motives by which he had been actuated, viz. " that it neyther was reason, nor in any wise to be suffered, that the young king, their master and kinsman, should be in the hands and custody of his mother's kindred; sequestered in manner from theyr companie and attendance;"[2] the which, " quod he, is neither honourable to hys majestie, nor unto us."[3] Gloucester, nevertheless, is represented as treating the young monarch with honour and reverence, and as behaving to his captive friends with courtesy and kindness[4], until himself and his council could meet in further deliberation

---

[1] " Now there came one not longe after midnight from the lord chamberlayn unto the Archbishop of York, then chancellor; and after communicating to his grace the arrest of the king and his attendant lords, adds, ' Notwithstanding sir,' quod hee, ' my lorde sendeth your lordship worde, that there is no fear; for he assureth you that all shall be well.' " — *More*, p. 29.

[2] More, p. 19.   [3] Ibid.   [4] Ibid. p. 28.

relative to matters which had been privately communicated to them. The nature of this information
is indicated by the result. On the following day the
royal duke consigned to imprisonment those lords
whose conduct gave proof of the unworthy motives
imputed to them; sending the Lord Rivers, the Lord
Richard Grey, and Sir Thomas Vaughan to Pomfret
Castle and other fortresses in " the north parts,"[1]
and taking upon himself " the order and governance of the young king,"[2] whom the said lords, his
counsellors, had sought to mislead, and over whom
they had obtained such dangerous ascendency.
And here it is important to show that this monarch was not at his accession a mere infant—not
" a child in his little tunic—a babe habited in loose
robes," as represented in many a fanciful engraving
designed to elucidate his obscure history—but a
youth almost arrived at man's estate, certainly old
enough to exercise judgment, and competent to
discriminate in most matters in which he was personally concerned. Indeed, he had been early prepared by able preceptors for that position to which
he would probably be one day elevated; and had
well nigh attained at his father's demise that age
of discretion[3] which would have entitled him, in
accordance with the common law of the land, to
claim participation in the affairs of state, however,

---

[1] Rous, p. 212. [2] Chron. Croy., p. 565.; More, p. 28.
[3] " A male at twelve years of age may take the oath of allegiance ;
at fourteen he is at discretion ; and if his discretion is actually
proved, may make his testament of his personal estate."—*Blackstone's Com.*, vol. i. p. 463.

duly controlled by the preponderating wisdom of a
regency.

Edward V. was in his thirteenth year when he
was proclaimed king; and the education which
was ordinarily bestowed on the heir apparent of
the throne, but more especially in those heroic
and momentous times, removed him at that age
far beyond mere childhood, although he may still
be considered as of " tender years." [1] The guardianship of Henry VI. was limited by his valiant
parent to the age of sixteen; the office of protector of the realm ceased when he was nine;
and, in his fourteenth year, this monarch was
advised to remonstrate with the council of regency at being too much excluded from public
business. [2]

Richard II. was two years junior to Edward V.
when he was crowned king; and the age of this
sovereign, when with a self-possession and determined courage that betokened a more efficient reign
he dispersed the infuriated mob assembled by Wat
Tyler, was only two years beyond that which Edward had attained when his progress was stayed,
and his attendants dispersed, by the authority of
his uncle of Gloucester. [3]

But the temperament of this young prince is
affectingly demonstrated in the sequel of Sir Thomas More's narrative of the proceedings at North-

---

[1] More, p. 51.   [2] Turner's Middle Ages, vol. iii. p. 34.
[3] " They sente awaie from the kynge whom it pleased them, and
sette newe servantes about him, such as lyked better them, than
hym."—*More*, p. 27.

ampton: " At which dealing hee wepte, and was nothing contente; but it booted not."[1]

Rous states that he had been " virtuously educated, was of wonderful capacity, and, for his age, well skilled in learning:"[2] and learned and virtuous he may have been; for Sir Thomas More bears similar testimony both as regards himself and the young Duke of York[3]; although he qualifies his evidence by intimating that Edward was " light of belief, and sone persuaded."[4]

Nevertheless, judging from the few verified details of this ill-fated monarch, together with the impression conveyed by Shakspeare[5], doubtless that which then generally prevailed of his calm and submissive deportment, he would seem to have been tender, affectionate, and docile, warm in his attachments[6], confiding and unsuspicious, resembling Henry. VI. in the gentle virtues that would have graced domestic life, and giving such promise of future excellence as regards erudition[7] as might have rendered him the " Beauclerc" of his time. But he was clearly deficient in the hereditary manhood of his race[8], and sympathised not in the fierce and stormy passions which marked the age. De-

[1] More, p. 27.   [2] Hist. Ang., p. 212.
[3] " Having in themselves also as many gifts of nature, as many princelye virtues, as much goodlye towardness, as their age could receive." — *More*, p. 5.
[4] More, p. 20.
[5] See Rich. III., act iii. sc. 1.   [6] More, p. 64.
[7] Rous, p. 212.
[8] Sir Thomas More states, that when Edward V. was told that his uncle was crowned king, he began to sigh, and said, " Alas! I would my uncle would let me have my life, though I lose my kingdom." — *More*, p. 130.

void of energy[1], of " a weak and sickly disposition,"[2] meek rather than courageous, studious rather than enterprising[3], the reign of Edward V. thus bade fair to revive those fearful calamities which had characterised that of Edward II., owing to the intrigues of the queen mother, a factious administration, an irritated and discontented nobility, and the ascendency exercised over a too yielding disposition by unpopular and unworthy favourites.

The accounts at this period are at the best too obscure and too concise to afford a clear exposition even of the leading events by which it was distinguished; but sufficient may be gathered to form a tolerable estimate as to the true cause of Richard's proceedings, and to comprehend many startling facts which resulted from his conduct. Ardently devoted to his country, and politically, if not personally, opposed to the queen and her kindred, it was Gloucester's object to save the one from the threatened evils likely to ensue from the uncontrolled ambition of the other; but he acted towards the young prince, his nephew, with the greatest tenderness and compassion[4], and is represented as having besought him on his knees to banish fear and apprehension, to place confidence in his affection, and reliance on the necessity of those summary measures which occasioned him such deep affliction.

Had the young Edward so acted, had he con-

---

[1] " After which time the prince never tyed his points, nor ought wrought of himself, but with that young babe hys brother lingered in thought and heaviness." — *More*, p. 130.

[2] Buck, lib. iii. p. 85.   [3] More, p. 27.

[4] Lingard, vol. v. p. 240.

fided in his father's brother, his natural guardian, and possessed sufficient moral courage and energy of character to co-operate manfully with one so fitted to guide, and so implicitly trusted by his deceased parent, instead of affectionately but effeminately weeping[1] for those who had misdirected the inexperience of his youth, the unhappy but amiable successor of King Edward IV. might have ascended in tranquillity and retained quiet possession of that throne which his father had won in his minority, and twice secured by his valour; and thus have perpetuated a dynasty, which, from the brilliancy of its commencement, bid fair to shine as one of the most glorious of any recorded in British history.

But so peaceful a state of affairs was neither in accordance with the unruly passions which hastened the downfal of the Plantagenets, nor the turbulent era in which that kingly race flourished, and at last became utterly extinct.

The annalist of that epoch will best narrate in his own brief manner the result of the proceedings at Stoney Stratford, and the miserable state of disunion into which the metropolis was already plunged, owing to the kingdom being without a head, and the realm without an acknowledged leader. On the following night after the capture of the Lords Rivers and Grey, rumours having reached London of "the king's grace" being in the hands of the Dukes of Gloucester and Buckingham, Queen Elizabeth betook herself to the

[1] More, p. 27.

Sanctuary at Westminster, with her children. "You might have seen, on that morning, the fautors of one and the other party, some truly, others feignedly, as doubtful of the events, adhering to this or that side: for some congregated and held their assemblages at Westminster, in the queen's name; others at London, under the shadow of Lord Hastings,"[1] who was the leading adviser of the late king, and the member of his council most inimical to the queen and her kindred.

The Marquis of Dorset, awed by the determination which was evinced at this critical juncture by the Duke of Gloucester, abandoned the Tower, and the unjustifiable assumption of authority which he had there exercised as its governor, and fled for refuge to the same sacred asylum whither his mother had again sought refuge, and where both herself and her infant progeny were secure from personal violence, and the evils that had already overtaken a portion of their race. "After the lapse of a few days," continues the annalist[2], "the aforesaid dukes brought the new king to London," conveying him thither with every testimony of respect; and on the 4th of May, the ill-omened day originally fixed for his coronation, the youthful prince entered the metropolis in state, escorted by Gloucester, Buckingham, and a suitable retinue, all habited in deep mourning, except the monarch himself[3], who was clothed in his kingly mantle of blue velvet. A short distance from the city, the royal cavalcade was met by the civic authorities, and 500 citizens

[1] Chron. Croy., p. 566.   [2] Ibid.
[3] More, p. 34.

sumptuously attired[1]; followed by whom, and preceded by the Duke of Gloucester, — who, uncovered, rode before his nephew, and in passing along said with a loud voice to the people, " Behold your prince and sovereign " — the king was conducted to the bishop's palace at St. Paul's; where he was lodged with every accompaniment of regal state and etiquette. There his uncle, acting as his guardian, forthwith compelled the lords spiritual and temporal, and the mayor and aldermen of the city of London, to take the oath of fealty to their lawful and legitimate sovereign[2]; which, it is recorded, " as the best presage of future prosperity, they did most willingly." [3]

Perfect tranquillity was the consequence of this unanimous feeling; and the legislature and municipal powers fully co-operated with Gloucester in carrying out measures which had restored confidence to all parties, and allayed the feverish excitement of the populace. [4] " The laws were administered," says Rous[5], " money coined, and all things pertaining to the royal dignity were performed in the young king's name, he dwelling in the palace of the Bishop of London from his first coming to London." The exigencies of the state required the immediate assemblage of a general council, which was as speedily summoned by the Protector, to give sanction to proceedings which

[1] Buck, lib. i. p. 11.
[2] Chron. Croy., p. 566.   [3] Ibid.
[4] " Then was there greate commotion and murmur, as well in other places about, as specially in the city."— More, p. 31.
[5] Rous, p. 212.

had been already carried into effect, and to guard
against future embarrassment arising from the
king's minority ; some executive power, legally
constituted, being essential, not merely up to the
period of his coronation, but until such time as he
should be of age to govern on his own responsibility.
" This council assembled daily at the bishop's palace,
because there the young Edward was sojourning ;
but as this imposed upon the prince unnecessary
restraint, it was suggested that he should be
removed to some more free place of abode." [1]

Various dwellings were proposed. " Some recommended the Priory of St. John, others the Palace of Westminster ; but the Duke of Buckingham
naming the Tower, it was agreed to, even by those
who disliked it." [2] Prejudice has been unduly exercised against this decision, from the Tower of
London being better known in modern times as
a state prison, than as the ancient palace of the
English sovereigns, which it really was during the
middle ages [3] ; and also because at an epoch a full
century removed from the period under present
consideration a feeling of undefinable terror was
associated with this gloomy pile, in consequence of
the dark and terrible deeds said to have been perpetrated therein.   But, as regards Edward V., this
idea is erroneously entertained.   In his day, it was
the king's palace, the metropolitan citadel, which
guarded alike the treasure of the kingdom, and
protected the person of its monarch, whenever the

[1] Chron. Croy., p. 566.   [2] Ibid.
[3] See Bayley's Hist. of the Tower.

safety of the latter was likely to be endangered. Examination into the history of this ancient national fortress will show that from the accession of Henry III., who first made it the regal abode and almost exclusively dwelt there, the Tower of London was the dwelling-place, during some portion of their reign, of every succeeding monarch who intervened between that king and the youthful Edward V. [1]; the unsettled state of the kingdom at this period of its history rendering a fortified abode as indispensable for the security of the monarch, as of the great feudal barons their subjects.

Within the precincts of the Tower, Joane Queen of Scotland, eldest daughter of King Edward II., was born [2]; and Elizabeth, sister to the young prince under present consideration, and eventually the queen of Henry VII., died within its walls in giving birth to the Princess Katherine of the line of Tudor.[3] The father of Edward V. resided there before he was driven from his throne, and in that stronghold his mother was left for protection when her royal consort was compelled to fly the kingdom.[4]

Whatever, then, may have been the after-consequences as regards his youthful successor, it is a most mistaken notion to suppose that, when it was suggested by his council that Edward V. should be removed to " some more free abode," [5] one apart from the necessary business of state, the Tower was selected either as a place of captivity, or be-

---

[1] See Appendix B.   [2] Sandford, book iii. p. 155.
[3] Holinshed, p. 709.   [4] Sandford, book v. p. 387.
[5] Chron. Croy., p. 566.

cause it was less accessible to his partizans than the bishop's palace at St. Paul's, the priory of St. John's Clerkenwell, the regal dwelling at Westminster, or any other metropolitan abode.

The Tower of London was moreover, by ancient usage, the ordinary abiding place of English monarchs preparatory to their coronation : and as the chief point for which the council had been assembled was to deliberate and determine upon the earliest fitting day for the celebration of that important ceremony, not only were those counsellors who proposed the Tower as the temporary residence of Edward V. justified in their selection of it, but it was the abode established by precedent[1], as well as, under the embarrassing circumstances in which the son of Elizabeth Wydville ascended the throne, the one best calculated to insure his personal safety, and inspire confidence in the citizens. Both these points were objects of great importance ; for all ranks in the metropolis had betrayed extreme agitation at the rumours which had preceded the public entry of the young prince ; and it required the most strenuous exertions on the part of the Lord Hastings to appease the multitude, and to justify the strong measures that had occasioned so much apprehension.

The wavering conduct of Rotheram, archbishop of York and lord chancellor, tended greatly to increase

---

[1] " It had for a long while been the custom of the king or queen to take up their residence at the Tower for a short time previous to their coronations, and thence they generally proceeded in state through the city, to be crowned at Westminster."— *Bayley's History of the Tower*, vol. ii. p. 263.

the fears which were entertained by the populace[1] of impending evil ; for on receiving private intelligence, about midnight, of the arrest of the Lords Rivers and Grey, he " thereupon caused, in all haste, his servants to be called up, and so, with his own household about him, and every man weaponed, he tooke the great seal with him, and came yet before day unto the queen," [2] delivering unto her hands this important badge for the " use and behoof" of her son.[3]

Repenting him, however, of the imprudence which he had committed in voluntarily resigning the signet of state to the queen, " to whom the custody thereof nothing pertained without especial commandment of the king," [4] he secretly sent for the seal again on the ensuing day, and brought it with him to the council chamber, when summoned by his compeers in the late administration to assist them in allaying the public ferment, which had assumed so alarming an aspect that the citizens went " flock-mele in harness," [5] and open insurrection was hourly apprehended.

The appearance, however, of Edward V. in royal progress at this crisis, and the respectful homage displayed by the Duke of Gloucester, when, bareheaded, he pointed out their young king to the multitude, set all fears at rest[6] ; and the great council of state, assembled by this prince in his sovereign's name, forthwith commenced their deliberations in tranquillity, and carried out their measures without interruption.

---

[1] More, p. 29.   [2] Ibid. p. 31.   [3] Ibid.   [4] Ibid.
[5] Ibid. p. 31.   [6] Ibid. p. 34. ; and Fabyan, p. 513.

Their first act was to appoint the Duke of Gloucester protector of the king and his realm. " Hee was
fallen in so great trust," observes Sir Thomas More[1],
that he was " the only man chose and thought most
mete " to be nominated to this responsible office; and
the Chronicler of Croyland [2], corroborating this fact,
adds, that " Richard received the same power as
wasc onferred on Humphrey Duke of Gloucester
during the minority of Henry VI., with the title
of Protector;" and likewise that " this authority
he used by the consent and good pleasure of all the
lords, commanding and forbidding in everything
like another king, as the case required." [3] A meeting of the senate, as constituted under the late
reign, was convened for the immediate despatch of
business; and a new parliament was summoned
for the 25th of the ensuing month (June), as shown
by an ancient document preserved in the Lambeth
register. [4] On the 16th of May the Archbishop of
York, after being severely reproved for having delivered up the great seal to the queen, the which
act had spread such alarm in the city, was deprived of his office; and Dr. Russel, late privy
seal and bishop of Lincoln, was appointed high
chancellor in his place; " a wise manne and a good,
and of much experience," [5] as testified by Sir
Thomas More, " and one of the best learned men,
undoubtedly, that England had in hys time." [6]
Divers other lords and knights were displaced, and
new counsellors appointed in their stead ; but the

[1] More, p. 34.   [2] Chron. Croy., p. 566.
[3] Ibid.   [4] Royal Wills, p. 347.
[5] More, p. 35.   [6] Ibid.

Lord Hastings, late chamberlain of the household, the Lord Stanley, the Bishop of Ely, and other personal friends of the deceased monarch, kept still " theyr offices that they had before." [1]

Various grants were issued by the youthful Edward; the functions of government were orderly and wisely executed; and the feast of St. John the Baptist (22d June) having been fixed as the day whereon the king's coronation was without fail to take place, all now hoped and expected the peace and prosperity of the realm. [2]

The 19th of May was decided upon for the presentation of the new monarch to the estates in parliament assembled, when, being conducted by his uncle to Westminster, he delivered a speech from the throne [3], claiming their fealty and asserting his royal prerogative and right of succession. " First to you, right noble lords spiritual and temporal ; secondly to you, worshipful syres, representing the commons, God hath called me at my tender age to be your king and sovereign." [4]

He then appeals to their liberality to make the usual grants for the " sure maintenance of his high estate," [5] and after eulogising " the right noble and famous prince the Duke of Gloucester, his uncle, protector of the realm, in whose great prudence, wisdom, and fortunes restyth at this season the execution of the defence of his realm," and noticing the dangers to be apprehended from the

---

[1] More, p. 35. [2] Chron. Croy., p. 566.
[3] Sharon Turner, vol. iii. p. 419.
Cott. MSS., Vitel. E. 10. [5] Ibid.

opposing party, " as well against the open enemies
as against the subtle and faint friends of the same,"
the royal speech concludes by urging " thys
hygh court of parliament " to confirm the Duke of
Gloucester in the protectorate, to which he had
been previously nominated by the council of state.[1]
" The power and authority of my Lord Protector is
so behoffull and of reason to be asserted and established by the authority of this hygh court, that
among all the causes of the assemblyng of the
parliament in thys tyme of the year, thys is the
greatest and most necessary to be affirmed." [2]

And truly it was so, as regards the necessities of
the state, and the factious spirit that pervaded the
court. This Richard felt; and he wisely desired
that the kingly authority, which as lord protector
had temporarily devolved upon him, should be confirmed beyond all controversy by legislative enactment.

His title to be so confirmed was admitted by all
parties. The early death of the young Edward's
natural parent had left his uncle, as stated in the
speech from the throne, " next in perfect age of the
blood royal to be tutor and protector "[3] to his royal
nephew; and his unblemished character up to this
unlooked-for exaltation is demonstrated by his being
proposed to the young monarch at the ratification

---

[1] Cott. MSS., Vitel. E. 10.
[2] Ibid.   The whole of this interesting document, a copy of which
was preserved by Sir Robert Cotton in his invaluable collection of
MSS., is still extant, although much defaced by the great fire which,
in the commencement of the last century, destroyed so many records
in his ancient library then deposited at Westminster.
[3] Cott. MSS., Vitel. E. 10.

of his protectorate by the assembled peers, as an example of "majoral cunning [mature wisdom], felicity, and experience."[1]

Gifted as he was with the distinguishing merits of his time, invincible courage and profound military sagacity and skill, it had been better perhaps for Richard of Gloucester had circumstances not conspired to elevate him to so lofty a position in the government of his country; for he was endowed with qualifications that lead to greatness, and he was superior to the times in which he lived — times, be it remembered, when morality was at a very low ebb, and when the virtues of private and domestic life were little estimated, in comparison with brilliant exploits, daring courage, and warlike renown.

But the Duke of Gloucester had no competitor for the kingly office to which he was elected. He stood alone in his just pretensions to the uncontrolled exercise of that dangerous power which had so suddenly dawned upon him; and, the sole guardianship of Edward V. having been committed to his charge by the unanimous voice of the legislature, he yielded to the lofty feelings of his race, and henceforth issued the vice-regal mandates under the high-sounding titles of " Duke of Gloucester, brother and uncle of kings, protector and defender of the realm, great chamberlayne, constable, and lord high admiral of England."[2] It is, however, but justice to this prince to observe, that in adopting a style so invariably adduced as a proof of

[1] Cott. MSS., Vitel. E. 10.
[2] Chron. Croy., p. 566.; also Fœdera, xii. p. 184., and Drake's Ebor., p. 115.

his vain-gloriousness and intolerable pride, that Richard only adhered to the precedent afforded by Humphrey Duke of Gloucester, who held the same office in a former reign, and whose protectorate was the example given when the same power with which he was invested was now conferred upon the uncle of Edward V.[1]

The removal of this monarch from the bishop's palace at St. Paul's to the regal apartments occupied by his predecessors in the Tower, appears, by his signature to certain instruments[2], dated from both those places, to have occurred somewhere between the 9th and the 19th of May; during which brief period many weighty appointments were made by the young king, the most remarkable of which was the nomination of the Duke of Buckingham to those high military commands in South Wales and the English counties adjoining[3] which had so recently been possessed by his uncle the Lord Rivers, and which it must have caused Edward extreme pain to have bestowed upon another.[4] This fact, however, joined to the circumstance, before named, of the Earl of Northumberland's investiture with corresponding authority in the north[5], clearly demonstrates who were the par-

---

[1] The titles used by the uncle of King Henry VI., after his nomination to the protectorate, were "Humphrey, by the grace of God son, brother, and uncle to kings, Duke of Gloucester, Earl of Henault, &c., Lord of Friesland, Great Chamberlain of the Kingdom of England, Protector and Defender of the said Kingdom and Church of England."—*Sandford*, book iv. p. 308.

[2] See Harl. MSS., 435. p. 221.

[3] Rymer's Add. MSS., 4616., art. 6.

[4] Fœdera, vol. xii. p. 180.   [5] Drake's Ebor., p. 111.

ties that incited the Duke of Gloucester to the severe measures he adopted; owing to the alleged plot for the destruction of himself, which is detailed by all contemporary writers, and the particulars connected with which, there can be no doubt, were communicated to Richard by the two lords, thus speedily recompensed with such powerful and honourable offices. One thing connected with these is remarkable: that although the appointments above named, and all others indeed that were made by Edward V. after his removal from Stoney Stratford, — the very day subsequent to which, it should be noticed, Northumberland's indenture is dated, viz. 1st of May, 1483 [1],— must have been executed by the advice, if not at the instigation, of his uncle of Gloucester; and although Richard's assumption of the protectorate was confirmed within a few days by the council of state, and the election of these counsellors ratified before the close of the month by the higher authority of parliament, yet his name never appears in any of the official documents issued by his royal nephew[2], until after his formal induction into that high preferment by the lords spiritual and temporal duly convened for that purpose by Edward V.[3] From that day, however, all and each instrument issued in the young king's name [4] concluded with the words " by the advice of our dearest uncle the Duke of Gloucester, protector of our realm of England during our youth," [5] and

---

[1] Harl. MSS., 433. p. 228.
[2] See Fœdera, vol. xii. p. 179, 180.   [3] Royal Wills, p. 347.
[4] Fœdera, vol. xii. p. 184.
[5] Whatever difference of opinion may have prevailed relative to

the almost despotic power which centred in him
after his title was thus confirmed past all dispute
— power, as states the annalist of that period,
" used by the consent and good pleasure of all the
lords "— was such, " that it empowered him," he
adds, as has been before stated, " to command and
forbid in everything like another king." [1]

Richard of Gloucester was now in effect the
ruler of the kingdom, its sovereign, all but in title:
and the regal authority which thus so unexpectedly
devolved upon him—changing his condition in the
short space of five weeks from the dependent station of the sovereign's younger brother to a position so elevated that it entitled him to govern the
monarch himself as well as to wield the destinies
of the nation, as sole arbiter of the acts and actions
of a minor prince—rekindled, there can be little
doubt, in his heart the germs of that hereditary
ambition which had lain dormant since his earliest
infancy.

Formed by nature for command, and possessing
clear and enlarged views of the exigencies of the
times, and the wants of the country over whose

the motives or conduct of Richard Duke of Gloucester, he has ever
been considered a fast and steady friend. This is curiously instanced in the first occasion on which he signed himself Protector.
By an instrument bearing date the 19th of May, 1483, his early
companion and associate in arms, the Lord Lovell, was appointed to
the valuable office of chief butler, which had been bestowed by
Edward IV. on the Lord Rivers. The nomination is thus expressed
in the original grant : — " Viscount Lovell, appointed chief butler of
England by the advice of our most entirely beloved uncle the Duke
of Gloucester, protector of our realm : anno 1 Edw. V." — *Harl.
MSS.*, 433. fo. 221. b.

[1] Chron. Croy., p. 566.

interests he was called upon to preside, Richard felt himself qualified to regulate with zeal and ability the complicated machinery of that government, which was now entrusted to his guidance. But, however much he may have been fitted by temperament as well as ability to control and to direct an executive so complex and involved as that which his consanguinity to Prince Edward entailed upon him, it must surely be admitted that the dangerous power which Gloucester so unhappily attained was the result of no illegal measures pursued by himself, but was the voluntary gift, first of the privy council, and finally, of the whole legislature itself assembled in parliament. The council of state convened for this purpose, before the dissolution of the old parliament and the assembling of the new one, was sufficiently powerful to have resisted the duke's assumption of the high office which he claimed as his birthright had the haughty nobles in that age of baronial dignity considered it to have been unjustifiably seized and unlawfully exercised. The young King was securely lodged in his royal citadel; he had been there placed expressly to admit of free discussion, so that his person was no longer subject to his uncle's detention, when parliament confirmed Richard in the protectorate: neither had this prince an army in the metropolis, nor resources either civil or military, sufficient to intimidate his opponents, even had he evinced such a disposition to violence. But he rested his pretensions on ancient usage, he based his claims on a character free from stain and reproach; and the result of the solemn

assembly of the land, which met to consider the
policy of investing the brother of King Edward IV.
with the sole guardianship of his heir and successor
in his non-age, attests their belief at that crisis of
Richard's fate, of the just, prudent, and upright
manner in which, as quaintly expressed in the language of that day " my said lord protector will
acquit himself of the tutele and oversight of the
king's most royal person during his years of tenderness[1]," thus giving the most convincing proof
of the injustice which has been exercised for three
centuries against the character, actions, and motives of Richard Duke of Gloucester, up to the
critical period, when by universal consent and un-
fettered by restraint he was entrusted with the
helm of state, and appointed " protector and defender of the realm."

[1] Cott. MSS. Vitel. E. fo. 10.

CHAP. XII.

THE eyes of the whole nation were now fixed upon the Duke of Gloucester. Upon his wisdom hung the fate of the empire, upon his integrity the welfare of its monarch. In the very face of a political convulsion, more formidable than any which had threatened the peace of the kingdom since the disastrous feuds which terminated in the elevation of his brother to the throne, he had secured the tranquil accession of Edward V., quelled the divisions in the late king's council, revived the sinking spirits of the people, and restored faith and confidence in the government. And all this without striking a blow, without causing the death of one human being, or sullying the efforts of his vigorous mind by acts of cruelty, vengeance, or retaliation.[1]

At no period of his life was Richard of Gloucester so truly great as when he thus achieved a moral victory over powerful adversaries, whom he awed not more by his military renown than he subdued by his sagacity and self-possession. Civil war must inevitably have ensued had no legitimate claimant for the protectorate existed. A succession of insults inflicted by the Wydville family[2], and of jealousies long endured by the ancient nobility of the realm, rendered an appeal to the sword unavoidable; and the fear of this impending collision, there can be little doubt, led to Gloucester's being so unanimously confirmed in the protectorship by the friends of both parties, after he had forcibly seized that dignity, whether in virtue of former precedents, or, as asserted by Buck[3], in pursuance of the deceased king's command.

In consequence, however, of the embarrassing circumstances which arose almost immediately after this event, and which so completely disorganised the whole state of public affairs, attention has never been sufficiently directed to the threatened evils and miserable feuds that must inevitably

[1] " Without any slaughter, or the shedding of as much blood as would issue from a cut finger." — *Chron. Croy.*, p. 566.

[2] Buck, in noticing "the insolency of the queen's kindred," states, that they " stirred up competitions and turbulencies among the nobles, and became so insolent and public in their pride and outrages towards the people, that they forced their murmurs at length to bring forth mutiny against them." Again, " they extended their malice to the princes of the blood and chief nobility, many times by slanders and false suggestions, privately incensing the king against them." — Lib. i. p. 12.

[3] Buck, lib. i. p. 11.

have desolated the land, had the youthful monarch, in conjunction with his mother and her family, been opposed to the ancient lords of the realm[1]; at an era as remarkable for the insufficiency of the regal prerogative as for the preponderating influence of the nobility. Gloucester, by his constitutional calmness, and his experience in the civil government of men, saw the dangers which threatened the destruction of his royal house, and the heir of the Yorkist dynasty. Bold in design, and enterprising in spirit, his ready genius discerned, and his prudence selected, a middle path, between open rebellion to his sovereign[2] and ignoble submission to the queen mother; and seizing upon the opportunity which the actions of Dorset and Rivers afforded of crushing these impending hostilities, without either party having recourse to arms, he entered with alacrity and zeal upon the daring career which he had seen the urgent necessity of adopting, and from which he never withdrew until he had secured to himself the power of carrying into effect, under the sanction and authority of parliament, those resolute measures which he had boldly commenced on his own responsibility.

And so far not a shadow of blame can attach to

---

[1] If the queen's kindred "should assemble in the king's name much people, they should give the lords (atwixt whom and them had been sometime debate) to fear and suspect lest they should gather this people, not for the king's safeguard, whom no man impugned, but for their destruction. . . . . For which cause they [the nobles] should assemble on the other party much people again for their defence," "and thus should all the realm fall on a roar." — *More*, p. 22.

[2] Ibid.

the memory of Richard of Gloucester. In his ambition to rule the state during his nephew's minority he was borne out by the usage of the times,
and by that pride of birth inherent in every branch
of the Plantagenets; but there is nothing in this
desire to indicate that Gloucester had formed any
sinister design for usurping the throne, or that he
contemplated the death of the Lords Rivers and
Grey when he caused these nobles to be arrested
and imprisoned until such time as he had thoroughly investigated the reports[1] which were generally circulated against them.[2] There can scarcely,
indeed, be a greater proof that the severities subsequently practised against the prisoners were not
the mere result of casual reports, than the fact of
the young monarch's preceptor, Dr. Alcock, bishop
of Worcester, who was seized at the same time
with the other royal attendants[3], being released
from captivity and set at large in the metropolis
within a fortnight[4] of his arrest at Stratford:
added to this, that the treasurer of the young
prince's household, Sir Richard Croft, was speedily
rewarded for his services by a pension for life[5];
and that no imputation of any kind was ever cast

[1] The Lord Hastings assured the council that Rivers and Grey
should no longer remain under arrest " than till the matter were
(not by the dukes only, but also by all the other Lords of the king's
council) indifferently examined, and by other discretion ordered,
and either judged or appeased." — *More*, p. 32.

[2] " They were accused of having conspired the death of the protector." — *Rous, Hist. Reg. Ang.*, p. 217.

[3] These were Dr. Alcock, preceptor and president of his council;
Sir Thomas Vaughan, lord chamberlain; Sir Richard Hurst, treasurer
of the household.

[4] Royal Wills, p. 345.

[5] Harl. MSS., No. 433. fo. 58.

upon King Edward's chancellor, upon his lord
steward, or any other members of his establishment[1] who remained behind at Ludlow, although
Sir Thomas Vaughan[2] and Sir Richard Hurst, arrested at Stratford with the Lords Rivers and
Grey, were detained in prison, and eventually
executed with those noblemen.

The conduct indeed of the duke of Gloucester
up to this period, considering the temper and character of the times, was irreproachable. His proceedings, though startling, from the stern decision
which they indicated, were not acted in the dark;
not clandestinely pursued, but openly, before the
gaze of the people.[3]

There was, moreover, no necessity for plotting
or intrigue, inasmuch as his interposition at Stratford was forced upon him by the noblest in the
land, and sanctioned by the highest in authority.
And that honourable position which Gloucester so
speedily attained, owing to the jealousies of other
and less noble minds, was never, it ought to be
remembered, made a reproach to him until the
same spirit of jealousy and craving for power, the
same conflicting interests in the rival lords[4], who,

[1] The other members of the prince's establishment were, the
Bishop of St. David's, chancellor; Sir Wm. Stanley, steward of the
household; Sir Richard Croft, treasurer. — *Sloane MSS.*, No. 3.
479.; and *Harl. MSS.*, No. 433. fo. 665.

[2] Sir Thomas Vaughan was nearly related to the Wydville family,
and through the interest of the queen he had been appointed by
Edward IV. treasurer of the king's chamber, and master of his
jewels. — *Cal. Rot.*, p. 311.

[3] Polydore Virgil, lib. i. p. 11.; and More, p. 29.

[4] "In especial twayne, Henry Duke of Buckingham and William
Lord Hastings . . . . these two not bearing eche to other, so
much love, as hatred both, unto the queen's party." — *More*, p. 21.

to promote their own selfish ends, had rekindled
that inordinate ambition which was the evil genius
of Richard's house, made them seek to enslave the
victim whom they had exalted, solely to advance
their own aspiring views. Thus embarrassed and
surrounded with difficulties, keenly alive to the important charge confided to his care, but unable
from the rivalry and envy of his compeers to
follow the dictates of his own better judgment,
Gloucester was gradually tempted to adopt measures so offensive to the young king, that he soon
found his personal safety had become compromised[1],
in consequence of which he was led to depart from
that virtuous and honourable path which had characterised his youth and his manhood, and to enter
upon a course which probably he never would have
attempted had he not been swayed by evil counsellors, and made the tool of treacherous and time-
serving allies.

Succeeding ages have dwelt on this epoch as one
of the most corrupt in English history, and justly
so. " The state of things and the dispositions of
men were such," writes Sir Thomas More, " that a
man could not tell whom he might trust, or whom
he might fear[2];" and almost similar sentiments are
expressed in a letter written by one high in office
at this identical time, — " every man doubts the
other." [3]   It has been already shown, that from the

---

[1] " The matter was broken unto the Duke of Bukingham by the
protector," who declared unto him "that the young king was
offended with him, for his kinsfolk's sake, and that if he was ever
able, he would revenge them." — *More,* p. 64.
[2] Ibid.   [3] Excerpt. Hist., p. 17.

period of the birth of Richard of Gloucester up to the date of his elevation to the protectorate, the worst passions had disgraced, and the most unworthy motives influenced, the highest in rank and station.

The Duke of Gloucester well remembered that the leading members of the very council who were now associated with him in carrying out the measures of government were those peers and prelates who had been bribed by the wily monarch of France[1], Louis XI.; who had sacrificed honour to gold, and in whom the love of wealth was stronger than the love of their country. He well knew, also, that their unanimity when raising him to be " defender of the realm" arose more from hatred to the queen and her family than from respect to himself, or devotion to their youthful sovereign; and with his keen perception of human character, he could entertain little doubt that the support which they now gave him, and the loyalty they professed towards their prince, had no more solid basis than the wavering and time-serving policy that had twice elevated his royal brother to the throne, and twice deposed his unhappy rival.

In selecting the Duke of Gloucester, then, as a peculiar object of execration, and as seeming to

---

[1] Jean Tillet, with Phil. de Comines, tells us that the Lord Howard, in less than two years, had the value of 24,000 crowns in plate, coins, and jewels, over and above his annual pension; the Lord Hastings at one time to the value of 2000 marcs in plate, besides his pension; and Dr. Rotherham, bishop of Lincoln, lord chancellor of England, and Dr. Morton, bishop of Ely, master of the rolls, with other noblemen and councillors of special credit with the king, had 2000 crowns apiece per annum. — *Buck*, lib. i. p. 29.

concentrate in himself, in an extreme degree, the
evil principles which characterised an age so selfish
and demoralised, great injustice has been done to
this prince; no mention ever being made of his
nobler qualities, as a palliative to those vices which
have been alone perpetuated, or attention drawn
to the particular merits of his character, his fidelity,
his patriotism, and his integrity, in the many offices
of trust and importance which he had filled with
equal honour to himself and benefit to his country.
He did not, it is true, escape the infection of the
corrupt times in which he lived, or remain un-
tainted by the love of power, which in that day
seemed to supersede all other feelings saving the
desire of wealth alone. And who, imbued from
infancy with these the leading features of his age,
stimulated by a father's example, strengthened by
a brother's precepts, could have passed through
life uninfluenced by the pernicious education which,
from his very cradle, had taught him to covet a
crown? — not the imperious Plantagenets, whose
ascendancy was characterised by violence, usurpation and homicide[1] — not the race of York,
" greedy and ambitious of authority "[2] — not the
sole surviving brother of a fraternity, " great,
stately," "impatient of partners!"[3]

Had Richard of Gloucester died after his elevation to the Protectorate, and before he had tasted
the sweets of sovereignty, coupled with what different associations would his name have descended

---

[1] Biondi's Civill Warres, vol. i. lib. iv. p. 1.
[2] More, p. 7.   [3] Ibid.

to posterity ! Evil, there can be little doubt would equally have befallen his ill-fated nephew ; but Richard would have been commemorated as the prince who had stayed the demon of war at the accession of young Edward, and blunted the arrows of discord when the bow was bent, and the shaft had well nigh winged its flight at the victims of ambition, of hatred, and of revenge. Then would his motto, " Loyalty bindeth me," have been strictly realised by his actions [1]; then would his memory have been united with that of Edward V. in the literal manner in which, by a singular coincidence, the only specimens of their autographs combined (of which the subjoined is a fac-simile) have been transmitted to posterity, — the protector's name beneath that of his youthful sovereign, followed by the words " Loyaultè me liè."

The want of confidence that pervaded the highest in rank, both temporal and ecclesiastical, is strikingly

[1] " His loyalty bearing a most constant expression in his motto," says Sir George Buck, " ' Loyaultè me liè' (loyalty bindeth me) ; which I have seen written by his own hand, and subscribed Richard Gloucester." The autograph here mentioned is still extant, having been preserved in the Cott. MSS., Vesp. F. xiii. fo. 53.

displayed by the refusal of the late king's executors to carry into effect the provisions of their royal master's will.

As a contrast, however, to this melancholy picture, a pleasing instance is afforded of the high estimation which, at this corrupt period, Cecily Duchess of York still maintained in public estimation [1]; for Baynard's Castle, her metropolitan abode [2], and the place where she was at this time sojourning, was selected by the two archbishops and eight other prelates, for holding the meeting which placed her late son's property under ecclesiastical sequestration [3], and for depositing also the king's jewels [4], which were thenceforth entrusted to his mother's

[1] Although the name of the Duchess of York seldom occurs in connection with the political events of Edward the Fourth's reign, yet there are not wanting a few brief notices of this illustrious lady, that carry on her personal history up to that monarch's decease. Among the Tower records is preserved a privy seal bill (temp. 8th Edw. IV.), conveying to the Lady Cecily a grant of certain lands in the vicinity of the monastery of St. Benett, "for so moche as our dearest lady mother hath instantly sued unto us for this matter, and for so much also as our very trust is in her." At the back of the instrument, written in the king's own hand, are these words : — "My Lord Chauncellor, this must be done." (Dr. Stillington was at that time lord chancellor of England.) During King Edward's invasion of France, in 1475, the following mention is made of the Lady Cecily in the Paston Letters (vol. ii. p. 181.) : " My Lady of York and all her household is here at St. Benett's, and purpose to abide there still, till the king come from beyond the sea, and longer if she like the air there as it is said." (St. Benett's was a mitred abbey at Holm, in the parish of Horning, county of Norfolk, then a structure of great importance, now a mere ruin in the midst of a dreary level marsh.) In 1480 (20th Edw. IV.), it appears that Cecily Duchess of York and her sister Anne Duchess of Buckingham both professed themselves religious, at Northampton, on the same day." — See *Nicholl's Hist. and Antiq. of Fotheringay.*

[2] Archæologia, P. xiii. p. 7.

[3] Roy. Wills, p. 345.   [4] Ibid.

charge, as it would seem, because the executors
were mutually distrustful of each other.

The Duke of Gloucester was present at this
meeting;—another cause for believing that he must
in some measure have been connected with, or interested in, the contents of his brother's last testament. The length of time which separates this
distant period from the present age precludes the
possibility of ascertaining precisely how far Richard
Duke of Gloucester and the Lady Cecily participated in the same sentiments: but it appears that,
on reaching London, he repaired at once to the
abode of his venerable parent, and continued for
some days an inmate with her; which circumstance
affords reason for surmising that the Lady Cecily
approved of the measures he had pursued, and was
in all likelihood a party concerned in instigating
him to adopt them, from the frequent messengers
which are said to have met him upon his arrival at
York, and on the road to Northampton.[1] This
fact is important, for as this illustrious lady had
recently become a member of the Benedictine order[2],
her religious vows[3] would seem a sufficient surety
that she would not lend herself to any nefarious
projects, either for disinheriting her grandchild, or
for unjustly elevating her son to the throne; although there can be little doubt that the death of
the Duke of Clarence, promoted as it had been by
the queen and Lord Rivers, still rankled deeply
and painfully in the heart of every member of the

---

[1] More, p. 35., and Drake's Eborac., p. 111.
[2] Cott. MSS., Vitel. L. fo. 17.
[3] See Appendix C.

house of York, at an era more remarkable for re-
talition and revenge than for the Christian virtues
of mercy and forgiveness.

Unhappily for all parties, this rancorous feeling
was constantly fed by the knowledge that the
enormous wealth of the deceased and attainted
prince, together with the person, guardianship,
and marriage of his youthful heir, the Earl of
Warwick, instead of enriching his own kindred,
had been conferred upon, and was still in the hands
of, a Grey, the Lord of Dorset.[1]   Neither, indeed,
could Gloucester or the Lady Cecily entertain a
doubt that if the same aspiring and not over scru-
pulous race, who had ruined the fame of one
brother and procured the execution of the other,
could but secure the ear of the new sovereign[2],
himself likewise, the late monarch's only surviving
brother, would speedily fall a victim to their hatred
and ambition.[3]

Thus on the demise of Edward IV., or rather at
the accession of Edward V., a struggle for pre-
eminence, altogether apart from all merely political
questions, arose between the young monarch's royal
kindred and his maternal relatives.   The natural
consequence was, that the protector was instigated
and supported in his resolute measures by every
branch of his own princely house[4]; but chiefly by

---

[1] Cal. Rot., p. 325.

[2] " Howbeit, as great peril is growing, if we suffer this young
king in our enemies' hand, which, without his willing, might abuse
the name of his commandment, to any of our undoing, which thing
God and good provision forbid."—*More*, p. 20.

[3] " As easily as they have done some other, already as near of his
royal blood as we."— *Ibid.*

[4] The Duke of Buckingham, as already shown, was a Plantagenet

his mother, whose heart had ever inclined to Richard, the youngest but most judicious of her sons; and that her own kindred, the lordly Nevilles, were equally zealous in espousing his cause[1], is shown by one of the first acts of his protectorate being to endow the Lord Neville with the constableship of the Castle of Pontefract[2], in reward for his faithful adherence.

The month of May, ushered in so ominously by the seizure of Edward V. and the dispersion of his attendants, and rendered, afterwards, so remarkable by its comprehending, in the brief space of days, acts that in the ordinary course of things it would take months, if not years, to carry into effect, glided on more tranquilly towards its close than the portentous events which heralded its dawn would have seemed to prognosticate. Richard presided with his characteristic energy at the helm of state, assisted, there is reason to suppose, by a council appointed at the time when he was nominated to the protectorate; and although no document is known to be extant recording the names of such nobles as were deputed, according to ancient precedent, to assist Gloucester in his ar-

by descent from Thomas of Woodstock, the fifth son of Edward III.; and the Lord Howard, whose fidelity to Richard is a subject of historical notoriety, was also a Plantagenet, being lineally descended from Thomas of Brotherton, younger son of King Edward I.

[1] Sir George Neville, lord Bergavenny, and Henry Neville, his son, nephews of the Duchess of York, were also among his zealous partizans, and were rewarded with proofs of his gratitude. Henry Percy, earl of Northumberland, his chief supporter, was likewise allied to the Nevilles, that nobeman's brother having married Ellinor, the Lady Cecily's sister.

[2] Harl. MSS., 433. fo. 223.

duous duties, yet the connection of the most firm of King Edward's friends, and of the most zealous of Gloucester's supporters, with the measures of the protector enables a tolerable judgment to be formed as to who were his political associates in the administration.[1]

The new acts of the young monarch being attested at Westminster, as well as at the Tower[2], intimates also that the council assembled at both of these places; and trivial as it may appear, this circumstance conveys an important fact, inasmuch as it proves that the youthful monarch was under no undue restraint, but that he occasionally joined his council at Westminster, or was visited by its members at his apartments in the Tower, after " the court was removed to the Castle Royal and chief house of safety in the kingdom;"[3] thus proving him to have been accessible to his lordly subjects, and by no means under the restraint generally reputed to have been imposed on him by the protector.

A state of things so tranquil. and harmonious could not, however, long continue, taking into consideration the secret views entertained by the dif-

---

[1] The names of these nobles are — Hastings, lord chamberlain to Edward IV. ; Stanley, lord steward of the late king's household ; Rotherham, archbishop of York, and Morton, bishop of Ely. These servants of the late king were also his executors. (See *Royal Wills*, p. 347.) Of Gloucester's peculiar and especial party may be named, Buckingham, created constable of the Duchy of Lancaster ; Northumberland, warden of the North ; Howard, seneschal of the Duchy of Lancaster ; and Lovel, chief butler of England. The neutral party were, Bourchier, archbishop of Canterbury ; Russel, bishop of Lincoln, the new lord chancellor ; and Gunthorp, dean of Wells, his successor in the office of privy seal.

[2] See Fœdera, xii. p. 180. ; and Harl. MSS., 433. p. 221.

[3] Buck, lib. i. p. 11.

ferent parties of which the council was composed, and the discordant feelings which influenced the advisers of young Edward's administration. They had all united in opposing the queen and her family, when they had reason to dread their aiming at the regency[1]; and both had joyfully elevated Gloucester to the guardianship of the king, the more effectually to crush his rivals in power.

But in so doing they had not designed to invest this prince with the absolute power conferred on him by the senate, "commanding and forbidding in every thing like another king!"[2] and could ill brook the haughty independence, the proud decision, and the regal superiority which Gloucester immediately assumed, both in the councils of state and in the style of his decrees. They felt that nothing more had been done than the transfer of the government of the realm from the "queen's blood to the more noble of the king's blood[3];" and that the benefit and patronage anticipated by the opposing parties, instead of being neutralised, as they had hoped, by the protector, was now altogether concentrated in his hands. Peaceably, therefore, as Richard had obtained the ascendency, it was an office too much bordering on despotic authority to be viewed otherwise than with distrust and envy by his compeers; and occasions speedily occurred for making this feeling apparent. The first symptom of discontent, says the annalist of Croyland, arose from "the detention of the king's

[1] Buck, lib. i. p. 12.
[2] Chron. Croy., p. 566.   [3] Ibid.

relatives and servants in prison, and the protector not having sufficiently provided for the honour and security of the queen."[1] For the late monarch's servants, although opposed to the royal Elizabeth when in her prosperity she abused the indulgence of her illustrious consort, had relented towards their widowed mistress in this her hour of adversity; and the more so, as their own jealous feelings had now become excited against a rival whom they suspected to be fully as aspiring, and felt to be far more powerful, than either the queen or her obnoxious kindred. These sentiments, at first slowly admitted, gained strength as it was seen that all vacant offices of profit or trust were bestowed on Gloucester's adherents; and a visible disunion in the council was the natural result. This disunion was displayed in various ways, but chiefly by secret meetings held at the private dwelling-house of the Duke of Gloucester; and that, too, not unfrequently at the same time when such members of the council as favoured the young king and his mother were formally and officially assembled elsewhere.[2]

Richard had quitted Baynard's Castle upon the removal of his nephew to the Tower, and had established himself at his metropolitan abode[3] in Bishopsgate Street[4]; whither, says Sir Thomas More, "little by little, all folk withdrew from the

---

[1] Chron. Croy., p. 566.   [2] More, p. 66.

[3] "Richard Duke of Gloucester and lord protector, afterwards king by the name of Richard III., was lodged in Crosby Place." — *Stowe's London*, p. 106.

[4] Fabyan, p. 513.

Tower, and drew to Crosbie's Place, where the Protector kept his household."[1]

This open display of pre-eminence and strength on the part of Gloucester increased the mistrust and doubt which had already taken possession of the minds of his adversaries[2]; and it is related that the Lord Stanley in particular, between whom and the Lord of Gloucester there was little love,[3] " said unto the Lord Hastings, that he much misliked these two several councils; for while we (quod he) talk of one matter in the tone place, little wot we whereof they talk in the tother place."[4] Nevertheless, for a time the important affairs of state continued to progress without serious interruption, and the month of June was ushered in by active preparations for the coronation of Edward V. This ceremonial was officially announced as definitively fixed for the 22d inst.; and letters were addressed to numerous persons in the king's name[5], charging them " to be prepared to receive the order of knighthood at his coronation, which he intended to solemnize at Westminster on the 22d of the same month."[6] Costly robes[7] were ordered for this

---

[1] More, p. 67.   [2] Ibid.

[3] In an old MS. poem, written by Robert Glover, Somerset herald in the reign of Queen Elizabeth, there is a quaint description of two quarrels between the Lord Stanley and Richard of Gloucester when in the north, both of which were decided by force of arms. In the last encounter Stanley's men defeated Richard's forces near Salford Bridge; and the poem says, —

> " Jack o' Wigan, he did take
> The Duke of Gloucester's banner,
> And hung it up in Wigan church,
> A monument to his honour."

[4] More, p. 67.   [5] See Appendix D.
[6] Fœdera, vol. xii. p. 185.   [7] See Appendix E.

" honourable solemnitie,"[1] of which the time appointed "then so near approached that the pageants
and subtleties[2] were in making day and night at
Westminster, and much victuals killed therefore
that afterwards was cast away."[3] The nobles and
knights from all parts of the realm were summoned
by the Duke of Gloucester[4], and came thick to

[1] The entry in the Wardrobe accounts, setting forth that robes
were ordered for " the Lord Edward, son of Edward IV., for his
apparel and array," the which entry Lord Orford first brought to
notice in his " Historic Doubts" (p. 64.), there can exist no doubt,
formed part of the preparations mentioned by Sir Thomas More as
devised by the lords in council for " the honourable solemnitie" of
the young king's coronation. By the annexed entry, preserved
among the Harl. MSS. (No. 433. art. 1651.), these preparations
appear to have been carried on almost up to the very day fixed upon
for the ceremonial. "Warrant for payment of 14l. 11s. 5d. to John
Belle, in full contentacion of 32l. 2s. 7d., for certain stuff of wildfowl
of him bought by Sir John Elrington, ayenst that time that the
coronation of the bastard son of King Edward should have been
kept and holden." Now the marked distinction in the wording of
these two memoranda show at once that one was inserted *before*, and
the other *after*, the illegitimacy of the prince had been established ;
and removes all doubts as to the robes having been ordered for the
young king's coronation, at the time when the letters announcing the
ceremony as fixed for the 22d June were issued. Preparations for
the coronation of Richard III. were not commenced until after the
illegitimacy of the young princes had been admitted. From that
time all notices relative to the deposed sovereign are couched in the
same language as the entry above quoted from the Harl. MSS., the
epithet, " bastard son of King Edward," being invariably affixed,
because from this defective title of his nephew arose the Protector's
elevation to the crown.

[2] Subtleties or sotilties signified paste moulded into the form of
figures, animals, &c., and grouped so as to represent some scriptural or
political device. At the coronation of King Henry VI. "a sotiltie
graced every course ;" a description of one of which will suffice to
exemplify the nature of the emblematical confectionery that was so
much estimated at this period. "At the third course was exhibited,"
states Fabyan, " a sotiltie of the Virgin with her Child in her lap,
and holding a crown in her hand : St. George and St. Denis kneeling
on either side, presenting to her, King Henry with a ballad in his
hand."—*Fab. Chron.*, p. 419.

[3] More, p. 76.   [4] Ibid. p. 66.

grace that ceremonial; and the Duchess of Gloucester, having been sent for by the Protector, " reached
the metropolis on the aforesaid 5th instant,"[1] and
joined her husband at Crosby Place.

Meanwhile the difficulties of Gloucester's position
daily increased. He feared to release the Lords
Rivers and Grey, yet he knew that each day's captivity alienated the young king's affection farther
from himself. The royal youth had been too early
and too strenuously imbued with affection for his
mother's kindred, whose interest it had been from
childhood to conciliate his love, not to bemoan
deeply and bitterly their continued separation from
him: their " imprisonment," we are told, " was
grievous to him!"[2] Whether it was that the mild
and gentle Edward V. was deficient in that moral
energy and daring spirit which formed the chief,
nay, sole recommendation of the period in which he
lived, or that he betrayed a physical incapacity for
exercising the regal prerogative in such troubled
times, cannot at this distant period be determined;
but the assertion of Sir Thomas More, that the
increased popularity of Gloucester " left the king
in manner desolate,"[3] would seem to indicate that
there must have been some stronger motive for
this palpable desertion of the young king, and for
the deference paid to Richard, than could have
arisen merely from the power attached to an office
which the latter had exercised but a few weeks,
and which all men knew, in a yet shorter period of
time, would cease altogether.

[1] Excerpt. Hist., p. 17.
[2] More, p. 64. [3] Ibid. p. 66.

The high dignity of protector of the realm always lapsed after the coronation of the monarch, whose regal authority, during infancy, it was the peculiar province of that office to maintain[1]; and setting aside the knowledge that such had been invariably the case in all minorities preceding that of Edward V., the legislature, in nominating Richard as protector, expressly restricted him to " the same power [2] as was conferred on Humphrey Duke of Gloucester during the minority of Henry VI."

The disastrous fate of this excellent and noble prince was of too recent occurrence for all matters connected with his lamentable end to be forgotten; and Richard well knew that the Lancastrian monarch, whom his brother had deposed, was crowned in his eighth year, with the express design of terminating the office and power of his uncle the lord protector ; neither was he likely to forget that the murder of Humphrey Duke of Gloucester [3] resulted from the jealous and determined malice of his political enemies. The subject of these memoirs flourished in an age of dark superstition — one in which omens and presages, soothsaying and necromancy held an unbounded influence over the minds of all men; and the uncle of Edward V., beset as he was with perplexities of no ordinary kind, became feelingly alive, there can be little doubt, to the ill-omened title which he bore[4], and the presage of evil which seemed especially to attach to its being con-

---

[1] Rot. Parl., vol. iv. p. 326. [2] Chron. Croy., 566.
[3] Hall, p. 209. [4] See Appendix F.

joined to that of lord protector.[1] Had the brother of Edward IV. been nominated regent instead of protector, or had the disturbed state of the realm led to the extreme measure of a prolonged protectorate until his nephew was of age to govern in his own person, Richard of Gloucester in all likelihood had never aspired to be king; but his proud spirit could ill brook the prospect that awaited him of sinking into a mere lord of council[2], after having ruled for some months in the capacity of protector of the realm; and life possessed too many charms at the age of thirty for him calmly to reflect on the more than probability that he would fall a victim to the same dangerous elevation which had proved the death-warrant of preceding Dukes of Gloucester.

Two paths alone seemed opened to him; either to conciliate the young king by releasing Rivers and Grey, and acting thenceforth in conjunction with the queen and her kindred, or boldly to form a distinct interest for himself under the hope of its leading to some more permanent authority. In the former case he must sacrifice Hastings[3], Buckingham, Northumberland[4], and his noblest supporters, and sink into one of the Wydville train,

[1] Holinshed, p. 211.   [2] Parl. Roll, vol. iv. p. 338.
[3] " Hastings feared that if the supreme power fell into the hands of those of the queen's blood, they would avenge upon him the injuries which they had received." — *Chron. Croy.*, p. 564.
[4] Buckingham and Northumberland were the chief accusers of the Wydvilles, and the instigators of the arrest of the Lords Rivers and Grey; who " would prick him (the king) forward thereunto if they escaped; for they wolde remember their imprisonment." — *More*, p. 64.

— a degradation from which his pride of birth as a Plantagenet recoiled; — and in the latter case he was so much beholden to the above-named nobles, that his honour was, as it were, pledged to them; although he was already convinced, from the jealousy which they had evinced in the executive deliberations, that it was doubtful whether he would be enabled to carry out any measures of farther aggrandizement. With his usual sagacity, then, and a keen perception of the desperate character of the times, he resolved on being prepared for either extreme; accordingly, on the eighth instant, by the hand of one of his faithful adherents, Thomas Brackenbury, he renewed his former connection with the city of York, by writing to the authorities of that place [1], in reply to " letters of supplication which they had recently addressed to him, preferring some request to which he promised speedy attention [2]; and when accused of " cajolery," in thus keeping himself alive in the remembrance of his friends in that city, it seems always to have been forgotten that York and the northern towns had been for nearly ten years under Richard's immediate jurisdiction; that he was warmly and firmly beloved in that part of England; and that the letter which he has been charged with writing " artfully, to curry favour," was, in effect, an official answer to an earnest appeal

[1] See Appendix G.

[2] Drake, who has published this letter from the original MS. preserved among the records of the city of York, states that " York and the northern parts were his strongest attachment; and, in order to make the city more in his interest, a remarkable letter was sent from him and delivered to the lord mayor by Thomas Brackenbury." — *Drake's Ebor.*, p. 111.

sent by a special messenger from the mayor and commonalty of the city of York, who evidently rested their hopes of success " on the loving and kind disposition" shown to Gloucester in former times, and which that prince in his letter acknowledges that " he never can forget." [1] — Scarcely, however, was this pacific despatch transmitted than some intimation of approaching danger appears to have reached Gloucester's anxious and susceptible ear. Of the exact nature and extent of this threatened evil no minute details remain; but that it was some plot to compass Richard's destruction appears certain, from a second letter written by this prince, and addressed to the citizens of York [2], praying them to send armed men to town to assist in " guarding him against the queen" and " her affinity, which have intended, and do daily intend, to murder and utterly destroy us and our cousin the Duke of Buckingham and the blood of the realm." This communication was not conveyed secretly to the mayor, but addressed to him from his post as " protector of the realm ;" and that this fresh outbreak decided the fate of the prisoners in the North seems certain, from Sir Richard Ratcliffe, the bearer of the above [3], being also charged with commands from Gloucester to the Earl of Northumberland to proceed to the castle of Pontefract, there to preside at the trial of Lord Rivers [4], and from his also carrying a warrant for the immediate execution of Grey, Vaughan, and Hurst. [5]

[1] Drake's Ebor., p. 111.   [2] See Appendix H.
[3] Cont. Croy., p. 567.   [4] Rous, Hist. Reg. Ang., 214.
[5] Drake's Ebor., p. 111.

The following day (11th of June) Gloucester further addressed an earnest appeal for support to his kinsman, the Lord Neville; and as this is conveyed in a private letter, and that such confidential communications form the most authentic source for biographical memoirs, a document so materially affecting Richard's actions at this important and mysterious period of his life demands unabbreviated insertion.

"To my Lord Nevylle[1], in haste.—

"My Lord Nevylle, I recommend me unto you as heartily as I can, and as ye love me, and your own weal and surety and this realm, that ye come to me with that ye may make defensibly arrayed in all the haste that is possible; and that ye will give credence to . . . . . Richard Radclyff, this bearer, whom I now do send to you instructed with all my mind and intent.

"And, my lord, do me now good service, as ye have always before done, and I trust now so to remember you as shall be the making of you and yours. And God send you good fortunes.

"Written at London, the 11th day of June, with the hand of

"Your heartily loving cousin and master,

"R. GLOUCESTER.[2]

"London, Wednesday, 11th June, 1483.
(1 Edw. V.)"

Notwithstanding the merciless feeling so invariably imputed to him, Richard Duke of Gloucester

---

[1] It does not clearly appear who this Lord Neville was. Sir George Neville, lord Abergavenny, attended the coronation of Richard III. as a baron, but he was never called Lord Neville.

[2] Paston Letters, vol. v. p. 303.

was not cruel by nature. [1] Circumspect and wary
he undoubtedly was; but the habit of concealing his
designs resulted more from prudence and a lively
sense of the perfidious character of the age than
from deliberate hypocrisy and hardness of heart.
Up to this period no accusation of homicide, either
as prince or protector, has been laid to his charge
by contemporary writers, which is the more remarkable considering that he flourished at an epoch
singularly ferocious, and pre-eminently distinguished for the infliction of summary vengeance,
and utter disregard of the value of human life.[2]
Consistently, therefore, with his temperate and
watchful habit, although he wrote both officially
and privately, on the 10th and 11th of June, providing for his safety by requiring his northern partizans to assemble at Pontefract, and as speedily as
possible to be conducted to London by the Lords
Northumberland and Neville, he appears to have
carefully concealed from those around him his apprehension of danger—or rather that he had received
any direct intimation of it—until he was enabled to
test the fidelity of Hastings, and other members of
the council implicated, by report in the scheme for
his destruction. Unhappily for all the parties concerned, Richard had admitted to his councils and
confidence one of those plausible but wretched
instruments of treachery and dissimulation, who,

---

[1] " There were instances enough of his bounty and humanity, but
none of his cruelty, till, being protector, he was pushed on by
Buckingham and Hastings to put the queen's brother and son to
death; and which involved Hastings himself in the same ruin."—
Carte's Hist. Eng., vol. ii. p. 819.

[2] Turner's Middle Ages, vol. iv. p. 398.

sheltered by their own insignificance, are nevertheless often the active agents for producing moral and
political convulsions. Catesby, " a man well learned
in the laws of this land," and, by the especial favour
of the lord chamberlain, " in good authority," [1] had
so far insinuated himself into the protector's regard
as to assist at his private deliberations. In addition
to the fact stated by Sir Thomas More, that " no
man was so much beholden to Hastings as was this
Catesby [2], it appears that a brotherly affection and
close intimacy had long subsisted between them.
He was " of his near secret council," he adds, " and
whom he very familiarly used, and in his most
weighty matters put no man in so special trust." [3]
Now the Lord Hastings was but the echo of Stanley,
Rotheram, and Morton. The annexed words, therefore, of Sir Thomas More [4] on this point are very
important, when it is considered that his information
was almost certainly derived from Morton himself;
and the conviction consequently resulting is, that
Catesby, by his subtlety and hypocrisy, had discovered and divulged the treasonable designs which
led to the foregoing letters,—" but surely great pity
was it, that he (Catesby) had not had either more
truth, or less wit ; for his *dissimulation only* kept all
that mischief up."

The unsuspecting frankness of the Lord Chamberlain proved indeed his destruction ; yet it seems
that Richard struggled hard to save Hastings' life :
" the Protector loved him well, and loath was to
have lost him, saving for fear lest his life should

---

[1] More, p. 68.   [2] Ibid.   [3] Ibid.   [4] Ibid.

have quailed their purpose."[1] "For which cause he moved Catesby, whether he could think it possible to win the Lord Hastings into their party," and to consent, neither to the death of young Edward, nor even to that prince's deposition, but (as admitted by the Duke of Buckingham himself to Morton) to the taking "upon him the crown till the prince came to the age of four-and-twenty years, and was able to govern the realm as an able and sufficient king."[2] Little opposition was likely to arise on this matter from the Lord of Buckingham. He had too closely allied himself to his cousin of Gloucester to hope for aggrandisement from the opposite faction; and his vanity was fed by a proposed marriage[3] between Richard's "only lawful son" and his eldest daughter.[4]

But Hastings was not so easily managed. He hated Rivers indeed, and he loved not the queen; but he was devotedly attached to the late king, and faithfully espoused the interests of his offspring. He well knew that power once obtained is very seldom voluntarily relinquished; and he also knew that Gloucester, by ambition as well as by lineage, was a Plantagenet and a Yorkist.

Unfortunately for the Protector, as well as for Hastings, Catesby, the perfidious spy on the actions of both his patrons, on both the friends whom he feigned to serve[5], was the agent em-

---

[1] More, p. 68.
[2] Grafton, Cont. of More, p. 153.   [3] More, p. 65.
[4] The Duke of Buckingham had two daughters whose ages agreed with either being the wife of the young prince.
[5] From this despicable character was lineally descended that Catesby in whom originated the Gunpowder Plot. Other members of the family, too, were notorious for the same intriguing and un-

ployed "to prove with some words cast out afar off"[1] the true state of the Lord Hastings' mind towards the Protector. " But Catesby, whether he essayed him, or essayed him not, reported that he found him so fast, and *heard him speak so terrible words*, that he durst no further break: and of truth the Lord Chamberlain of very trust shewed unto Catesby the mistrust that others began to have in this matter."[2]

Alas, for the too confiding Hastings! this imprudent openness, confirming as it did the alleged conspiracy to destroy the Lord Protector, effectually sealed the fate of the queen's kindred, decided the death of the Lord Chamberlain himself, and stimulated Richard to the desperate course he henceforth resolved on pursuing.

Catesby, in his double capacity of friend and betrayer, appears indeed to have possessed himself of some plans and schemes that involved either the destruction of Gloucester or of his foes:—" On my life, never doubt you (quod the Lord Hastings"), when warned to be circumspect; " so surely thought he that there could be none harm toward him in that counsel intended, where Catesby was,"[3]—" for while one man is there, which is never thence, never can there be thing once minded that should sound amiss toward me, but it should be in mine ears ere it were well out of their mouths." " This meant he by Catesby."[4] But honour and integrity, and trust between man and man, had little influ-

principled habits which cast so deep a shade over this period of Gloucester's career.

[1] More, p. 69.   [2] Ibid.   [3] Ibid. p. 67.   [4] Ibid.

ence on this degenerate age; for, as emphatically
stated in a remarkable letter written at this precise
period, and describing the state of the metropolis
as it was then constituted, " With us is much trouble, and every man doubts the other."[1]   Catesby
reported to Gloucester " the so terrible words" he
had heard the Lord Chamberlain speak; — and
having, through the misplaced trust of this nobleman, ascertained or feigned so to do, the evil intended and the extent of the mischief, the arrest
and condemnation of Hastings was decreed; the
which strong measure was probably taken, fully as
much in consequence of the danger likely to ensue
from the hints thrown out by Catesby to the Lord
Chamberlain as from the treasonable designs unfolded by that perfidious lawyer[2], " in whom, if the
Lord Hastings had not put so special trust, many
evil signs that he saw might have availed to save
his life."[3]

But the die was cast, and Richard's decision was
made ! Accordingly, on the 13th of June, " the protector having with singular cunning devided the
council, so that part should sit at Westminster
and part at the Tower, where the king was, Hastings, coming to the Tower to the council, was by
his command beheaded.   Thomas, Archbishop of

---

[1] See Excerpta Historica, for two valuable letters from Simon
Stallworth, one of the officers of the Bishop of Lincoln, to Sir William
Stoner, knight, giving an account of the state of London, and the
political news, shortly before the accession of Richard III. — *Excerp.
Hist.*, p. 17.

[2] " He, fearing lest their motions might with the Lord Hastings
minish his credence (whereunto only all the matter leaned), procured
the Protector hastily to rid him." — *More*, p. 69.

[3] Ibid. p. 68.

York, and John, Bishop of Ely, although on account of their order their lives were spared, were
imprisoned in separate castles in Wales."[1]

Such is the brief account given by the faithful
historian of that time. Fabyan, the city chronicler, repeats almost verbatim this statement, only
in less concise terms; but he gives no further particulars, excepting that "an outcry, by Gloucester's
assent of treason, was made in the outer chamber;"[2]
and that "the Lord Protector rose up and yode
himself to the chamber door, and there received in,
such persons as he had before appointed to execute
his malicious purpose."   "In which stirring the
Lord Stanley was hurt in the face, and kept awhile
under hold."[3]   Sir Thomas More, in the spirit of
romance which pervades his work, embellishes this
portion of his narrative, as he does all the descrip-
tive parts, by a display of his oratorical powers;
and by making his rhetoric available towards in-
corporating with the admitted facts of contemporaries the marvellous tales of a wonder-loving age.
But these descriptions, graphic as they are, and
attractive as they proved, unhappily for Richard,
both to the dramatist, the Tudor chroniclers, and
the mere copyist of later times, can no longer pass
current for, or be received as, authentic history.
Without attempting to handle arguments, and to
reiterate descrepancies which have been exposed
and examined by writers[4] of repute and superior

[1] Chron. Croy., p. 566.
[2] Fabyan's Chron., p. 514.   [3] Ibid.
[4] See Sir George Buck, lib. i. p. 13. ; Walpole's Hist. Doubts, 47. ;
Laing (in Henry), xii. p. 415. ; together with Carte, Rapin, Lingard,
Turner, and many others.

abilities, it must surely be sufficient in this enlightened age to ask any reasonable person with reference to Sir Thomas More's additions, whether a prince, who was distinguished as the ablest general of his time, a time in which the mode of warfare was remarkable for ponderous armour and weapons of almost gigantic size[1], could have had from his birth "a werish withered arm," when that arm at Barnet was opposed to the mighty Warwick himself, and by its power and nerve defeated Somerset, the most resolute warrior of the age, at the desperate battle of Tewkesbury ?

Still more improbable is the statement that the Lord Chamberlain of England should have been made to suffer death, and led out to instant execution without trial, because Jane Shore, the unhappy victim of King Edward's passion, was alleged to have leagued with the widowed queen whom she had so irreparably injured, "in wasting the Protector's body by witchcraft and sorcery :"[2] yet these traditions have been gravely perpetuated for ages; and no portion of Shakspeare's tragedy more com-

---

[1] Specimens of the armour worn in the reign of Richard III., the age in which that suit termed "ribbed" had arrived at the greatest perfection, may be seen in the present day in the armoury at the Tower, together with the helmet then used, and its weighty oreillets, the rondelles and jambs for protecting the arm-pits and legs, and several of the weapons which, had they been models, instead of actual relics of the fifteenth century, might have made many sceptical as to the possibility of their having been wielded by persons of ordinary size and strength.

[2] " Then said the Protector, ' Ye shall all see in what wise that sorceress, and that other witch of her counsel, Shore's wife, with their affinity, have by their sorcery and witchcraft wasted my body.' And therewith he plucked up his doublet sleeve to his elbow upon his left arm, where he shewed a werish withered arm and small, as it was never other."— *More*, p. 72.

pletely developes the corrupt source from which
he drew his information, than the literal manner in
which the dramatist has rendered this part of Sir
Thomas More's narrative.

Perhaps, as far as it is possible at this distant
period of time to remove the extraneous matter
which has so long cast an air of distrust over the
records of this confused era, the real facts of the
case may be summed up in the words applied to
the Protector's father by his great political antago-
nist, Edmund Duke of Somerset, under somewhat
parallel circumstances, " that if York had not
learned to play the king by his regency, he had
never forgot to obey as a subject." [1]

Richard, as has been before observed, was peculiarly fitted for sovereignty ; his legislative abilities
were of a very high order ; and having once inhaled
the intoxicating fumes of absolute power, he resolved
upon continuing his rule at any cost.   The Lords
Hastings, Rivers, and Grey would never have
sanctioned his accession to the throne, either temporarily or definitively; and that the latter were
concerned in some league to get rid of the Protector,
and therefore afforded him some show of justice for
their execution, seems to have been admitted even
by Hastings himself; for Sir Thomas More states [2],
that these nobles " were by *his assent before devised*
to be beheaded at Pontefract this self-same day, in
which he was not aware that it was by others devised that himself should be beheaded in London." [3]

---

[1] Echard, vol. i. p. 214.   [2] More, p. 74.
[3] " He was brought forth into the green beside the chapel, within
the Tower, and his head laid on a log of timber, and there stricken

The news of the Lord Chamberlain's execution,
together with the imprisonment of the bishops, the
Lord Stanley, and others "suspected to be against
the Protector," quickly spread throughout the
metropolis, and caused extreme consternation; but
Gloucester, in anticipation of this result, sent a
herald, within two hours, through the city, " in the
king's name," proclaiming the fact that " Hastings,
with divers other of his traitorous purpose, had
before conspired that same day to have slain the
Lord Protector and the Lord Buckingham sitting
in the council; and after to have taken upon them
to rule the king and the realm at pleasure, and
thereby to pil and spoil whom they list uncon-
troulled." [1]

How far this charge was well founded, it would
be vain to argue : although Sir Thomas More's
positive implication of Catesby—as regards " the
terrible words" which he asserts that he reported
to Gloucester — affords reasonable ground for supposing that there was at least some foundation for
the reported conspiracy. Moreover, as the information of this historian was derived from Bishop
Morton himself, who was implicated in the plot,
and one of the conspirators accused and imprisoned
for it, it accounts for the marvellous tales which
he gave out[2], and for his concealment of facts

off; and afterward his body, with the head, was interred at Windsor,
beside the body of King Edward IV." — *Fabyan*, p. 513.
[1] More, p. 80.
[2] " The artificial glare with which the whole is surrounded
generates a suspicion that some treason was detected and punished,—
a conspiracy in which Morton had participated with Hastings, and
was therefore desirous to remove from view." — See *Laing* (*Appendix to Henry*), vol. xii. p. 417.
G 2

that would possibly have held the Protector fully justified in his promptitude and stern decision.

Whatever was the true cause of Hastings's death, however, the effect produced was such as his enemies desired; for it is recorded by the Chronicler of Croyland, that "being removed, and the king's other adherents intimidated, the two dukes did from henceforth what they pleased."[1]

The precipice on which Gloucester stood was one that might have well daunted a less daring spirit; but, courageous and determined by nature, he felt that he had now advanced too far to admit of the possibility of retreat; and, with the desperation common to aspiring minds, he gave the full reins to that ambition which had already mastered his better feelings.

As a prelude to the views that he now began to entertain of securing the crown altogether, he felt it advisable to remove the young Duke of York to the Tower, so that, the princes being together, he might be better enabled to máture his plans and carry them into effect.[2] Without testing the ultimate designs of Richard, or drawing conclusions resulting from subsequent events, it must be admitted, that by virtue of his responsible office as

---

[1] Chron. Croy., p. 566.

[2] " Wherefore incontinent at the next meeting of the Lords at the council he proposed unto them that it was a heinous deed of the queen, and proceeding of great malice towards the king's councillors, that she should keep in sanctuary the king's brother from him, whose special pleasure and comfort were to have his brother with him. And that (by her done), to none other intent but to bring all the lords in obloquy and murmur of the people; as though they were not to be trusted with the king's brother, that by the assent of the nobles of the land were appointed, as the king's nearest friends, to the tuition of his own royal person." — More, p. 36.

Lord Protector of the realm he was, in some degree, justified in striving to obtain possession of the person of the infant Duke of York, as heir presumptive to the crown[1]; the more so since the king desired, as was indeed natural, the companionship of his brother[2]; and also because a report had been circulated that it was intended to send the young prince out of the kingdom.[3] Now Richard was not so advanced in years as to forget the almost parallel case when himself, at the very age of the Duke of York, was, with his brother of Clarence, privately conveyed to Utrecht, owing to the anxiety and misgivings of his mother; neither was he ignorant of the fact that the Marquis Dorset, the Lord Lyle, and Sir Edward Grey, his young nephews' maternal relatives, had already effected their escape[4], although Lionel Wydville, Bishop of Salisbury, yet remained in sanctuary to counsel and aid his royal sister.

Resolute, however, as was the Protector in his determination to withdraw, if possible, the young prince from Westminster, the strongest test and greatest surety for the lawfulness of his proceedings up to this time rests upon the fact that he was supported in his design by the heads of the church and the chief officers of the crown, "my Lord Cardinale, my Lord Chauncellor, and other many lords temporal."[5]

Sir Thomas More's elaborate account of the transaction, together with the lengthened orations

---

[1] More, p. 43. [2] Chron. Croy., p. 566.
[3] More, p. 36. [4] Rous, Hist. Reg. Ang., p. 212.
[5] Stallworth Letters, Ex. Hist., p. 15.

of the queen and Cardinal Bourchier, have long been considered as the effusions of his own fertile imagination[1]; but the simple statement of the Croyland Chronicler, the soundest authority of that day, embraces, there can be little doubt, the entire facts of the proceeding. "On Monday, the 15th of June, the Cardinal-Archbishop of Canterbury, with many others, entered the sanctuary at Westminster for the purpose of inducing the queen to consent to her son, Richard Duke of York, coming to the Tower for the consolation of the king his brother. To this she assented, and he was accordingly conducted thither by the archbishop."

Fabyan's account is even more laconic; but the silence of both these contemporaries, as well as that of the writer of the above-named letters[2], exonerates Richard from the alleged violence imputed to him by More; and proves beyond dispute that the young prince was removed by the consent of his

[1] Lingard, vol. v. p. 244.

[2] Simon Stallworth, the writer of these coeval letters, was one of the officers of the Lord Chancellor, into whose hands, he states, the young duke was placed; and, consequently, had personal violence been intended, he must have known it. But, although he relates that there were "at Westminster great plenty of armed men," the natural consequence of the troubled state of the metropolis which he had just been describing, he in no way couples them with what he terms "the deliverance of the Duke of York." He mentions the princely reception given to the royal child; and in this *particular point*, which is one of great importance, he agrees with Sir Thomas More, viz. that the Duke of Buckingham met the young prince in the middle of Westminster Hall, and that the Lord Protector received him at the door of the star-chamber "with many loving words, and in the company of the cardinal took him to the Tower." The armed men, there can be little doubt, were intended to guard this public procession; for the soldiers in the fifteenth century would have shrunk from forcibly violating a sanctuary.

mother, who was his natural guardian, and not by any exercise of Richard's authority as Protector. It is worthy of remark, that the City Chronicler confirms two assertions of Sir Thomas More which tell greatly in the Protector's favour; namely, the one, that Cardinal Bourchier, the Archbishop of Canterbury, pledged his life for the young prince's safety[1], so implicitly did he rely on the honour and integrity of the Duke of Gloucester; and the other, that if their royal parent would voluntarily quit the sanctuary, her sons should not be separated from her:—but he adds, " the queen, for all fair promises to her made, kept her and her daughters within the foresaid sanctuary."[2]

Had Elizabeth yielded, how different might have been the fate of Edward V.! Had she but possessed sufficient moral energy to risk her own life for her sons, as did the parents of Edward IV. and Henry VII., how far brighter might have been her own lot and that of her infant progeny! " Here is no man (quod the Duke of Buckingham) that will be at war with woman. Would God some of the men of her kin were woman too, and then should all be soon at rest."[3]

But both the princely brothers were now in the Protector's power; and those friends who had conspired against their uncle's life, and who would have opposed his elevation, were either dead or in close imprisonment. Only seven days intervened

---

[1] " He durst lay his own body and soul both in pledge, not only for his surety, but for his estate."—*More*, p. 79.

[2] Fabyan, p. 513.   [3] More, p. 41.

before that fixed for young Edward's coronation; only one short week remained, in which to aim at sovereignty, or to sink back into the position of a subject.

Richard, in an evil hour, yielded to the worldliness of a corrupt age and a pernicious education; and by this dereliction of moral and religious duty he cast from him the glory of being held up to the admiration of posterity as an example of rigid virtue and self-denial, instead of being chronicled as an usurper and the slave of his ungovernable ambition.

From this day, the 15th of June, the two Dukes of Gloucester and Buckingham no longer concealed their designs. The despatch forwarded to York by Sir Thomas Radcliff on the 10th did not reach that city for five days; but on the 19th its contents were acted upon by a proclamation[1] requiring as many armed men as could be raised to assemble at Pontefract by the 22d instant; and on the following day, the 23d, Lord Rivers, having been removed from his prison at Sheriff-Hutton, was there tried and executed by the Earl of Northumberland, that peer acting both as judge and accuser.[2] However harsh this proceeding may appear, it is clear that this unfortunate nobleman was himself satisfied that his sentence was conformable to the proceedings of the age, and had been merited by his own conduct.[3] That he had confidence also in the

---

[1] Drake's Ebor., p. 111.   [2] Rous, Hist. Reg. Angl., p. 213.

[3] The historian, who has recorded the particulars of his execution, has preserved a ballad written by Earl Rivers after he was condemned to death: it breathes a spirit of resignation and firmness

Protector's justice, although he entertained no hope of awakening his mercy, is likewise shown by the annexed conclusion to his will dated at Sheriff-Hutton 23d of June, 1483[1], " Over this I beseech humbly my Lord of Gloucester, in the worship of Christ's passion and for the merit and weal of his soul, to comfort, help, and assist, as supervisor (for very trust) of this testament, that mine executors may with his pleasure fulfill this my last will."[2]

The Duke of Gloucester, renowned as he was for bravery and military skill, was wholly averse to civil war; and, in the present instance, although he was firmly resolved on displacing his nephew, and ruling the empire as king actually, and not merely

that is very pleasing, but contains no expression either of injustice at his sentence or reproach to the Protector.—*Rous*, p. 214.

[1] Excerpt. Hist., p. 248.

[2] The commiseration ordinarily expressed at the violent end of Anthony Earl Rivers has arisen in great measure from the lamentations bestowed upon him by Caxton; whose first book (from the English press), with the date and place subjoined, was a work of this nobleman's, entitled " Dictes or Sayings of Philosophers," the MS. of which, elaborately illuminated, represents Edward IV., his son, and the queen, and Earl Rivers in the act of offering his work to the king, accompanied by Caxton.— See *Oldy's Brit. Lib.*, p. 65.; and *Ames' Typ.*, p. 104. But this accomplished nobleman, although learned, chivalrous, and excelling his compeers in the more graceful attainments of the age, was by no means free from the vices which characterised his family and the times in which he lived. He was universally unpopular, from the selfish and covetous ambition which marked his political conduct during the ascendency of his royal sister. He was the cause of King Edward's committing to the Tower his " beloved servant" Lord Hastings. He instigated the queen to insist on the Duke of Clarence's execution.—See *Fœdera*, xii. p. 95. He grasped at every profitable or powerful appointment in King Edward's gift; and would, there can be no doubt, have sacrificed the Duke of Gloucester to his insatiable ambition, had not that prince, from intimation of his designs, felt justified, in accordance with the relentless custom of that period, in committing him to prison, and commanding his execution.

by sufferance, yet his energies were altogether directed towards accomplishing this end by means the most speedy and the least turbulent. An opening had presented itself to his calculating sagacity for securing the crown, not only without bloodshed, but even with some appearance of justice, arising from an important secret with which he had been intrusted some years antecedent to this period.

The marriage of Edward IV. with Elizabeth Wydville was not valid[1], inasmuch as that monarch had before been privately married[2] to the Lady Elinor Butler.[3] Not only was this fact well known to Gloucester[4], and to the Duke of Buck-

---

[1] Rot. Parl., vol. vi. fol. 241.

[2] " The lady to whom the king was first betrothed and married was Elinor Talbot, daughter of a great peer of this realm, of a most noble and illustrious family, the Earl of Shrewsbury; who is also called in authentick writings the Lady Butler, because she was then the widow of the Lord Butler; a lady of very eminent beauty and answerable virtue, to whom the king was contracted, married, and had a child by her." — *Buck*, lib. iv. p. 122. Sir Thomas More, by some oversight, substitutes the name of Elizabeth Lucy for that of Elinor Butler: the former was King Edward's mistress, and mother of his illegitimate son Arthur Lord Lisle; the latter was his affianced and espoused wife. — See *More*, p. 96.

[3] Milles's Cat. of Honour, p. 743.

[4] On the authority of Philip de Comines (lib. v. p. 202.), Buck states, that Dr. Stillington was induced by the Lady Butler's family, to inform the Duke of Gloucester of King Edward's marriage, " as the man most inward with the king" during that monarch's life; who, upon the matter being mentioned to him by Gloucester, became so incensed against the bishop, saying, he had " not only betrayed his trust, but his children, that he dismissed him from his council, and put him under a strict imprisonment for a long time; which at length Stillington redeemed himself from by means of a heavy fine paid shortly before the king's death, as testified by Bishop Goodwin in his Catalogues Episcoporium."—*Buck*, lib. iv. p. 122.

ingham, who was the Lady Elinor's cousin [1], but Dr. Stillington, Bishop of Bath and Wells (the prelate by whom the parties had been united [2], and through whose means the circumstance had become known to the Protector), yet lived to attest the fact; and so likewise did Cecily Duchess of York, who had exerted herself both by entreaties and remonstrances [3] to prevent the second marriage [4], entered into by her son in direct violation of a sacramental oath, and in open defiance of the law, ecclesiastical as well as civil. [5] Here, then, was solid ground on which to base his own pretensions, and

[1] Elinor Talbot, daughter of John Talbot, Earl of Shrewsbury; her mother was the Lady Katherine Stafford, daughter of Humphrey Stafford, Duke of Buckingham; and she was the widow of Thomas Lord Butler, Baron of Sudely.—*Buck*, lib. iv. p. 116.

[2] " This contract was made in the hands of the bishop, who said that afterwards he married them, no person being present but they twayne and he, the king charging him strictly not to reveal it."— *Phil. de Com.*, lib. v. p. 151.

[3] More, p. 93.

[4] " The duchess, his mother, who, upon the secret advertisement of his love to this Lady Gray, used all the persuasions and authority of a mother to return him to the Lady Elinor Talbot, his former love and wife (at least his contracted), to finish and consummate what he was·bound to by public solemnity of marriage."—*Buck*, lib. iv. p. 119.

[5] Buck states, that the announcement of the king's second marriage " cast the Lady Elianora Butler into so perplext a melancholy, that she spent herself in a solitary life ever after." — Lib. iv. p. 122. The same historian also states, that the king's " remembrance of his pre-contract after a time moved him by such sensible apprehensions, that he could not brook to have it mentioned; which was the cause of his displeasure against his ancient chaplain, Dr. Stillington, because he did what his conscience urged to God and the kingdom in discovering the marriage."—*Ibid.* The Lady Eleanor did not long survive the king's infidelity: retiring into a monastery, she devoted herself to religion, and dying on the 30th of July, 1466, was buried in the Carmelites' church at Norwich. She was a great benefactress to Corpus Christi College in Cambridge, as she was likewise to the University.—*Weaver*, p. 805.

to invalidate his nephew's right of succession. Nor was Richard slow to profit by it.

The Lord Mayor, Sir Edmund Shaw, together with the sheriffs of London, were well inclined towards the Protector; and Dr. Raaf Shaw, an ecclesiastic of eminence and brother to the mayor, in conjunction with Dr. Penker, the superior of the Augustin friars, undertook to advocate the Duke of Gloucester's claims publicly from the pulpit. They were " both doctors of divinity, both great preachers, and both greatly esteemed amongst the people." [1]

When attention is directed to this point, together with the eagerness which had been so recently shown by the mayor and sheriffs above named to testify their loyalty to Edward V. on his entrance into the city [2], and their promptitude in taking the oath of allegiance to him, it cannot but suggest the conviction that Richard's claims must have been better founded, and his conduct less flagitious, than is ordinarily reported, if he could thus speedily, and without force of arms enlist both the clergy and the city magistracy in his cause.

Political expediency—the alleged source of all the miseries connected with these direful times—may have operated with Richard, as an individual, in accelerating the death of his opponent, Hastings, or his rival, the Earl Rivers; but it can scarcely be supposed to have had sufficient weight to influence the clergy and the city authorities publicly to advocate what must have appeared open perjury

---

[1] More, p. 88.   [2] Chron. Croy., p. 566.

and usurpation. The bonds of social union, it is well known, were dissevered, and the national character had become grievously demoralised by the civil wars; but it is beyond all belief that one individual, even were he as vicious and depraved as the Protector has long been represented, could have corrupted a whole nation — peers, prelates, and legislators, in the brief span of fifty days; much less have obtained sufficient mastery over the people to induce them to advocate the deposition of their acknowledged sovereign, and to seek his own advancement, unless there were palpable grounds for so strong a measure.

Little doubt can remain that many more facts must have been known to the community at large than have been perpetuated in the ex-parte statements that have alone been transmitted to posterity; a few concise notices, unfortunately, being all that is left in the present day whereby to guide the historian in his efforts to unweave that mass of fiction and deceit in which the period under consideration is enveloped.

As a prelude to the stigma which he was about to affix on Edward IV. and his offspring, Richard determined upon delivering over to the ecclesiastical power Jane Shore, his brother's favourite mistress, who was said to have been living in the same unlawful manner[1] with the Lord Hastings up to the very period of his execution.

She was arrested by the Lord Howard, or, as some say, the sheriffs of London, immediately after the lord chamberlain's death, on suspicion of being

[1] More, p. 80.

implicated in the conspiracy for which he suffered; and her vast wealth was also seized, " less," says Sir Thomas More, " from avarice than anger."[1]

It is by no means improbable that Jane's attachment to the late king may have led to her being a party concerned in schemes for securing the well-being of Edward V.; and that her house in consequence was the chosen resort of the young king's friends: but it was her immorality, not her political offences, that it best suited Gloucester at this crisis to make apparent. Consequently, after being imprisoned and examined on the latter accusation, she was delivered over to Dr. Kempe, the Bishop of London, for punishment on the former charge; and by him sentenced to perform open penance on the Sunday following the Lord Hastings' execution. Her saddened look and subdued manner, united to her rare beauty and accomplishments, excited general commiseration; but as a native of London[2], and well known to the citizens as the unfaithful partner of one of their eminent merchants, a goldsmith and banker[3]; she was a notable instance of the late king's licentious habits, and therefore a fitting instrument to prepare the minds of the people for the desperate measure which her public degradation was intended to strengthen.

On the ensuing Sunday, the 22d instant, Dr. Shaw, whose high reputation, perpetuated by Fa-

[1] More, p. 81.

[2] " This woman was born in London, worshipfully friended, honestly brought up, and very well married, saving somewhat too soon; her husband an honest citizen, young and goodly, and of good substance."— *More*, p. 83.

[3] Graph. Illust., p. 49.

byan, seems strangely irreconcilable with the part which he is said to have acted on this occasion[1], ascended St. Paul's Cross[2], " the Lord Protector, the Duke of Buckingham, and other lords being present,"[3] and selecting an appropriate text from the Book of Wisdom[4] (ch. iv. v. 3.), he directed the attention of his mixed congregation to the dissolute life which had been led by the late king. After dwelling forcibly on the evils resulting to the state from his indulgence in habits so derogatory to his own honour and the well-being of the kingdom, he " there showed openly that the children of King Edward IV. were not legitimate, nor rightful inheritors of the crown;" concluding his discourse by pointing out the preferable title of the Lord Protector, disannulling that of the young king, and urging the immediate election of Richard as the rightful heir to the throne.[5]

Such is the brief account given by Fabyan, a contemporary, a citizen[6], and most probably an au-

[1] "And the more he was wondred of, that he could take upon him such business, considering that he was so famous a man both of his learning and his natural wit."—*Fabyan,* p. 514.

[2] A pulpit in form of a cross which stood almost in the middle of St. Paul's Church-yard, raised in an open space before the cathedral; the which, says Pennant, " was used not only for the instruction of mankind by the doctrine of the preacher, but for every purpose ecclesiastical or political; for giving force to oaths, for promulgating laws, and for the defaming of those who had incurred the royal displeasure."

[3] Fabyan, p. 514.

[4] " 'Spuria vitulimina non agent radices altas;' that is to say, Bastard slips shall never take deep root."—*More,* p. 100.

[5] Fabyan, p. 514.

[6] Fabyan, who was a merchant and alderman of London, and living on the spot at this momentous crisis, is high authority for all matters which occurred in the neighbourhood of London; and as he

ditor, respecting this celebrated sermon, which, after being distorted and exaggerated to a degree almost inconceivable (unless the additions of succeeding annalists are compared with the plain testimony of such as were coeval with the event), makes Gloucester perform a part better befitting a strolling player[1] than the Lord Protector of the realm, and even act in so revolting a manner as that of instructing[2] the preacher to impugn the reputation of his own mother![3] fixing the stain of illegitimacy on all her sons but himself; and he, be it remembered, was her youngest and eleventh child![4]

Monstrous indeed is the charge! a fitting accompaniment to the common story of Clarence's death, and Gloucester's " werish and withered arm."

All reply to this gross accusation against the Protector may be summed up in the simple fact,

did not write his Chronicle until party spirit had distorted Richard's actions, and malice had blackened his reputation, he is not likely to have favoured the deceased king by withholding facts which there was then no danger in narrating.

[1] " Now was it before devised, that in the speaking of these words, the Protector should have come in among the people to the sermon, to the end that those words, meeting with his presence, might have been taken among the hearers as though the Holy Ghost had put them in the preacher's mouth, and should have moved the people even there to cry ' King Richard! King Richard!' that it might have been after said that he was specially chosen by God, and in manner by miracle. But this device quailed either by the Protector's negligence, or the preacher's over-much diligence." — *More*, p. 102.

[2] Ibid. p. 99.

[3] " The tale of Richard's aspersing the chastity of his own mother," says Horace Walpole, " is incredible ; it appearing that he lived with her in perfect harmony, and lodged with her in her palace at that very time."—*Hist. Doubts*, p. 125.

[4] See Archæol., xiii. p. 7.; Hist. Doubts, p. 42.; and Buck, lib. iii. p. 82.

that every contemporary writer is silent on the matter; making no allusion whatever to the Lady Cecily, or the unnatural and uncalled-for part said to have been acted by her son.

The Prior of Croyland and Rous of Warwick seem to have considered Dr. Shaw's sermon too unimportant even to call forth remark. Fabyan's account merely shows it to have been the means employed to prepare the citizens of London for the claims that were about to be legally submitted to the council of lords at the approaching assemblage of parliament; and .Sir Thomas More, the next writer in chronological order[1] (and the first who relates the calumny)[2], " which the worshipful doctor rather signified than fully explained,"[3] not only certifies that Richard was acquitted of all share in the transaction, but also that the entire blame was laid on the over-zeal of the time-serving, obsequious Dr. Shaw[4], assigning this outrage on the Protector's mother as the cause of that disgrace[5] which Fabyan, as well as himself, perpetuates.

---

[1] The Prior of Croyland wrote his Chronicle in 1484. Rous of Warwick wrote his history in the year 1487. Fabyan's Chronicle was compiled somewhere about 1490. Sir Thomas More wrote his Life of Richard III. in 1508. Polydore Virgil was sent to England by Pope Innocent VIII. to collect the Papal tribute in the year 1500. He commenced his history shortly after his establishment at the English court, and completed it in 1517.

[2] More, p. 99.   [3] Ibid. p. 111.

[4] " That the preacher attacked the chastity of the Protector's mother to put the late king's legitimacy in doubt, is scarcely credible, because it was unnecessary ; and if this were done, it did not originate with Richard. It was one of the articles of Clarence's attainder (Rot. Parl., vi. p. 194.), that he accused his brother, Edward IV., of being a bastard."—*Turner*, vol. iii. p. 456.

[5] " This drift had been too gross for King Richard . . . . . and to quit him of it Sir Thomas More, Richard Grafton, and Mr. Hall

It is from Polydore Virgil, the annalist of
Henry VII., whose history was compiled under
the auspices[1] of the rival and bitter enemy of
Richard III., and from which corrupted source has
sprung those calumnies which for ages have supplied the stream of history, that we must look for
the source of those accusations which so long have
darkened the fame of Richard of Gloucester. He it
was who affixed on the Protector this most uncalled-
for infamy. He makes the aspersions on the Lady
Cecily's honour to comprise the whole of the offensive portion of Dr. Shaw's sermon, even denying
that he attacked the legitimacy of King Edward's
children, although admitting that such a report was
spread at the time.[2] But Polydore Virgil was not
contemporary with that time, as were Fabyan and
the Croyland doctor. He wrote what he had heard
at the court of Henry VII., many years after

say that he was much displeased with the doctor when he heard the
relation, which the Duke of Buckingham also affirmed in his speech
to the Lord Mayor of London, viz. ' That Dr. Shaw had incurred
the great displeasure of the Protector, for speaking so dishonourably
of the duchess his mother.' That he was able of his own knowledge
to say he had done wrong to the Protector therein, who was ever
known to bear a reverend and filial love unto her."—*Buck*, lib. iii.
p. 82.

[1] Laing (in Henry), vol. xii. p. 450.

[2] Polydore Virgil says that Dr. Shaw attacked the chastity of the
mother of Edward IV., and alleged the want of resemblance between
that monarch and his father in proof of his accusation. He proceeds to state (after commenting upon the astonishment of the people
at the impudence and wickedness of this libel) that it was reported
that he had attacked the legitimacy of the sons of Edward IV., but
in proof that such was not the accusation of Dr. Shaw, adds that immediately after the sermon, " Cecilia, the mother of Edward, before
many noblemen, of whom some are yet alive, complained that so
great an injustice should have been done to her by her son Richard."
—*Pol. Virg.*, p. 454.

Richard's death, while they testified that which they had seen and known during the reign of Richard III. Polydore Virgil undertook his history at a period when one of those very children, whose legitimacy had been admitted by parliament, was queen of England and mother of the heir apparent, and likewise after the reigning monarch had commanded the obnoxious statute to be expunged from the rolls, "annulled, cancelled, destroyed, and burnt,"[1] fine and imprisonment being threatened to all possessed of copies, who did not deliver them to the lord chancellor[2] for destruction."[3]

The Croyland writer, however, had previously inserted in his chronicle the purport of the bill that was presented to the assembled lords; and Fabyan, uninfluenced by the political changes which rendered it expedient in Polydore Virgil to remove the stigma of illegitimacy from the queen consort, and fix the imputation on the children of the deceased Duchess of York[3], recorded from his own knowledge the exact substance of Dr. Shaw's sermon;

[1] Year Book, Hilary Term, 1 Hen. VII.

[2] "The statute was abrogated in Parliament, taken off the rolls, and destroyed; and those possessed of copies were directed, under the penalty of fine and imprisonment, to deliver them to the chancellor, "so that all things said or remembered in the bill and act be for ever out of remembrance and forgotten."—See *Henry*, vol. xii. App. p. 409.; *Carte*, vol. ii. p. 824.

[3] Rot. Parl., vol. vi. p. 289.

[4] Cecily Duchess of York survived her illustrious consort thirty-five years, and, after outliving her royal sons, Edward IV. and Richard III., she died in retirement at her castle of Berkhampstead in the year 1495 (10th Henry VII.), and was buried by the side of her husband in the collegiate church of Fotheringay. — *Sandford*, book v. p. 369.

at the delivery of which, as one of the civic authorities, he was, in all probability, present.[1] Resident
in London, and one of its aldermen and merchants,
he had ample means of knowing the terms on which
the Protector lived with his venerable parent. He
could not be ignorant of the remarkable scene at
Baynard's Castle, which almost immediately followed the proceedings at St. Paul's Cross—that
important assemblage of the lords and commons,
the prelates and great officers of state, at the
Lady Cecily's mansion; in the audience chamber
appertaining to which, those overtures were made
which raised her son to the throne, and whither,
says Sir Thomas More, "the mayor, with all the
aldermen, and chief commoners of the city, in their
best manner apparelled, assembling themselves together resorted—an honourable company, to move
a great matter to his grace."[2] There can, indeed,
remain no doubt that he would have noticed a
proceeding so utterly revolting as the attack, had
it been made by the Protector upon his mother's
honour, if there had been any just ground for the
accusation, when he particularly states that the
announcement of the illegitimacy of the young
princes, by Dr. Shaw, "and the dislanderous words
in the preferring of the title of the said Lord Protector and in disannulling of the other," was "to the
great abusion of all the audience except such as
favoured the matter."[3]

---

[1] Fabyan was a member of the Drapers' Company, and actively
employed in the city on many public concerns. He was sheriff
of London in the 9th year of the reign of Henry VII., and resigned his aldermanic gown in 1502, to avoid the mayoralty. —
Biog. Dict.

[2] More, p. 117.   [3] Fabyan, p. 514.

It would be vain to attempt following up the alleged effect of this sermon, or refuting the groundless calumnies which have sprung from it. The result of the revolution it was intended to prelude is well known. Discarding then the irreconcilable discrepancies of a later period, and adhering scrupulously to the coeval accounts transmitted by Fabyan and the Prior of Croyland, from whose original and then unpublished manuscript Sir George Buck copied and first made known[1] the existence of a bill which at the expiration of nearly three centuries was corroborated by the discovery of the identical roll of parliament which confirmed the facts the Croyland doctor had recorded[2], the change of government which elevated Richard of Gloucester, and excluded his nephew from the throne, may be thus briefly summed up in the concise terms of the city chronicler. " Then upon the Tuesday following Dr. Shaw's address, an assembly of the commons of the city was appointed at the Guildhall, where the Lord of Buckingham in the presence of the mayor and commonalty rehearsed the right and title that the Lord Protector had to be preferred before his nephews, the sons of his brother King Edward, to the right of the crown of England. The which process was so eloquent-wise shewed, and uttered without any impediment," he adds, — thus implying that he was present, and heard the discourse, — " and that of a long while with so sugred words of exhortation and according sentence, that many a wise man that

---

[1] Buck, lib. i. p. 23.   [2] Hist. Doubts, p. 43,

day marvelled and commended him for the good ordering of his words, but not for the intent and purpose, the which thereupon ensued."[1]

It is traditionally reported that in consequence of this powerful address, the mayor and civic authorities, accompanied by Buckingham and many knights and gentlemen, proceeded direct from the Guildhall to Crosby Place[2], the private dwelling-house of the Protector, and there formally solicited him to assume the regal dignity.

A room in this venerable structure, which still exists, retaining as it has done for nearly four centuries the name of the " council chamber[3]," together with one immediately above it, bearing the appellation of the " throne room,"[4] gives weight to the supposition that the city council may have assembled in the one, and that the throne was offered and accepted in the other.

Neither is it altogether unworthy of record, in substantiating this tradition, that Bishopsgate Street thenceforth bore the name of King Street[5], in commemoration doubtless of the residence of Richard III. within its precincts, although it has long since returned to the primitive appellation[6] which it to this day retains.

Certain it is, that on the following day, the 25th instant, for which parliament had been legally

---

[1] Fabyan, p. 514.   [2] See Harrison's Survey of London, p. 124.
[3] Carlos, Hist. of Crosby Hall, p. 36.   [4] Ibid.
[5] Blackburn's Hist. and Antiq. of Crosby Place, p. 14.
[6] Bishopsgate, the ancient name it had borne from St. Erkenwold, bishop of London, founder of the gate by which the street was formerly divided into " within and without," and which was ornamented by his effigy. — *Harrison's Survey of London*, p. 435.

convened[1] by Edward V., a supplicatory scroll was
presented to the three estates assembled at Westminster[2], although not " in form of parliament,"[3]
in consequence of the question which had arisen
respecting the legality of the young king's title to
the throne.

" There was shown then, by way of petition, on
a roll of parchment, that King Edward's sons were
bastards, alleging that he had entered into a pre-
contract with Dame Alionora Butler, before he
married Queen Elizabeth ; and, moreover, that the
blood of his other brother, George Duke of Clarence,
was attainted, so that no certain and incorrupt lineal
blood of Richard Duke of York could be found
but in the person of Richard Duke of Gloucester.
Wherefore it was besought him on behalf of the
lords and commons of the realm, that he would
take upon him his right."[4] Such is the clear and
explicit account of the contemporary historian ;
and "here," observes Horace Walpole, " we see
the origin of the tale relating to the Duchess of
York—nullus certus et incorruptus sanguis: from
these mistaken or perverted words, flowed the report of Richard's aspersing his mother's honour ; "[5]
a report the calumnious nature of which is rendered more apparent by the fact, that the Protec-

[1] Royal Wills, p. 347. [2] Rot. Parl., vol. vi. p. 240.
[3] " From which I should infer that the parliament was summoned,
but that it was not opened in due form ; Richard not choosing to do
it as Protector, because he meant to be king, and for the same reason
determining that Edward should not meet it."—*Turner,* vol. iii.
p. 458.
[4] Chron. Croy., p. 566. [5] Hist. Doubts, p. 43.

tor owed his elevation to the throne solely to the effect produced by the contents of the above-named petition.[1] " Whereupon the lords and commons, with one universal negative voice, refused the sons of King Edward,"[2] not for any ill-will or malice, but for their disabilities and incapacities, the opinions of those times holding them not legitimate.[3] For these and other causes the barons and prelates unanimously cast their election upon the Protector."[4]

Importuning the Duke of Buckingham to be their speaker, the chief lords, with other grave and learned persons, having audience granted to them at the Lady Cecily's mansion " in the great chamber at Baynard's Castle[5], then Yorke House, addressed themselves to the Lord Protector ; and after rehearsing the disabilities of Edward V., and reciting the superiority of his own title, petitioned him to assume the crown.

The result of this solemn invitation is thus narrated in the parliamentary report[6], which attests

---

[1] Rot. Parl., vol. vi. p. 240. [2] Buck, lib. i. p. 20.

[3] The king might have avoided the inconveniency of the post-contract, or later marriage, that gave the imputation of bastards to his children, and so have avoided all the ensuing calamities, if first he had procured a divorce of the former contract with the Lady Elinor from Rome. — *Ibid.* lib. iii. p. 123.

[4] Ibid. lib. i. p. 20. ; More, p. 110.

[5] Some confusion has arisen from four places being indifferently mentioned by contemporary historians as associated with the meetings of the council and the Protector during this memorable period, viz. the Tower, Westminster, Baynard's Castle, and Crosbie Place. The two former would seem to have been selected for public discussion, and the latter reserved for private deliberation. Richard choosing his mother's abode at St. Paul's Wharf for general consultation with his kindred and supporters, but giving audience, on matters of personal interest, at his own private abode in Bishopsgate Street.

[6] Rot. Parl., vol. vi. p. 240.

this remarkable fact, — " Previously to his coronation, a roll containing certain articles was presented
to him on behalf of the three estates of the realm,
by many lords spiritual and temporal, and other
nobles and commons in great multitude, whereunto
he, for the public weal and tranquillity of the land,
benignly assented." This corroboration of the plain
account given by the contemporary chroniclers,
both as regards the cause that led to Richard of
Gloucester being elected king, and the mode of
proceedings observed on the occasion, exonerates
this prince altogether from two of the odious
charges brought against him by subsequent historians, viz. his alleged unnatural and offensive conduct to his venerable mother, disproved, not alone
by her mansion being selected for the audience that
was to invest him with the kingly authority, but
also from the aspersion of the Lady Cecily's character
being totally uncalled for, when valid grounds [1]
existed for displacing and excluding his brother's
children, without calumny or injustice to her. And,
secondly, that although the principles and feelings
which operate at this present time may lead to
Richard's being considered to a certain degree, in a
moral sense, as an usurper, since fealty had been
sworn to Edward V., both as Prince of Wales, and
subsequently as king, yet, in a legal and constitutional sense, he has been undeservedly stigmatised
as such, inasmuch as he neither seized the crown

[1] The doubts on the validity of Edward's marriage were better
grounds for Richard's proceedings than aspersion of his mother's
honour. On that invalidity he claimed the crown and obtained it;
and with such universal concurrence, that the nation undoubtedly was
on his side. — *Hist. Doubts*, p. 40.

by violence, nor retained it by open rebellion in defiance of the laws of the land.

The heir of Edward IV. was set aside by constitutional authority [1] on an impediment which would equally have excluded him from inheritance in domestic life ; and Richard having been unanimously elected [2] by the three estates of the realm, took upon him the proffered dignity by their common consent.

Hereditary succession to the crown [3], at this period of English history, was but feebly recognised [4], and the right of parliament [5] to depose one monarch and elevate another had been admitted,

[1] " The jurisprudence of England," says Archdeacon Paley, " is composed of ancient usages, acts of parliament, and the decisions of the courts of law ; those, then, are the sources whence the nature and limits of her constitution are to be deduced, and the authorities to which appeals must be made in all cases of doubt."

[2] Rot. Parl., vol. vi. p. 240.

[3] The grand fundamental maxim upon which the *jus coronæ*, or right of succession to the throne of Britain depends, Sir Wm. Blackstone takes to be this : that the crown is, by common law and constitutional custom, hereditary, and this in a manner peculiar to itself ; but that the right of inheritance may from time to time be changed or limited by act of parliament, under which limitations the crown still continues hereditary.

[4] " We must not judge of those times by the present. Neither the crown nor the great men were restrained by sober established forms and proceedings as they are at present ; and from the death of Edward III. force alone had dictated. Henry IV. had stepped into the throne contrary to all justice. A title so defective had opened a door to attempts as violent ; and the various innovations introduced in the latter years of Henry VI. had annihilated all ideas of order. Richard Duke of York had been declared successor to the crown during the life of Henry and of his son Prince Edward, and, as appears by the Parliamentary History, though not noticed by our careless historians, was even appointed Prince of Wales."—*Walpole's Hist. Doubts*, p. 30.

[5] If the throne becomes vacant or empty, whether by abdication or by failure of all heirs, the two houses of parliament may, it is said by Blackstone, dispose of it.

not only in the previous reign of Edward IV. [1], —
whose election to the throne took place in the identical chamber of the Lady Cecily's mansion, in
which the crown was now offered to his brother, —
but also in the case of Edward III. and Henry IV.,
examples grounded on far less valid pretences than
that which led to the deposition of Henry VI. and
Edward V. The indignation, therefore, which has
been heaped on Richard's memory for centuries,
even if merited in a moral sense, ought rather to
have fallen on the peers, prelates, and " noted persons of the commons," who raised him to the
throne. They as well as himself had taken [2] and
broken the oath of allegiance to his nephew, but
in them as a body was vested a power, which
Gloucester, as an individual, could not possess —
that of deposing the prince whom they had sworn
to protect and serve, and of naming as his successor the person whom they considered to be more
lawfully entitled to the throne. The crown, therefore, assumed by the Protector was consequently
not a crown of usurpation, but one that, having
become void by alleged failure of legitimate heirs,
was legally proffered to him.

Richard of Gloucester must have been born in

---

[1] Compare Mr. Sharon Turner's account of the election of Edward IV., together with his hesitation at accepting the crown he had
fought to obtain, on account of his oath to Henry VI., with Dr.
Lingard's description of King Richard's election — his scruples in
ascending a throne he too had laboured to secure, from motives of
delicacy to his nephew — and the ambition which led both brothers
to surmount all obstacles that risked the loss of a kingdom they so
much coveted to possess. — *Middle Ages*, vol. iii. p. 240. ; *Lingard*,
vol. v. p. 250.

[2] Rot. Parl., vol. vi. p. 234.

another era than that in which he flourished, and have been imbued with feelings altogether distinct from such as characterised the nobles of England in the fifteenth century, could he have resisted such an appeal, or rejected a throne which under such plausible circumstances he was unanimously called upon to fill. Kings do but exemplify the character of the times in which they live, and the spirit of the people whom they rule. In them are reflected the prevalent virtues or vices of their age; and those princes who have either risen up or been chosen by the nation to contest the sceptre, will be generally found to have been imbued in more than a usual degree with the predominant passions of their epoch, and such as influenced chiefly the actions and conduct of their compeers.

The Duke of Gloucester was neither more vicious nor more virtuous than the great body of the people who chose him for their ruler. True—ambition was the predominant passion of his race, · but a craving for power influenced alike all ranks, and was exercised in all stations: it was the fruit of that pernicious education in which the seeds were sown, and the natural result of the haughty independence which at this era had attained its climax.

Richard was petitioned to ascend a throne which had been previously declared vacant. Assenting, therefore, to a choice freely made by the constituted authorities of the realm, he assumed the proffered sovereignty on the 26th of June, 1483.[1]

" The said Protector," says Fabyan[2], " taking then

---

[1] Chron. Croy., p. 566.
[2] Fabyan, although usually correct in all matters that occurred in

upon him as king and governor of the realm, went with great pomp unto Westminster, and there took possession of the same. Where he, being set in the great hall in the seat royal, with the Duke of Norfolk[1], before called the Lord Howard, upon the right hand, and the Duke of Suffolk[2] upon the left hand, after the royal oath there taken, called before him the judges of the law, exhorting them to administer the laws and execute judgment, as the first consideration befitting a king."[3] Addressing himself forthwith to the barons, the clergy, the citizens, and all gradations of rank and professions there

London and its vicinity, is evidently in error respecting the date of King Richard's accession, which he fixes on the 22d June. The Croyland continuator, and Buck, on his authority, fix it on the 26th June, and their testimony is confirmed by the instructions forwarded, by command of King Richard himself, to the governor of Calais and Guisnes two days after his accession.—*Harl. MSS.*, 433. fo. 238. Hall, Sir Thomas More, Grafton, and the continuator of Hardyng's Chronicle state that Richard III. ascended the throne on the 19th ; Rapin, on the 22d ; Hume, about the 25th ; Laing, the 27th ; Sharon Turner and Lingard, with their usual correctness, on the 26th. " These discrepancies," observes Sir Harris Nicolas, " are not surprising, considering that Richard himself states that ' doubts' had existed on this point." — *Chronology of Hist.*, p. 326.

[1] John Lord Howard, " one of the fairest characters of the age," and the most devoted of Richard's friends, was raised to the peerage by Edward IV. On the decease of Anne, only child and heiress of John Duke of Norfolk, he became the legal heir to her vast possessions; the which, however, together with the title, had been previously conferred by a royal grant on the infant Duke of York, when he espoused the Lady Anne in 1477. — *Rot. Parl.*, vol. vi. p. 168. The Lord Howard coveted the ducal rank, which had heretofore accompanied the lands that now reverted to him by heirship ; consequently, on the illegitimacy of King Edward's offspring being admitted, Richard deprived his youthful nephew of the dignity he had to that period enjoyed, and bestowed the dukedom of Norfolk on the Lord Howard, and on his son the earldom of Surrey.

[2] The Duke of Suffolk was brother-in-law to the Protector, having espoused the Lady Elizabeth, his eldest surviving sister.

[3] Fabyan, p. 514.

assembled, he pronounced a free pardon for all offences against himself, and ordered a proclamation to be openly made of a general amnesty throughout the land.[1]

Having thus taken possession of the regal dignity amidst the acclamations of the multitude, he proceeded in due state to Westminster Abbey, there to perform the usual ceremonies of ascending and offering at St. Edward's shrine; being met at the church door by the leading ecclesiastics, the monks singing " Te Deum laudamus," while the sceptre of King Edward was delivered to him by the abbot.[2] From thence he rode solemnly to St. Paul's, " assisted by well near all the lords spiritual and temporal of this realm, and was received there with procession, with great congratulation and acclamation of all the people in every place and by the way, that the king was in that day."[3] After the customary oblations and recognition in the metropolitan cathedral, the Protector " was conveyed unto the king's palace within Westminster, and there lodged until his coronation,"[4] being that same day "proclaimed king throughout the city, by the name and style of Richard III.,".[5] just two months and twenty-seven days after the demise of Edward IV., and from the period when that monarch's hapless child succeeded to a crown which he was destined never to wear, although his name survives on the regnal annals of England as the second monarch of the Yorkist dynasty, and the last Edward of the Plantagenet race.

[1] More, p. 125.   [2] Buck, lib. i. p. 24.
[3] Kennet, vol. i., note to p. 522.   [4] Buck, lib. i. p. 24.
[5] Fabyan, p. 515.

CHAPTER XIII.

Richard takes possession of the throne, not as an usurper, but as a
legitimate sovereign. — His conduct greatly misrepresented. —
Commencement of his reign. — Preparations for his coronation. —
State progress through the city. — Richard's election analogous to
the change of dynasty in 1688. — Coronation of King Richard
and Queen Anne at Westminster. — Peculiar magnificence of the
ceremony. — The banquet which followed. — Early measures of
Richard III. — His wisdom, justice, and attention to his domestic
duties. — Commences a progress through his dominions. — Flattering reception at Oxford. — Liberality to the city of Gloucester.
— Holds a court at the castle at Warwick. — Is there joined by
the queen. — Receives letters of credence from foreign princes.
— Embassy from Ferdinand and Isabella. — Resumes his regal
progress. — Decides on a second coronation. — Is joined by his
son the Earl of Salisbury, at Pontefract. — Enthusiastic reception
at York. — King Richard and his queen crowned a second time
in that city. — His son created Prince of Wales. — Dismissal of
the foreign envoys to their respective courts.

RICHARD of Gloucester was now king of England—
king, by the common consent of the nation, by the
unanimous choice of the nobles, the clergy, and the
people.[1] For upwards of four centuries he has been
designated as an usurper; but has consideration
ever been duly bestowed on the literal acceptation
of the term, or of its application to this monarch?
It would appear not! as, if attention is directed to
the one leading point, that Richard neither deposed
Edward V., nor forcibly seized the crown, but that
the regal dignity was tendered to him voluntarily

[1] Chron. Croy., p. 567.

and peaceably[1] by that branch of the constitution whose peculiar province it is to mediate between the monarch and the people, and to examine into the just pretensions of the new sovereign before he is irrevocably anointed ruler of the kingdom, it must be admitted that in this point, at least, Gloucester has been most unjustly accused. To quote the words of a modern eminent writer, who minutely examined every available document connected with this momentous inquiry, " Instead of a perjured traitor, we recognize the legitimate sovereign of England; instead of a violent usurpation, we discover an accession, irregular according to modern usage, but established without violence on a legal title."[2] Whatever difference of opinion may prevail respecting the disability alleged against Edward V., there can exist none as to his having been dethroned by the "lords and commons of the realm,"[3] whose assent had alone rendered valid his former accession to the crown.[4] If then parliament may settle so important a question as the right of succession to the throne of these kingdoms, parliament assuredly may unsettle and reform the same; but the laws of inheritance, like the moral laws, are framed on mental obligations which cannot be infringed, even by parliament, without raising a

---

[1] Buck, lib. i. p. 20.   [2] Laing, App. to Henry, vol. xii. p. 414.
[3] Chron. Croy., p. 567.

[4] " The power and jurisdiction of parliament," says Sir Edward Coke, " is so transcendent and absolute, that it cannot be confined either for causes or persons within any bounds. It can regulate or new model the succession to the crown. It can change and create afresh even the constitution of the kingdom, and of parliaments themselves." — *Coke, quoted by Guthrie,* p. 26.

sense of injustice. Consequently, the fruitful source of that odium which has ever been attached to Richard's memory as king may be traced to the early suppression, by Henry VII.[1], of that statute which admitted the disqualifications of Edward V., and also to want of sufficient attention having been given to the fact that the young prince was rejected by his subjects on the ground of disqualification alone, and his uncle elected to the throne in his place because that throne was about to be vacated.

The peers and prelates of England felt themselves aggrieved at fealty having been exacted for a prince against whose legitimacy doubts might be entertained, and who had therefore no legal claims to their oath of allegiance, either as heir apparent or as king, owing to the irregularity of his father's marriage. It was this conviction that proved the great support of the Lord Protector's cause when the matter was formally submitted for discussion to the assembled peers, and was confirmed to them

---

[1] " Henry's policy in suppressing that statute affords additional proof of Edward's marriage with Elenor Butler," observes Mr. Laing; who adds : — " The statute would have been destroyed without the ceremony of being reversed, but an act was necessary to indemnify those to whose custody the rolls were intrusted." — See *Year Book, Hilary Term,* 1 Hen. VII. The statute was abrogated without recital in order to conceal its purport, and obliterate, if possible, the facts it attested ; and a proposal for reading it — that Stillington, bishop of Bath, might be responsible for its falsehood — was overruled and stifled by the king's immediate declaration of pardon."— *Ibid.* " Its falsehood," continues Mr. Laing, " would have merited and demanded detection, not concealment ; and Stillington, whose evidence had formerly established the marriage, was, if perjured, an object of punishment, not of pardon." — *Laing's Dissertation, Appendix to Henry's England,* vol. xii. p. 409.

by the production of competent witnesses and authentic legal documents.[1]

The presumed rights of Edward V. being thus impugned, the constituted authorities elected his uncle their king, less from any notion that Gloucester had been wronged by his nephew's accession, than because they were impressed with the conviction that what parliament had sanctioned under false premises parliament had a right to nullify when legitimate cause was shown for thus exercising their prerogative. This momentous question rests, not upon any present consideration of justice or injustice, but upon the view then taken of the matter by the lords and commons of the kingdom; and even admitting that they acted under mistaken impressions, one deduction can alone be made as regards King Richard himself, viz. that instead of usurping the crown, it was bestowed upon him by others, — a gift, which, it is true, little doubt can exist as to its having been obtained chiefly by his keen sagacity, and that seducing eloquence and insinuating address which was peculiar to Richard when his abilities were called forth on any favourite project.

The youth of the hapless Edward, his innocence, his gentleness, have led to many accusations being heaped on Richard that must vanish whenever they are tested by the standard of justice; for however much sympathy may be elicited, or indignation

---

[1] " He then brought in instruments, authentick doctors, proctors, and notaries of the law, with depositions of divers witnesses, testifying King Edward's children to be bastards." — *Grafton, Cont. More*, p. 153.

be roused, for the calamities of a prince so roughly handled, the victim of error not his own, yet the mere act of his deposition and the elevation of his uncle to the throne, which is the sole point under consideration, was the decree of the nobles, the decision of the people, and therefore, it must be admitted, not the act of the Lord Protector himself.

Richard III. ascended the throne of England on the 26th of June[1], 1483, aged thirty years and eight months. The last known signature of Edward V. bears date the 17th of that same month[2]; and the first instrument attested by Gloucester after his accession is dated the 27th of June[3], on which day the great seal was delivered to him by the Bishop of Lincoln, who was re-appointed chancellor, and " received the seals from the new king

[1] Sir Harris Nicolas, in his Chronology of History (p. 326.), says: " As scarcely any two authorities agree respecting the date of the accession of this monarch, it is fortunate that he himself should have removed all doubt on the subject by an official communication. On the memoranda rolls of the exchequer in Ireland the following letter from Richard III. occurs, which fixes the date of the commencement of his reign to the 26th June, 1483: —

" 'Richard, by the grace of God king of England and of France and lord of Ireland. To all our subjects and liegemen within our land of Ireland, hearing or seeing these our letters, greeting. Forasmuch as we be informed that there is great doubt and ambiguity among you for the certain day of the commencing of our reign, we signify unto you for truth, that by the grace and sufferance of our blessed Creator, we entered into our just title, taking upon us our dignity royal, and supreme governance of this our royaume of England, the 26th day of June, the year of oui Lord 1483 : and after that we will that ye do make all writings and records among you.

" ' Given under our signet, at our Castle of Nottingham, the 18th day of October, the 2d year of our reign.' "

(Printed in the report of the commissioners of the records of Ireland, where a fac-simile of this letter may be seen.)

[2] Fœdera, vol. xii. p. 187.   [3] Ibid. p. 189.

in a chamber near the chapel in the dwelling of the
Lady Cecily Duchess of York, near the Thames,
called Baynard's Castle, in Thames Street, London[1];
a fact which seems, even more decisively than all
which have hitherto been alleged, to disprove the
charge of impugning the character of his venerable
parent, or of her having openly expressed indignation at her son's unfilial conduct.   Before entering on the proceedings which occupied the brief
interval between Richard's accession and his coronation, two points of some importance towards the
justification of his character require particular notice at this crisis, resting as they do upon contemporary authority: the one, that Lord Lyle, closely
allied to Edward V. and his mother's family, and
who had openly opposed the Duke of Gloucester
upon his elevation to the protectorate, now joined
his party and espoused his cause[2]; the other, that
the followers of the late Lord Hastings entered the
service of the Duke of Buckingham: thus affording a decisive proof that a portion, at least, of the
deposed monarch's kindred[3] were satisfied with the
justice of Richard's conduct; and likewise, that the
partizans of the late king's most favoured adviser,
so far from resenting the execution of their master,
actually joined themselves to one of the two dukes
who are charged with having so unjustly compassed
the Lord Hastings' death.   Neither must another

[1] Fœdera, vol. xii. p. 189.
[2] " The Lord Lyle is come to my Lord Protector, and awaits
upon him." — *Stallworth Letters, Excerpt. Hist.*, fo. 15.
[3] " The Lord Lyle was brother-in-law to the widowed queen of
King Edward IV., and consequently uncle to the Marquis of Dorset
and to the Lord Richard Grey, recently executed at Pontefract." —
Dugd. Bar., vol. i. p. 719.

fact, derived from the same source, be overlooked, from its connection with the alleged usurpation, as it affords evidence that the armed men sent for from York were indeed required as a protection to Richard and a safeguard to the metropolis, and were not summoned, as has been asserted, under a false plea to aid him in forcibly seizing the crown. " It is thought," writes Stallworth to Sir William Stoner, after describing the disturbed state of the city, " there shall be 20,000 of my Lord Protector's and my Lord Buckingham's men in London this week, to what intent I know not, but to keep the peace ; "[1] yet Stallworth's letter, from whence the above is extracted, was dated the 21st of June—the day previous to Dr. Shaw's sermon, and before any attempt had been made to promote Richard's accession, or to oppose the coronation of his nephew ; consequently the disturbed state of the metropolis arose not, it is very evident, from revolt instigated by the Protector, the very letter in question making express mention of preparations for Edward's coronation,—a fact altogether at variance with the supposition that measures had been ripening for weeks to dispossess him of the crown. Stallworth's attestation is confirmed by Fabyan, who, after narrating the particulars of Richard's elevation to the throne, adds : " Soon after, for fear of the queen's blood, and other, which he had in jealousy, he sent for a strength of men out of the North, the which came shortly to London a little before his coronation, and mustered

[1] Excerpt. Hist., p. 560.

I 3

in the Moorfields, well upon 4000 men." [1] These two accounts, the one written by an officer in the Lord Chancellor's household, the other narrated by a citizen of London contemporary with him, confirm the truth of Richard's assertions to the citizens of York, that a conspiracy had been formed to compass his destruction.[2]

This desperate state of things, and the severe measures consequent upon its discovery, decided Richard, there can be little doubt, to aspire to the crown, and also led to the counter-revolution which raised him to the throne instead of removing him from the protectorate, — a change in affairs which was effected actually before sufficient time had elapsed for his northern partizans to have reached the metropolis.

Not an effort, indeed, seems to have been made in favour of Edward V. — not a voice raised, even by the rabble, in behalf of the youthful king. The nobles, the clergy, the citizens, the people at large, hailed the accession of Richard III. with as much earnestness and unanimity as if Edward V. had died a natural death, and the crown had, of necessity, reverted to his uncle. Popular feeling, however, was too fleeting to be trusted by one so wary as Richard beyond the shortest possible period. The barons and knights who had elected him king were still remaining in the metropolis, whither they

[1] Fabyan, p. 516.

[2] Polydore Virgil (p. 540.) distinctly asserts that Lord Hastings speedily repented of the share he had taken in advocating the part pursued by Gloucester relative to the young king ; and that he privately convoked a meeting of the deceased monarch's most attached friends to discuss the proceedings most expedient for the future.

had been summoned to assist at the coronation of his royal nephew; and the preparations and festivities, so nearly completed for the deposed monarch, were in readiness for the immediate solemnisation of his uncle's enthronement.[1] Richard resolved on availing himself of so happy a coincidence, the more so, as the trusty followers whom he had summoned from the North for other purposes, and who were hourly expected, would, he knew, be at hand, either to swell the procession, or to repress tumult and prevent disorder. Assembling, then, the lords of the council, and the great officers of state, the day for the coronation of himself and his queen was definitively fixed, and the usual preliminaries forthwith commenced.[2] The following day, June 28th, instructions were despatched to Lord Mountjoy and others, the governors of Calais and Guisnes, commanding them to make known to the garrison of these important fortresses " the verrey sure and true title which our sovereign lord that now is, King Richard III., hath and had to their fealty;"[3] and to exact from them anew the oath of allegiance, which had become void by the dethronement of his nephew.[4] He presided in person at the judicial courts, declaring it to be " the chiefest duty of a king to minister to the laws."[5] He withdrew his personal enemies from sanctuary[6], that he might openly pardon their

---

[1] " And that solemnity was furnished for the most part with the self-same provision that was appointed for the coronation of his nephew." — *More*, p. 126.

[2] Fœdera, vol. xii. p. 190. [3] Harl. MSS., 433. fol. 238.

[4] See Appendix I. [5] More, p. 244.

[6] Ibid.

offences before the people; and, calculating on
the effect which courtesy produces, more especially
when emanating from princes to their subjects, he
followed the example set by Edward IV. on his
accession, of mingling familiarly with the populace,
addressing to the noble and opulent fair words and
speeches, and acknowledging, with urbanity and
condescension, the homage even of the most lowly.[1]
On the 30th of June, the Duke of Norfolk, who
upon Richard's accession had been created earl
marshal, was appointed steward of England for the
approaching coronation[2]; and the honourable offices
and high distinctions consequent upon that solem·
nity were dispensed with a liberal and impartial
spirit, being alike distributed on the avowed enemies as upon the warm friends of the Protector.

On the 4th of July, Richard proceeded in state
to the Tower[3] by water, accompanied by his royal
consort; and, after creating several peers, he invested many gentlemen and esquires with the order
of knighthood. He released the Lord Stanley from
confinement, pardoned his reputed connection with
the conspiracy of Lord Hastings, and, with a generosity and disregard to personal danger that
seems little in accordance with the evil deeds imputed to him, sought to bury the past in oblivion,
and to make him his friend, by appointing him lord
steward of his household.[4] He likewise set at
liberty the Archbishop of York[5], and, confirming
him in his primacy, permitted him to depart to his

[1] More, p. 245.   [2] Fœdera, vol. xii. p. 191.
[3] Harl. MSS., No. 293. fol. 208.   [4] Grafton, p. 799.
[5] Buck, lib. i. p. 26.

diocese. Morton, Bishop of Ely, whose after-career fully confirmed the reports of his having conspired for Richard's destruction, although also liberated from the Tower[1], was committed to the charge of the Duke of Buckingham, that a nominal restraint in that nobleman's hereditary abode at Brecknock might be placed upon the turbulent prelate until such time as he evinced less violent opposition to the newly-elected king.

It is probable that the greater indulgence shown to the archbishop arose from an urgent appeal addressed to Richard on his behalf by the University of Cambridge. This monarch was much attached to that seminary of learning, to which he had shown himself a great benefactor; and he was in consequence generally beloved and estimated by its members their earnest entreaties, therefore, in favour of their chancellor, whose munificent acts attested alike his piety and his goodness, was not likely to pass unnoticed by the king when the fitting time arrived for his enlargement, the more so as the language of the petition[2] did full justice to his own beneficence,

[1] Grafton, p. 797.

[2] " Right high and mighty prince, in whom singularly resteth the politic governance, peace, and tranquillity of the realm of England. Your humble orators commend them to your good grace. And forasmuch as we have felt in times past your bountiful and gracious charity to us your daily bedemen, not only in sending by your true servant and chancellor, Master Thomas Barrow, to his mother the University a great and faithful lover, your large and abundant alms ; but as well founding certain priests and fellows, to the great worship of God and to the increase of Christ's faith in the Queen's College of Cambridge ; we, upon that comfort, make our writing to your good grace, for such things concerning the weal of the University, beseeching your noble grace to show your gracious and merciful goodness, at this our humble supplication, to the Right Reverend Father in God

and testified most pleasingly the estimation in which he was held at that university.

On the 5th of July, Richard, accompanied by the queen, rode from the Tower through the city in great state[1], attended by all the chief officers of the crown, the lord mayor, the civic authorities, and the leading nobility and commons, sumptuously arrayed[2], — the king, as it is related, " being robed in a doublet and stomacher of blue cloth of gold, wrought with netts and pine-apples, a long gown of purple velvet furred with ermine, and a pair of short gilt spurs[3]; and the queen in a kirtle and mantle of white cloth of gold, trimmed with Venice gold and furred with ermine, the mantle being additionally garnished with seventy annulets of silver and gylt."[4] During the procession not the slightest disturbance occurred, nor was any indi-

---

the Archbishop of York, our head and chancellor, and many years hath been a great benefactor to the University and all the colleges therein, and, through the help of God and your gracious favour, shall long continue. Most Christian and victorious prince, we beseech you to hear our humble prayers, for we must needs mourn and sorrow, desolate of comfort, until we hear and understand your benign spirit of pity to him-ward, which is a great prelate in the realm of England. And we to be ever your true and humble orators and bedemen ; praying to him that is called the Prince of Mercy for your noble and royal estate, that it may long prosper to the worship of God, who ever have you in His blessed keeping.

         " Your true and daily orators,
              " THE UNIVERSITY OF CAMBRIDGE.
" To the right high and mighty prince Duke of Gloucester,
        " Protector of the realm of England."
         (Printed in Cooper's Annals of Cambridge, p. 226.)

[1] Buck, lib. i. p. 26.

[2] " But the Duke of Buckingham carried the splendour of that day's bravery, his habit and caparisons of blue velvet, embroidered with golden naves of carts burning, the trappings supported by footmen habited costly and suitable." — *Buck*, lib. i. p. 26.

[3] Brit. Costume, part ii. p. 212.   [4] Ibid. p. 218.

cation given by the populace, either of compassion
for Edward V. or disapprobation at the accession of
his uncle; and although Richard took the precaution of issuing a proclamation[1] tending to preserve
peace, yet the undisturbed state of the metropolis
seemed to render the edict unnecessary, unless in accordance with ancient usage or political expediency.
Surely this very extraordinary unanimity in all
classes of the community must cast a doubt upon
the imputation of hatred towards Richard which has
been so long entertained, more especially when the
national character of the English people is taken
into consideration, and due weight attached, not
only to the difficulty with which they are persuaded to adopt a new order of things, but also to
the innate generosity of spirit which induces them
as a body invariably to side with the oppressed,
and fearlessly to oppose both king and nobles, if
tyranny is exercised or despotism evinced. But
the utmost indifference to the position of Edward V. seems universally to have prevailed; and
that masterly scene of the immortal Shakspeare,
which so forcibly depicts the hapless position of
Richard II., from whose disastrous reign may be
dated the calamities which fell so heavily on the
innocent young princes of the house of York, is as
applicable to the dethroned and forsaken Edward,
and to his uncle the monarch of the nobles, as it was
to Henry of Bolingbroke, when he, like Richard of
Gloucester, rode in triumph through the city, and
received the homage of the multitude.[2]

[1] See Appendix K.
[2] "He rode from the Tower through the city," says Buck,

> " The duke, great Bolingbroke,
> Mounted upon a hot and fiery steed,
> Which his aspiring rider seemed to know,
> With slow but stately pace kept on his course,
> While all tongues cried, ' God save thee, Bolingbroke !'
> You would have thought the very windows spake,
> So many greedy looks of young and old
> Through casements darted their desiring eyes
> Upon his visage ; and that all the walls
> With painted imag'ry had said at once,
> ' Jesu preserve thee !   Welcome Bolingbroke !'
> Whilst he, from one side to the other turning,
> Bare-headed, lower than his proud steed's neck,
> Bespake them thus : ' I thank you, countrymen ;'
> And thus still doing, thus he pass'd along."
>
> *Richard II.*, act v. scene 2.

A more peaceful or tranquil accession can scarcely be adduced from the regnal annals of England than that of King Richard III. But if wonder is excited at the undisturbed manner in which this prince obtained possession of the throne, still greater astonishment must be felt at the unanimity which prevailed at his coronation ; the celebration of which solemnity is not only perpetuated as one of the most gorgeous pageants on record, but as perhaps the most magnificent ceremonial which can be adduced from our national archives. It was alike remarkable for the vast attendance of the aristocracy, and for the extraordinary magnificence[1] displayed by the influential leaders of the Lancastrian and Yorkist factions.

" The great regularity with which the coronation was prepared and conducted," observes Lord

" with three dukes and nine earls, twenty-two viscounts and simple barons, eighty knights, esquires and gentlemen not to be numbered." — Lib. i. p. 26.

[1] Appendix L.

Orford, "and the extraordinary concourse of the nobility at it, have not at all the air of an unwelcome reception, accomplished merely by violence; on the contrary, it bore great resemblance to a much later event, which, being the last of the kind, we term 'the Revolution.'"[1] And a revolution truly it was, in its extreme sense, although not an usurpation; and, considering that it was accomplished without bloodshed, without the aid of an armed force, — for the description of Richard's "gentlemen of the north," as given by Fabyan[2], is little in keeping with desperate or determined rebels, — and that a fortnight was occupied in calm and deliberate preparations for solemnising the ceremony, with the most minute attention to regal splendour, court etiquette, and the observance of ecclesiastical and judicial forms, the question with which Lord Orford concludes his examination into this remarkable event cannot fail to recur to the mind of every reflective person : " Has this the air of a forced and precipitate election? or does it not indicate a voluntary concurrence in the nobility?"[3] The circumstances of Richard's election were indeed singularly analogous to those which took place on

---

[1] " The three estates of nobility, clergy, and people, which called Richard to the crown, and whose act was confirmed by the subsequent parliament, trod the same steps as the convention did, which elected the Prince of Orange ; both setting aside an illegal pretender, the legitimacy of whose birth was called in question : in both instances it was a free election." — *Historic Doubts*, p. 45.

[2] . . . . " In their best jackes and rusty salettes, with a few in white harness not burnished to the sale." — *Fabyan*, p. 516. Hall and Grafton speak even more opprobriously : " Evil apparelled, and worse harnessed," they say, " which, when mustered, were the contempt of beholders." — *Drake's Ebor.*, p. 115.

[3] Hist. Doubts, p. 17.

the change of dynasty in 1688. Upon that great occasion, states Blackstone, "the lords and commons, by their own authority, and upon the summons of the Prince of Orange, afterwards King William, met in a convention, and therein disposed of the crown and kingdom."[1] Blackstone goes on to remark that this assembling proceeded upon a conviction that the throne was vacant, and "in such a case," he says, "as the palpable vacancy of the throne, it follows *ex necessitate rei* that the form of the royal writs must be laid aside, otherwise no parliament can ever meet again."[2] And he puts the possible case of the failure of the whole royal line, which would indisputably vacate the throne: "In this situation," he says, "it seems reasonable to presume that the body of the nation, consisting of lords and commons, would have a right to meet and settle the government, otherwise there must be no government at all." It was upon this principle that the conventions of 1483 and 1688 both proceeded. Both presumed the throne to be vacant; the former by reason of the illegitimacy of the children of Edward IV., the latter on account of the abdication of James II. Both met without writ, as they must do if they assembled at all, on account of the vacancy of the throne; both declared the throne to be vacant; both tendered the crown to sovereigns selected by themselves; and both procured a subsequent parliamentary ratification of their proceedings. So far, therefore, as relates to strict legal form, the proceedings on the election of Richard

---

[1] Blackstone's Comm., vol. i. p. 152.   [2] Ibid.

III. were exactly similar to those adopted on the transfer of the throne from James II. to William and Mary.

Copies of the oath of allegiance to Richard III., taken by the lords spiritual and temporal[1], are still in existence; as also are the names of the individuals who were created knights by this monarch on the Sunday before his coronation.[2]

Many other very minute particulars are preserved in the Heralds' College, and also in the Harleian manuscripts[3], relative to the gorgeous ceremony which finally invested Richard of Gloucester and " Warwick's gentle daughter" with the regal honours[4]; but as they embrace many obsolete customs and observances that are more curious than interesting in the present day, it will perhaps be deemed sufficient to give merely a general outline of the proceedings from the above-named contemporary documents.[5]

On the 6th of July, King Richard and Queen

---

[1] Rymer's Add. MSS., No. 4616. art. 17, 18.

[2] Harl. MSS., No. 293. art. 208.   [3] Ibid. No. 433. art. 211.

[4] The termination of the MS. in the Harleian library is defective, but the corresponding instrument deposited in the College of Arms enables it to be completed. A literal transcript of the whole has been published in the Excerpta Historica, p. 380.; and Sir George Buck has likewise given a correct programme of the ceremony.

[5] They are thus entitled : " Here beginneth the coronation of King Richard III. and Queen Anne, in the year of our Lord God 1483, and in the 6th day of July, the first year of his noble reign ; and of the royal service that was done at the said coronation at Westminster. In the year and date aforesaid the king and queen coming out of the Whitehall to Westminster Hall, unto the King's Bench, the king and the queen going upon red cloth barefoot ; and so they went, until time they came to St. Edward's shrine, with his noble lords before him, both spiritual and temporal, every lord in his estate, according as ye shall have hereafter written."

Anne, with the royal household and great officers of the crown, preceded by trumpets, clarions, and " heralds with the king's coat-armour," passed from the Tower, through the city, to Westminster Hall, where they were met by the priests, abbots, and bishops, with mitres and crosiers, who conducted them to the Abbey. The Bishop of Rochester bare the cross before Cardinal Bourchier, Archbishop of Canterbury; two earls following, the one bearing the golden spurs, and the other " with Saint Edward's staff for a relic."[1] The Earl of Northumberland carried the pointless sword of mercy; the Lord Stanley the mace of constableship (an arrangement that ought not to pass without comment on account of its impartiality, considering that the one nobleman had been chiefly instrumental in promoting Richard's present elevation, and that the other had been but a few days released from imprisonment in the Tower for conspiring to effect his destruction); the Earl of Kent and the Viscount Lovel carried the naked swords of justice, ecclesiastical and temporal, on the right and left hand of the king ; the Duke of Suffolk[2] bare the sceptre, and his son, the Earl of Lincoln[3], the ball and cross; the Earl of Surrey carried the sword of state in a rich scabbard, followed by his illustrious parent the

---

[1] St. Edward's staff is of pure gold ; on the top is an orb and a cross, and it is shod with a steel spike : a fragment of the real cross is said to be deposited in the orb.

[2] The Duke of Suffolk was Richard's brother-in-law, having married the eldest surviving sister of that monarch and of the deceased king.

[3] The Earl of Lincoln was King Richard's nephew, his sister's eldest son.

Duke of Norfolk, earl marshal of England, bearing the crown. Immediately after this nobleman came the king himself, under a canopy borne by the Barons of the Cinque Ports, sumptuously habited in robes of purple velvet furred with ermine; his hose, coat, and surcoat of crimson satin, and his sabatons (shoes) covered with crimson tissue cloth of gold. On one side Richard was supported by the Bishop of Bath [1], on the other by the Bishop of Durham; his train being borne by the Duke of Buckingham, holding his white staff of office as seneschal or hereditary lord high steward of England.

The queen's procession succeeded to that of her royal consort, the Earl of Huntingdon bearing the sceptre, the Viscount Lyle the rod with the dove. Here, also, another instance of strict impartiality is remarkable, the Lord Huntingdon [2] being by betrothment the destined son-in-law of King Richard, and the Lord Lyle [3] the brother to the dowager queen, and, until within a brief period, one of the most violent and bitter enemies of the new monarch. The Earl of Wiltshire carried the crown; and next to him followed the queen herself under a gorgeous canopy corresponding with that of her royal consort, but with the addition of a bell of

[1] This prelate was Dr. Stillington, formerly chaplain to King Edward IV., whose testimony of that king's former marriage led to the deposition of Edward V. and to the elevation of Richard III.

[2] The Lord of Huntingdon was betrothed to the Lady Katharine Plantagenet, King Richard's illegitimate daughter.

[3] The Lord Lisle, or Lyle, so created by the deceased monarch, was a Grey; he was brother by marriage to the widowed queen, and uncle to her sons by the Lord Grey.

gold at every corner. Like him, too, she was habited in robes of purple velvet, furred with ermine, her shoes of crimson tissue cloth of gold. Her head was adorned with " a circlet of gold, with many precious stones set therein," and her train was upheld by Margaret of Lancaster, Countess of Richmond, followed by the Duchess of Suffolk, the Duchess of Norfolk, and a retinue of twenty of the noblest ladies of the land. According to the accounts that have been transmitted to posterity, nothing could exceed the grandeur and magnificence of the procession.[1] Entering the west door of the Abbey, the royal pair proceeded direct to their chairs of state, and there rested until " divers holy hymns were sung;" then ascending the high altar, and being divested of their surcoats and mantles of velvet, they were solemnly anointed from a vessel of pure gold[2] by the bishop. New

---

[1] A full description of the coronation robes worn by the king and queen, by the chief officers of state, the principal nobility, and the henchmen or pages, together with the silks of various colours given as liveries and perquisites, has been preserved in the wardrobe accounts for the reign of Richard III. ; to which is prefixed an indenture, witnessing " that Piers Curteys, the king's wardrober, hath taken upon him to purvey by the 3d of July next coming the parcels ensuing, against the coronation of our sovereign lord." The materials furnished for the ceremony were of the most costly description : velvets, satins, and damasks of every hue; purple, crimson, and scarlet cloths of gold, richly embroidered ; ermine, minever pure, and other costly furs ; mantles trimmed with Venice gold ; stuffs of the most dazzling appearance for canopies, banners, and pennons ; horse furniture wrought in gold and silver, together with every appurtenance of dress ; shoes, vests, kirtles, hose, bonnets, feathers with jewelled stems, cauls (or caps) of gold net, and transparent veils, paved or chequered with gold, all of corresponding magnificence, whether as regards richness of texture, variety of colour, or costliness of material.

[2] The " ampullæ, or golden eagle," containing the oil with which

robes of cloth of gold were in readiness for the
concluding scene; being arrayed in which, they
were both crowned with great solemnity by the
Archbishop of Canterbury, the king being supported by two bishops, as also by the Dukes of
Buckingham and Norfolk, the Earl of Surrey upholding the sword of state upright before him.
The queen was likewise supported by two prelates,
the Bishops of Exeter and Norwich, and having a
princess of York[1] on her right hand, a princess of
Lancaster[2] at her left, and the Duchess of Norfolk
kneeling behind. High mass was performed by
the cardinal archbishop, and the holy communion
administered by him. " The king and queen,"
states the contemporary MS., " came down to the
high altar and there kneeled down, and anon the
cardinal turned him about with the holy sacra-
ment in his hand and parted it between them, and
there they received the good Lord and were absolved both." Yet this venerable ecclesiastic, this
high dignitary of the church of Rome, the primate
of all England, who thus absolved Richard from his
sins and sealed his pardon with the most holy
symbol of Christ's passion, was the same lord cardinal who had pledged " his own body and soul "
to the widowed queen, when receiving the infant
Duke of York from sanctuary scarcely three weeks

the sovereigns of England were anointed, is of great antiquity, as
likewise the " anointing spoon," used for the same purpose.

[1] The Duchess of Suffolk, second daughter of Richard Duke of
York and the Lady Cecily.

[2] Margaret Beaufort, Countess of Richmond, was the great grand-
daughter of John of Gaunt, Duke of Lancaster, fourth son of Edward IV.

before, not only for " his surety, but also for his
estate."[1]   Can there, then, remain any longer a
doubt that some just cause existed for young
Edward's deposition ; or that Richard's election
to the throne was free and unbiassed ?

The character of the archbishop who set the
crown on Richard's head has never been impeached.[2]
He was not raised to that high office for the occasion, or in reward of former services to the Lord
Protector, but had been a bishop nearly forty years,
and primate of Canterbury even before the accession of the house of York.[3]   Venerable by age
and eminent for his talents and virtues, lineally descended from Edward III.[4], nearly allied to Edward
IV.[5], whom he had also anointed king and invested
with the regal diadem, and pledged to his youthful
heir, Edward V.[6], to whom he had twice sworn allegiance, — any remonstrance from such a quarter
could scarcely have passed unheeded ; not to mention
the power of a cardinal, which was in those days so
great that their persons were sacred, and their high

---

[1] More, p. 59.   [2] Hist. Doubts, p. 55.

[3] Thomas Bourchier, son of William Bourchier, Earl of Essex, was
in 1434 elected chancellor of Oxford.   From the see of Worcester
he was translated to Ely, and enthroned archbishop of Canterbury in
1453.

[4] Thomas Bourchier, archbishop of Canterbury and cardinal of
St. Cyrac, was the third son of the Lady Anne Plantagenet, by her
second husband, William Bourchier, Earl of Essex ; she was the
eldest daughter of Thomas Duke of Gloucester, fifth son to King
Edward III.

[5] Richard Earl of Cambridge, the grandsire of Edward IV. and
Richard III., left two children, viz. Richard Duke of York, father of
the above-named monarchs, and Isabel, married to Henry Bourchier,
Earl of Essex, brother to the cardinal. — *Sandford*, book iii. and v.
chap. xv. p. 365.

[6] Rot. Parl., vi. p. 234. ; and Chron. Croy., p. 566.

office considered inviolate.[1] Yet Cardinal Bourchier, with the appeal to his God yet fresh upon
his lips, that "the estate as well as safety" of the
young princes should be required at his hands,
consecrates Richard of Gloucester ruler of the
kingdom, and absolves him from all sin. But one
conclusion, surely, can result from this extraordinary proceeding, sanctioned as it was by the
whole body of the clergy[2], by the judges, and by
the knightly representatives of the people; viz.
that the nobility met Richard's claim to the throne
at least half way[3], from their hatred and jealousy
of the queen-mother's family, and their conviction
of the fact of King Edward's former marriage.
Perceiving the calamities that would probably ensue from this defective title during a long minority[4], and appreciating the high talent for government evinced by the Lord Protector, they hailed
a legitimate plea for quietly deposing the youthful
son of Elizabeth Wydville, and elevating for their
ruler one of the popular race of York, whose
abilities they had tried, whose firmness they had
witnessed, and whose military reputation would
alike conduce to peace at home, and, should the

---

[1] " Our reverend father here present, my lord cardinal, who may
in this matter (alluding to the removal of the Duke of York from
sanctuary) do most good of any man, if it please him to take the
pains." — *More*, p. 36.

[2] " And anon came up to the king two bishops kneeling before him,
and so rose and went up to the king, and kissed him, one after
another, and so stood before the king, one on the right and one on
the left hand." — *Harl. MSS.*, 433. fol. 2115.

[3] Hist. Doubts, p. 45.

[4] " And that the great wise man well perceived, when he sayde,
' Veli regno cujus rex puer est,'—Woe is that realme that hath a child
to their king." — *More*, p. 113.

honour of the kingdom require it, command respect for the English arms abroad.

To return, however, from this necessary digression, to the gorgeous pageant of Richard's coronation. The religious ceremonies terminated by the king's going to St. Edward's shrine, and offering up St. Edward's crown, with many relics; after which devotional acts, being invested with the regal tabard[1], and the sacred coif of fine lawn, and assuming the regal coronet, the illustrious pair, bearing their insignia of sovereignty in their hands, returned to Westminster Hall in the same state and in the same order of procession as they had entered the Abbey. Mounting the raised dais[2], the splendid cortège dispersed, the king and queen leaving thereon their regal mantelets, and retiring for a brief period to their private apartments. The banquet which followed was conducted with the same magnificence and grandeur that had characterised the performance of the morning's solemnity. During the short interval in which the king and queen "retired themselves for a season," the Duke of Norfolk, riding into the hall with his horse trapped with cloth of gold down to the ground, cleared it of the vast concourse of people who had thronged to witness the spectacle. Yet, with all this multitude, — this indiscriminate assemblage of all ranks, — no tumult, no murmuring is recorded;

[1] " Like unto a dalmatica, or upper garment of white sarsnet."— *Brit. Cost.*, part 2. p. 212.

[2] The dais was the place of honour in banqueting rooms, and signified a raised platform on which the king, or the noble in his baronial halls, dined apart from their retinue or vassals, who were seated at tables somewhat removed from their illustrious chief.

all was peaceable and joyous. The turbulent spirit mentioned by Stallworth as agitating the metropolis not a fortnight before was now altogether hushed; and the trouble and anxiety, which then filled men's hearts with fear, was turned into unanimity and concord, and a universal display of cordiality, confidence, and loyalty.

About "four of the clock," Richard and his royal consort are described as having entered the hall, "arrayed in fresh robes of crimson velvet embroidered with gold, and furred with minever pure," and advancing to the high dais, there sat down to dinner, under canopies supported by peers and peeresses; the king in the centre of the table and the queen on his left hand: there being present the Archbishop of Canterbury, the lord chancellor, the lord mayor, the lord marshal, the lord steward, the bishops, the chief judges of England, and an immense assemblage of the nobility and the most illustrious ladies of the English court. All was in keeping with the passion for splendour and the spirit of magnificence which so especially characterised the age. Nothing was omitted that could grace or dignify the entertainment. The royal couple were waited upon by the noblest persons in the realm, and the king was served "with one dish of gold and another of silver, the queen in gilt vessels, and the cardinal bishop in silver." At the second course, Sir Robert Dymoke, the king's champion, came riding into the hall, "his horse trapped with white silk and red, and himself in white harness," and inquired "before all the people, if there be any man will say against King

Richard III., why he should not pretend to the crown; and anon all the people were at peace awhile." Then making proclamation that "whosoever should say that King Richard III. was not lawfully king, he would fight with him with all utterance," the champion threw down his gauntlet for gage thereof, "when all the people cried, King Richard! God save King Richard!" Eighteen heralds, four of them wearing crowns, forthwith advanced before the king, and, after garter king-at-arms had proclaimed his styles and title, the remainder cried, "a largesse"[1] three times in the hall[2], when, "the day beginning to give way to the night," wafers and ippocras were served, and anon the king and queen arose up, and went to their chambers. "Great light of wax torches and torchets" speedily illumined the hall, and "every man and woman," the contemporary Chronicle in conclusion states, "departed and went their ways where it liked them best."[3]

Such was the inauguration of the last monarch of the Plantagenets, a fitting close to the most powerful, magnificent, and chivalrous dynasty that ever filled the English throne. No personal fear was evinced by Richard, no deception practised on the multitude: bold and decisive, gorgeous, magnificent, and wholly unopposed, the enthronement of Richard III. is the best reply to all the calumnies that proclaimed him a dark and a stealthy

[1] "Largesse, a free gift or dole, signifying, in this particular instance, coins scattered among the people."

[2] The following entry is preserved in the Harl. MSS.: "To garter king-at-arms, and to other heralds and poursuivants, 100l. for the king's largesse the day of his coronation."—No. 433. fol. 22.

[3] Excerpt. Hist., 383.

usurper. Friends and foes were marshalled side by side, and the kindred of the deposed sovereign[1] shared with the relatives of the new monarch the most dignified and honourable places, both in the procession and the banquet.

A daughter of the house of York[2], the sister of the late and aunt of the rejected king, occupied with her husband and son the most prominent places about the persons of Richard and his queen; while the heads of the royal house of Lancaster, the Duke of Buckingham and Margaret Countess of Richmond[3], were selected to fill the most favourite positions, and upheld the trains of the illustrious pair. No single observance was disregarded that could give effect or add weight to the ceremony, neither was there any display of despotism or partiality that could convert the solemn rite into a compulsory act, or one of abject servility to a tyrant; peers and prelates, judges, knights, and citizens, all united with one accord in honouring the choice of the legislature, and in confirming the elevation of King Richard III.

[1] The Earl of Kent, as also the Duke of Buckingham, were, by marriage, brothers to the widowed queen, and uncles to the deposed sovereign ; these two noblemen having espoused Jaquetta and Katherine Wydville, the royal Elizabeth's sisters : and it cannot but be considered as a striking circumstance that not one of the noble peers thus closely allied to the ex-queen as the husbands of her five sisters—and the greater proportion of whom had been enriched or received honourable appointments through her influence with Edward IV.—were absent from King Richard's coronation.

[2] Elizabeth Duchess of Suffolk, sister of Edward IV. and Richard III.

[3] Margaret Countess of Richmond was the relict of Edmund Tudor, half-brother of King Henry VI., and the mother of King Henry VII. This illustrious lady, as also Margaret Countess of Stafford, the parent of Henry Duke of Buckingham, were great grand-daughters of John of Gaunt, Duke of Lancaster.

There is one circumstance connected with this monarch's coronation which must not pass unnoticed; viz. the absence of Richard's heir, the youthful Earl of Salisbury, who had no place apportioned to him either at the solemnity in the Abbey or the festive banquet which succeeded. Whether the omission arose from a feeling of delicacy to the young princes in the Tower, or from the apprehension that the sight of Edward of Gloucester might call to remembrance his deposed cousin, and thus excite sympathy in the populace for the reverse of fortune which had so blighted his seemingly high destiny, cannot of course be determined; but certain it is that none of the ill-omened offspring of Edward IV., of George of Clarence, or Richard of Gloucester, graced the pageant which fixed the crown of England on the head of the youngest of three brothers, whose joint history and career is perhaps unparalleled.

King Richard being irrevocably seated on the throne, and fully invested with that sovereign power for which, by nature and by education, he was so peculiarly fitted, speedily showed his capacity for government, and his peculiar talents for the high office to which he had been raised, by the wisdom of his measures, and the vigour and resolution which characterised the opening of his reign. Mystery hangs, indeed, over his early days, and few and widely scattered are the memorials of his youth. Not so his career as monarch of this realm. No testimony that could be given by historian or biographer, no panegyric that could be passed by follower or friend, on his talents, vigilance, and energy, could so truly depict his actual character, or develope the wonderful powers of Richard's masterly mind, as the evidence of his own acts both as lord protector and king, which have fortunately been transmitted to posterity. Amongst innumerable documents connected with the history of the Plantagenet monarchs, there is preserved in the Harleian library a most curious folio volume in manuscript, formerly belonging to the Lord Treasurer Burleigh[1], containing a copious register of the grants and public documents which passed the privy seal or sign manual during the reigns of Edward V. and Richard III., consisting of no less than *two thousand three hundred and seventy-eight articles!* "[2] When it is remembered that these entries commemorate the proceedings of little more than two short years, and that, apart from mere official edicts, they abound in instances of generosity and benevolence, together with proofs of his just, equable, and prudent administration, it will be seen how great injustice has been done to Richard III. as king, whatever difference of opinion may prevail as regards his character as a man. Perhaps no monarch who ever ascended the throne of these

---

[1] Sir Harris Nicolas, whose authority on these points is indisputable, and who obligingly favoured the Authoress with his opinion, considers that this work of Lord Burleigh's was probably what is called a " docket," and that it may have passed into Lord Burleigh's hands out of some public office, or by purchase, by plunder, or by gift. There cannot be any doubt that the book is contemporary with Richard III. ; its authenticity, too, is equally removed from all suspicion ; and, whether compiled officially, or collected to serve some official purpose, its contents are invaluable, as throwing new light on Richard's true character and that of his remarkable reign.

[2] See Catalogue Harl. MSS., preface.

realms was so competent to exercise the royal prerogative; and it is doubtful if the archives of this
country could produce a corresponding instance of
activity, zeal, and devotion to the cares of government, in so brief a space of time, and under such
trying and difficult circumstances.

So clear and explicit are the entries, that they
form a complete diary of Richard's proceedings
from his accession to his death, there being scarcely
a day in which some notification may not be adduced to show where he was sojourning, and what
great event occupied prominently either his time
or his attention.[1] Conjecture, then, may henceforth be discarded as regards the regal career of
Richard III.; and as wonder is excited at the
energy and activity of mind and body so astonish-
ingly developed therein, regret must equally be
felt that any informality should have marked the
elevation of a monarch whose intelligence and political wisdom was far in advance of the times in
which he lived.

King Richard's first act, after creating the usual
number of knights of the Bath[2] customary at a
coronation, was immediately to assemble and dis-
miss to their homes the lords spiritual and tem-

[1] So numerous are these documents, that even a partial selection
would fill a volume of considerable size ; for the most important
entries are inserted at full length, and the substance is given of all
the rest.   The last possessor of this invaluable manuscript was the
antiquary and historian, John Strype, and it appears to be the same
MS. (observes Mr. Sharon Turner) which is a few times quoted in
the annotations appended to Bishop Kennett's Collection of English
Monarchs, under the name of " King Richard's Diary," and signed
" J. S."—*Middle Ages*, preface to vol. iii. p. 21.

[2] Harl. MSS., No. 293. p. 208.

poral[1], and the barons and knights of the shires, with a strict charge, as magistrates and men in authority, to exercise their power in maintaining tranquillity and punishing the lawless in their several districts, appointing commissioners of array " for the security and defence of the king and of his realm, and for the conservation of the peace."[2] He likewise assembled the judges, and in an eloquent address enjoined them to a firm and impartial administration of justice within their jurisdiction and upon their circuits. He communicated to them his resolution of proceeding forthwith to the North " to pacify that country, and to redress certain riots there lately done;"[3] and in this, his intended progress through the kingdom, intimated his determination of personally examining into the wants of his subjects, exacting a reformation of abuses, and suppressing with severity all insubordination or disregard of the laws. The 4000 men whom he had summoned from York when the metropolis was in so disordered a state " that Richard dared not to trust the Londoners for fear of the queen's blood,"[4] and whom he afterwards retained to swell the pageant of his coronation, he countermanded home " shortly after that solemnity, with sufficient rewards for their travail."[5]

On the 9th of July (three days after he was anointed king) Richard by letters patent appointed the " right high and mighty prince Edward[6], his

[1] Buck, lib. i. p. 27.   [2] Rymer's Add. MSS., 4616. art. 26.
[3] Fabyan, fol. 154.   [4] Drake's Eborac., p. 115.
[5] Fabyan, fol. 154.   [6] Harl. MSS., 433. fol. 242.

first-begotten son," to be lieutenant of Ireland[1],
despatching a special messenger to that portion of
his dominions to show that " the king, after the
establishing of this his realm of England, principally afore other things intendeth for the weal of
this land of Ireland,"[2] and appointing Gerald. Earl
of Kildare " the young prince's deputy."[3] His
sense of justice in the liquidation of debts duly incurred is strikingly evinced in the next instrument
which passed the royal signet, letters patent, bearing date the 18th of July anno 1mo Richard III.
being issued " for the payment of 52*l.* and 20*d.*,
resting due to divers persons for their services
done to his dearest brother the late king, and to
Edward bastard, late called Edward V."[4]

Having arranged all matters of import within
the metropolis calculated to give confidence to
the citizens and promote the peaceable disposition
evinced by the populace, King Richard, with his
queen, quitted London for Greenwich and Windsor,
at which royal demesnes he sojourned a brief period to arrange the ceremonial of his progress
through the kingdom, and to requite the services

[1] The wording of this entry sufficiently refutes the assertion of
some few historians that King Richard created his son " Prince of
Wales" upon his coronation at Westminster, the 6th day of July.

[2] On the 18th of July King Richard gave evidence of his sincerity in this declaration, by reforming and raising the value of the
Irish coinage, in which, it appears by his official declaration, great
abuses had prevailed, both as regards deficiency in weight and mixture of alloy with the silver bullion at the Irish mint.   To guard
against repetition of this evil, he commanded that the new silver
coinage should bear " on one side the arms of England, and on the
other three crowns."—*Harl. MSS.*, 433. fol. 233.

[3] Ibid. 433. fol. 243.   [4] Ibid. 433. fol. 104.

of those trusty friends whose zeal had been the means of elevating him to the throne. To the Duke of Buckingham, the most devoted of his partizans, and whom he styles " his right trusty and entirely beloved cousin," he awarded all the manors, lordships, and lands of Humphrey de Bohun, Earl of Hereford[1], which Edward IV. had unjustly appropriated to himself[2], concluding the letters patent which conveyed to him this munificent recompence for his zeal, and which are dated " at Greenwich, the 13th day of July, in the first year of our reign," by the following testimonial, that it was given for " the true, faithful, and laudable service which our said cousin hath, in many sundry wise, done to us, to our right singular will and pleasure."[3] His gratitude to this nobleman is indeed abundantly displayed. Besides receiving many valuable donations, as " a special gift" from the king, very speedily after the coronation ceremony he was successively created constable of England for life[4], confirmed in his former appointments of chief justice and chamberlain of North and South Wales[5], made steward of many valuable crown manors, and

[1] Humphrey de Bohun, Earl of Hereford, at his decease left two daughters, co-heirs to his enormous wealth ; the one espoused King Henry IV., the other the progenitor of the Duke of Buckingham. On the death of Henry VI. the posterity of the eldest sister became extinct, and Buckingham, as the lineal descendant of the youngest co-heir, claimed the property formerly divided between them. It was, however, refused to the duke by King Edward IV., who took possession of the lands ; and it has also been asserted that King Richard was equally unmindful of Buckingham's just claim ; but the entry in the Harl. MSS. (433. fol. 107.), and the testimony of Dugdale (vol. i. p. 168.), afford satisfactory proof to the contrary.

[2] Dugdale's Bar., vol. i. p. 168.   [3] Harl. MSS., 433. fol. 107.

[4] Rymer's Add. MSS., 4616. art. 23.   [5] Ibid. art. 6.

appointed governor of the royal castles in Wales.[1]
The Duke of Norfolk was nominated admiral of
England, Ireland, and Aquitaine for life.[2]   The
Earls of Surrey and Lincoln, the Lords Lovel and
Nevil, Bishop Stillington, Sir James Tyrrel, Sir
Thomas Ratcliffe, Brackenbury, Catesby, Kendall,
and innumerable other followers and friends, were
all distinguished by some manifestation of their
sovereign's especial favour or regard.[3]   No individual, indeed, appears to have been overlooked
who had either served him long or faithfully. Yet,
in the midst of all this pressure of business, and
the important avocations of state necessarily attendant on the commencement of a new reign,
Richard did not neglect his domestic duties, but,
with his characteristic foresight and vigilance,
gave a due portion of time and thought towards
regulating his establishment at Middleham, and
providing for the rule and management of his son's
household there, deprived as the young prince
must necessarily henceforth be of the constant residence of one parent and the active superintendence
of the other.   " This is the ordinance made by the
king's good grace," states the ancient and curious
MS. which has thus perpetuated Richard's attention to the well-being of his family at his favourite
Middleham, " for such number of persons as shall
be in the North as the king's household, and to
begin the 24th day of July." [4]   An attentive observance to the hours of God's service is the first

---

[1] Rymer's Add. MSS., 4616. art. 6.   [2] Ibid.
[3] See Harl. MSS., No. 433.   [4] See Appendix M.

thing enjoined, after which the utmost care is given towards providing for the just and equitable government of the whole establishment, and to the forming of such rules as could contribute to the welfare even of the humblest retainer. The expenses of the household were to be examined, and paid monthly : and this ordinance, so remarkable as affording evidence of Richard's sound principles of order and justice, concludes with these remarkable words—" that convenient fare be ordained for the household servants, and strangers to fare better than others." [1]

The young Lord of Lincoln, Richard's favourite nephew, appears to have been nominated by this monarch to the lucrative office of governor of his household and ruler of his extensive demesnes in the North ; the above quoted fragment, containing not only various items providing for the comfort of the earl and the support of his exalted rank, but also the following decree, " that the costs of my Lord of Lincoln, when he rideth to sessions or any meetings appointed by the council," are to be paid by the treasurer, but that at all ridings, huntings, and disports, " my said lord to be at his own costs and charges." Who, or what is meant by " the children," so especially named in this interesting document, or what is to be understood by so vague a term, is, as has been before noticed, a mystery that justifies many conjectures, but is altogether difficult of any satisfactory solution. That the young Earl of Salisbury was one of these

[1] Harl. MSS., 433. p. 269.

adults admits not of doubt, for, in King Richard's household book of costs at Middleham, the expenses of the lord prince at this abode, and at that particular period, are distinctly and minutely detailed [1], not only prior to the framing of the abovenamed ordinance, but for many weeks after it was acted upon. Possibly the Lady Katharine Plantagenet, betrothed in "her young age" [2] to William Herbert, Earl of Huntingdon, and the Lord John Plantagenet, both illegitimate by birth, but acknowledged as his children by Richard [3], may have been resident at Middleham, and early associated with the Earl of Salisbury. Nevertheless, coupling the term "children" with the king's remarkable expression in the letters patent, issued within a few days of this domestic arrangement, "Edward, his first begotten son," it justifies the surmise, as has been before argued, that the Earl of Salisbury was not the sole child of Richard and the Lady Anne, although the monarch's illegitimate offspring may probably have been included among the youthful members so distinctly specified in the household regulations of Middleham.

All preliminaries, public and private, being arranged, King Richard, on the 23d of July, 1483, commenced his royal progress, quitting Windsor for Reading; his stay in which town was marked by an act of liberality that is greatly at variance with the heartless spirit so universally imputed to him. He granted to Katharine Lady Hastings his

---

[1] Harl. MSS., 433. p. 118.
[2] Banks, Dormant and Extinct Baronage, vol. ii. p. 273.
[3] Harl. MSS., No. 258. fol. 11. ; and No. 433. fol. 211.

full and entire pardon[1] for the offences of her recently executed lord, released the title and estates from attainder and forfeiture, confirming her son and the rest of her children in all their possessions and just rights, and promising " to protect and defend the widow and to suffer none to do her wrong."[2] Thence he passed on to Oxford, and at the entrance of that city was welcomed with great reverence by the chancellor and heads of the university, where, " after they had expressed their love and duty to him, he was honourably and processionally received in Magdalen College[3] by the founder, Bishop Waynflete, the president and scholars thereof, and lodged there that night."[4] The king was accompanied by the Bishops of Durham, Worcester, St. Asaph, and St. David's, the Earls of Lincoln and Surrey, the Lords Lovell, Stanley, Audley, Beauchamp, and many other knights and nobles."[5]

The reception given to Richard at Oxford as little implies hatred or unpopularity, as does the public support afforded to him by the bishops, on this and other occasions, favour the tradition of his reputed crimes. He was welcomed with loyalty, respect, and affection. Every honour that could be paid to him by the university was abundantly shown[6]; and this monarch's visit to the university is perpetuated by its famed antiquary, Anthony

[1] Dated at Reading, 23d July, anno 1 Richard III.
[2] Harl. MSS., 433. p. 108.
[3] Magdalen College is required by its statutes to entertain the kings of England and their eldest sons, whenever they come to Oxford. — *Chalmers' Hist. of Oxford,* p. 211.
[4] Gutch's Hist. of Oxford, p. 638.   [5] Ibid.
[6] See Appendix N.

Wood[1], as one of the most interesting and memorable scenes connected with the early history of this seat of learning. The day after his arrival, solemn disputations on moral philosophy and divinity were held in the hall, by command and at the desire of the king; when the disputants, one of whom was that celebrated reviver of learning, Grocyn, "the friend and patron of Erasmus,"[2] were honourably rewarded. On the ensuing day, King Richard, with his noble retinue, visited several of the colleges, and heard disputations also in the public schools, "scattering his benevolence very liberally to all that he heard dispute or make orations to him;"[3] and, in conformity with a promise made to the scholars at his reception, he confirmed the privileges of the university granted by his predecessors. He was equally mindful, also, of the town of Oxford, for which he showed his love by releasing it from the usual crown fee due to each sovereign at his accession. Richard III. was indeed a great benefactor to both the universities; for although Cambridge, so often distinguished by his bounty, came not at this time within the royal progress, yet it did not escape his attention. In addition to other marks of royal favour to that seminary of learning, he endowed Queen's College, the foundation of which, begun by the unfortunate Margaret of Anjou, had been completed by the widowed[4] queen of Edward IV.[5], with 500 marks per annum;

---

[1] Wood's Hist and Antiq. of Oxon., vol. i. p. 233.
[2] Gutch, p. 638.   [3] Ibid. p. 639.
[4] Ibid. p. 639.
[5] Elizabeth Woodville, consort of Edward IV., obtained his licence

and for the benefit of both Oxford and Cambridge, he caused an act to be made, that strangers might bring printed books into England, and sell them by retail, — a matter of great importance to these seminaries of learning in the infancy of printing.[1] But although most histories that treat of the eventful times in which this sovereign lived are abundantly filled with accounts of his misdeeds and his alleged depravity, how few notice the undeniable evidence of his bounty, his patronage of literature, and the high estimation in which he was evidently held by the learned and the good![2] Yet the golden

in the sixth year of his reign, to complete the foundation of Queen's College, Cambridge, begun by her predecessor, Margaret of Anjou, but left incomplete, owing to her exile and the deposition of Henry VI. — *Sandford,* book iii. p. 385.

[1] Gutch, 639.

[2] The piety, erudition, and eminent virtues of Waynfleet, bishop of Winchester, the founder of Magdalen College, where the king lodged, and who went there expressly to receive the monarch, and to superintend in person the arrangements that were to welcome the illustrious visitor, is attested equally by his own biographers, as by the historians of Oxford and Winchester. So high was the reputation of this exemplary ecclesiastic, that King Henry VI. solicited him to superintend the progress, constitution, and discipline of Eton College, of which he appointed him provost in 1443; and on the death of Cardinal Beaufort, in 1447, the king advanced him to the see of Winchester, honouring with his presence the ceremony of Waynfleet's enthronement. He was selected to baptise the monarch's princely son, and in the year 1456 he was appointed by him lord high chancellor, which office he resigned on the deposition of his royal patron and benefactor. Nevertheless, Waynfleet was treated by Edward IV. with marked attention, and on his founding Magdalen College, this monarch condescended to visit it, unasked, and simply from respect to his high character and talents.

This eminent prelate, having received three crowned heads as visitors in his college, viz. Henry VI., Edward IV., and Richard III., lived to see the union of the Houses of York and Lancaster, by the marriage of Henry VII. with the Princess Elizabeth, and to be twice honoured with the company of their eldest son, Arthur Prince of Wales." — *Chalmers' Oxford,* vol. i. pp. 191—193.

opinions which he reaped during his stay at Oxford are registered in the college archives, and would seem to have universally prevailed ; — such, at least, is a fair inference from the glowing description which records his visit, and thus describes its termination : — " So that after the Muses had crowned his brows with sacred wreaths for his entertainment, he, the same day, went to Woodstock ; the University then taking leave of him with all submission."

The act which certifies this monarch's sojourn at Woodstock fully proved the honesty of the resolution he expressed to the judges, of personally examining into the wants of his subjects, and redressing their grievances. The inhabitants presented to him a petition, setting forth that his brother King Edward had, unjustly and " against conscience, annexed and incorporated to the forest of Wichwood, — and placed it under forest law, — a great circuit of country,"[1] to the serious injury of the dwellers in those parts. Richard not only received their appeal most graciously, but, after due inquiry into the merits of the case, he disafforested the tract of land, together with " other vast woods adjacent,"[2] confirming the restitution to the inhabitants by charter.[3]

At Gloucester, to which place the royal progress was next directed, he was received with the utmost loyalty and affection. This city, whence Richard derived his youthful title of duke, had remained firm to King Edward and himself amidst all their reverses of fortune. " When Queen Margaret be-

[1] Rous, p. 216. [2] Buck, lib. v. p. 138.
[3] Lingard, vol. vi. p. 349.

sieged the city of Gloucester with the king's power, the citizens stood at defiance with her army, and told her it was the Duke of Gloucester his town, who was with the king, and for the king, and for him they would hold it."[1]

Richard never forgot a kindness. True, indeed, as asserted by his bitter enemy Sir Thomas More, with "large gifts he got him unsteadfast friendship,"[2] but his grateful remembrance of former benefits, his justice, and his munificence, even in this royal progress alone, exemplify in a striking degree the additional evidence of this historian, that "he was free of dyspence," and "above his power liberal." The city of Gloucester was most abundantly rewarded for the love that the citizens had borne him. He granted them many exemptions and immunities[3], appointed a mayor and sheriffs[4], and, after annexing "two adjoining hundreds, made it a county of itself, calling it the county of the city of Gloucester."[5] Tewkesbury, the scene of his early military renown, was the next station on his progress. He reached it on the 4th of August, and after visiting the abbot, and bestowing large sums on the abbey[6], he passed on with his noble train to Worcester, the bishop of which diocese had attended Richard to Oxford[7], and had accompanied him throughout his tour. This prelate, it will be remembered, was one of the executors[8] of Edward IV., and preceptor and president

---

[1] Buck, lib. iii, p. 83. ; also Fleetwood, Chron., p. 26.
[2] More, p. 9.   [3] Buck, lib. i. p. 28.
[4] Lingard, vol. vi. p. 349.   [5] Heylin, p. 326.
[6] Harl. MSS., No. 433. p. 110.   [7] Gutch, p. 639.
[8] See Royal Wills, p. 347.

of the council[1] to the deposed Edward V., and had been arrested and imprisoned as such by the Lord Protector at Stoney Stratford; yet is he chronicled as one of the four bishops who by their presence imparted sanctity and added dignity to the new king's progress through his dominions. Such support seems wholly incomprehensible, if Richard were the monster of depravity usually represented; the more so, as Dr. Alcock, the bishop of Worcester, was highly celebrated in his day for his virtues, his learning, and his piety. Still more irreconcilable with the odious character so long affixed to this king is the popularity which greeted him wherever he sojourned. The city of Worcester, following the example set by the commonalties of London and Gloucester, tendered him " a benevolence,"[2] or sum of money to defray his expenses. Richard, however, was too wise a legislator not to perceive the evil of a tax which pressed so heavily on the industrious portion of his subjects; he therefore thanked them for their liberality, but, in each case, declined the money offered, stating that he "would rather possess their hearts than their wealth."[3] Surely, incidents of this kind disprove, infinitely beyond the most laboured arguments, the calumnies of a later age, and imputations based only on oral conjecture, originating in political rancour, and propagated by angry opponents and prejudiced writers. "Every one that is ac-

[1] Sloane MSS., No. 3479.

[2] The severe imposition called " benevolence" — a despotic mode of raising money, by exacting large sums as voluntary gifts from the great body of the people — was devised by King Edward IV., and abolished by Richard III. — *Harl. MSS.*, No. 980. art. 23.

[3] Rous, p. 215.

quainted with English history," observes Drake, who rescued from obscurity so many original documents connected with Richard III., "must know that there is hardly any part of it so dark as the short reign of this king: the Lancastrian party which destroyed and succeeded him took care to suppress his virtues, and to paint his vices in the most glaring colours."[1]

From Worcester the monarch proceeded to the city of Warwick, the birth-place of his royal consort. Here he was joined by the queen, who came direct for the purpose from Windsor with a numerous retinue; and in this place he delayed his progress for a brief space, to hold a court, which was characterised by every demonstration of regal pomp and splendour, there being present most of the great officers of the crown, the chief justice of England, the Duke of Albany brother to the Scottish king, Edward the youthful Earl of Warwick, and a numerous assemblage of bishops, earls, barons, and "other lords and illustrious ladies in like manner with the queen."[2] During the king's sojourn at Warwick Castle,— an abode well fitted for the ceremonial of such recognition,— ambassadors met him from the courts of Spain, France, and Burgundy, to deliver their letters of credence[3] from

---

[1] See Drake's "Eboracum," or History and Antiquities of York, p. 118.— a work of great research, containing literal copies of all King Richard's letters and proclamations sent to the mayor and citizens of York, together with the daily orders in council about the state of affairs to this king's death, extracted from the city registers.

[2] Rous, p. 216.

[3] These letters are preserved in the Harl. MSS., together with King Richard's replies to them. They are thus entitled : —

" Letter of Credence of Isabella Queen of Spain to the King, dated

their sovereigns, acknowledging his title, and paying him that homage which could alone render the royal diadem valuable in his eyes. And in this princely dwelling of his child's grandsire, the mighty Warwick, who raised and dethroned kings " at pleasure,"[1] he received the highest honours which could be conferred on him by foreign potentates; a proposal being made by the Spanish ambassador for a marriage between the king's only son, Edward Earl of Salisbury, and the daughter of Ferdinand and Isabella[2], the most powerful sovereigns of Europe. The same envoy, whose mission was so flattering to Richard's pride and ambition, also publicly made known to the English nobility the affront which had formerly been offered to the illustrious Isabella[3] by Edward IV. " in refusing her, and taking to his wife a widow of England"[4] —a communication invaluable to the new monarch,

6th June, A. D. 1483, written in Spanish and in English." —No. 433. fol. 236.

" Letter of Louis XI., the French king, to Richard III., thanking him for the news of his accession to the crown." It is written in French, signed Loys, and dated 31st July. — *Ibid.*

" Letter of Philip of Austria, duke of Burgundy, &c., to King Richard III.," in French, dated at Gand, 30th July, 1483. — *Ibid.*

The letter of the Spanish queen being dated before the deposition of Edward V., it would seem that the Spanish government mistook Richard's elevation to the protectorate for his election to the throne. It was undoubtedly delivered to this monarch by the ambassador in person, and was evidently designed for him, not only from the proposal for his son's marriage with which the envoy was charged, but also from the nature of the verbal relations which Queen Isabella informs Richard she has empowered "her orator to show his Majesty."

[1] " He made kings and put down kings, almost at pleasure, and not impossible to have attained it himself, if he had not reckoned it a greater thing to make a king than to be a king."—*More*, p. 98.

[2] Rous, p. 216.   [3] Appendix O.

[4] Harl. MSS., 433. fol. 235.

at this particular crisis, from its lessening the dignity of Elizabeth Wydville, so scornfully designated by Granfidus de Sasiola, " a widow of England! " and strengthening the recently admitted follies and unkingly proceedings of the deceased monarch.

At the expiration of a week [1], accompanied by his queen, the ambassadors, and a considerable addition to his retinue, King Richard quitted Warwick Castle for Coventry, the city where, in childhood, he had been delivered with his mother a prisoner into the hands of Henry VI., and where his father was attainted, his brothers outlawed, and the aspiring hopes of his proud race apparently crushed for ever. Now he entered it monarch of the realm, and with every accessory which could dignify the ruler of a great and powerful kingdom. The precise date of his stay here is made known by his signing, on the 15th August at Coventry, an order for payment for articles furnished to " Queen Anne, the king's consort," [2] preparatory to her regal progress.

Richard next proceeded to Leicester, where some symptoms of disaffection appear to have reached his ears; for on the 17th August he issued a mandate in that town, commanding " 2000 Welsh bills or glaives" to be made for him in all haste, and authorising one of the officers of his household " to impress as many smiths " as were requisite for the completion of the order. [3] Official documents were also despatched from the same city to " seventy knights and esquires of Yorkshire, and the neigh-

---

[1] Rous, p. 216.   [2] Harl. MSS., 433. fol. 109.   [3] Ibid. fol. 110.

bouring counties [1], commanding them to await his
coming at the castle of Pontefract by a given day [2]:
and, previous to his departure, he wrote a letter in
French to the Duke of Burgundy, dated " at the
Castle of Leicester, 18th of August, 1483." [3]

At Nottingham, which town King Richard entered on the 19th instant, the first indications were
given of his contemplating a second coronation ;
a letter being addressed by his private secretary,
John Kendall, to the mayor, recorder, aldermen,
and sheriffs of York, announcing his approach to
that city, and enjoining them to " receive his highness and the queen at their coming, as laudably as
their wisdom can imagine ;" Kendall advising that
the streets through which the king's grace shall
pass should be hung " with cloth of arras, tapestry-
work, and other ; for that there come many southern
lords, and men of worship with them, which will
mark greatly your receiving their graces." [4]   Proclamations were also issued, commanding the attendance at York of the surrounding nobility and
gentry, that they might be awaiting the monarch's
arrival to take the oath of allegiance, and to greet
the prince, who had so long dwelt among them ;
and from this time the most active preparations
appear to have been made by Richard III. for re-

[1] Harl. MSS., 433. fol. 111.

[2] " Trusty and well beloved." ... " For certain causes and considerations us moving, such as shall be shewed unto you at your
coming, we command you to give your attendance upon us, upon our
coming unto our castle of Pomfret, which, by God's grace, shall be
the 26th day of the present month of August.   Given at Leicester
the 18th of August, anno 1 Richard III., 1483."—*Harl. MSS.*, 433.
fol. 101.

[3] Harl. MSS., 433. fol. 237.   [4] Drake's Eborac., p. 116.

newing in the northern metropolis the gorgeous scene which had marked his enthronement at Westminster. Whether this repetition was induced by a desire of displaying to the foreign ambassadors the unanimity with which his accession was hailed, or whether the proposed alliance with Spain made Richard regret the absence of his princely son Edward, the youthful Earl of Salisbury, on the former occasion, and resolve on making his title to the throne not only evident to Granfidus de Sasiola, the proud " orator of Spain," but a prominent part of the ceremony, by associating him publicly in the procession, and by his subsequent investiture with the principality of Wales, must remain matter of conjecture. There is, however, ground for this latter surmise; for, independent of the remarkable expression in Kendall's letter, " the men of worship, which will mark greatly your receiving their graces," the young Earl of Salisbury, who has before been noticed as absent from London at his parent's coronation on the 6th of July, is known to have remained uninterruptedly at Middleham from the time of his father's accession until the 22d of August following, the very day that the notification was sent to York relative to the king's contemplated renewal of his installation.

This fact is clearly established by reference to the household book before named[1], entries for my lord prince's expenses with his attendants being there charged from Midsummer-day, June 21st, to the 2d day of August; and again, from that date

[1] Harl. MSS., 433. fol. 118.

to the 22d of the same month, when the Earl of
Salisbury evidently quitted Middleham to join his
royal parents at Pontefract, preparatory to their
triumphal entry into York. The cost of " my lord
prince's" household on his journey thither are distinctly and minutely specified.[1] Wages are charged
for his running footmen[2], and several even of the
stages enumerated, showing that he rested at
Wetherby and Tadcaster prior to reaching Pontefract Castle, where Richard and Queen Anne
arrived on the 27th of August. The monarch did
not forget his former abode at this renowned castle,
nor his early connection with the inhabitants. He
awarded to them many valuable grants, appointed
a mayor[3] and corporation, and bestowed large sums
of money in charity and religious donations prior
to departing for York, which city he entered in
great state on the 29th of August, 1483.

The royal party were welcomed by the citizens
with a display of enthusiasm and zealous attachment
that fully confirms the accounts given by local historians[4] of the devotion with which Richard was
beloved, not alone in York, but throughout the
whole of the northern counties. The feeling appears
to have been reciprocal. " This place," says Drake,
" he seems to have paid an extraordinary regard
to ; " and that portion of Kendall's letter which
announces " to the good masters, the mayor and

---

[1] Extracts from the original document will be found on reference
to Appendix M M, Vol. I. p. 367.

[2] Harl. MSS., 433. p. 118.   [3] Rous, p. 216.

[4] Richard III., whatever may be the crimes imputed to him, was
personally popular in the north. — *Surtees's Durham,* p. 60.

aldermen of York," King Richard's purposed visit
to their city, is couched in words too remarkable
to be omitted in these pages.[1] " The cause I write
to you now is, forasmuch as I verily know the
king's mind and entire affection that his grace
beareth towards you and your worshipful city, for
manifold your kind and loving designings to his
grace showed heretofore, which his grace will
never forget ; and intendeth therefore so to do
unto you [beyond] that [which] all the kings that
ever reigned bestowed upon you, did they never so
much." This letter, as may be supposed, produced
extraordinary emulation in the citizens to outvie
other places, and even to rival one another in " the
pomp and ceremony of the king's reception," and
" Richard, on coming to the goodly and ancient
city of York, the scope and goal of his progress,
was received with all possible honour and festivity." [2] Plays, pageants, feasts, and goodly
speeches occupied the week that preceded the coronation; to increase the splendour of which solemnity, King Richard sent an order to Piers Curteys, keeper of the wardrobe[3], to forward apparel
for the occasion, of so costly a description that it
exceeded, if possible, the magnificence of that worn
at his first inauguration.

On the 8th of September the solemn rite was performed in the most imposing manner : the gorgeous
procession was led by the clergy, fully vested in
their pontifical robes, followed by the mayor and aldermen and a large attendance of the spiritual and

[1] Drake's Eborac., p. 116.   [2] Ibid.
[3] See Appendix P.

temporal peers.[1] Supported by the great officers of
the crown[2], and attended by a lordly retinue of
nobles, barons, and knights, the king walked in
regal splendour, wearing his crown and bearing his
sceptre.[3] The queen, preceded in like manner by
the lords of her household, and attended by a
suitable number of prelates, peers, and peeresses,
graced the procession, wearing her regal coronet,
and holding by the left hand her princely son,
whose brow was encircled with the diadem appertaining to the heir apparent of England.[4]
Five heralds in coat-armour ; banners of " our
Lady," the Trinity, St. George, St. Edward, and
St. Cuthbert ; lastly, standards of the richest
sarsenet embroidered with king Richard's badge,
" the silver boar:" forty trumpet banners, and
hundreds of pennons, pensils, and streamers of
dazzling hues and rich materials, closed the procession, which was received at the cathedral doors
with all homage and dutiful respect by Archbishop
Rotheram ; in the chapter house[5] appertaining to

[1] Drake, p. 116.

[2] The presence of the Lord Chief Justice of England, Sir Wm.
Hussey, who, from his being mentioned as with the king at Warwick,
would seem to have accompanied Richard throughout in his progress,
is shown by a remarkable instrument, signed at York, which illus-
trates in a striking degree the odious custom of enriching the royal
coffers by the disposal of the wardship of rich minors : —

" Sale of the ward and marriage of Anne, daughter and heir of
John Salvayne, knight, to Sir William Husse, knight, chief justice,
for 1000 marks. Given at York, the 7th day of September, anno
1 Richard III." — *Harl. MSS.*, No. 433. fol. 113.

[3] Drake, p. 117.

[4] This crown is of plain gold, and unornamented with jewels ;
and where there is an heir apparent to the throne, it is placed, during
his infancy, on a velvet cushion before the seat of the Prince of
Wales in the House of Lords on all state occasions.

[5] Drake, p. 117.

which[1], amidst the tumultuous acclamations of thousands who had known him "long and well," King Richard III. and Anne his queen were, by " the lord primate of England,"[2] solemnly crowned a second time, sovereigns of the realm.

The imposing service concluded, the procession, after passing through the chief streets of the city, returned in the same state to the palace[3], where the king created his son, the young Earl of Salisbury, " Prince of Wales and Earl of Chester,"[4] investing him with the principality " by a golden rod, a co-ronet of gold, and other ensigns."[5] At the same time he conferred the honour of knighthood on Granfidius Sasiola, the Spanish envoy, who was present at the ceremony, and " put round his neck a golden collar in memory of the event;"[6] striking

---

[1] It is said that the chair at the north of the altar on York Min-ster, in which King Richard III. was crowned, is older than the cathedral itself; being that in which several of the Saxon kings were also invested with the symbols of royalty. — *Poole's Lectures on the Decorations of Churches.*

[2] The Archbishop of York, by whom Richard III. was crowned the second time, was lord high chancellor at the decease of King Edward IV., by whom he was distinguished with particular marks of favour and regard. This ecclesiastic, upon hearing of the arrest of Edward V. by the Lord Protector, proceeded to the widowed queen, and delivered into her hands the great seal for the " use and behoof of her son," with which he had been intrusted by his deceased parent. " Madam," quoth he, " be of good cheer, for I assure you, if they crown any other king than your son, whom they now have with them, we shall on the morrow crown his brother whom you have here with you."—*More*, p. 30.

[3] Formerly the kings of England had a palace at York, on the north side of the river Ouse, from which it had a gradual ascent. It was almost demolished during the civil wars, although sufficient was left of the ruins to convey an idea of its original magnificence.

[4] Warrant for a new great seal for the palatine of Chester, to be made for the prince, was given at York, the 16th day of September, anno 1 Richard III. — *Harl. MSS.*, No. 433. p. 114.

[5] Fœdera, vol. xii. p. 200.   [6] Ibid.

him " three times upon his shoulders with the
sword, and, by other marks of honour, according
to the English custom, with agreeable words
added; in testimony whereof the king gave him
his letters patent, dated at his court at York."[1]
Triumphal sports, masks, and revels concluded the
solemnities; and the most sumptuous entertainment was given at the palace to all the illustrious
personages who had taken part in the ceremony
of the day—" a day," says Polydore Virgil, " of
great state for York;" there being " three princes
wearing crowns — the king, the queen, and the
prince of Wales."[2] But, flattering to the citizens
as was the renewal of this imposing rite within
their ancient walls, it is an error to suppose that
Richard III. by a second coronation exceeded his
prerogative, or committed any outrage on the ordinary usages of the realm, by thus honouring a city
which had always been remarkable for zeal and
attachment to his race, and from which the dynasty which he now represented derived its title.
It is, indeed, but justice to this monarch here to
take the opportunity to exculpate him from two
charges which, although apparently unimportant in
themselves, yet help to swell the catalogue of those
offences, the summing up of which complete the
measure of the ill fame of Richard III. A second
coronation has been represented an outrageous and
unparalleled event; but, so far from such being the
case, a repetition of the ceremony was usual, if not
invariable, among the Anglo-Saxon kings. Although this custom was discontinued by the Nor-

---

[1] Drake's Eborac., p. 118.   [2] Pol. Virg., p. 547.

man monarchs, yet the founder of that race adopted
the coronation oath of the Anglo-Saxon kings[1], and
Henry I. restored to the English, on the day of his
coronation, their Anglo-Saxon laws and privileges.[2]
The two-fold coronation itself was revived very
speedily by the Plantagenet dynasty, King Henry
III. having been crowned with great solemnity at
Gloucester in 1216, and again at Westminster in
1219[3]; and Henry VI., after being crowned in
London in 1429, was a second time anointed king
at Paris in the year 1431.[4] Thus it is shown that
Richard III., who for three centuries has laboured
under the most disparaging imputations, arising
from his second investiture with the symbols of
royalty, only revived an ancient custom, of which
a precedent was afforded him by Edward IV., who
was crowned king in this very city after the battle
of Hexham.[5] The splendid apparel worn by Richard at York, and on all state occasions, has likewise been made a subject of reproach to him[6],
whereas, in bestowing attention on his personal
appearance, he merely acted in conformity with the
spirit of the age in which he lived. Display in
dress, during the fifteenth century, was carried to

[1] Ord. Vitel., p. 503.   [2] Turner's Middle Ages, vol. i. p. 171.
[3] Sandford's Geneal. Hist., book ii. p. 87.
[4] Ibid. book iv. p. 289.
[5] " Richard III. only followed the example of Edward IV. in
being crowned at York.   Edward, marching from York, met
Henry VI. at Hexham, where victory declared for him ; the unfortunate monarch escaped only by the fleetness of his horse.   The
royal equipage falling into Edward's possession, he immediately used
it, by being solemnly crowned in that city, May 4. 1464.   Henry's
rich cap of maintenance, or abacot, having a double crown, was
placed upon his head."—*Noble's Hist. Coll. of Arms*, p. 53.
[6] Turner's Middle Ages, vol. iii. p. 479.

such an excess that the most severe legislative
enactments became necessary to keep within bounds
all ranks that were privileged to appear otherwise
than in the " russet garb" which indicated vassal-
age and servitude ; and a very slight glance at the
wardrobe accounts of the Plantagenet monarchs,
and of the sumptuary laws enacted to repress the
absurd extravagancies of the fourteenth and fifteenth centuries, will at once prove the fallacy of
these personal accusations which have rendered
Richard III. an object of censure[1] for displaying the
rich and gorgeous attire which the custom of the
times rendered not only imperative but a positive
duty incumbent on· princes and all men of high
birth and exalted stations.[2]

[1] Turner's Middle Ages, vol. iii. p. 479.

[2] " These inferences," observes Sir Harris Nicolas (in refuting
the arguments of Mr. Sharon Turner), " with respect to the character of Richard III., are, it is submitted, drawn from a mistaken
estimate of evidence, rather than from erroneous data ; and they prove
the necessity of an historian, not merely using research, but of being
able to attach a proper value to his materials. The grounds upon
which the opinion of Richard's vanity is built are, the account of the
articles delivered out of the wardrobe for his coronation ; the descriptions of chroniclers of his pompous appearance on public occasions ;
and the clothes for which he sent from York. Viewed without
reference to similar accounts, in previous and subsequent reigns, the
conclusion is natural, that the sovereign to whom they relate was " a
vain coxcomb," especially if the opinion be correct, that that list
was prepared by the monarch himself. But when records of this
nature are compared with others, and it becomes evident that the
splendid dresses worn by Richard formed the general costume of
persons of rank of the age ; and when the minuteness of detail, which
is ascribed to his own taste, is proved to be the usual form in which
wardrobe keepers and their officers entered the articles intrusted to
their custody, the error of supposing that the splendour or the accu-
rate description of the robes are in any degree indicative of Richard
the Third's character, is manifest. A reference to these wardrobe
accounts, or to any other list of apparel or jewels in the 14th or 15th
and 16th centuries, will prove that there is not a single circumstance

The festivities at York, which had preluded the ceremony of the coronation, were continued for many days after it was solemnised: but, amidst "tilts, tournaments, stage-plays, and banquets, with feasting to the utmost prodigality,"[1] Richard devoted a considerable portion of his time to receiving petitions, redressing grievances, and administering justice.   Some of the northern soldiers, who, in their march back from London, had committed gross outrages, were executed for their lawless proceedings[2]; and although the Croyland writer states, that Richard proceeded to York, "wishing to display his newly acquired authority,"[3] yet the actions of this monarch are more corroborative of Rapin's assertions, that his going down there "was to minister justice everywhere."   That he did so, and with strict impartiality, is proved by the local records that have perpetuated his progress from town to town during his journey to the north, and is likewise confirmed by a statement in Kendale's letter, addressed to the authorities at York, communicating to them the nature of the monarch's proceedings.   " Thanked be Jesu," writes the royal secretary, "the king's grace is in good health, as is likewise the queen's grace, and in all their progress have been worshipfully received with pageants and other &c. &c., and his lords and judges in every place, sitting determining

connected with Richard which justifies the opinion that he was more fond of splendour than his predecessors, much less that he was either ' a fop ' or ' a coxcomb.' " — *Privy Purse Expenses of Elizabeth of York*, edited by Sir Harris Nicolas, p. 4.

[1] Drake, p. 117.   [2] Ibid. p. 116.

[3] Chron. Croy., p. 567.

the complaints of poor folks, with due punition of offenders against his laws."[1] It is, indeed, most clear that Richard did not contemplate a second coronation, when, following the example of his predecessors[2], he resolved on visiting the chief cities of the kingdom; neither did he direct his steps to York, merely with the vain desire of exhibiting his kingly position; for, setting aside the short period allotted to the citizens for arranging so important a ceremony, the circumstance of this monarch having been altogether unprepared for the gorgeous pageant, must alone establish that point. Independent of the messenger who was sent to London for the state robes and regal apparel, it appears that another was despatched for the crown jewels, his costs on the journey, together with his expenses whilst executing his mission, being charged in Richard's private accounts.[3]

Immediately after his second investiture with the symbols of royalty, the monarch dismissed the foreign envoys with letters to their respective sovereigns, and closed his stay at York by confirming overtures of peace and amity with the courts of Spain[4] and Scotland.[5] His illegitimate son, the Lord John Plantagenet, he also knighted, conferring the same honour upon many northern gentlemen[6]; and willing to do the city and citizens some extraordinary bounty " for old services and new," he sent

[1] Drake, p. 116.

[2] The example set by King Henry I. of making a progress into the remote parts of the land for the administration of justice, was followed by most of his successors. — *Harl. MSS.*, No. 980. fol. 34.

[3] Harl. MSS., 433. p. 118.　　　　　[4] Fœdera, xii. p. 200.

[5] Harl. MSS., 433. fol. 246.　　　　　[6] Drake, 117.

for the mayor, the aldermen, and commons on the 17th of September, and, "without any petition or asking," bestowed upon the city of York a charter of great value and importance. " Richard's munificence to our city at this time," observes Drake[1], who has published a transcript of the original instrument, " whether it proceeded from gratitude or policy, was a truly royal gift.... I never found him, amongst all his other vices, taxed with covetousness, and he had many reasons, both on his own and his family's account, to induce him even to do more for a city which had always signalised itself in the interest of his house."

After a fortnight passed in a district so interesting to him from long residence and early associations, and now endeared yet more by the proofs of attachment and loyalty so recently and enthusiastically displayed, Richard III. departed from York ; carrying with him abundant proofs of the love of her citizens and of that personal attachment which was never diminished, never withdrawn,—no, not even when calumny had blighted Richard's fair fame, or death had rendered him powerless to reward the fidelity with which his grateful northern subjects cherished the memory and upheld the reputation of their friend and benefactor.[2]

[1] Drake, p. 117.

[2] What opinion our citizens of York had of King Richard will best appear by their own records ; in which they took care to register every particular letter and message they received from him. And as his fate drew nigh, they endeavoured to show their loyalty or their gratitude to this prince in the best manner they were able. — *Drake,* p. 117.

CHAPTER XIV.

KING Richard, accompanied by Queen Anne and
the Prince of Wales, recommenced his royal progress about the middle of September, proceeding
direct from York to Pontefract, which town he
entered on the 20th of that month, with the view
of returning to London through the eastern counties, and visiting the principal towns connected
with that portion of the kingdom. But the festivities and apparent harmony which characterised
this monarch's double coronation, and the peaceful

state of things which marked his progress through so considerable a part of his dominions, was at an end : it had been but a temporary calm, the prelude of scenes of violence and disaffection, far more in keeping with that turbulent era, than the uninterrupted tranquillity which formed so remarkable a feature in the dawn of this monarch's reign.

It has been shown that no effort was made to rescue Edward V. ; no arm was raised in defence of the youthful princes, by the many and powerful lords who had been ennobled and enriched by their deceased parent : yet was there a feeling of commiseration in the humbler classes of the community ; a still small voice of sympathy and affection for the royal orphans, which, like the mournful sound that betokens a coming storm, even under a cloudless sky, swept through the land and ended in a political convulsion that speedily brought home to Richard's heart the sense of the uncertain tenure of public applause, and the disquietude attendant upon a throne. From a proclamation sent to the mayor and bailiffs of Northampton[1], forbidding the inhabitants to " take or receive any liveries or recognizances of any person of what estate, degree, or condition soever he be of," induced by a report that " great divisions and dissentions had arisen in consequence of oaths, the giving of signs and recognizances of time past," it is probable that some intimation of impending danger was communicated to the king, even before his arrival at York. But an order sent from thence to Lord Dynham, lieu-

---

[1] Harl. MSS., 433. fol. 111.

tenant of the town and marches of Calais, to discharge a portion of the garrison on account of the expense, and because, as asserted, " the season of any great danger of adversaries is of all likelihood overpast for this year, "[1] would seem to imply that Richard's mind was thoroughly at ease before he left that city ; and the nature of his edicts from Pontefract, 'at the fortress of which he remained for a brief period, convey no symptoms of alarm either from foreign or domestic enemies. He addressed a letter on the 22d inst., dated from " Pomfret Castle," to the mayor of Southampton, assuring him, in reply to some official communication, that he would not allow " his dearest son, the prince, to deal or intermeddle with their franchises."[2] He also wrote to the Earl of Kildare from the same place, acquainting him that he had appointed the Lord of Lincoln, his nephew, to be lieutenant of Ireland, and the said earl to be his deputy [3], requesting him to accept the office, which office, it will be remembered, was conferred upon the Earl of Kildare on the 9th of July, when King Richard had nominated his young son, now Prince of Wales, to the command of that country. Various communications to different individuals in Ireland[4], some high in rank, others in a humbler station[5] of life, thanking them for their assistance against his enemies, or acknowledging past kindnesses, either to himself or his kindred, may also be found in this portion of Richard's diary, together

[1] Harl. MSS., 433. fol. 113.   [2] Ibid. fol. 115.
[3] Ibid. p. 267.   [4] Ibid.   [5] Ibid.

with instances of his impartial administration of the laws, in cases where proof was given that persons had been oppressed or wrongfully treated.[1] No portion indeed of Richard's singularly eventful life more thoroughly disproves the accusation of his being destitute of natural affection, callous to the ties of kindred, the endearments of " household love," than the actions which perpetuate his brief sojourn at Pontefract, the only period of repose which occurred during his short and troubled reign. He sent instructions to the Bishop of Enachden empowering him to receive the allegiance of the Earl of Desmond, also to thank that nobleman for his offers of personal service, and to accept them " in consideration of the many services and kindness shown by the earl's father to the Duke of York, the king's father, the king then being of young age."[2] These instructions were accompanied with munificent gifts, together with a letter from the king himself to the Earl of Desmond, dated the 29th of September, wherein he says, " It is our intent and pleasure for to have you to use the manner of our English habit and clothing ; for the which cause we send you a collar of gold of our livery and device, with our apparel for your person[3] of the English fashion, which we will ye

[1] Harl. MSS., 433. p. 267.

[2] The debt of gratitude to his father here acknowledged has reference to the shelter afforded the Duke of York in Ireland, when, with his son, the Earl of Rutland, he escaped from Ludlow, and sought refuge in that country. King Richard was at that time about six years of age. In another part of this document allusion is made to the Earl of Desmond's father having suffered a violent death arising from his devotion to the house of York, for which the king says he has always felt great " inward compassion."

[3] See Appendix Q.

shall receive in our name, trusting, that at some
convenient season hereafter we shall have you to
come over to us hither, and be more expert both in
the manners and conditions of us, and our honorable and goodly behaving of our subjects."[1] King
Richard also confirmed the annuity granted by
Edward IV. for ministering divine service in the
chapel which was erected on the bridge at Wakefield[2] in memory of his father and brother slain
in the vicinity of that town. He commanded payment of 40*l*., of the king's gift[3], towards the building of the church at Baynard's Castle, and issued
a "warrant to the auditors of Middleham to allow
Geoffrey Frank, receiver of the same, the sum of
196*l*. 10*s*. in his accounts, for monies laid out upon
several occasions, the particulars whereof are specified, and are mostly "the expences of my lord
prince,"[4] which remarkable payment, so often
quoted in these pages, has furnished to posterity
almost the only known records of Richard's illustrious child. Offerings to religious houses[5], charitable donations[6], and the disbursement of all just
debts, not alone for himself, his offspring, and his
household[7], but even those incurred by his political
enemies[8], might be adduced with advantage, to exemplify the consideration which Richard bestowed

---

[1] Harl. MSS., 433. fol. 265.   [2] Ibid. fol. 116.
[3] Ibid. fol. 119.   [4] Ibid. fol. 118.
[5] "The king's offerings to religious houses," observes Whitaker,
"appear to have been very liberal." — *Whit. Hist. Richmondshire,*
vol. i. p. 346.
[6] Harl. MSS., 433. fol. 118.   [7] Ibid. fol. 58. 118. 120.
[8] "For money paid to Sir Thomas Gower, by him laid out for
the expences of the Lord Rivers." — *Harl. MSS.*, 433. fol. 118.

equally on the private duties of life, as on the important functions of royalty. But these minute details, though important in themselves from displaying the true nature of Richard's disposition, could not be followed up without tedious prolixity. Nevertheless it is due to this monarch to state, that the closest examination of the register that has recorded his acts at this period, will show, that numerous as are the documents associated personally with him, and varied as are the edicts that bear the sign manual, and mark his progress from town to town, yet no one entry can be produced that convicts King Richard of being " dispitious[1] and cruel."[2] He was bountiful to the poor, indulgent to the rich, and generous in all his transactions, whether in recompensing the friends of his family[3], or seeking to appease the animosity of his enemies. To the widow of Earl Rivers, who had " intended and compassed his destruction," he ordered the payment of all duties accruing from the estates which had been settled on her as her jointure.[4] He presented the Lady Hastings with the wardship and marriage of her son, and intrusted her with the sole charge of his vast estates after taking off the attainder[5]; a boon that might have been greatly abused, and which would have been a munificent recompence to many of his faithful followers. But the most remarkable instance that

---

[1] Dispitious—full of spite.   [2] More, p. 9.

[3] In the register of Richard's acts at this particular period is " a grant of an annuity of 60l. to Thomas Wandesford, for his good service done to the right excellent prince of famous memory, the king's father, whom God pardon." — *Harl. MSS.*, 433. fol. 117.

[4] Harl. MSS., 433. fol. 166.   [5] Ibid. fol. 27.

could perhaps be adduced of Richard's kind and
forgiving disposition, was the commiseration he felt
for the destitute state of the unfortunate Countess
of Oxford, the wife of the bitterest enemy of himself and his race, on whom he settled a pension of
100*l.* a year[1] during the exile of her noble lord,
notwithstanding he was openly and avowedly arrayed in hostility against him.

The last instrument which received his signature
prior to his departure from Pontefract is singularly
illustrative of the religious scruples and sense of
justice which formed so leading a feature in
Richard's character. " The king, calling to remembrance the dreadful sentence of the church of
God given against all those persons which wilfully
attempt to usurp unto themselves, against good
conscience, possessions or other things of right
belonging to God and his said church, and the
great peril of soul which may ensue by the same;
commands that twenty acres and more of pasture
within the park at Pontefract, which was taken
from the prior and convent of Pontefract about the
tenth year of king Edward IV., be restored unto
them." [2] Sentiments such as these, emanating from
himself, attest better than any inferences drawn by
others that Richard considered he had been legally
and lawfully elected to the throne. The man who
feared God's judgments, if he withheld twenty acres
of land which had been unjustly taken " against
good conscience," would surely have paused before
usurping a crown! — calling to remembrance as he
did the dreadful sentence of the church, and the

---

[1] Harl. MSS., 433. fol. 53.   [2] Ibid. fol. 121.

great peril of soul which might ensue from such an act of injustice; or have risked his eternal salvation by wilfully perpetrating the most heinous crimes to secure possessions thus unlawfully obtained. Happy would it have been for this monarch had he been judged by his own acts, rather than by the opinions of others: his reign would not then have been represented in the annals of his country as alike disgraceful to himself and to the land over which he ruled.

Richard departed from Pontefract early in October[1], and from mention being made of alms having been bestowed at Doncaster[2], he probably rested at that town on his progress to Gainsborough, where the regal party were abiding on the 10th of October, as appears by Richard's signature to two instruments bearing that date both of time and of place.[3] Widely different, however, was the aspect of affairs during this portion of the monarch's tour, compared to the peaceful and unruffled state of things which his welcome reception at Oxford, Gloucester, and York had seemed to portend at the commencement of his progress. The clouds, which for many weeks had begun to shadow the brightness of his sunny path, now more darkly obscured the political horizon, and gave presage of that coming storm which was about to burst so heavily over

---

[1] Harl. MSS., 433. fol. 121.

[2] "iijs. iiijd. to a wyff (a poor woman) besides Doncaster, by the king's commandment." — *Harl. MSS.*, 433. fol. 118.

[3] Warrant for the payment of 500 marks "for the expences of our household at our castle of Carlisle," and of 5l. to the prior of the monastery of Carlisle, which the king had given towards the making of a glass window therein. Given at Gainsborough, 10th October, anno 1 Richard III., 1483. — *Harl. MSS.*, 433. fo. 120.

the head of Richard : nor was he altogether unprepared for the change, being too well acquainted with the workings of the human heart to overlook any indications, however trivial, that betokened ill, whether arising from jealousy in friends or hostility in enemies. Symptoms both of personal and political enmity had become apparent to the king at an early stage of his proceedings ; but he was too wise to accelerate the impending evil by any premature or injudicious disclosure of his suspicions, until compelled to do so in self-defence. Many circumstances, however, prove that from the time he quitted York until he arrived at Lincoln on the 14th of October, he had been preparing himself to meet the exigency whenever it should occur. This exigency, and its momentous occasion, involves the most important consideration associated with Richard's career ; not alone from the spirit of disaffection which it raised, and which was never afterwards subdued, but because it implicates this monarch in a transaction of the blackest dye, the truth of which, up to the present time, continues to be wrapt in the most impenetrable obscurity. So interwoven indeed with fable, with errors in date and discrepancies in detail, are the alleged facts of this mysterious occurrence, that perplexed as is the general tenor of king Richard's eventful life, yet this one point in particular has baffled effectually the labours of the antiquary, the historian, and the philosopher, to unravel the tangled web of falsehood and deceit in which it is enveloped. It need scarcely be said that these observations have reference to the ultimate fate of Edward V. and his young brother the Duke of York, which is so completely veiled in mystery, that notwithstanding tradition has long fixed on their uncle the odium of their deaths, yet no conclusive evidence has ever been adduced which can fasten upon him so revolting an act, or convict Richard the Third as a murderer or " a regicide."

The progress of public opinion, on which alone the imputation rests, will be best illustrated by examining the contemporary accounts, which are limited to three writers,—the Croyland historian, Rous the Warwick antiquary, and Fabyan the city chronicler. Fabyan, though the last in order as regards the time of the compilation of his work, is best fitted to describe the earliest indication of popular feeling, not only because he was resident in London at the time of Richard's election, but because he makes known the sentiments of the populace from the very earliest period of that monarch's regal career.

After narrating his accession to the throne, he says: " Then it followeth anon, as this man had taken upon him, he fell in great hatred of the more party of the nobles of this realm, insomuch that such as before loved and praised him, and would have jeoparded life and good with him, if he had so remained still as protector, now murmured and grudged against him in such wise, that few or none favoured his party, except it were for dread, or the great gifts that they received of him.".[1]

In this account, three strong points present themselves to notice: 1st, That Richard, up to the period

---

[1] Fabyan's Chron., p. 516

of his accession, was so beloved and estimated, that his contemporaries would have risked life and fortune in his cause; which admission very materially weakens the imputation of after ages, that he was innately cruel, vicious, and depraved. 2dly, That " he fell in hatred" because the turbulent nobles, who had elevated him to the throne, forthwith grudged him the exalted position which they had invited him to fill: it was not, let it be observed, the abuse of his newly acquired power which made Richard unpopular, but the power itself with which the nobles had invested him. 3dly, That from his accession he was treacherously dealt with, and surrounded by time-servers, who enriched themselves by his liberality, and after courting his favour, rewarded him with deceit. Such is the statement of Fabyan, writing under the Tudor dynasty, and with a strong Lancastrian bias. No allusion is made by him of public indignation at the injustice committed against Edward V., or of detestation at the cruelty practised against him. Envy and jealousy at Richard's being *king*, instead of continuing " *still as protector*," is the reason assigned by Fabyan why the lordly barons of England "murmured and grudged against him."

The Croyland writer, after briefly relating his coronation at Westminster, his progress and his second enthronement at York, thus concludes his concise account:—" Whilst these things were passing in the North, King Edward's two sons remained under certain deputed custody, for whose release from captivity the people of the southern and western parts began very much to murmur." [1]

---

[1] Chron. Croy., p. 567.

Thus it appears that up to the period of Richard's departure from York no apprehensions were entertained for the safety of the young princes ; and moreover, from the expression " certain deputed custody," it would seem as if they had been officially consigned to some person or persons well known or fitted for the charge, in accordance with the usual custom observed on similar occasions [1] ; the murmurs of the people, be it remarked, arising solely from their captivity. These murmurs would, in all probability, have yielded gradually to the popularity which Richard gained during his state progress, by his wise and temperate exercise of the kingly prerogative, if the commiseration for his nephews, thus recorded by the Croyland writer, had not been fomented into open rebellion by the treachery of those disaffected nobles, who, Fabyan states, " grudged" King Richard the regal authority that they had been the means of conferring upon him. " And when at last," continues the Croyland chronicler, " the people about London, in Kent, Essex, Sussex, Hampshire, Dorsetshire, Devonshire, Wilts, Berkshire, and other southern counties, made a rising in their behalf, publicly proclaiming that Henry Duke of Buckingham, who

[1] By reference to a former chapter of this work it will be seen that Henry IV., after he had deposed Richard II. and usurped his crown, imprisoned the legitimate heirs to the throne, (the two young princes of the house of March,) for many years in Windsor Castle, placing them under "continued and safe custody" there : and also, that the infant Duke of York, who was next to them in lawful succession to the crown, was similarly incarcerated by King Henry V. ; who sent the orphan prince to the Tower, after the execution of his parent, the Earl of Cambridge, placing him under "the custody and vigilant care" of Robert Waterton. — See Vol. I. ch. ii. p. 23.

then resided at Brecknock in Wales, repenting the course of conduct he had adopted, would be their leader, it was spread abroad that King Edward's sons were dead, but by what kind of violent death is unknown." [1] That plots and conspiracies would be formed in favour of the deposed prince was a result which Richard must have anticipated: it was also a natural supposition that the partizans of the widowed queen, and the friends of the deceased king, would rally by degrees, and seize any diminution of Richard's popularity to reinstate their deposed sovereign. But that Buckingham, the most zealous of the new monarch's supporters, the active agent by whom his elevation was effected [2], should be the first to rebel against the kinsman to whom he had so recently vowed fealty and allegiance, affords, perhaps, one of the most remarkable instances on record of the perverseness of human nature. Yet such was the case; and, judging from the testimony of the Croyland historian, the report which has so blackened King Richard's fame may be traced also to this unstable and ambitious peer: but whether considered to be made on just grounds, or propagated purely from malevolence and political animosity, must depend on the view taken of his general conduct, and the degree of credit to be attached to his alleged assertions.

If the young princes, through the agency of their friends, were secretly conveyed out of the kingdom upon their uncle's elevation to the throne, as was currently reported in the succeeding reign [3],

[1] Chron. Croy., p. 568.

[2] " By my aid and favor, he of a protector was made king, and of a subject made a governor." — *Grafton*, p. 154.

[3] " Neither wanted there even at that time (anno 1 Henry VII.)

— a circumstance by no means improbable, considering the disturbed state of the country, and the peculiar position of the respective parties, — the rising of their friends, and the defection of Buckingham, may possibly have induced King Richard himself to assert that his nephews were dead, with the view of setting at rest any further inquiry concerning them. The greater probability, however, is this: that the Duke of Buckingham, aware of their disappearance from the Tower, but not made acquainted with the place of their exile, spread the report with a view of irritating the populace against the new monarch, and thus advancing more effectually his own selfish and ambitious views; and that King Richard, unwilling, and indeed unable, to produce his nephews, was driven to sanction the report[1], as his only defence

secret rumours and whisperings, which afterwards gathered strength, and turned to great troubles, that the two young sons of King Edward IV., or one of them, which were said to be destroyed in the Tower, were not indeed murdered, but conveyed secretly away, and were yet living." — *Bacon's Henry VII.*, p. 4. " And all this time (anno 2 Henry VII.) it was still whispered every where that at least one of the children of Edward IV. was living." — *Ibid.* p. 19. " A report prevailed among the common people that the sons of Edward the king had migrated to some part of the earth in secret, and there were still surviving." — *Pol. Virg.*, p. 569. " Whose death and final infortune hath natheless so far comen in question that some remain yet in doubt whether they were in his (King Richard's) days destroyed or no." —- *More's Rycharde III.*, p. 126.

[1] A precisely similar report was spread in the reign of Henry VII., with the view of making that monarch produce the young Earl of Warwick, or acknowledge what had become of him. He had not been seen or heard of since his close imprisonment in the Tower; and " a fame prevailed," states Polydore Virgil, p. 69., " and was every where spread abroad, that Edward Count of Warwick had met with his death in prison." Lord Bacon likewise states (p. 19.) that it was generally circulated " that the king had a purpose to put to death Edward Plantagenet, closely in the Tower ; whose case was so

against their friends, and the surest method of keeping secret from his enemies their actual place of concealment.   Hence, in all probability, the origin of the tale ; for it cannot be denied that the words of the ecclesiastical writer with reference to Buckingham are very remarkable, and tend more strongly to fix the report on that nobleman and his party, than any allegation afterwards brought forward by tradition as evidence of the fact against Richard III. : — " Henry Duke of Buckingham, repenting the course of conduct he had adopted, would be their leader," are the words of the chronicler; and he immediately follows this statement by the assertion, that " it was reported," as if in consequence of the change in Buckingham's views, " that King Edward's sons were dead, but by what kind of violent death was unknown." [1]

Richard, indeed, was ill prepared for opposition from such a source, for so implicitly had he relied on Buckingham's honour and fidelity, that he had intrusted to his custody his most violent enemy, Morton, Bishop of Ely ; and it is more than probable that the active eloquence of this crafty prelate [2],

nearly paralleled with that of Edward the Fourth's children, in respect of the blood, like age, and the very place of the Tower, as it did refresh and reflect upon the king a most odious resemblance, as if he would be another King Richard."   In order to disabuse the public mind, the king commanded the young prince " to be taken in procession on a Sunday through the principal streets of London, to be seen by the people." — Page 27.

[1] Chron. Croy., p. 568.

[2] " This man," writes Sir Thomas More, p. 139., " had gotten a deep insight into political worldly drifts.   Whereby perceiving now this duke glad to commune with him, fed him with fair words and many pleasant praises."   Sir Thomas More's " History of Richard III." terminates abruptly in the midst of the conversation held between Morton and Buckingham.   The narrative is, however, resumed by Grafton, who, it has been conjectured, had access to the

working on an envious, jealous, and fickle temperament, roused into action in Buckingham those
rebellious feelings, which otherwise might have
rankled secretly in his own discontented bosom.
King Richard might well style him "the most untrue
creature living,"[1] for he remained firm to no party
and to no cause, beyond that which fed his rapacity
and insatiable ambition. He espoused the sister of
the royal Elizabeth, when the Wydville connection
was the road to preferment[2], and he was the first
to desert the widowed queen[3] and her now powerless
kindred, when he fancied it would be to his interest
to accelerate the advancement of Richard Duke of
Gloucester.[4] He proclaimed the illegitimacy and
advocated the deposition of Edward V.[5], when he
wished to place Richard III. on the throne, and he

same sources of original information which were open to Sir Thomas
More. — *Singer*, p. 145.

[1] In a letter addressed to his chancellor, which is preserved among
the Tower records, and will be inserted at length in a future chapter,
when considering the circumstances that led to its being written.

[2] "When King Edward was deceased, to whom I thought myself
little or nothing beholden, although we two had married two sisters,
because he neither promoted nor preferred me, as I thought I was
worthy and had deserved ; neither favoured me according to my
degree or birth ; for surely I had by him little authority and less
rule, and in effect nothing at all ; which caused me the less to favour
his children, because I found small humanity, or none, in their
parent." — *Singer's Reprint of More*, p. 152.

[3] "I remembered an old proverb worthy of memory, that often
rueth the realm, where children rule and women govern. This old
adage so sank and settled in my head, that I thought it a great
error and extreme mischief to the whole realm, either to suffer the
young king to rule, or the queen, his mother, to be a governor over
him." — Ibid.

[4] "I thought it necessary, both for the public and profitable
wealth of this realm, and also for mine own commodity and better
stay, to take part with the Duke of Gloucester." — *Ibid.*

[5] More, p. 112.

circulated a report of the murder of the princes[1], when he coveted their uncle's position and entertained the presumptuous hope of becoming king in his stead.[2] He aimed at being a second Warwick — another "king maker;"[3] but, possessing only the frailties of that lordly baron, unaccompanied by the vigorous intellect and those chivalrous qualities which fling such a romantic colouring over the career of the renowned and illustrious Richard Neville, he rushed headlong to his own destruction: equally with Warwick, the victim of ungovernable pride, and affording another but far less interesting example of the haughty and turbulent spirit which characterised the English nobles at this strange eventful era.

But as the alleged cause of the rebellion which sealed Buckingham's fate, and put so sudden a stop to the king's peaceful progress, was ostensibly to avenge the young princes' death[4], it becomes necessary to pursue the investigation into the

---

[1] Chron. Croy., p. 567.

[2] " I phantasied, that if I list to take upon me the crown and imperial sceptre of the realm, *now* was the time propitious and convenient." — *More*, p. 155.

[3] "I began to study and with good deliberation to ponder and consider how and in what manner this realm should be ruled and governed." — *Ibid.* p. 152.

[4] " But when I was credibly informed of the death of the two young innocents, his own natural nephews, contrary to his faith and promise (to the which, God be my judge, I never agreed nor condescended), O Lord ! how my veins panted, how my body trembled, how my heart inwardly grudged! insomuch that I so abhorred the sight, and much more the company of him, that I could no longer abide in his court, except I should be openly avenged. The end whereof was doubtful, and so I feigned a cause to depart ; and with a merry countenance and a despiteful heart, I took my leave humbly of him (he thinking nothing less than that I was displeased), and so returned to Brecknock to you." — *Grafton, Cont. of More*, p. 155.

reputed circumstances of that tragedy, before continuing the history of the Duke of Buckingham's
revolt, in order that it may be shown how vague
and unsatisfactory is the source from whence
sprang these accusations which have affixed to the
memory of Richard III. a crime that has made him
for many ages a subject of universal horror and
disgust. Fabyan, in addition to the passage before
quoted, says, after describing the accession of the
Lord Protector, "King Edward V., with his brother
the Duke of York, were put under sure keeping
within the Tower, in such wise that they never came
abroad after." [1] And again, that " the common fame
went that King Richard put unto secret death the
two sons of his brother." [2] Rous of Warwick is the
next contemporary authority; but, although coeval
with King Richard, it must not be forgotten that
he, like Fabyan, wrote the events which he records
after that monarch's decease; and the fact of his
having dedicated his work to King Henry VII. is
alone sufficient to demonstrate his Lancastrian bias,
even if proof did not exist that his character of
King Richard, when exercising sovereign power,
was altogether opposed to that which he afterwards
gave, when writing under the auspices of his rival
and successor. [3] " The Duke of Gloucester, for his

[1] Fabyan's Chron., p. 515.   [2] Ibid. p. 516.
[3] Whatever Rous chose to say of Richard, in compliment to
Henry VII., he gave a very different account of him in his roll,
which he left to posterity as a monument of the earls and town of
Warwick, to which he was so much attached. Here is the inscription, as it was written by Rous's own hand : " The most mighty
prince Richard, by the grace of God king of England and of
France, and lord of Ireland : by very matrimony, without discon-
tinuance, or any defiling in the law, by heir male lineally descending
from King Harry the Second, all avarice set aside, ruled his subjects

own promotion, took upon him to the disinheriting
of his lord, King Edward V., and shortly imprisoned
King Edward with his brother, whom he had obtained from Westminster, under promise of protection ; so that it was afterwards known to very
few what particular martyrdom they suffered." [1]
This writer, however, places the death of the princes
during the protectorate : "Then ascended the royal
throne of *the slain*, whose protector during their
minority he should have been, the tyrant Richard ; "
an assertion so utterly at variance with every contemporary [2], that it materially weakens the effect of
his other assertions.

Bernard Andrews, the historiographer and poet
laureate of Henry VII., states that "Richard ordered

in his realm full commendably, punishing offenders of his laws,
especially extortioners and oppressors of his commons, and cherish-
ing those that were virtuous, by the which discreet guiding he got
great thank of God and love of all his subjects, rich and poor, and
great laud of the people of other lands about him."
(From the original MS. roll, now in the College of Arms,
published in Lord Orford's works, vol. ii. p. 215.)

[1] Rous, Hist. Reg. Ang., p. 213.

[2] See the recently quoted statement of Fabyan and the Chronicler
of Croyland. Sir Thomas More's narrative is even more conclusive :
— "The prince," says that historian, in allusion to Edward V.,
"as soon as the protector left that name, and took himself as king,
had it showed unto him that he should not reign, but his uncle
should have the crown ; at which words the prince, sore abashed,
began to sigh, and said, 'Alas ! I would my uncle would let me
have my life yet, though I lose my kingdom.' Then he that told
him the tale used him with good words, and put him with the best
comfort he could. But forthwith was the prince and his brother
both shut up, and all other removed from them, only one called
Black Will, or William Slaughter, except, set to serve them, and see
them serve. After which time the prince never tied his points, nor
aught wrought of himself ; but with that young babe, his brother,
lingered in thought and heaviness, till this traitorous death delivered
them of that wretchedness." — *More*, p. 130.

the princes to be put to the sword,"[1] a fact that must have been known to the contemporary annalists, had a positive order to that effect been given[2]; and Polydore Virgil, who compiled his work under the immediate patronage and at the express desire of the same monarch, after intimating the uncertainty of the manner of their death, states that it was generally reported and believed *that the sons of Edward IV. were still alive, having been conveyed secretly away, and obscurely concealed in some distant region.*[3] Thus it appears that neither the contemporary writers of the period, nor those who wrote by royal command in the ensuing reign, give any distinct account of the fate of the young princes: the former all agree that they were imprisoned, and that it was "commonly reported" that they were dead; but when or how the event occurred, or whether there was foundation for the report, has never been sought to be established, excepting by Sir Thomas More. This historian was not coeval with Richard, he was a mere infant at the time of that monarch's death[4]; but, being educated, as before observed, in Bishop Morton's house, he is supposed to have derived the materials of his history from that personage. But Morton,

---

[1] Cott. MSS., Dom. A. xviii.

[2] Bernard Andrews could only narrate matters connected with this period from the reports of others, as he was a Breton by birth, and did not reside in England until after the accession of Henry VII., to whose suite he was attached, and whose fortunes he followed.

[3] Pol. Virg., p. 569.

[4] Sir Thomas More was born in 1482, the year preceding King Richard's accession; he was therefore three years of age at that monarch's decease, and in his nineteenth year when Bishop Morton expired in 1500. — *Turner*, vol. iii. p. 373.

although coeval with the events related, gloried in avowing himself Richard's bitter enemy. He united with Hastings in conspiring against him as the lord protector[1], and he goaded Buckingham to open rebellion after Richard was anointed king.[2] He deserted the latter nobleman as soon as he had weaned him from his allegiance; and escaping to the Continent[3], within a few weeks of Richard's coronation, there remained an exile and an outlaw during the rest of his reign. It must therefore be apparent that any information derived from him relative to affairs in England during that period could only be by report; and the colouring which his own prejudice and enmity would give to all rumours spread to the disadvantage of King Richard, would render his testimony not only doubtful, but most unsatisfactory, unless confirmed by other writers or proved by existing documents. Sir Thomas More himself seems to have felt

[1] " Thomas Archbishop of York, and John Bishop of Ely, although, on account of their order, their lives were spared, were imprisoned in different castles in Wales." — *Cont. Croy.*, p. 560.

[2] " But now, my lord, to conclude what I mean toward your noble person, I say and affirm, if you love God, your lineage, or your native country, you must yourself take upon you the crown and diadem of this noble empire; both for the maintenance of the honour of the same (which so long hath flourished in fame and renown) as also for the deliverance of your natural countrymen from the bondage and thraldom of so cruel a tyrant and arrogant oppressor." — *Grafton, Cont. More*, p. 149.

[3] The bishop, being as witty as the duke was wily, did not tarry till the duke's company was assembled, but, secretly disguised, in a night departed (to the duke's great displeasure) and came to the see of Ely, where he found money and friends, and he sailed into Flanders, where he did the Earl of Richmond good service, and never returned again till the Earl of Richmond, after being king, sent for him, and shortly promoted him to the see of Canterbury.—*Ibid.* p.163.

doubtful of the facts which he narrates, for he prefaces his account of the murder of the princes by these remarkable words : " whose death and final infortune hath natheless so far come in question, that some yet remain in doubt whether they were in Richard's days destroyed or no;" [1] and in detailing the commonly received tradition of their tragical end, he admits that the reports were numerous, and certifies that even the most plausible rested on report alone. [2] " I shall rehearse you the dolorous end of those babes, not after every way that I have heard, but after that way that I have so heard by such men and by such means as me thinketh it were hard but it should be true." If by these words Sir Thomas More meant Morton [3], that prelate, in consequence of his imprisonment at Brecknock, must have gained his information from the Duke of Buckingham, whose unprincipled conduct [4] and double dealing, even by his own admission [5],

---

[1] More, p. 126.   [2] Appendix R.

[3] " Could More," inquires Lord Orford, " have drawn from a more corrupted source ? Of all men living, there could not be more suspicious testimony than the prelate's, except the king's (Henry VII.)." — *Hist. Doubts*, p. 18.

[4] " Outwardly dissimuling that I inwardly thought, and so with a painted countenance I passed the last summer in his company, not without many fair promises, but without any good deeds." — *Grafton, Cont. More*, p. 155.

[5] The conversation between Buckingham and Morton, commenced by Sir Thomas More and continued by Grafton, is so explicit as to leave little doubt of its authenticity ; many circumstances related could only have been known to the bishop, — his dexterous management of Buckingham, the particulars of his imprisonment at Brecknock, and his escape from the duke ; these, and many other leading points in their reported conference, confirm the assertion of Sir George Buck (whose work was printed in 1646), that the reign of King Richard was written by Bishop Morton. " This book in

would rather be the means of acquitting Richard than of convicting him.

The narrative of the murder, as given by Sir Thomas More, is as follows[1]:—During the royal progress tö Gloucester, King Richard's mind misgave him that "men would not reckon that he could have right to the realm" so long as his nephews lived. Whereupon he sent John Green, "whom he especially trusted," unto Sir Robert Brackenbury, the constable of the Tower, with a letter, "and credence also," commanding him to put the two children to death. Green rejoined the king at Warwick, acquainting him that Brackenbury had refused to fulfil his commands. Greatly displeased at this result, the king gave vent to his discomfiture, by complaining to the page in waiting that even those he had brought up and thought most devoted to his service had failed him, and would do nothing for him. The page replied, that there was a man upon a pallet in the outer chamber, who, to do him pleasure, would think nothing too hard, meaning Sir James Tyrrel, "a man of right goodlye personage, and, for nature's gifts, worthy to have served a better prince." He was, however, it is intimated, jealous of Sir Richard Radcliffe and Sir William Catesby; which thing being known to the page, he, of very special friendship, took this opportunity of "putting him

Latin," he says, "was lately in the hands of Mr. Roper of Eltham, as Sir Edward Hoby, who saw it, told me." — *Buck,* lib. iii. p. 75.

Mr. Roper was an immediate descendant of Sir Thomas More's (see preface to Singer) his eldest and favourite daughter, the estimable Margaret Roper, having left a numerous offspring.

[1] More, p. 127.

forward" with his royal master, hoping to " do him
good." Richard, pleased with the suggestion, and
well aware that Tyrrel " had strength and wit,"
and an ambitious spirit, he called him up, and
taking him into his chamber, " broke to him
secretly his mind in this mischievous matter." Sir
James undertook the revolting office, whereupon
on the morrow the king sent him " to Brackenbury
with a letter, by which he was commanded to
deliver to Sir James all the keys of the Tower for
one night, to the end that he might there accomplish the king's pleasure in such thing as he had
given him commandment.". .. " After which letter
delivered and the keys received, Sir James appointed
the night next ensuing" to destroy the princes.
" To the execution thereof, he appointed Miles
Forest, one of the four that kept them," a known
assassin, and John Dighton, his own groom, a big,
broad, square, strong knave." All other persons
being removed, the ruffians entered the chamber
where the princes were sleeping at midnight, when,
wrapping them up in the bed-clothes, and keeping
them down by force, they pressed the feather-bed
and pillows hard upon their mouths, until they
were stifled and expired. When thoroughly dead,
they laid their bodies naked out upon the bed, and
summoned Sir James Tyrrel to see them; who
caused the murderers to bury them at the stair-
foot, deep in the ground, under a great heap of
stones. " Then rode Sir James in great haste to
the king, and showed him all the manner of the
murder, who gave him great thanks, and, as some
say, there made him a knight." " But it was

rumoured," continues Sir Thomas More, " that the king disapproved of their being buried in so vile a corner; whereupon they say that a priest of Sir Robert Brackenbury's took up the bodies again, and secretly interred them in such place as by the occasion of his death could never come to light."

The more closely this statement is examined, the more does its inconsistency appear, from the very commencement of the narrative. For example: as King Richard had been solicited to accept the crown, because his nephews' illegitimacy was admitted, and as he had been successively elected, proclaimed, and anointed king with an unanimity almost unparalleled, he could have had no reason, at this early period of his reign, to dread the effects of his nephews' reassumption of their claims; still less cause had he for apprehension, when journeying from Oxford to Gloucester, at which university he had been so honourably received, that, even allowing that his mind misgave him when he first entered upon his kingly career, his popularity during his royal progress was alone sufficient to set all doubts at rest. Again: if so revolting a deed as murdering the princes to insure the stability of his throne had gained possession of Richard's heart, was it probable that he would not have taken measures to effect his purpose before quitting the Tower, or whilst sojourning at Greenwich or Windsor, instead of delaying his commands for the perpetration of the dark deed until he was necessitated to commit the order to paper, and thus intrust a design so destructive to his reputation to the care of a common

messenger on the chance of its falling into his enemies' hands. King Richard was proverbially " close
and secret," being upbraided by his enemies as " a
deep dissimular;"[1] traits, however, which to the un-
prejudiced mind will rather appear a proof of his
wisdom when the subtlety of the age is taken into
consideration. Would, then, a wise and cautious
man, a prince evidently striving for popularity, and
desirous, by the justice of his regal acts, to soften
any feeling of discontent that might attach to his
irregular accession—would such a person be likely
to lay himself open to the charge of murder?—and
this, after he had peaceably attained the summit of
his ambition, and was basking in the very sunshine
of prosperity, and when the oath had scarcely faded
from his lips, by which he pledged himself to preserve the lives of the princes, and maintain them
in such honourable estate that all the realm should
be content?[2] Would any one, indeed, endued with
common foresight have risked two letters, which
innumerable casualties might convert into positive
proof of an act that would bring upon him the
hatred of his own kindred and the detestation of
the kingdom at large,—the one sent by an ordinary·
attendant, " one John Green," to Brackenbury,
with " credence also," commanding that " Sir Robert should, in any wise, put the two children to
death;" the other, by Sir James Tyrrel to Brack-

---

[1] More, p. 9.

[2] " He promised me, on his fidelity, laying his hand on mine, at
Baynard's Castle, that the two young princes should live, and that
he would so provide for them and so maintain them in honourable
estate, that I and all the realm ought, and should be content." —
Grafton, Cont. More, p. 154.

enbury, commanding him to deliver to Sir James
the keys of the Tower, that he might accomplish
the very crime which that official had previously
refused himself to perform ? It is scarcely within
the bounds of probability, unless the letter and
" credence" were extant, together with the formal
warrant which was sent to Brackenbury, justifying
him as governor of the Tower in delivering up
the keys of the fortress committed to his charge. [1]
" And has any trace of such a document been discovered ?" asks the historian of the Tower [2]; "Never,"
he adds: " it has been anxiously sought for, but
sought in vain ; and we may conclude that Sir
Thomas More's is nothing but one of the passing
tales of the day." [3]

If this assumption is warranted by the incon-
sistencies and contradictory statements which mark
the tradition generally, still more will such a conclusion appear to be well grounded if the several
statements connected with the chief individuals
named are strictly examined. Sir Thomas More
says, that King Richard took " great displeasure
and thought" at Sir Robert Brackenbury's re-

[1] " King Richard, having directed his warrant for the putting
of them to death to Brackenbury, the lieutenant of the Tower,
was by him refused. Whereupon the king directed his warrant to
Sir James Tyrrel to receive the keys of the Tower from the lieutenant for the space of a night, for the king's special service." —
Bacon's Henry VII., p. 123.

[2] This valuable work, "The History and Antiquities of the Tower,"
was compiled, as stated by the author, Mr. Bayley, from state papers
and original manuscripts there deposited, and which he had peculiar facilities for examining as " one of her Majesty's sub-com-
missioners on the public records." — *Bayley's Hist. of the Tower,*
part i.

[3] Bayley's Hist. of the Tower, part i. p. 64.

fusal. Is this borne out by the monarch's subsequent conduct as proved by existing records?[1]
Did he remove him from the honourable office of
governor; or even tacitly and gradually evince his
anger against him? On the contrary, he not only
continued him in the command of the Tower, but
renewed the appointment, with the annual fee of
100*l*., some months after this reputed contumacy[2];
and throughout the whole of his reign, he bestowed
upon him places and emoluments that are perfectly
consistent with his desire of providing for a
favourite follower, but are altogether opposed to
indications either of dissatisfaction or annoyance.
There would be nothing surprising in the grants
here alluded to, had Brackenbury been guilty; because the king would naturally favour him under
such peculiar circumstances: but both Sir Thomas
More and Lord Bacon expressly state that he was
innocent of all participation in the crime, that he
spurned the royal command, and that the king was
in consequence greatly displeased with him.

King Richard was not a man to shrink from
making apparent his displeasure, if just grounds of
offence had been given to him; at least so his
enemies would make it appear. "Friend and foe
was muchwhat indifferent where his advantage
grew: he spared no man's death, whose life with-
stood his purpose."[3] Neither was he so weak and
unreflective as to have sent an order to the constable
of the Tower of so fearful an import as the destruc-

---

[1] Appendix S.   [2] Harl. MSS., No. 433. fol. 56.   [3] More, p. 9.

tion of two princes committed to his custody, unless
well assured of the manner in which his design
would have been received and carried into execution.
Sir Thomas More implies that he early adopted
Brackenbury himself, brought him up, and also
that he thought " he would surely serve him."
And he did serve him, even unto death; for he
fought and died for his patron: but it was glo-
riously, honourably, and as became a true knight
on the battle field [1], and not as a midnight assassin
in the secret chamber.   Sir Robert was a member
of a very ancient and distinguished family [2] in the
north [3]; and if, from his trusty qualities, early
evinced, he acquired the confidence of the Duke of
Gloucester, it is most clear that other features in
his character must also have been equally well
known to his patron.   Green is stated to have found
Brackenbury at his devotions. [4]   If, then, he was
religious and humane, — firm in rejecting evil commands, though emanating from his sovereign [5], and
faithful in the discharge of the trust reposed in him
by the state,—braving death with cheerfulness and
alacrity when called upon to defend the king to
whom he had sworn allegiance, but shrinking from
the cowardly act of murdering imprisoned and de-

---

[1] Surtees's Durham, p. 71.   [2] Ibid.

[3] Two other brothers of the same family as Sir Robert are named
by Drake as attached to Richard's service ; viz. John and Thomas
Brackenbury : the first sent to London upon a confidential mission
by the mayor of York ; the other despatched to that city with the
Protector's reply. — *Drake's Ebor.*, p. 3.

[4] " This John Green did his errand unto Brackenbury, kneeling
before our Lady in the Tower."— *More*, p. 128.

[5] " Who plainly answered, that he would never put them to death
to die therefore." — *More*, p. 128.

fenceless children, — such a man was not the agent
to whom Richard, without previously sounding
him, would have made known his detestable project,
or have selected for carrying it into effect. If he
did, however, then the far greater probability is
this,—that Brackenbury, during the interval that
elapsed between Green's departure and the arrival
of Tyrrel, conveyed the hapless children abroad;
and thus gave foundation for the report mentioned
by More[1], Polydore Virgil, Bacon, and others, that
the children of Edward IV. had escaped, and were
concealed in a foreign land.

Sir James Tyrrel, the other leading personage in
the reputed tragedy, has been even more obviously
misrepresented than Sir Robert Brackenbury. Instead of being an obscure individual, at the period
when tradition would make it appear that he was
first recommended to the notice of his sovereign by
a page in waiting, his name, as a great officer of
the crown, is associated with the reign of Edward
IV.; and his prowess had been both acknowledged
and rewarded by Richard of Gloucester long antecedent to the period in question, and possibly
before the page was born. Tyrrel was a man of
ancient and high family.[2] His brother, Sir Thomas
Tyrrel, was one selected for the honourable distinction of bearing the mortal remains of Edward IV.

---

[1]. More, p. 126.; Pol. Virg. p. 569.; Bacon, p. 4.

[2] " Tyrell's situation was not that in which Sir Thomas More represents him; he was of an ancient and high family, had long before
received the honour of knighthood, and engaged the office of master
of the horse." — *Bayley's Hist. of the Tower*, vol. i. p. 62.; see also
Walpole's Reply to Dr. Milles, Archæol. for 1770.

to the tomb [1]; and Sir James himself was nominated by that monarch a commissioner for executing the office of high constable of England, an
office suppressed by Henry VIII. on account of its
dangerous and almost unbounded power. [2] So far
from this warrior being created a simple knight by
King Richard for murdering his royal nephews, he
is known to have borne that distinction full ten
years previously; " Sir James Tyrrel," as appears
by the Paston Letters [3], having been appointed
shortly after King Edward's restoration to convey
the Countess of Warwick from Beaulieu sanctuary
to the north. He was made a knight banneret [4]
by Richard in Scotland [5]; a mark of high distinction
never bestowed but on great and special occasions.
He was master of the horse to King Edward IV.,
and walked in that capacity at the coronation of
Richard III. [6], and at the identical period when
an obscure page, "of special friendship," availed
himself of the confidence reposed in him by his
royal master, to advance the interests of " a man
who lay without in the pallet chamber," [7]— Sir
James Tyrrel, the individual in question, was
master of the king's hengemen or pages [8]! a place
of great trust, and one which required him, as a

---

[1] Harl. MSS., No. 6. p. 3.
[2] Walpole's Reply to Milles. — *Archæol.* for 1770.
[3] Paston Letters, vol. ii. p. 145.
[4] Knight bannerets were created only by the king or commander-
in-chief when they themselves were present in the field ; and
nothing but signal bravery entitled any man in those martial ages
to so distinguished an honour." — *Walpole's Reply to Milles.*
[5] Harl. MSS., No. 293. fol. 208.   [6] Hist. Doubts, p. 55
[7] More, p. 128.   [8] Walpole's Reply to Milles.

part of his duty, to be personally attendant on his sovereign[1], and to keep guard, not repose, in the antechamber so long as the monarch was stirring. In the fifteenth century, that era of feudal power, kings were not in the habit of talking thus familiarly with their attendants, and communicating their feelings of pleasure or displeasure at the conduct of men in authority. It would have been derogatory even to the dignity of a baron to have so condescended ; and Richard, who, in common with all the princes of the house of York, was " great and stately[2], ambitious of authority, and impatient of partners," was as little likely to have needed his page to enlighten him as to the character of those by whom he was immediately surrounded[3], as to have communicated to so humble an individual as much of the nature of his fearful secret as is implied by the words which terminated the page's recommendation of Sir James Tyrrel, — " the thing were right hard that *he* would refuse." [4]

But, admitting that King Richard had so acted under the blind influence of a shallow policy, and the absence of every feeling of humanity, was it probable that facts known to so many unprincipled men, whose fortune would have been ad-

---

[1] Harl. MSS., No. 642. fol. 196.

[2] More, p. 7.

[3] Sir James Tyrrel's reputed jealousy of Catesby and Radcliffe could not have existed, as he was at this time in a far higher and more confidential position than either of those knights, being one of King Richard's body-guard and counsellors ; and before this alleged introduction to his sovereign, he had been invested by him with the lucrative and valuable appointment of steward of the duchy of Cornwall. —See *Harl. MSS.*, No. 433. fol. 40.

[4] More, p. 131.

vanced by divulging to Henry VII. the criminality
of his rival,—and this, too, so speedily after the transaction, that the facts could have been proved, and
peaceable possession of the crown secured to him and
the royal Elizabeth of York, — should never have
been narrated until after a lapse of twenty-five or
thirty years? Yet it was at this distance of time
that it was first detailed by Sir Thomas More[1],
only given by him as an acknowledged report, and
as the most plausible of the different rumours[2]
which had been circulated relative to the unexplained disappearance of the illustrious children.
Green, Brackenbury, Tyrrel, and the page; Forest,
Dighton, Slaughter, and the priest of the Tower;
setting aside the three others who waited conjointly with Forest[3] upon the princes;—these individuals could, each and all, have implicated or
cleared King Richard, had the above accusation
been made by his enemies during his lifetime.
But the utmost that was then alleged against him,
as shown by contemporaries, was, that he held his
nephews in captivity, and that report stated that
they were dead[4]; and all that can with any certainty be proved amounts to the summing up of
Fabyan[5]: " They were put under sure keeping within
the Tower, in such wise that they never came

---

[1] The History of Richard III. appears from the title affixed to
have been written about the year 1513, when More was one of the
under-sheriffs of London, and was printed in Grafton's Continuation
of the Metrical Chronicle of John Hardyng, in 1543. — See preface
to *Singer's Reprint of More*, p. 12.

[2] Buck, lib. iii. p. 84.

[3] " To the execution whereof, he appointed Miles Forest, one of
the four that kept them."—*More*, p. 131.

[4] Chron. Croy., 567.   [5] Fabyan, p. 515.

abroad after." Whether they ended their days speedily, or after years of imprisonment within that gloomy fortress, or were conveyed early and secretly abroad by command of their uncle, or later through the agency of Brackenbury, Tyrrel, or the personal friends of their parents on the commencement of the insurrection in the southern counties to effect their liberation, are points which cannot be determined, unless the discovery of other documents than are at present known to exist should throw further light on this mysterious subject.[1] There is, however, one very important record favouring the belief that the princes may have been sent out of the kingdom, in the acknowledged fact that plots were formed for carrying into effect precisely the same measure in the persons of the princesses, even before it was rumoured that their brothers were dead. " It was reported," says the Croyland historian[2], " that those men who had taken sanctuary advised that some of the king's daughters should escape abroad in disguise; so that if any thing happened to their brothers in the Tower, the kingdom might nevertheless, by their safety, revert to the true heirs. This having been discovered, a strict watch was set over the abbey and all the parts

---

[1] " Others," relates Sir George Buck, " say confidently the young princes were embarked in a ship at the Tower Wharf, and conveyed from thence to sea, so cast into the black deeps ; others aver they were not drowned, but set safe on shores beyond seas. And thus their stories and relations are scattered in various forms, their accusations differing in very many and material points ; which shakes the credit of their suggestion, and makes it both fabulous and uncertain, one giving the lie to the other." —*Buck*, lib. iii. p. 84.

[2] Chron. Croy., p. 567.

adjacent, over whom John Neffield, Esq. was appointed captain in chief, so that no one could enter or come out of the abbey without his knowledge." This summary proceeding would have naturally been adopted had King Richard been duped by the disappearance of the princes from the Tower; and the report of their death, which speedily followed this enactment, would as naturally be spread, both by those whose suspicions would have been roused by their absence, and those who had risked their own lives to compass the children's escape. It would also satisfactorily explain the cause why their violent death was so generally rumoured, and why no contradiction was given to the rumour by King Richard, who, as the whole of the southern counties were in open rebellion, would scarcely be so impolitic as to add to his danger by proclaiming the escape of Edward V. and his brother, and thus feed the very opposition to his newly-enjoyed dignity which it was his object to crush at the outset.

The occurrences of another reign being foreign to the subject of these pages, it would be irrelevant here to notice the appearance and discuss the apparent claims or reputed imposture of Perkin Warbeck, a youth who, about ten years after the period of the alleged murder of the princes, proclaimed himself the young Duke of York[1], and laid claim to the crown ; nevertheless, much might be said on a subject so replete with interesting matter, whether as regards the illustrious persons who suffered from

---

[1] Lord Bacon's Henry VII., p. 149.

their belief in his identity[1], — from the seeming
confirmation given to his tale by the King of Scotland bestowing upon him his near kinswoman in
marriage[2], — from the length of time in which he
struggled with Henry VII.[3], owing to the support
given to him by foreign courts; by the unfortunate Earl of Warwick (Clarence's son) being beheaded without even a shadow of cause[4], but that
of endeavouring to escape from prison, where
Perkin, with that prince, was inveigled to his destruction[5]; the absence of all satisfactory proof
that the confession imputed to Warbeck was ever

[1] The Lord Fitzwater, Sir William Stanley, Sir Simon Mount-
ford, Sir Robert Ratcliffe, Sir William Daubeny, as martyrs of state,
confirmed their testimonies with their blood; so did the king's sergeant Ferrier, also Corbet, Sir Quinton Belts, and Gage, gentlemen
of good worth, with 200 more at least, put to death in sundry cities
and towns for their confidence and opinions in this prince.— *Buck,*
lib. iii. p. 100.

[2] " King James entertained him in all things as became the person
of Richard Duke of York, embraced his quarrel, and, the more to
put it out of doubt that he took him to be a great prince, and not a
representative only, he gave consent that this duke should take to
wife the Lady Katharine Gordon, daughter to the Earl of Huntley,
being a near kinswoman of the king himself, and a young virgin of
excellent beauty and virtue." — *Lord Bacon's Henry VII.,* p. 153.
She was also nearly related to the English monarch; the youngest
daughter of James I. and Joan Beaufort his queen, having espoused
the Earl of Huntley: the consort of Perkin Warbeck was therefore
second cousin to Henry VII.—See *Sandford's Geneal. Hist.* book iv.
p. 312.

[3] " It was one of the longest plays of that kind that hath been in
memory, and might perhaps have had another end, if he had not
met with a king both wise, stout, and fortunate."—*Bacon,* p. 195.

[4] All men knew he was not only a true and certain prince, but
free from all practice; yet he was restrained of his liberty, and a
prisoner the most part of his life from the time of his father's attainder: this was after he had survived King Richard, his uncle,
fifteen years.—*Buck,* lib. iii. p. 96.

[5] " The opinion of the king's great wisdom did surcharge him
with a sinister fame that Perkin was but his bait to entrap the Earl
of Warwick."—*Bacon,* p. 193.

made[1]; and the positive evidence of contemporary writers, that the imposture, if acknowledged, was not promulgated or generally known at the time.[2]

These, and various other points of real import in testing the validity of Perkin's tale, might be dwelt on with advantage to his reputed claims ; but, as the entire drama which comprises the wonderful career of this remarkable individual belongs exclusively to the reign of Henry VII., and has no connection with that of Richard III., unless clear and undisputed evidence existed proving the escape of one or both of the princes, the inquiry into his identity or imposture cannot with propriety be pursued in this memoir. No allusion, indeed, to the appearance of Warbeck would have been required, but that his alleged imposture is said to have produced from the murderers of the hapless brothers that confession which Sir Thomas More

[1] " He was not only sharply restrained in the Tower, but the fame was, the question or gehenne (the rack) was given to him ; until at length, by torments and extremities, he was forced to say any thing, and content to say all they would have him, by a forced recantation of his family, name, and royal parentage ; and with a loud voice to read the same, which might pass at present with the multitude for current, who knew not how it was forced from him." —*Buck*, lib. iii. p. *93*, 94.

[2] " It was unknown to Fabyan and Polydore Virgil, both comtemporaries." — *Laing* (in Henry), vol. xii. p. 444. Bernard Andreas states that it was printed.—*Archæologia*, vol. xxvii. p. 153. Had it been printed on authority, it could not have escaped the knowledge of Fabyan, an alderman and sheriff of London, or been unknown to Polydore Virgil, who wrote professedly by command of Henry VII. ; neither is it probable that Lord Bacon would have substituted a different confession from that which, if printed at the time, as asserted by Andrew, must have been regarded as a legal document. " But Lord Bacon did not dare to adhere to this ridiculous account," observes Lord Orford, in noticing the gross and manifest blunders in Warbeck's pretended confession (see *Hall*, fol. 153.), but forges another, though in reality not much more credible."—*Hist. Doubts*, p. 131.

has incorporated in his history; and the examination into the truth of which reputed confession
furnishes perhaps the strongest evidence of the untenable nature of those calumnies which have so
long been believed and perpetuated. Shortly after
the appearance of Perkin Warbeck, the confidence
in his identity became so general that King Henry
had cause for serious alarm. To have recourse to
arms he thought would "shew fear;"[1] therefore, says
his biographer, " he chose to work by countermine.
His purposes were two: the one, to lay open the
abuse ; the other, to break the knot of the conspirators."[2] To detect the imposture, it was essential
to make it appear that the Duke of York was dead.
There were but four persons that could speak upon
knowledge of the murder; viz. Tyrrel, Dighton,
Forest, and the priest of the Tower[3] that buried
the princes; of which four, Forest and the priest
were dead, and there remained alive only Sir James
Tyrrel and John Dighton. " These two," states
Lord Bacon, " the king caused to be committed to
the Tower, and examined touching the manner of
the death of the two innocent princes. They agreed
both in a tale,— *as the king gave out*,"— and that
tale is the same promulgated by Sir Thomas More.
But what does Lord Bacon state—that consummate
lawyer and politician — after terminating his relation of the narrative? He makes this remarkable
admission: " Thus much was then delivered abroad
to the effect of those examinations; but the king,
nevertheless, made no use of them in any of his

---

[1] Bacon's, Henry VII., p. 122.   [2] Ibid.   [3] Ibid, p. 123.

declarations; whereby it seems that those examinations left the business somewhat perplexed : and as for Sir James Tyrrel, he was soon after beheaded in the Tower Yard for other matters of treason; but John Dighton, *who, it seemeth, spake* best for the king, was forthwith set at liberty, and was the principal means of divulging this tradition. Therefore, this kind of proof being left so naked, the king used the more diligence in the tracing of Perkin."[1]

On a tale, then, that " the king gave out," and that king he who had defeated and slain his calumniated rival, and possessed himself of the throne, — a tale " left so naked of proof," that even the politic and wily Henry VII. could make no use of it for exposing the imposture of the alleged Duke of York, — has Richard III. been upbraided as a murderer, the destroyer by wholesale of his own kindred : and this, on no other proof but the reputed confession of a low " horsekeeper," — a suborned witness, — a self-convicted regicide, traitor, and midnight assassin, — the truth of whose testimony may be judged of by Lord Bacon's expression, " who, it seemeth, *spake best* for the king," and who was therefore set at liberty, and was the chief means " of divulging this tradition." Surely, the very term " tradition " divulges Lord Bacon's want of confidence in the validity of the tale.

But it may naturally be inquired, how came Henry VII. to cause Sir James Tyrrel and Dighton to be thus suddenly committed to the Tower, and examined, at the expiration of ten years, touching the

---

[1] Bacon, p. 125.

murder of the young princes? Was he previously in possession of the facts that are reputed to have been confessed by them? If so, how came these individuals not to have been subpœnaed as witnesses on Lambert Simnel's imposture, and thus have proved facts that would have preserved the king from future imposture, and would have saved him from executing Sir William Stanley, his mother's brother-in-law, his faithful friend and zealous follower? How was it that no means were taken, at the accession of the monarch, whose invasion was tolerated chiefly from indignation at the mysterious disappearance of the young princes, either to expose the villany, or to bring to condign punishment the reputed murderers of the two brothers of his betrothed queen — a measure that would have rendered him so popular, and made Richard an object of unqualified execration? How was it that Sir James Tyrrel was spared, " when the Duke of Norfolk and Lord Lovel, Catesby, Radcliffe, and the real abettors or accomplices of Richard, were either attainted or executed?"[1] and that " no mention of the murder was made in the very act of parliament that attainted King Richard himself, and which, could it have been verified, would have been the most heinous aggravation of his crimes?" Sir James Tyrrel, instead of being an object of execration, continued unblemished in reputation up to the period under consideration, having been honoured and trusted, not only by Richard III., but by his political rival, Henry VII., from whom

---

[1] Hist. Doubts, p. 58.　　　　[2] Ibid. p. 59.

he received the high and confidential appointment of governor of Guisnes, and was nominated, even after Warbeck's appearance and honourable reception at Paris, one of the royal commissioners for completing a treaty with France[1]; facts that are altogether irreconcilable, if it was so well known that he was "the employed man from King Richard"[2] for murdering his nephews. Henry VII., desirous as he was to prove the fact of their destruction, neither accuses Sir James of the act in his public declarations, nor gives any foundation whatever throughout his reign for a rumour that rests on no other ground than common report[3]; for Tyrrel, instead of being beheaded "soon after" Warbeck's appearance, as erroneously stated by Lord Bacon, was actually living twenty years after that event on terms of intimacy and friendship with the kindred of the murdered children; having been committed to the Tower in 1502, not to be examined touching the death of the princes, but relative to the escape of their cousin, the persecuted Duke of Suffolk.[4] For succouring this

---

[1] Laing, in Henry, vol. xii. p. 446.   [2] Bacon, p. 122.

[3] See Bacon's Henry VII., p. 125.; Buck's Richard III., p. 84.; Walpole's Hist. Doubts, p. 57.; Laing, in Henry, vol. xii. p. 446.

[4] Edmund Duke of Suffolk was the eldest surviving son of Elizabeth Duchess of Suffolk, sister of Edward IV. and Richard III. His elder brother, John Earl of Lincoln, whose name occurs so frequently in these pages, was slain in the battle of Stoke, shortly after the accession of Henry VII., and had been in consequence attainted in parliament. Edmund, the second son, was entitled to the honours and estates on the demise of his father, the Duke of Suffolk; but King Henry, jealous of all who claimed kindred with the house of York, deprived him, most unjustly, of his inheritance; and under the frivolous pretence of considering him the heir of his attainted brother, rather than the inheritor of his father's titles and possessions, he compelled him to accept, as a boon, a small stipend, and substituted the inferior rank of earl for the higher title of duke.—*Rot. Parl.*, vi. p. 474.

prince in his misfortunes, and for aiding the flight
of the eldest surviving nephew of his former benefactors, Edward IV. and Richard III., Sir James
Tyrrel was, indeed, " soon after executed;" his
ignominious end proving his devotion to the house
of York, and disproving, as far as recorded proofs
of fidelity can disprove mere report, the startling
accusation that has singled out a man of ancient
family, a' brave soldier, a gallant knight, and a
public servant of acknowledged worth, one who
filled the most honourable offices under three suc-
cessive monarchs,—the parent of the young princes,
their uncle, and the possessor of their throne, — as
a hireling assassin, a cool, calculating, heartless
murderer.

The unfortunate duke whom he assisted to
escape could hold out no hope of recompence to
those friends who sympathised in his persecutions[1];
he wandered for years over France and Germany
in a state of abject penury, — houseless, an exile,
" finding no place for rest or safety;"[2] whereas
certain danger was incurred by braving the indignation of the monarch, whose political jealousy had
committed Suffolk to prison.[3] Nevertheless, Sir
James Tyrrel, the long-reputed destroyer of the

---

[1] William de la Pole, the Earl of Suffolk's brother, Lord Courtenay, who had espoused a daughter of King Edward IV., Sir William Wyndham, and Sir James Tyrrel, with a few others, were
apprehended. To the two first no other crime could be imputed than
their relationship to the fugitive; the other two were condemned and
executed for having favoured the escape of the king's enemy. —
Lingard's Hist. Eng., vol. vi. p. 322.

[2] Sandford, Geneal. Hist., book v. p. 379.

[3] " It was impossible to attribute the king's conduct to any other
motive than a desire to humble a rival family." — *Lingard*, vol. vi.
p. 331.

young princes, had the moral courage to risk life
and fortune, and was condemned to suffer imprisonment, death, and attainder, for co-operating to
save the life of a friendless persecuted member of
that race, two of the noblest scions of which he is
alleged to have coolly, determinately, and stealthily
murdered!

The examination of the various questions resulting from the conflicting testimony that suggested the foregoing observations cannot, however
(from the reasons before assigned), be farther
discussed ; although one conclusive remark, one
on which the entire condemnation or acquittal of
Richard III. may fairly be permitted to rest, is
not alone admissible, but imperative, as relates to
his justification. If Tyrrel and Dighton made the
confession so craftily promulgated by Henry VII.,
although not officially disclosed by his command,
how was it that Sir Thomas More, bred to the law,
and early conversant with judicial proceedings[1],
did not make use of this proof of Richard's criminality, and of Tyrrel and Dighton's revolting conduct,— not as one only out of " *many reports*," but
as affording decisive evidence of the FACT ? " If
Dighton and Tyrrel confessed the murder in the
reign of Henry VII., how," asks Lord Orford,

---

[1] Sir Thomas More was the son of Sir John More, one of the
judges of the King's Bench. He was bred to the bar, and was early
chosen law-reader in Furnival's Inn. At the age of twenty-one, he
obtained a seat in parliament. He was a judge of the sheriff's court,
a justice of the peace, and made treasurer of the exchequer shortly
after being knighted by King Henry VIII. In 1523 he was chosen
speaker of the House of Commons; in 1527, chancellor of Lancaster,
and in 1530 he succeeded Cardinal Wolsey as lord high chancellor
of England.— *Biog. Dict.*

" could even the outlines be a secret, and uncertain, in the reign of Henry VIII. ? Is it credible that they owned the fact, and concealed every one of the circumstances ? If they related those circumstances, without which their confession could gain no manner of belief, could Sir Thomas More, chancellor of Henry VIII., and educated in the house of the prime minister of Henry VII., be ignorant of what it was so much the interest of Cardinal Morton to tell, and of Henry VII. to have known and ascertained ?"[1]

Fabyan, who lived and wrote at the precise time when the events are said to have occurred, and the value of whose chronicle rests mainly on his correctness as relates to matters happening in London and its vicinity, neither records the examination, nor the alleged confession, although he expressly mentions the imprisonment and execution of Sir James Tyrrel for facilitating the escape of Suffolk.[2] On no other ground, then, than one of the passing tales of those days, —"days so covertly demeaned, one thing pretended and another meant,"[3] writes Sir Thomas More, when admitting the uncertain basis of the tradition,—was Sir James Tyrrel alleged to have made a confession never published, and not imputed to him until after he had excited the jealousy of Henry VII., and had been executed for reputed treason against the Tudor race, and acknowledged fidelity to that of the house of York. The high reputation of the Lord Chancellor gave an interest and force to his

[1] Supplement to Hist. Doubts, p. 215.
[2] Fabyan, p. 533.   [3] More, p. 126.

narrative, that led to its being adopted by the succeeding chroniclers, without the slightest regard to
the truth or consistency of the tale. It was dramatised by Shakspeare, gravely recorded by Lord
Bacon, and, passing gradually from mere report to
asserted fact, has for ages been perpetuated as truth
by historians, who felt more inclined to embellish
their writings with the " tragedyous story," than
to involve themselves in the labour of research and
discussion which the exposure of so ephemeral a
production would have imposed upon them. " The
experience of every age justifies the great historian
of Greece[1], in the conclusion to which he was led
by his attempts to ascertain the grounds on which
so much idle fable had been received as truth by
his countrymen : Men will not take the trouble to
search after truth, if anything like it is ready to
their hands."[2] Disclaiming all intention of being
the advocate or extenuator of Richard III. unless
when contemporary documents redeem him from
unmerited calumny, and without presuming even
to risk an opinion relative to so mysterious an
occurrence as the disappearance of the young princes
from the Tower, and the share which their uncle
might, in an evil hour, have been led to take in
their destruction, it is incumbent on his biographer
to state that no proof is known to exist of his
having embrued his hands in the blood of his
nephews[3] ; and that co-existent accounts afford no

[1] Thucydides, lib. i. c. 20.
[2] Hind's " Rise and Progress of Christianity," vol. ii. p. 58.
[3] The industrious antiquary, Master John Stowe, being required
to deliver his opinion concerning the proofs of the murder, affirmed,

basis on which to ground accusations altogether
irreconcilable with Richard's previous high character and unblemished reputation.[1]

Even after his decease, neither the influence of
sovereign power, of regal bribes, kingly favour, or
kingly threats, could succeed in fixing upon him the
unhallowed deed[2]; and however much, on a cursory
review of mere exparte evidence, and with minds
prepared to admit the most exaggerated statements,
appearances may seem to convict of murder a
prince who, previously to his accession, was so
estimated and beloved by his compeers that they
would have risked " fortune and life"[3] to have
served him, yet, when the points upon which the
accusation rests are examined singly, it will be
found that the imputation, long as it has been perpetuated, is neither justified by the contradictory
reports given by his political enemies, nor is it
borne out by the undecisive and prejudiced evi-

it was never proved by any credible witness, no, not by probable
suspicions, or so much as by the knights of the post, that King Richard
was guilty of it.   And Sir Thomas More says, that it could never
come to light what became of the bodies of the two princes ; Grafton,
Hall, and Holinshed agreeing in the same report, that " the truth
hereof was utterly unknown."—*Buck*, lib. iii. p. 106.

[1] " No prince could well have a better character than Richard had
gained till he came to be protector and dethroned his nephew ; this
action, and the views of the Lancastrian faction, gave birth to the
calumnies with which he was loaded." — *Carte's Hist. Eng.*, vol. ii.
book xiii. p. 818.

[2] " The proof of the murder being left so naked, King Henry
used the utmost diligence towards obtaining more sure information.
He furnished these his employed men liberally with money to draw
on and reward intelligence, giving them in charge to advertise continually what they found, and nevertheless still to go on." — *Lord
Bacon's Hen. VII.*, p. 124.

[3] Fabyan, p. 515.

dence whereon his condemnation has hitherto been founded.

Inferences unfavourable to King Richard have been drawn arising from his liberality to Sir James Tyrrel[1] as well as to Sir Robert Brackenbury[2], and likewise from the names of the several persons stated to be concerned in the murder being all mentioned as benefiting in some degree by this monarch's favour. But, in condemning him on this ground only, the customs of the age and corresponding gratuities, heaped upon old and faithful followers, alike in previous as in subsequent reigns, have altogether been overlooked. Brackenbury and Tyrrel were attached to Richard's service as Duke of Gloucester; and if a comparison is instituted between the grants bestowed upon them and any two favourite partizans of other English kings, it will be seen that instances abound of similar marks of favour. If Brackenbury and Tyrrel are to be implicated in the murder on this pretence, every supporter of King Richard may be implicated in the fearful deed, for his diary abounds in instances of his liberality and munificence to such as served him with fidelity. Sir William Catesby and Sir Richard Ratcliffe, John Kendall the monarch's secretary, and Morgan Kydwelly his attorney, with many others whose names are less publicly associated with his career, received grants and lucrative appointments fully as great as those bestowed upon Tyrrel and Brackenbury; while the lords of Buck-

[1] Harl. MSS., No. 433. pp. 26. 205.
[2] Ibid. pp. 23. 247.

ingham, Norfolk, Surrey, Northumberland, Lincoln, Neville, Huntingdon, and Lovell, with innumerable knights, esquires, and ecclesiastics of every grade, may be adduced as examples of the liberality with which the king dispensed his gifts in requital for zeal in his cause, or recompence for personal attachment.

John Green, whom Sir Thomas More admits to have been a "trusty follower".[1] of Richard's, and who was "yeoman of the king's chamber," was not inappropriately recompensed for his long servitude, —apart from all connection with the murder,—in being appointed receiver of two lordships and of the castle of Portchester[2]; while the names of Dighton as "bailiff of Aiton in Staffordshire, with the accustomed wages,"[3]—or Forest as "keeper of the Lady Cecily's wardrobe,"[4]—would have excited no more suspicion, or even attention, than that of the many other unimportant individuals whose names occur in King Richard's diary, if prejudice had not predisposed the mind to associate these entries with the reputed assassination of the princes. Indeed the very office assigned to Forest would rather tend to exculpate than condemn him; for it can scarcely be imagined that Richard would place the murderer of her grandsons in a trustworthy situation in the mansion of his venerable parent; while the subsequent entry of a small annuity to Forest's widow[5] would favour the belief that he

---

[1] More's Rycharde III., p. 127.   [2] Kennet, vol. i. p. 552.
[3] Harl. MSS., No. 433. fol. 55.   [4] Ibid. fol. 187.
[5] Ibid. fol. 78.

was an old and tried servant of the Duchess of
York, rather than an hireling attached but a few
months to her household.   It has been farther
argued that Green's culpability is implied by an
entry in the Harl. MSS. granting him " a general
pardon;"[1] another example this, of the false inferences which may be drawn by pronouncing
judgment without due consideration being given
to the usages of the era in which the entry was
made.

The Fœdera[2] abounds with instances of " a
general pardon."   In its pages will be found one
granted to Dr. Rotheram, Archbishop of York, for
all " murders, treasons, concealments, &c.;"[3] and
this, after he had crowned King Richard in his
northern capital, and long after he had been released from imprisonment and restored to his sovereign's favour.   The Archbishop of Dublin in the
reign of King Henry VII. is in like manner " pardoned " for a catalogue of crimes[4] which is truly
appalling: and many such pardons might be adduced as granted to the most exemplary persons.
Indeed, the very diary which records Green's pardon
contains corresponding entries to William Brandone,
to Robert Clifford, and to Sir James Blount, the
Governor of Hammes.[5]   Yet these brave men have
neither been suspected nor in any way implicated
in heinous offences or revolting crimes.   Nor was
there any basis for condemning Green on such evi-

---

[1] Harl. MSS., No. 433. fol. 28.   [2] Hist. Doubts, p. 50.
[3] Ibid.   [4] Ibid.
[5] Harl. MSS., No. 433. fol. 58. 83. 101.

dence: similar entries were customary in the middle ages at the commencement of a new reign; and but for the traditional notoriety attached to Green, arising from Sir Thomas More's narrative, his pardon and his appointments would have excited as little suspicion as would otherwise have been called forth by the very natural and ordinary gift to Bracken-bury, as governor of the Tower, of "the keeping of the lions" in that fortress, or the "custody of the Mint," established within its precincts.

Lengthened as has been this discussion, yet, as the truth of the tradition narrated by Sir Thomas More and Lord Bacon has been considered to have received confirmation from the discovery in after years of the supposed remains of the young princes, a brief notice of that occurrence is also indispensable.

"In the year 1674," states Sandford [1], whose relation is given on the testimony of an eye-witness, one, he says, principally concerned in the scrutiny, "in order to the re-building of several offices in the Tower, and to clear the White Tower from all contiguous buildings, digging down the stairs which led from the king's lodgings to the chapel in the said tower, about ten feet in the ground were found the bones of two striplings in (as it seemed) a wooden chest, which upon the survey were found proportionable to the ages of those two brothers (Edward V. and Richard Duke of York), about thirteen and eleven years; the skull of one being entire, the other broken, as were indeed many of

---

[1] Sandford, Geneal. Hist., book v. p. 404.

the bones, as also the chest, by the violence of the
labourers, who, not being sensible of what they had
in hand, cast the rubbish and them away together;
wherefore they were caused to sift the rubbish, and
by that means preserved all the bones."... "Upon
the presumption that these were the bones of the
said princes, His Majesty King Charles II. was
graciously pleased to command that the said bones
should be put into a marble urn, and deposited
among the relics of the royal family in the chapel
of King Henry VII. in Westminster Abbey."

It may be doubted if any stronger instance could
be adduced of the mischief that may result from
a desire of reconciling historical traditions with co-
incidences which, chancing to agree with local legends, blind the enthusiastic and prejudging to all
the many minor proofs that can alone substantiate
the truth sought to be established. The discovery
of these very bones, which for nearly two centuries
has been considered to remove all doubt of
Richard's guilt, is the silent instrument of clear-
ing him from the imputation, if Sir Thomas More's
statement, by which he has been condemned, is
considered to be verified by their discovery. This
historian, it will be remembered, relates that "about
midnight" the young king and his brother were
murdered; that after "long lying still to be thoroughly dead," their destroyers "laid their bodies
naked out upon the bed, and fetched Sir James to
see them; which, after the sight of them, caused
these murderers to bury them at the stair-foot
metely deep in the ground, under a great heap of

stones."[1] No mention is made of a chest; they were laid out " naked upon the bed;" and the nights in July (the reputed period of the dark deed) afford small time after midnight for two men to commit such a crime, to watch long over their expiring victims, to lay them out for the inspection of their employer, and, by his command, to dig a space sufficiently large to bury a chest deep in the ground; although the bodies of two youths might be hastily cast into " a deep hole"[2] under the stairs, and some stones cast upon them.[3] Sandford states that the chest was found when " digging down the stairs, about ten feet deep."[4] More asserts that the bodies were buried at the " stair-foot, metely deep in the ground."[5] In addition to this, the discovery was made in the stairs which led from the king's lodgings to the chapel; now Sandford, in his previous narrative of the murder, distinctly asserts that " the lodgings of the princes being in the building near the water-gate, which is therefore to this day called the Bloody Tower, their bodies were buried in the stair-foot there, somewhat deep in the ground."[6] Both these statements are at variance with Sir Thomas More, the first promulgator of the tradition, and the source from whence all subsequent historians have derived their information. If the young princes died in the Bloody Tower, and were buried at the stair-foot there, then it could not be their remains which were discovered in the

[1] More, p. 131.
[2] Buck, p. 84.
[3] Bacon, p. 123.
[4] Sandford, p. 404.
[5] More, p. 131.
[6] Sandford, p. 404.

stairs leading to the chapel; and if they inhabited the king's lodgings, and were buried where the remains were discovered, it at once invalidates the assertion of More[1], and of Lord Bacon[2] likewise, that they were removed from " so vile a corner" by the king's command, who would have them buried in a better place because they were " a king's sons."

If reference is made to the early history of the Tower of London, it will be found that the portion of that fortress so long reputed to be the scene of the young princes' tragical end was in their days merely a porter's lodge[3], and not likely to be in the smallest degree connected with the dark deed which its particular appellation is believed to have perpetuated. Nay, so far from the gateway being thus designated in consequence of the alleged murder within its narrow precincts, the very epithet itself, originating from other causes nearly a century after the disappearance of the princes, seems to be the sole origin of a rumour which gained strength in consequence of certain peculiarities in its structure appearing to coincide with Sir Thomas More's description.[4] Hence, towards the close of the Tudor

---

[1] More, p. 132.   [2] Bacon, p. 123.

[3] " This gateway was erected in the time of Edward IV. It is about thirty-four feet long and fifteen wide. Each end of the entrance was originally secured by gates and a strong portcullis, and on the eastern side, between these defences, was a small circular stone staircase, leading to the superstructure which formed the lodging or watch, and consisted of two gloomy apartments, one over the other, and a space for working the portcullis." — *Bayley's Hist. of the Tower*, vol. i. p. 262.

[4] " At the end, towards the south, both the gates and the portcullis still exist: they are extremely massive, and carry with them every appearance of high antiquity. The staircase leading to the

dynasty, it began to be reported as the scene of the dark transaction; and surmise passing current with the multitude for fact, it has long since[1] been confidently pointed out as the actual site of the tragedy.[2] " In the careful and minute survey which was taken of the Tower of London," observes its elaborate historian, " in the reign of Henry VIII., this building is called the Garden Tower, by reason of its contiguity to the constable's or lieutenant's garden, which now forms a part of what is termed the Parade.[3] In the year 1597, another survey was made of the fortress by order of Queen Elizabeth, and it was then known by its present appellation; which it is generally supposed to have derived from the circumstance of the two young princes, Edward V. and his brother Richard Duke of York, having, as it is said, been put to death in this particular spot, by order of their uncle, the Duke of Gloucester, afterwards King Richard III. " The whole story of the two royal brothers," continues this writer, " having been destroyed in the Tower, comes to us in so questionable a shape, that it can never be entertained without some serious doubts.

porter's lodge, though not now made use of, also remains; but the gates, as well as the portcullis, which were at the northern end, have long since been removed." — *Bayley*, vol. i. p. 262.

[1] " All the domestic apartments of the ancient palace within the Tower were taken down during the reigns of James II. and William and Mary." — *Bayley's Londiniana*, vol. i. p. 109.

[2] " It is a very general opinion that the building called ' The Bloody Tower' received its appellation from the circumstance of the royal children having been stifled in it, and it is commonly and confidently asserted that the bones were found under a staircase there; yet both of these stories seem wholly without foundation." — *Bayley*, vol. ii. p. 64.

[3] Bayley's History of the Tower, p. 264.

If we admit, however, that the young princes really
came to a violent death in the Tower, the idea of
this place having been the scene of their destruction rests on no authority; and the story which
the warders, whose trade it is " to tell a wondrous
tale," so gravely propagate respecting the discovery
of these bones under the little staircase above
alluded to (in the Bloody Tower), is still more
glaringly false. Bones, it is true, were found in the
Tower in the reign of Charles II., and they were
looked upon to be those of children corresponding
with the two princes; but it is most decidedly
known that they were discovered in a very different part of the fortress to that in which tradition
reports them to be interred, viz. on the south side
of the White Tower, and at the foot of the staircase which leads to the chapel in that building.[1]

Few traditions propagated on such high authority
as Sir Thomas More and Lord Bacon—men eminent
for their learning, and yet more for their exalted
stations as lord chancellors of England — would
bear such strict scrutiny, with a view of disproving
the rumour on which both admit that the tradition
sprung. Thus it appears that the legend of the
Bloody Tower, as connected with the murder of the
princes, vanishes by testing its validity on the sole
basis on which it was reported to rest[2],—the appel-

[1] This chapel, which is within the White Tower, and is altogether distinct from the sacred edifice wherein divine service has
been for many years performed, is now called the Record Office. —
Bayley, vol. i. p. 263.

[2] " A stronger proof we need not have that the name of the
building did not originate in the circumstance in question, is its not
having assumed the appellation till upwards of a century after the
supposed act."—*Ibid.* vol. i. p. 264.

lation supposed to commemorate the dreadful act not having been assumed until 100 years after the murder was reported to have been perpetrated[1]; and the bones, the discovery of which were considered to confirm the tradition, were found in another staircase, and in a part of the fortress far removed from that gateway, which, nevertheless, to this day continues to be shown as the place of their death and burial, notwithstanding the royal interment of the remains found elsewhere. Had Sir Thomas More and the biographer of Henry VII. ended their tale by the mere relation of the massacre and hurried interment, then indeed there might have appeared some ground for belief that the remains were those of the young princes; for the stairs leading from the royal apartments — a far more probable abode for the royal children than the porter's lodge[2] — would have seemed a

[1] " Between the reign of Henry VIII., when this building was called the Garden Tower, and the year 1597, when it was known as the Bloody Tower, the Tower was crowded by delinquents of all descriptions ; and as the structure in question was no doubt then frequently used as a prison, it more probably derived its present name from some of the horrid deeds which distinguished that era." —*Bayley*, vol. i. p. 264.

[2] It may be alleged, that King Richard took possession, in all likelihood, of the royal apartments after his coronation, and removed his nephews to the Bloody Tower. In the absence of proof on that point, the fact can only be judged by analogy. King Edward IV. continually resided at the Tower, and for many years held his court in the palace there, where his predecessor was imprisoned ; yet no mention is made of Henry VI. having been immured in apartments unbecoming his high estate ; and notwithstanding this latter monarch is reputed to have been murdered in the Tower, neither history nor tradition commemorate menial apartments as the site of that dark and mysterious event. Even Sir Thomas More, who perpetuated the lamentation of Edward V. when informed of his uncle's coronation, makes no mention whatever of any removal

natural place for the assassins to have chosen for the concealment of the desperate act, and therefore conclusive evidence of the truth of the tale. But both these eminent men distinctly report that the bodies were removed by Richard's order, and buried " in a less vile corner;" " whereupon, another night, by *the king's warrant renewed*," (such are the strong words of Lord Bacon[1],) " their bodies were removed by the priest of the Tower, and buried by him in some place which by means of the priest's death soon after could not be known ; " and Sir Thomas More's[2] expression is, " whither the bodies were removed, they could nothing tell." If, therefore, credit is given to their having been first interred in or under the stairs, some credit must attach to the assertion, from the same source, of their having been removed from those stairs, and their remains fitly deposited by the governor's chaplain in consecrated ground, and in a spot suitable to their noble birth. He was not commanded to remove the bodies from apprehension of discovery or suspicion of treachery, but, as asserted, from

from the place usually appointed to the royal prisoners. Richard III. was much too reserved, cautious, and reflective to have prematurely laid himself open, by unnecessarily degrading the royal children, to subsequent suspicion as regards his conduct towards them. " Is it to be supposed," asks Mr. Bayley, " whatever might have been the Protector's design as to the ultimate fate of his nephews, that the princes were not lodged in royal apartments, and paid all the respect due to their rank ? Is it likely that Richard should have had them shut up in the dark and wretched dwelling of one of the porters of the gates ? If he had wanted in humanity, would policy have dictated such a course ? No : it must at once have betrayed some foul design, without adding a jot to the facility of the perpetration." — *Bayley*, vol. i. p. 264.

[1] Life of Henry VII., p. 123.
[2] Life of Rycharde III., p. 132.

Richard's considering their burial at a "stair-foot," derogatory to the former exalted position of his nephews, "being too base for them that were king's children,"[1] an important consideration in testing the validity of these relics, because it coincides with Richard's general character, and with the religious feeling of the times. Apart, however, from this view, it would be preposterous to suppose that they would be exhumed from one stairs to be interred in another; or that, if exhumed, their remains would be otherwise than laid at rest with the ordinary attentions to the illustrious dead, however secretly performed or scrupulously concealed.[2] Although the ecclesiastic, who is reputed to have undertaken the office, was dead, and that the place was known only to himself, yet Sir George Buck states that Dighton and Tyrrel's reputed confession was followed up by the examination of the spot where their victims were said to have been buried.[3] But nothing was discovered, although the digging at a "stair-foot," when the precise spot was pointed out, was as practicable in the reign of Henry VII. as that of Charles II. Little consideration seems to have been bestowed on the friable condition to which, in this latter reign, the remains would probably have been reduced after the interment of centuries, or that the detached bones would have crumbled into dust

[1] Bacon, p. 123.

[2] "They might have added, it was done *sub sigillo confessionis*, which may not be revealed." — *Buck*, lib. iii. p. 85.

[3] "For true it is, there was much diligent search made for their bodies in the Tower: all places opened and digged, that was supposed, but not found." — *Ibid.*

on exposure to the air. Decomposition almost immediately follows a violent death, above all, such an one as is reputed to have terminated the existence of the royal brothers, that of suffocation; " the featherbed and pillows" being kept down by force " hard into their mouths, that within a while smothered and stifled them ;"[1] and a situation so damp as that of the Tower of London, erected on the banks of a river, would scarcely have favoured their preservation. Although relics carefully secured might possibly continue to a distant era sufficiently entire to admit of discussion with reference to identity if forthwith commenced, yet it is contrary to the ordinary course of nature that either the mortal remains of the young princes, or the chest into which they were hurriedly thrown, could endure for the space of 200 years in the same state in which they were deposited under the peculiar circumstances stated. These mutilated remains were long exposed to the air, and subjected to the violence of the labourers, before even a rumour began to prevail respecting their probable identity with the missing princes. " The skull of one was broken, and many of the bones likewise," we are told ; and also that " the workmen cast them and the rubbish away together." [2] Yet these broken, scattered, and decomposed remains, — to collect which labourers were obliged to sift this refuse when the report gained ground as to their connection with Sir Thomas More's tradition, — were definitively recognised as the skeletons of the young princes, and

[1] More p. 131.   [2] Sandford, p. 404.

gravely pronounced to be the remains of adults, precisely of the ages required.

On a discovery thus vague and inconclusive has Richard the Third's guilt been considered incontestably proved, despite of the untenable legend of the " Bloody Tower," the absence of all proof of Tyrrel and Warbeck's reputed confessions[1], and the admitted fact that the revolting personal portrait so long given of this monarch has as little foundation in truth as the asserted removal of the bodies by the king's command, if, indeed, these were the remains of the royal youths said to be murdered by their uncle. " The personal monster whom More and Shakspeare exhibited has vanished," states a powerful writer of the present day[2], but the deformity of the revolting parricide was surely revealed in the bones of his infant nephews!" Had these been the only bones which the credulity of later times transformed into the murdered remains of one or both of the princes, the power which a favourite hypothesis, once established, possesses to warp the judgment even of the most reflective might, in this instance, be admitted as the cause why evidence so weak, and identity so vague, was overlooked in the plausibility which seemed to attach to the discovery.

---

[1] " King Henry's great and culpable omission in this instance," (the alleged confession of Warbeck) " as in the case of the examination of Tyrrel and Dighton, was, in not openly publishing a statement, signed and verified by competent authorities, which would have been far more satisfactory than ' the court fumes,' which, adds Bacon, ' commonly print better (*i. e.* more strongly impress themselves on the public mind) than printed proclamations.'"—*Documents relating to Perkin Warbeck, Archæologia,* vol. xxvii. p. 153.

[2] D'Israeli, " Amenities of Literature," vol. ii. p. 105.

But the case of the relics found in the time of Charles II., and by him honoured with a royal interment, is not a solitary instance of remains coming to light which were fully believed to substantiate the tradition of King Richard's criminal conduct; and however ludicrous the statement may appear, yet it is an historical fact, that bones discovered years before these that are now under discussion in a lofty and unoccupied turret, and which were at the time generally believed to be the remains of the unfortunate Edward V., were afterwards allowed to be the skeleton of an ape! who, escaping from the menagerie, had clambered to the dangerous height, and, too feeble to retrace his steps, had there perished.[1]

[1] " The weak constitutions and short lives of their sisters, may be a natural proof, to infer it probable enough that this prince died in the Tower ; which some men of these times are brought to think, from certain bones, like to the bones of a child being found lately in a high desolate turret, supposed to be the bones of one of these princes ; others are of opinion it was the carcase of an ape, kept in the Tower, that in his old age had happened into that place to die in, and having clambered up thither, according to the light and idle manner of those wanton animals, after, when he would have gone down, seeing the way to have been steep and the precipice so terrible, durst not adventure to descend, but for fear stayed and starved himself ; and although he might be soon missed, and long sought for, yet was not easily to be found, that turret being reckoned a vast and damned place for height and hard access, nobody in many years looking into it." — *Buck,* lib. iii. p. 86.

" The identity of the bones," observes Mr. Laing, " is uncertain ; the Tower was both a palace and a state prison, the receptacle of Lollards, heretics, and criminals, within which those who died by disease or violence were always buried ; the discovery, therefore, of bones, is neither surprising nor perhaps uncommon ; but we must guard against the extreme credulity perceptible in the officers, who, persuaded that the princes were secretly interred in the Tower, appropriated every skeleton to them. Bones found at a former period in a deserted turret, were regarded as the remains of one of the princes ; though some entertained a ludicrous suspicion that they

So ready were the occupants of the Tower to appropriate every suspicious appearance towards elucidating a mystery, which, beyond all others of the startling events connected with the remarkable history of this national fortress, cast an air of melancholy interest and romance over its gloomy towers. Is it just, however, to convict a monarch of England, — a Plantagenet by birth and descent, the last of a noble and gallant race,—of crimes which the mind shrinks from contemplating, on no more solid basis than mere rumour, the alleged proofs of which are so inconclusive, that even the lowest and most hardened criminal in this present day would pass unscathed through the ordeal ? Has any other of our English sovereigns been convicted on such shallow evidence ? Has King Henry I., the usurper of his brother's rights, and the author of his fearful sufferings, or King John, who wrested the throne from his nephew, and has been suspected even of putting him to death with his own hand, been vituperated with equal rancour; does odium attach, except in a very modified degree, to Edward III., Henry IV., Edward IV., Henry VII., and Queen Elizabeth, all more or less implicated in the cruel execution of dethroned rivals or princely opponents? Whence then, is it, that to Richard III. has been applied every invective that can be heaped on the memory of the basest of men, and the most ruthless of kings ? It arose from this simple cause, that he was succeeded by the founder of a new dynasty, — a

belonged to an old ape, who had clambered thither and perished."— *Laing (in Henry)*, vol. xii. p. 419.

sovereign whose interest it was to load him with the vilest calumnies, and to encourage every report that could blacken his memory.[1] Hence later chroniclers, to court the favour of Henry VII. and his posterity, adopted as real facts those reports which were at first raised merely to mislead, or at least satisfy the populace. Desirous of transmitting Richard III. to future ages in the most detestable light, from mental depravity they passed to personal deformity — " representing him as crooked and deformed, though all ancient pictures drawn of him show the contrary."[2] Succeeding sovereigns sanctioning these accusations, so implicit became the belief in his guilt, that at length it mattered little whether it was the recent skeleton of a starved ape, or the decomposed remains of sifted bones, that aided to increase the odium, and still deeper to blacken the character of a prince prejudged as a ruthless murderer — condemned as an inhuman parricide. The mass of mankind are so prone to suspicion, that oft repeated and long received accusations will at length prevail even with the most ingenuous; and so feelingly alive is each individual to the frailty and weakness of human nature, that however noble may have been the career, or honourable the actions of the character vituperated, if once the poisoned tongue of malice has singled out its object, neither purity of heart, nor consciousness of innocence, will protect the unhappy victim of malevolence from the stigma sought to be established, either to gratify private pique or further the views of political animosity.

[1] Carte, vol. ii. book xiii. p. 818.   [2] Ibid.

Such was the position of Richard III. as regards the murder of his nephews. He may have been guilty, but this cannot be authenticated, for no evidence is on record, and no more substantial basis even for the accusation exists than the envenomed shaft of political malice. Although the plague raged many times fearfully within the metropolis[1], precluding alike regular interments, and explaining irregular burials[2]; although that greater scourge to mankind, religious persecution, together with civil warfare, led to deeds of such fearful import, that many a tale of horror might be unfolded if the walls of the Tower could divulge the tragical scenes acted within them,—and which are now only in part suspected, or remain altogether unknown,—yet no one cause has ever been suggested to account for the broken chest and scattered remains found in the passage leading to the chapel, but that grounded on such slight foundation as the allegation against King Richard III.

Mysterious indeed is the fate of the young princes, and so it is likely to remain, unless future discoveries should bring to light some more conclusive

---

[1] Shortly after the accession of King Henry VII. a fearful pestilence denominated "The Sweating Sickness," almost depopulated the metropolis ; and the execution of the young Earl of Warwick, in 1499, was followed by so devastating a plague, that the king, the queen, and the royal family were obliged to leave the kingdom, and were resident at Calais for many weeks.   During the "Great Plague" of 1665, the weekly bill of mortality amounted to 8000 ; and so awfully did it rage in the heart of the city, that between 400 and 500 a-week died in Cripplegate parish, and above 800 in Stepney.—*Brayley's Londiniana,* vol. iii. p. 220.

[2] "The numbers of dead in the outposts were so great that it was impossible to bury them in due form or to provide coffins, no one daring to come into the infected houses."—*Ibid.* p. 216.

cause for Richard's condemnation than "one," out
of "many rumours," not promulgated until he, like
his nephews, slumbered the sleep of death, and
which took its rise in times when the reputation of
the noblest characters were attacked with a disregard to truth and bitterness of feeling that is
truly appalling. But those times have passed away,
and the feuds that gave rise to such discordant
passions being no longer in operation, however
strongly appearances may seem to favour the imputation cast upon Richard III.; yet, as it is
already admitted, that "the personal monster whom
Sir Thomas More and Shakspeare exhibited has
vanished," it behoves all advocates for historical
truth to suspend judgment in a case which has so
long darkened the royal annals of England.

From the researches which are actively pursued
in the present day, it is by no means impossible
that some fresh documents may yet come to light
which will lead to a knowledge of the facts, and thus
afford legitimate cause. for condemning or acquitting a monarch, who, if not altogether free from the
vices which pre-eminently marked his turbulent
age, was not devoid of those nobler qualities which
equally characterised the same chivalrous period,
and which afford substantial ground for discredit-
ing reports that are wholly at variance with the
prudence and generosity of his youthful days, and
are yet more strongly opposed to the discretion
and wisdom which marked his kingly career.

CHAPTER XV.

THE entire reign of King Richard III. is composed
of such startling events, each succeeding the other
so rapidly, and all more or less wrapt in impenetrable mystery, that it more resembles a highly-
coloured romance, than a narrative of events of real
life. Perhaps no scene in the remarkable career of
this monarch is more strange, more irreconcilable
with ordinary calculations, than the insurrection of
the Duke of Buckingham; characterised as it was
by perfidy and ingratitude of the blackest dye, and
involving purposes as deep, and results as momentous, as the basis on which it was built was

shallow and untenable. No one appears to have been more thoroughly ignorant of the deep game playing by his unstable kinsman than the king himself; for however strongly his suspicions of some outbreak might have been excited as regards local or general disaffection, yet that his confidence in Buckingham remained unchanged, and his friendly feelings towards him undiminished, is evinced by one of the last official instruments issued by the monarch from York, his assent being affixed to " Letters from Edward Prince of Wales, to the officers and tenants of his Principality in North Wales and South Wales, commanding them to make their recognisances, and pay their talliages [1], to Humfrey Stafford, the Duke of Buckingham, and his other commissioners." That Richard had not merited the enmity which led to Buckingham's revolt is apparent from many documents which attest his generosity, and prove the honourable fulfilment of his promises to that nobleman. Setting aside several of these that were instanced as among the first acts of his reign, the historian Rous, the contemporary both of Richard and of Buckingham, states that the king conferred on the duke such vast treasure, that the latter boasted, when giving livery of the " Knots of the Staffords [2], that he

[1] Harl. MSS., No. 433. fol. 3.

[2] This observation refers to the Duke of Buckingham's badge. The cognisance of the Earl of Warwick, " the bear and ragged staff," was one of the most celebrated heraldic devices of the middle ages. The Stafford knott, however, was of great antiquity ; and the Dacre's knott, the Bourchier's knott, the Wake's knott, and the Harrington's knott were all distinguished as badges of high repute, and as denoting the retainers of ancient and honourable houses.

had as many of them as Richard Neville Earl of
Warwick formerly had of ragged staves."[1]   Simple
as is this anecdote, yet few could better have pour-
trayed the feeling which occupied Buckingham's
mind of assimilating himself in all respects to that
mighty chief.

That vanity, indeed, and the most inordinate
ambition were the true causes of the Duke of
Buckingham's perfidious conduct to his royal kinsman admits of little doubt, for although Sir
Thomas More asserts that, " the occasion of their
variance is of divers men, diversly reported;"[2]
yet he sums up the detail of these several rumours
by this important admission — "very truth it is, the
duke was an high-minded man, and evil could bear
the glory of an other, so that I have heard of some
that said they saw it, that the duke at such time as
the crown was first set upon the protector's head,
his eye could not abide the sight thereof, but wried
[turned aside] his head another way."[3]

The ordinarily reputed cause of his rebellion is
evidently devoid of truth, as shown by instruments
that effectually disprove the allegation.   The Duke
of Buckingham is stated to have taken offence at
King Richard's refusing him the Hereford lands[4],
whereas complete restitution, and in the fullest
manner that was in the power of the crown, was
almost the opening act of this monarch's reign :
nothing can be more forcibly worded than were
the letters patent[5] " for restoring to Henry Stafford

[1] Rous, p. 216.
[2] More, p. 135.
[3] More, p. 137.
[4] Ibid. p. 136.
[5] Harl. MSS., 433. fol. 107.

Duke of Buckingham, the purpartie of the estate of Humfrey Bohun late Earl of Hereford, at present till the same shall be vested in him by the next parliament, as fully as if no act of parliament had been made against King Henry VI."[1]

This was followed by " a cedule, or particular of this purpartie, amounting to a great sum yearly."[2] Sir Thomas More narrates, that up to the last moment of the duke's departure, although his discontent was apparent to Richard, yet that " it was not ill taken, nor any demand of the duke's uncourteously rejected, but he with great gifts and high behests, in most loving and trusty manner departed at Gloucester."[3]

Neither could indignation have been kindled in his heart, arising, as is generally believed, from the murder of the princes; for at the time that he is asserted to have united with Bishop Morton in deploring their death, the contemporary chronicler testifies that they remained " under certain deputed custody; "[4] and it is also recorded by Fabyan, that conspiracies were beginning to form in the metropolis for effecting their release.[5] Sir Thomas More, the sole narrator of the reputed manner of their destruction, distinctly relates that the assassins were not despatched to destroy them until the king arrived at Warwick[6]: nevertheless, Bucking-

---

[1] On the death of King Henry VI., who died without issue, all the estates of Lancaster (especially those of the royal family of Lancaster) escheated to King Edward IV., and from him they came to King Richard, as heir to his brother upon the deposition of Edward V. and the elevation of himself to the throne. — Buck, lib. i. p. 35.

[2] Harl. MSS., 433. fol. 107.   [3] More, p. 136.

[4] Chron. Croy., p. 567.   [5] Fabyan, p. 515.   [6] More, p. 128.

ham, who left Richard at Gloucester some days before the king's departure from that city, informs the bishop that the fearful event was communicated to him during his attendance on the king. "When I was credibly informed of the death of the two young innocents, his own natural nephews, contrary to his faith and promise, (to the which, God be my judge, I never agreed nor condescended,) O Lord, how my veins panted, how my body trembled, and how my heart inwardly grudged! insomuch that I so abhorred the sight, and much more the company of him, that I could no longer abide in his court, except I should be openly revenged." [1]

If this was indeed the case, then Sir James Tyrrel's reputed confession is still more completely negatived; and Sir Thomas More's statement becomes nullified altogether. Without, however, renewing discussions on this point, or dwelling on the suspicions that might fairly be pursued of Buckingham's connivance in the princes' destruction, if they were indeed so early murdered as he implies, or indulging in conjectures arising from his seeming knowledge of a crime that formed the alleged basis of his weak and wayward conduct; still ambition as regards himself, and envy as relates to King Richard, is apparent throughout that remarkable dialogue held by the duke and his prisoner, Cardinal Morton, the substance of which [2] there can be no doubt was reported by that prelate to Sir Thomas More, and hence narrated

---

[1] Grafton's Cont. of More, p. 135.   [2] Turner, iii. p. 505.

by him and by Grafton, the continuator of his
history.[1]

That the Duke of Buckingham coveted the regal
diadem is evident from his entire conduct, but
whether Bishop Morton indirectly fed his vanity
with the ultimate view of restoring the sceptre to
King Edward's offspring, or that Buckingham was
in reality so blind as to believe himself capable of
founding a new dynasty, is difficult of decision, from
the contradictory and altogether incredible circumstances with which the details are involved.[2]

The leading points of the occurrence, as popularly
received, are as follows : — Disgusted at the death
of the young princes, and abhorring the presence
of their uncle, Buckingham feigned a cause to leave
King Richard at Gloucester, and departed, as it is
said, with " a merry countenance but a despiteful
heart."[3] As he journeyed towards Brecknock his
angry passions had so far gained the ascendancy
over him, that he began to contemplate whether it
were practicable to deprive the king of his crown
and sceptre, and even fancied that if he chose himself to take upon him the regal diadem, now was
" the gate opened, and occasion given, which, if
neglected, should peradventure never again present
itself to him."[4] " I saw my chance as perfectly as
I saw my own image in a glass," he states, " and
in this point I rested in imagination secretly with
myself two days at Tewkesbury."[5] Doubting, how-

[1] Singer's More, p. 145.

[2] Buck, lib. iii. p. 76. ; Laing, in Henry VI., p. 415. ; Walpole,
p. 18.   [3] Grafton, p. 155.

[4] Ibid. p. 156.   [5] Ibid.

ever, how far his title to the throne would be
favourably received if acquired by conquest[1] alone,
he resolved upon founding his pretensions on his
descent from the house of Lancaster, the legitimate
branch of which having become extinct in Henry
VI., the descendants of the " De Beauforts," John
of Gaunt's illegitimate offspring, considered themselves the representatives of their princely ancestor.
Pleased with this scheme, and sanguine as to its
result, he made it known to a few chosen friends;
but while pondering within himself which was the
wiser course to pursue, whether publicly and at
once to avow his intentions, or " to keep it secret
for a while,"[2] as he rode between Worcester and
Bridgenorth he encountered his near kinswoman,
the Lady Margaret Countess of Richmond, wife to
the Lord Stanley, and the descendant of the eldest
branch of the above named " De Beauforts." This
illustrious lady, to whom in conjunction with the
Duke of Buckingham had been allotted so favoured
a position at the recent coronation of Richard and
Queen Anne, being well acquainted with the influence which her kinsman possessed at court, and
the favour with which he was regarded by the king,
availed herself of this opportune meeting to intreat
his good offices in behalf of Henry Earl of Richmond, who escaping into Brittany on the total
defeat of the house of Lancaster, was attainted by

---

[1] " I mused, and thought that it was not convenient to take upon
me as a conqueror, for then I knew that all men, and especially the
nobility, would with all their power withstand me for rescuing
of possessions and tenures, as also for subverting of the whole estate,
laws, and customs of the realm." — *Grafton,* 155.

[2] Ibid. p. 157.

Edward IV., and had been for the space of fourteen years an exile and a prisoner in that country. She prayed the duke for " kindred sake " to move the king to " license his return to England," promising that if it pleased Richard to unite him to one of King Edward's daughters [1] (in conformity with a former proposition of the deceased monarch), that no other dower should be taken or demanded, but " only the king's favour." [2] This was a death-blow to Buckingham's aspiring views, arising from his Lancastrian lineage. An elder branch lived to dispute with him any claims which he might urge on that ground, the Countess of Richmond being the only child " and sole heir to his grandfather's eldest brothers, which," he states, " was as clean out of my mind as though I had never seen her." [3] All hopes of the crown being thus at an end as regards his descent from John of Gaunt, the duke revolved his other possible chances of success. " Eftsoons I imagined whether I were best to take upon me, by the election of the nobility and commonalty, which me thought easy to be done, the usurper king thus being in hatred and abhorred of this whole realm, or to take it by power which standeth in fortune's chance and hard to be achieved and brought to pass." [4]

But neither of these plans gave promise of a happy result, the sympathy of the country was too much excited for the offspring of King Edward IV. for any fresh claimants to anticipate aid either from the nobles or commons of the realm, while the re-

---

[1] Cott. MSS., Dom. A. xviii.   [2] Grafton, p. 159.
[3] Ibid. p. 157.   [4] Ibid.

sources and alliances of his cousin, the Earl of Richmond, " which be not of little power," would, as Buckingham felt, even if he were elected to the throne, keep him ever " in doubt of death or deposition."[1] With a reluctance which only served to increase his hatred to King Richard, he found himself compelled to abandon all hope of obtaining that sovereign power to which he had been the chief means of elevating his kinsman.

Bent, however, on depriving Richard of a crown which he could not himself obtain, Buckingham again changed his purpose; and, improving on the modest request preferred by the Countess of Richmond, determined to devote his "power and purse"[2] to effect the release of her son: not, however, through the favour of Richard III., neither through measures of peace and amity; but in avowed hostility, as a rival to the reigning monarch, whose throne he decided should be promised to the Earl of Richmond, on condition that he espoused the Princess Elizabeth, and thus united the long-divided houses of York and Lancaster. That the Duke of Buckingham should have aspired to the regal dignity, or imagined it possible from mere personal malice to effect a counter-revolution within a few weeks of an election and coronation so seemingly unanimous as that of Richard III., seems utterly incomprehensible: but that he could, by any possibility, have forgotten that he was descended from the youngest branch of a family so remark-

[1] Grafton, p. 158.   [2] Ibid. p. 160.

as the house of Somerset, arising from the feuds which their struggle for power had occasioned for half a century, in turbulent but unavailing efforts to be recognised as legitimate[1] branches of the royal line of Lancaster[2], is altogether incredible, and casts an air of fable over the entire narrative that professes to relate his motives. Pride of birth, of lineage, and of kindred ties, was one of the leading characteristics of the age; and family intermarriages, arising from this pride of ancestry, constitute one of the most difficult features in the biography of these early times. The continued captivity of the Earl of Richmond had been too favourite a scheme, both with Edward IV. and King Richard himself, for the rivalry which existed between the house of York and the collateral branch of the house of Lan-

[1] The De Beauforts had been legitimated by act of parliament, February 1397, and enabled to enjoy all lands and hereditary seignories; but the charter, it was generally considered, conferred on them no pretensions to the crown, there being a special exception when the act was confirmed in the reign of Henry IV. with respect to the royal dignity. — *Life of Margaret Beaufort*, p. 80.

[2] Table showing the descent of Margaret Countess of Richmond and Henry Duke of Buckingham from John of Gaunt, Duke of Lancaster.

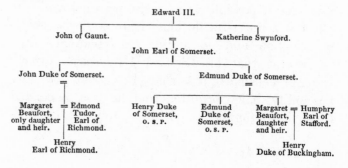

caster to have remained unknown to their cousin
of Buckingham: and, had such been the case, the
simple fact of himself and the Countess of Richmond having been selected to fill so prominent a
position as that of upholding the trains of the king
and queen at the coronation, in virtue of their
Lancastrian descent, was of itself sufficient to have
refreshed his memory. This unfortunate position,
indeed, was in all probability the true cause of con-
verting the envious Buckingham from Richard's
devoted friend to his bitterest foe.[1] He had been
the active instrument in raising him to the throne;
and, as the joint descendant with himself from
King Edward III.[2], he could ill brook to bear the
train of a prince for whom he had secured a crown.
It might be deemed a favoured place, and it certainly was one that implied confidence and friendship: but Buckingham was by descent a Plantagenet, and he above all things loved display and
coveted distinction. Moreover, he considered
himself entitled to the office of high constable of
England in virtue of his descent from the De

[1] " When the Protector rode through London towards his coronation, he [Buckingham] feigned himself sick, because he would not
ride with him. And the other, taking it in evil part, sent him word
to rise, and come ride, or he would make him be carried! Whereupon he rode on with evil will; and that notwithstanding, on the
morrow rose from the feast, feigning himself sick: and King Richard
said it was done in hatred and despite to him. And they say, that
ever after continually each of them lived in such hatred and distrust
of other, that the duke verily looked to have been murdered at
Gloucester; from which, natheless, he in fair manner departed." —
More, p. 136.

[2] Table showing the descent of Richard III. and Henry Duke of
Buckingham from King Edward III. (See next page.)

Bohuns, Earls of Hereford[1], whose lands he had so urgently claimed of Edward IV.; and he was mortified at the ensigns of that honourable office being borne by the Lord Stanley, though but temporarily, on the day of the coronation[2]; and yet more at the newly-created Earl of Surrey occupying its allotted position when carrying before the king the sword of state.

It is true that, as a descendant of the house of Lancaster, the Duke of Buckingham bore his wand of office as hereditary seneschal, or lord high steward of England, anciently the first great officer of the crown. But although his consanguinity to that royal line was thus made apparent, yet Buckingham felt humbled at displaying it as the appendage of a train-bearer to the rival dynasty, when the

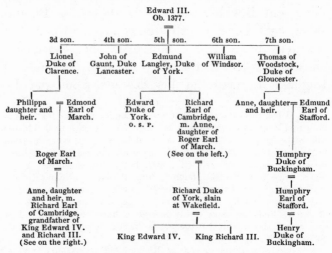

Edward III.
Ob. 1377.

3d son.	4th son.	5th son.	6th son.	7th son.
Lionel Duke of Clarence.	John of Gaunt, Duke Lancaster.	Edmund Langley, Duke of York.	William of Windsor.	Thomas of Woodstock, Duke of Gloucester.

Philippa daughter and heir. = Edmond Earl of March.

Edward Duke of York. o. s. p.

Richard Earl of Cambridge, m. Anne, daughter of Roger Earl of March. (See on the left.)

Anne, daughter and heir. = Edmund Earl of Stafford.

Roger Earl of March. =

Humphry Duke of Buckingham.

Anne, daughter and heir, m. Richard Earl of Cambridge, grandfather of King Edward IV. and Richard III. (See on the right.)

Richard Duke of York, slain at Wakefield. =

Humphry Earl of Stafford.

King Edward IV.   King Richard III.

Henry Duke of Buckingham.

1 Grafton, p. 154.; Edmondson's Heraldry, p. 154.
2 Buck, lib. i. p. 26.

Duke of Norfolk carried the crown, the Earl of Surrey the sword of state, and the Lord Stanley the much-coveted mace of constableship. True, this high office was secured to him immediately after the coronation, together with the lands of the De Bohuns[1]; but the canker-worm of envy and mortified vanity had previously turned the selfish love of Buckingham to hatred, — as selfishly and unworthily indulged.

Obscure as may be the ostensible cause, nevertheless the compact between the duke and his prisoner, Bishop Morton, admits not of doubt; neither, indeed, does the fact, that at its final ratification the southern countries were on the eve of open rebellion to release the young princes from the Tower.[2] The two conspirators at Brecknock felt assured, therefore, that no sooner could a report be circulated that the princes were dead, than the insurgents would readily fall into the plot which was about to be formed in favour of the Earl of Richmond, and of which Buckingham determined to propose himself as the captain and leader[3]; while King Richard could scarcely fail to be caught in the net thus doubly prepared to ensnare him,

---

[1] On the 13th of July, in the first year of Richard III., Henry Stafford, Duke of Buckingham, had livery of all those lands whereunto he pretended a right by descent as cousin and heir of blood to Humfrey de Bohun, Earl of Hereford and constable of England; and within two days after was advanced to the high and great office of constable of England, as also constituted by the king constable of all the castles and steward of all the lordships lying within the counties of Salop and Hereford, and likewise chief justice and chamberlain of all South Wales and North Wales. — *Edmondson's Constables of England,* p. 30.

[2] Chron. Croy., p. 567.

[3] Ibid.

by being compelled either to produce his nephews, and thus accelerate the operations of the insurgents, or be overwhelmed by the yet more formidable league, which would unite both parties in supporting the pretensions of the Earl of Richmond, if the belief gained ground of the murder of the princes.[1] Violently opposed to King Richard, and personally attached to his former royal masters, Henry VI. and Edward IV., Morton hailed with delight any proposition that would shake the stability of the newly-created monarch, and give ultimate hope of uniting the lineages of York and Lancaster[2]; con-

---

[1] The imposture of Lambert Simnell, in the succeeding reign, is attributed by Lord Bacon to a corresponding scheme for compelling King Henry to produce the person, or avow the death, of Edward Earl of Warwick. A report generally prevailed that that monarch had put to death, secretly within the Tower, this hapless prince, the last male heir of the line of Plantagenet. With the view of ascertaining this fact, and the better to advance his interest if alive, a youth of corresponding age and appearance was brought forward by the partizans of the house of York to counterfeit the person of the Earl of Warwick, with a report of his having escaped from his murderers; it being agreed that if all things succeeded well, he should be put down and the true Plantagenet received. King Henry, alarmed for the safety of his throne, caused " Edward Plantagenet, then a close prisoner in the Tower, to be shewed in the most public and notorious manner that could be devised unto the people : in part," continues Lord Bacon, " to discharge the king of the envy of that opinion, and bruite [report] how he had been put to death privily in the Tower, but chiefly to make the people see the levity and imposture of the proceedings." The part pursued by the ecclesiastic at Oxford and the Earl of Lincoln, the chief supporters of Simnell and the bitter opponents of Henry VII., bears a singular analogy to the conduct of Bishop Morton and the Duke of Buckingham as regards King Richard III. and the young princes. — See *Bacon's Henry VII.*, pp. 19. 36.

[2] " The bishop, which favoured ever the house of Lancaster, was wonderfully joyful and much rejoiced to hear this device; for now came the wind about even as he would have it; for all his indignation tended to this effect, to have King Richard subdued, and to have the

sequently the most resolute but cautious measures were speedily adopted by the duke and the bishop to carry their scheme into immediate execution. As a necessary preliminary, a trusty messenger, Reginald Bray, was sent to the Countess of Richmond, informing her of the high destiny contemplated for her son, and requiring her co-operation in the conspiracy. Transported with joy at intelligence so far exceeding her most sanguine expectations, the Lady Margaret willingly undertook to break the matter to the widowed queen and the young princess[1], both still immured in the Sanctuary at Westminster; which difficult office was ably accomplished through the medium of Dr. Lewis, a physician of great repute attached to the household of the Countess of Richmond, who was instructed to condole with the queen on the reported death of her sons, and forthwith to propose the restoration of the crown to her surviving offspring by the marriage of the princess royal with Henry of Richmond.[2] Oppressed with grief, as the dowager queen is represented to have been[3], when informed of the untimely end of her two sons, she yet hailed with great thankfulness a suggestion that gave promise of brightened prospects for her daughters; and, entering with alacrity into the scheme, she promised the entire aid of her late husband's friends and her own kindred, provided always that the Earl of Richmond would solemnly swear " to espouse and take to wife the Lady

lines of King Edward and Henry VI. again raised and advanced."— *Grafton*, p. 160.
[1] Grafton, p. 162.   [2] Ibid.   [3] Ibid. p. 164.

Elizabeth, or else the Lady Cecily, if her eldest sister should not be living." [1]

For the more speedy accomplishment of the project, the Countess of Richmond had returned to the metropolis, and taken up her abode at her husband's dwelling place within the city of London [2], so that daily communication passed between the countess and the queen in sanctuary, through the intervention of Dr. Lewis the physician; and a powerful ally of the Duke of Buckingham, Hugh Conway, Esquire, with Christopher Urswick the Lady Margaret's confessor, were speedily sent to Brittany " with a great sum of money," [3] to communicate to the Earl of Richmond the fair prospect that had dawned for terminating his captivity, and ensuring his honourable reception in England. In the west country, Buckingham and Bishop Morton exerted themselves with equal zeal and determination: but the wily prelate, whether through apprehension of the duke's stability, or from a desire of effectually securing his own safety by flight, took advantage of the trust reposed in him by his noble host, and stealthily departing from Brecknock Castle proceeded secretly to his see of Ely. There securing both money and partizans, he effected his escape into France, and, joining the Earl of Richmond, devoted himself to his interest during the remainder of King Richard's troubled reign. [4]

[1] Grafton, p. 166.

[2] Derby House, on the site of which the College of Arms now stands; a princely abode, erected on St. Benett's Hill, by the Lord Stanley, shortly before his marriage with the Countess of Richmond. — *Edmondson*, p. 143.

[3] Grafton, p. 166.   [4] Ibid. p. 163.

The Duke of Buckingham, although greatly discomfited and mortified by the treachery of Morton, who acted towards him the same disingenuous part which in a greater degree he was pursuing towards his sovereign, was nevertheless too deeply involved in the conspiracy to shrink from prosecuting his scheme, even after he had been abandoned by his coadjutor, and that at a time "when he had most need of his aid."[1]

He stedfastly persevered in his object, communicating with the Yorkist leaders, enlisting on his side the disaffected of all parties, and gaining over to his cause the chief supporters of the late king, together with many ancient partizans of the fallen house of Lancaster, who had slumbered but not slept over the calamitous events which marked the extinction of their party. Thus gradually, but guardedly pursuing his design, the Duke of Buckingham soon collected sufficient force to enable him to co-operate with Henry of Richmond, when the plot should be sufficiently ripened to admit of his projected invasion of the realm.[2] All these proceedings and secret schemes were planned and carried out during King Richard's progress from Warwick to York: but whether the confederacy had wholly escaped detection before his second coronation, or whether the monarch dissembled his knowledge of the league until such time as he could trace the object of the conspiracy and ascertain who were its leaders, is not altogether clear. Thus much is certain: that on the 24th of Sep-

[1] Grafton, p. 163. [2] Ibid. p. 169.

tember, a few days after Richard's return to Pontefract, the Duke of Buckingham sent to the Earl of Richmond, directing him to land in England on the 18th of October[1], on which day the conspirators had arranged to rise simultaneously in anticipation of his arrival. That Richard betrayed no suspicion of the impending danger, is evident from the whole tenor of his conduct at York; neither were any measures adopted at Pomfret that could admit of just inference that he apprehended the landing of a rival. It may be that he despised the pretensions of Richmond, arising as they did from an illegitimate source; or that he was too much engrossed with preparations for his second coronation to examine into the vague reports that reached him. This latter surmise, however, is scarcely consistent with Richard's active and wary character. If he felt the danger, it is more probable that his tranquillity was assumed, that it was a mere veil to conceal knowledge which it was not politic to disclose to the world: but the former view is on the whole the most likely, considering the slender claim which a spurious branch of the usurping House of Lancaster could have upon the throne.

The history of the Earl of Richmond is briefly told.[2] His connection with the extinct dynasty has been already detailed in a note at the commencement of this Memoir, when treating of the rivalship between the Lords of York and Somerset: but a brief recapitulation at this crisis

[1] Rot. Parl., vi. p. 245.
[2] Table showing the descent of Henry Earl of Richmond from John of Gaunt, Duke of Lancaster. (See opposite.)

will serve to render more apparent the shallow
grounds on which he asserted a claim to the crown.
John of Gaunt, fourth son of Edward III., had
three wives. By his first, the heiress of the house
of Lancaster (from marriage with whom he acquired that title), he had two daughters[1] and one
son, afterwards King Henry IV., the founder of
the Lancastrian dynasty. By his second wife, a
Castilian princess, he had an only child, a daughter[2]:
and by his third wife, who was previously his
mistress, he had four children[3], born before mar-

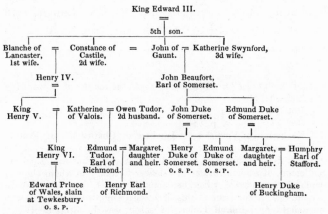

[1] Philippa, the eldest daughter, was united to John King of
Portugal, and her descendants for seven generations governed that
kingdom. Elizabeth, the second daughter, married John Holland,
Duke of Exeter.

[2] This princess, Katherine, espoused Henry Prince of Asturias,
the eldest son of the King of Spain. Their posterity continued
sovereigns of that realm until the year 1700.

[3] These children were —

1. John, afterwards created Earl of Somerset.

2. Henry, the renowned Cardinal Beaufort, Bishop of Winchester.

3. Thomas, created Duke of Exeter, and eventually chancellor of
England.

4. Joan, married to Ralph Neville, Earl of Westmoreland. She

riage, and surnamed De Beaufort, from the place of their birth. These children were eventually legitimated by act of parliament[1], although a special reservation was made (in the letters patent[2]), excluding them from succession to the crown.[3] From this corrupt source sprang the Duke of Somerset, father of the Countess of Richmond. She was united at the early age of fourteen to Edmond Tudor, Earl of Richmond, half-brother of King Henry VI.[4], and one child, a son, was the fruit of this union. Immense riches had centred in the Lady Margaret, herself an only child[5]; and her husband's near relationship to the Lancastrian monarch conferred upon their offspring at his birth a very distinguished position. This was increased

was the parent of Cecily Duchess of York, the mother of Edward IV. and Richard III.

[1] Rot. Parl., vol. iii. p. 343.   [2] Excerpta Hist., p. 152.

[3] Rot. Parl., vol. v. p. 343.

[4] Katherine of Valois, only daughter of Charles VI. of France, and the widowed queen of King Henry V., as also mother of his successor King Henry VI., selected for her second husband a private gentleman, of ancient lineage but slender fortune ; to whom she was clandestinely married when her son, Henry VI., was about seven years of age. The issue of this ill-advised union was three sons and one daughter : Edmund Tudor, the eldest, was the father of Henry of Richmond, afterwards King Henry VII., by marriage with the Lady Margaret Beaufort, heiress of John Duke of Somerset. Jasper Tudor, the second son, was a remarkable character during the rule of the house of York, and the chief agent in the preservation of the life of his nephew, Henry of Richmond, and of his subsequent elevation to the throne. Owen Tudor, the third son, and Katherine Tudor, their sister, died in the prime of life.

[5] John, first Duke of Somerset (grandson of John of Gaunt), died in the fourth year after his marriage, at the age of 39. His title, from default of male heirs, passed to his next brother, Edmond de Beaufort ; but in all else, his daughter and only child, then not quite three years old, became sole heiress to his vast possessions. — See *Life of Margaret Beaufort*, p. 17.

by the premature death of the Earl of Richmond, and likewise from King Henry VI. being reputed to have prognosticated great things of his infant heir, the young earl[1], who thenceforth became an object of jealousy to the house of York, and of corresponding interest to the line of Lancaster. At the brief restoration of King Henry VI., Henry of Richmond was in his fourteenth year. His prospects at that time were most promising, and he was completing his education at Eton[2], when the fatal battle of Tewkesbury having re-established the race of York on the throne, and effectually ruined the Lancastrian cause, he was secretly conveyed from England through the affectionate solicitude of his uncle, the Earl of Pembroke, himself also a half-brother of Henry VI.[3] A furious storm cast the fugitives upon the shores of Brittany[4], where, being treacherously dealt with by the reigning duke of that principality, the young earl was made captive, and detained a state prisoner, in which hapless position he had con-

---

[1] " One day, when King Henry VI., whose innocency gave him holiness, was washing his hands at a great feast, and cast his eye upon Richmond, then a young youth, he exclaimed, ' This is the lad who shall possess quietly that we now strive for.' "—*Bacon's Henry VII.*, p. 247.

[2] Sandford's Geneal. Hist., vol. vi. ch. 10.

[3] Buck's Richard III., p. 16.

[4] The wind being contrary, and its violence extreme, they were driven far out of their course, and after having been placed in imminent peril, and preserved by little less than a miracle, they were at length cast upon the shores of Brittany. They gained St. Maloes with some difficulty, and were resting there to recruit their exhausted energies, when information having been forwarded to Francis, the reigning duke of that state, he forthwith ordered them to be arrested and conveyed as prisoners to the castle of Vannes. — *Life of Margaret Beaufort*, p. 85.

tinued a victim to hopeless captivity up to the period when his mother so earnestly besought the intercession of the Duke of Buckingham towards effecting his release, and obtaining his pardon from Richard III.

Considering that a special reservation of the royal dignity had been inserted in the patent of legitimation exemplified and confirmed by Henry IV.[1] at the earnest request of his kinsmen the de Beauforts[2], the Yorkist sovereign would appear to have needlessly apprehended danger from the captive earl: but the deadly feud which had ever existed between Richard Duke of York, father of Edward IV., and John Duke of Somerset, grandfather to Henry Earl of Richmond, the two great leaders of the rival factions, had rendered the illustrious exile a subject of suspicion and hatred to the house of York.[3] The affection with which Henry VI. regarded his half-brothers, and the distinguished position which the young Richmond held as the nephew[4] of the reigning monarch,

[1] The patent of legitimation which was exemplified and confirmed by Henry IV. on the 10th of February 1407, at the request of the Earl of Somerset, is to this effect: — "We do, in the fulness of our royal power, and by the assent of parliament, by the tenor of these presents empower you to be raised, promoted, elected, assume, and be admitted to all honours, dignities (*except to the royal dignity*), pre-eminences, estates, and offices, public and private, whatsoever, as well spiritual as temporal." — *Rot. Parl.*, vol. iii. p. 343.

[2] Excerpta Hist., p. 152.

[3] One of the earliest proceedings of Edward IV. was to attaint the young Earl of Richmond (*Rot. Parl.*, 1 Edw. IV. p. 2.), and by letters patent he stripped him of his territorial possessions, and bestowed them upon his brother, George Duke of Clarence. —*Report on the Dignity of the Peerage*, p. 130.

[4] " In the act of attainder passed after his accession, Henry VII. calls himself nephew of Henry VI." — *Historic Doubts*, p. 100.

linked him so closely with the Lancastrian dynasty,
that it strengthened the apprehension inspired by
his being the heir male of the house of Somerset,
after the battle of Tewkesbury had rendered the
royal line extinct. Innumerable were the efforts
made by Edward IV. to obtain possession of the
attainted earl. Costly presents were sent to
Francis Duke of Brittany, and great sums offered
to ransom his victim[1]: these overtures failing,
King Edward, at the expiration of a few years,
adopted a different course; and under the plea of
sympathy for the young earl, and a desire to bury
past differences in oblivion, he sent ambassadors
to sue for his release, and to proffer him the hand
of his eldest daughter, the Princess Elizabeth.[2]
This subtle device had well nigh cost Richmond
his life; for the Duke of Brittany, deceived by the
well-dissembled protestations of King Edward, consented to release his captive. Happily, however,
for the earl, the plot was made known to him, and
escaping into sanctuary[3], he eluded and defied the
malice of his enemies. Francis of Brittany was a
wary prince. The custody of Henry of Richmond
was a constant source of emolument to himself and
his principality, from the bribes sent by Edward IV.
in the hope of obtaining the earl's release; and
moreover, from the evident importance attached to
his prisoner, his continued safety rendered him
always a hostage for unbroken and friendly alliance
with the English. Under these considerations,

---

[1] Philip de Comines, p. 516.   [2] Cott. MSS., Dom. A. xviii.
[3] Lobineau, l'Histoire de Britagne, vol. i. p. 751.

Francis again tendered his protection to Richmond, who quitted the sanctuary on receiving a pledge that, although he must still be considered as a state prisoner, he should no longer be subjected to rigorous confinement.   At the death of Edward IV. the attainted earl had been thirteen years an exile and a captive: nevertheless, the decease of his persecutor made no change in the conduct pursued by his captor.   True, his misfortunes, his gentleness, his noble bearing, and entire submission to his cruel lot, had gradually gained him many powerful friends at the court of Brittany; still the reigning duke kept a vigilant watch over his proceedings, and any faint hope of liberation in which he may have indulged during the brief reign of Edward V. was effectually crushed by the decisive measures pursued by Richard III. immediately after his accession to the throne.   One of this monarch's first acts was to despatch Sir Thomas Hutton to renew the existing treaty with Francis[1], and to stipulate for the continued imprisonment of Richmond[2]; and with the view of securing this latter desirable object, the most costly presents were sent, not alone to the duke himself, but also to his counsellors and the leading persons of his court.   Such was the position of Henry Earl of Richmond when the prospect of the English crown, together with the proffered hand of the princess royal[3], gave promise of future honours that contrasted very remarkably

---

[1] Harl. MSS., 433. fol. 241.   [2] Grafton, p. 169.

[3] " The Duke of Buckingham, by the advice of the Bishop of Ely, his prisoner at Brecknock, sent to him to hasten to England as soon as he could, to have to wife Elizabeth, elder daughter of the deceased king, and together with her, possession of all the realm." — Cont. Croy., p. 568.

with the forlorn situation which had characterised his early youth and manhood.[1] The presence and counsels of the Bishop of Ely inspired him with confidence, and the vast sums of money sent him by his mother enabled him privately to enlist in his cause many persons of high military reputation, exiled followers of Henry VI., who had for years lingered in the extreme of poverty. Richmond's next measure was frankly to make known his bright prospects to the Duke of Brittany[2], of whom he earnestly besought assistance; but the recent compact between Francis and Richard precluded the possibility of his sanctioning his enterprise. Nevertheless, touched with compassion for one who had so meekly submitted to the restraints imposed upon him for so many years, he so far yielded as to pledge himself not to oppose his undertaking; and under that assurance, Richmond exerted himself so strenuously, and was supported by so powerful a band, both of Yorkist and Lancastrian exiles, that he was enabled to respond to the call of Buckingham, and to pledge himself to arrive in England by the day fixed upon for the general rising, viz. the 18th of October.

However scrupulously the commencement of this formidable league was concealed, it had evidently reached King Richard's ears before its final ratification. "The conspiracy," says the Croyland his-

[1] Philip de Comines, who was well known to the Earl of Richmond, states, that he told him, even from his birth, he had scarcely known the blessings of liberty, having been either a fugitive or a captive from the age of five years. — *Philip de Comines,* vol. v. p. 514.

[2] Grafton, p. 168.

torian[1], "by means of spies was well known to Richard, who, in manner as he executed all his designs, not drowsily, but with alacrity and with the greatest vigilance, procured, as well in Wales as in all the marches there, in the circuit of the said Duke of Buckingham, that as soon as he set foot out of his house, esquires should be in prompt readiness, who, animated by the duke's great wealth, which the king for that purpose conferred upon them, should seize upon the same, and by all means impede his progress; which was done. For on that side of the castle towards Wales, Thomas, son of Sir Roger Vaughan deceased, with his brethren and relatives, most strictly watched all the circumjacent country; and the bridges and passages leading to England were partly broken down, and partly closed under strict guards by Humphrey Stafford."

It cannot but tell greatly in Richard's favour, that these last-mentioned individuals, the grandchildren of old Sir Thomas Vaughan, whom he has been reproached with unjustly executing, and Sir Humphrey Stafford, the near relative of Buckingham himself, should have so decidedly espoused the king's cause as to be willing agents for entrapping the rebellious duke; neither can it escape observation, that the reputed avenger of the princes' alleged murder, instead of bringing forward the Earl of Warwick, or advocating exclusively the rights of the Princess Elizabeth, lawfully the inheritor of the crown,—if indeed proof existed that

[1] Chron. Croy., p. 508.

her brothers were really dead, — should have selected as the successor to their throne an illegitimate scion of the extinct house of Lancaster, and by making the Princess Elizabeth a secondary consideration, have thus perpetuated to the house of York the very act of injustice for which they condemned King Richard.

It is more than probable from the wording of Dr. Hutton's instructions[1], on his mission to the court of Brittany, that the plot for restoring the Lancastrian dynasty in the person of Henry of Richmond had been contemplated before the deposition of Edward V., and that the report of the alleged death of the royal brothers was spread by the Lancastrian agents[2] to further views which had been contemplated at the accession of the young king, arising out of the disturbed state of the realm at that period, but which had been promptly dissipated by the firm and vigilant government of Richard, both as protector and king. That the Duke of Buckingham should have risked the uncertain favour of a kinsman to whom he was

[1] In instructions given to Dr. Thomas Hutton, who was sent to the Duke of Brittany for the ostensible purpose of renewing a commercial treaty, which " *by diverse folks of simple disposition* " was supposed to have expired in the death of Edw. IV., is the following passage : — " Item, He shall seek and understand the mind and disposition of the duke, anenst Sir Edward Wydville and his retinue, practising by all means to him possible, to unsearch and know if there *be intended any enterprise out of land,* upon any part of this realm, certifying with all diligence all the views and depositions there from time to time." — *Harl. MSS.,* 433. fol. 241.

[2] The Croyland historian, after stating that " it was reported that King Edward's children were dead," adds, " all those who began this commotion, seeing that they could not find a new captain, they called to mind Henry Earl of Richmond, who had now for many years dwelt in exile in Brittany." — *Cont. Croy.,* p. 568.

personally unknown, — one that had been long
estranged from his country, and was an alien to its
laws and customs, — when the monarch whom but
a few weeks previously he had aided to elevate
to the throne was manifesting on all occasions his
gratitude, and showering down his gifts most
liberally upon him, is a mystery that defies solution! How keenly Richard felt his treachery,
and how bitterly he resented it, is not, however,
subject of surmise, being recorded in his own handwriting, in a confidential postscript to a letter[1]
addressed to the Lord Chancellor, a document so
replete with interest as pourtraying the true nature
of the king's sentiments and feelings on this momentous occasion, that it demands unabbreviated
insertion in this memoir of his life.

" By the King.

" Right reverend Father in God, and right trusty
and well-beloved, we greet you well, and in our
heartiest wise thank you for manifold presents[2]
that your servants in their behalf have presented
unto us at this our being here, which we assure
you we took and accepted with good heart, and so

[1] This letter from Richard III. to Russel, Bishop of Lincoln, was,
extracted from the original in the Record Office in the Tower by
Strype. It was printed in a note to Buck's History of Richard III.,
in Kennet's Complete History of England; and was also published
by Singer in an Appendix to his revised and corrected edition of Sir
Thomas More's History of Richard III. The postscript is in the
king's own hand, and is most interesting for the earnestness with
which it dwells on Buckingham's treachery.

[2] The Bishop of Lincoln at this time filled the office of lord
chancellor, and these words allude to Richard's abode in his see,
and probably also to his residence at the ecclesiastical palace at
Lincoln.

have cause. And whereas we by God's grace intend to advance us towards our rebel and traitor
the Duke of Buckingham, to resist and withstand
his malicious purpose, as lately by our other
letters[1] we certified you our mind more at large;
for which cause it behoveth us to have our great
seal here, we being informed that for such infirmities and diseases as ye sustain, ye may not in
your person to your ease conveniently come unto
us with the same : Wherefore we will, and natheless charge you, that forthwith, upon the sight of
this, ye safely do cause the same our great seal to
be sent unto us; and such of the office of our chancery as by your wisdom shall be thought necessary,
receiving these our letters for your sufficient discharge in that behalf.

     " Given under our signet, at our city of
    Lincoln, the 12th day of October."

Then follows the postscript in the king's own
handwriting.

" We would most gladly ye came yourself, if that
ye may; and if ye may not, we pray you not to
fail, but to accomplish in all diligence our said
commandment to send our seal incontinent upon
the sight hereof, as we trust you, with such as ye
trust, and the officers perteining [appertaining] to
attend with it : praying you to ascertain us of your
news there. Here, loved be God, is all well, and
truly determined, and for to resist the malice of
him that had best cause to be true, the Duke of

---

[1] This expression justifies the inference that King Richard knew
of the conspiracy before his arrival at Lincoln.

Buckingham,—the most untrue creature living: whom with God's grace we shall not be long 'till that we will be in that parts, and subdue his malice. We assure you there was never falser traitor purveyed for; as this bearer Gloucester[1] shall show you."

This remarkable letter, as appears by its date, was written at Lincoln on the 12th October, a few days after the king is stated to have received from Buckingham an avowal of his perfidy, arising out of a refusal to attend the royal summons[2], the monarch having invited his personal attendance with the view of ascertaining the truth or falsehood of a report which he could not bring himself to believe without such substantial proof.

Richard's character was one of determined resolution; and although it can scarcely be said that he was devoid of suspicion, yet every record favours the belief, that he unwillingly credited reports to the disadvantage of his friends, and placed in all who were personally attached to his service a confidence that in many cases was shown to be miserably abused.[3]

Once roused, however, Richard was as firm in resisting his opponents as he was generous in recompensing his followers; and Buckingham, having openly avowed himself " his mortal enemy," and

---

[1] Richard Champney, the favoured king-at-arms of Richard III. This office was founded because it had been the name of Richard's ducal honour, a practice then usual; Edward IV. before, and Henry VII. after, making their heralds kings-at-arms, giving them the names of the titles they bore. — See *Noble's College of Arms*, p. 65.; likewise *Edmondson's Heraldry*, p. 99.

[2] Grafton, p. 171.

[3] More, p. 9.

hoisted the standard of rebellion, the monarch adopted the most rigorous measures for defeating the insurgents, and crushing the conspiracy. He despatched a letter[1] to the authorities of York, requiring their aid in this emergency, and desiring that such troops as they could furnish should meet him at Leicester on the 21st inst. This was followed by a proclamation, dated likewise at Lincoln, declaring the Duke of Buckingham a traitor; and he was proclaimed as such at York, as appears by the municipal records of that city, " on the 16th October."[2] This same day, the Lord Chancellor continuing too ill to attend the king, he delivered up the great seal " at the Old Temple, London, in a great chamber near the garden."[3] It was intrusted to the keeping of one of the clerks in Chancery, and was by him restored to the king himself[4] three days afterwards, " at Grantham, in a chamber called the kynge's chamber, in the Angel Inn, in the presence of the Earls of Northumberland and Huntingdon, and of Sir Thomas Stanley."[5] From

[1] See Appendix T.
[2] Drake's Eborac., p. 119.   [3] Fœdera, vol. xii. p. 203.
[4] The king retained the great seal until the 26th November, and sealed with it numerous writs, commissions, &c., and on that day returned it to the chancellor. — *Fœdera*, vol. xii. p. 203.
[5] This nobleman, who filled the most confidential situation about the person of the king, was the father-in-law of Henry Earl of Richmond, having espoused Margaret Countess of Richmond, whose exertions in behalf of her son have been recently described. The trust thus reposed in one so closely connected with the rebels, is perhaps one of the strongest instances that could be adduced of Richard's unsuspicious disposition ; it also induces the belief, that the Lady Margaret, whose wisdom and strength of mind was very remarkable, anxious for the restoration of her son, but unwilling to compromise the safety of her husband, had carefully concealed from him all knowledge of the league to which she was lending her aid.

Grantham, where Richard is thus shown to have rested on the 19th inst., he proceeded to Melton Mowbray, leaving that town on the 21st for Leicester. By this time the greater part of the kingdom was in open rebellion. The Marquis of Dorset, escaping from sanctuary, had gathered together a formidable band of men in Yorkshire. The Bishop of Exeter, and his brother Sir Edward Courtney, raised another army in Devonshire and Cornwall; in Kent, Sir Richard Guildford[1], heading a company of soldiers, had openly begun the war[2], and Henry Earl of Richmond, having collected " an army of 500 manly Bretons, and forty well-furnished ships," sailed from Brittany on the 12th inst., hoping to land at Plymouth, as instructed by the confederates, on the 18th of October.[3] But King Richard was by no means dismayed. Intrepid bravery was a leading feature in his character; nevertheless, his valour was always tempered with judgment. He met danger promptly, fearlessly, resolutely; yet he calmly revolved every auxiliary measure that might best secure to him final success; and, with a singular mixture of energy and coolness, would, within the same hour, direct military movements and issue civil processes, and this with a rapidity of thought, keen foresight, and calm deliberation, that awed his opponents, and inspired confidence in his partizans.

---

[1] The Guildfords were a distinguished family seated at Hempsted in Kent. Sir Edward Guildford, son of the above-named Sir Richard, was father-in-law to the celebrated John Dudley, Duke of Northumberland, whose son was united to Lady Jane Grey.

[2] Grafton, p. 171.   [3] Ibid. p. 177.

Rous [1] states that he forthwith hastened with a
large army into the south: other contemporary
documents show how little he trusted to mere force
of arms alone, and with what a master mind he
grasped the extent of the evil with which he was so
suddenly encompassed. During his stay at Leicester
he put forth a proclamation [2], offering 1000*l.*, or
100*l.* a year for life, on the capture of the Duke
of Buckingham; 1000 marks for the Marquis of
Dorset, or his uncle Lionel Bishop of Salisbury, the
son and brother of the widowed queen; and 500 on
the arrest of other leading insurgents, who are
therein specified. [3] The following day a vice-con-
stable [4] was nominated, and invested with extraordinary powers to judge and execute, without
delay, such of the rebels as were captured or betrayed into his hands. [5] The marches of Wales, the
bridges, fords, and ordinary passes [6], were guarded
by trusty bands of soldiers, well acquainted with
that part of the country, as well as with the person
of the Duke of Buckingham; men altogether opposed to his rebellious views, and well affected
towards the king. Vessels of war were stationed
in the channel to keep a careful watch, not alone
on any ships that were advancing to England, but

---

[1] Rous, p. 216. [2] See Appendix U.

[3] Fœdera, vol. xii. p. 204.

[4] This appointment was rendered necessary, because the Duke of
Buckingham filled the office of constable of England, to which, it will
be remembered, that he preferred an hereditary claim, and to which
high office he was nominated immediately after King Richard's
coronation. — *Edmondson's Heraldry,* p. 30.

[5] Fœdera, vol. xii. p. 205. [6] Chron. Croy., p. 568.

also on all boats that approached the coast, or were observed departing from its shores.[1]

Thus prepared at all points, the monarch quitted Leicester on the 23rd October, and arrived at Coventry on the 24th, proceeding from thence to Salisbury, in consequence of information that the coalition sought to be effected between Buckingham and Richmond was to take place in the southern counties.

Decisive and ably concerted as had been the king's arrangements, yet these were so evenly balanced by the vigilant and determined measures of the conspirators[2], that the issue would probably have been doubtful, had not a series of misadventures brought to a speedy close the turbulent and undisciplined career of the capricious Buckingham. On the 18th of October[3], in conformity with his pledge to the Earl of Richmond, the duke assumed the command of the Welsh rebels, proceeding from Brecknock Castle to Weobly, the seat of Walter Devereux, Lord Ferrers[4], enlisting on his route, either by violence or bribery, a strong addition to his force. He from thence marched rapidly through the Forest of Dean, and reached the confines of the city of Gloucester by the time the king had advanced within two days' journey of Salisbury[5], intending to cross the Severn at the former city, and thence to march southward and form a junction with the army raised in the west

---

[1] Chron. Croy., p. 568.   [2] Grafton, p. 169.
[3] Rot. Parl., vi. p. 245.   [4] Chron. Croy., p. 568.
[5] Grafton, p. 172.

by the Courtneys[1]; which " if he had done," says Grafton, " no doubt but King Richard had been in great jeopardy, either of privation of his realm or loss of his life, or both."[2]

But during the duke's progress through Wales, violent storms and a continual rain of ten days had caused the Severn to rise and overflow its banks[3], producing a sudden inundation so extensive that the bridges were broken down, the fords impassable; and the cattle being drowned in their pastures, a scarcity of provisions ensued, which increased the privations that his followers had already endured from the inclemency of the weather during their toilsome march to Gloucester. Unable to join his confederates, or to communicate with them, and destitute of the means of appeasing the soldiery, who murmured at being " without money, victual, or wages,"[4] Buckingham was reluctantly compelled to yield to their clamours, and return back to Weobly.[5] Dispirited at the failure of the enterprise, which they superstitiously viewed as an ill omen, the Welshmen dispersed, and departed to their homes; and for all the Duke's fair promises, threatenings, and enforcements, they would " in no wise neither go farther nor abide."

[1] " So great was the influence of the Courtney family at this period, that the inhabitants both of Devon and Cornwall flocked to their standard." — *Jenkins' Hist. of Exeter*, p. 88.

[2] Grafton, p. 172.

[3] " Insomuch that men were drowned in their beds, and houses with the extreme violence were overturned; children were carried about the fields swimming in cradles, beasts were drowned on hills; which rage of water lasted continually ten days, insomuch that in the country adjoining they call it to this day the Great Water, or the Duke of Buckingham's Great Water." — *Grafton*, p. 173.

[4] Grafton, p. 173.   [5] Chron. Croy., p. 568.

Thus deserted by his followers, the peril of the Duke of Buckingham became extreme. His own castle was in the hands of the Vaughans, who immediately after he had departed from Breck-nock, seized and plundered it, making captive his daughters[1] and their attendant gentlewomen.[2]

The proclamation issued by the king, offering so large a reward for his apprehension, and threatening such severe penalties for his conceal-ment, completed the measure of his misfortune, and rendered his situation so desperate that, finding himself closely watched even by his own kindred, and that he could " on no side make his egress with safety,"[3] he suddenly quitted his associates, and departed from Weobly in disguise; first, however, providing with fond affection for the concealment

---

[1] The Duke of Buckingham had two daughters, both older than his sons. Grafton states (p. 65.), that a compact was made during the brief reign of Edward V., that Buckingham should aid Richard's elevation to the throne, on condition that he pledged him-self to ally his only son, Edward Earl of Salisbury, to one of the duke's daughters. Buck farther asserts, that the Duke of Bucking-ham felt himself aggrieved at the breach of promise in the king for not joining the prince his son in marriage with the Lady Ann Stafford, his daughter. — *Buck*, lib. i. p. 35. If this was the case, Buckingham's jealousy must have been aroused by the favourable reception given by Richard to the Spanish ambassador, at Warwick, who sought an alliance with the youthful heir of the English crown and the eldest of the Princesses of Spain; but it must not be forgotten that Buckingham left the king in anger at Gloucester, which was previous to and altogether unconnected with the monarch's visit to Warwick.

[2] " Or ever my Lord of Buckingham departed out of Weobley, Brecknock was robbed, and [the assailants] fetched out the younger ladies and gentlewomen, and brought them to Sir Thomas Vaughan's place, the traitor which was captain of the said robbing." — From the *Stafford MSS.* published in *Blakeway's Shrewsbury*, vol. i. p. 241.

[3] Chron. Croy., p. 568.

of his infant' heir, the Lord Stafford, whose
preservation and wonderful escape from captivity
forms a fitting companion to the romantic history
of Lord Clifford's son, " the shepherd lord." [1] The
duke having effected his flight, in so secret a
manner that few or none of his household suspected his design [2], he sought shelter in the
dwelling of Humphrey Banastre, at Lacon near
Shrewsbury, hoping to find a sure but temporary
asylum with a follower "whom he above all men
loved, favoured, and trusted." [3] But the search
after the "proscribed traitor" had become too
active and unceasing to leave any probability of
Buckingham's escape. "One thousand pounds, or
one hundred a year for life," was a stimulus that
urged numbers to the most unwearied efforts to
discover his retreat: "whereof hearing," states
Fabyan, "the foresaid Banastre, were it for need
of the same reward, or fear of losing of his life and
goods, discovered the duke unto the sheriffs of the
shire, and caused him to be taken, and so brought
unto Salisbury, where the king then laid." [4]

How far Banastre merits the obloquy which has
attached to his memory, as the treacherous and mercenary betrayer of a kind and indulgent master, it
is hard to say; certainly the accounts transmitted
by the chronicler of Croyland, whose contemporary
authority on all points is so greatly esteemed, render
it doubtful whether, at least in the first instance, he
was accessory to the capture of his patron: "The

---

[1] See Appendix V.   [2] Fabyan, p. 517
[3] Grafton, p. 173.   [4] Fabyan, p. 517.

duke," as that historian states, " was at length discovered in a cottager's hut, in consequence of provisions of a superior kind being conveyed to him;"[1]
—a cause of suspicion so natural, that it contrasts
strikingly with the marvellous tales which cha-
racterise the relations of later chroniclers.[2] Without discussing a point which is so replete with
contradictions[3] that it adds another instance to the
many already adduced in this Memoir, showing
how little confidence can be placed in the reports
of a period[4] that, beyond all others in our national

---

[1] Chron. Croy., p. 568.

[2] " Whether this Banister betrayed the duke more for fear than
covetousness, many men do doubt ; but sure it is, that shortly after
he had betrayed the duke his master, his son and heir waxed mad,
and so died in a boar's sty ; his eldest daughter, of excellent beauty,
was suddenly stricken with a foul leprosy ; his second son very marvellously deformed of his limbs and made lame; his younger son in a
small puddle was strangled and drowned ; and he, being of extreme
old age, arraigned and found guilty of a murder, and by his clergy
saved."—*Grafton*, p. 176.

[3] Blakeway's Shrewsbury, vol. i. p. 256.

[4] Ralph, or Humphrey Banastre, as he is variously termed, was
not, as generally supposed, a humble servitor of the Duke of Buckingham, but a gentleman of ancient family and plentiful estate, who
had been brought up in the duke's house (see *Grafton*, p. 173.),
in accordance with the usage of those times ; and to whom his
patron presented himself as a guest, although an unhappy fugitive.
The Rev. J. B. Blakeway, in his valuable History of Shrewsbury
(vol. i. p. 236.), has entered minutely into the details of this interesting topic, and after proving that Banastre merited at first (and
possibly as long as it was in his power) the confidence reposed in
him, refutes the long-received tradition of retribution having
speedily followed his treachery ; arising from the fulfilment of curses
reputed to have been invoked upon the traitor, by the unhappy duke
upon his knees, in the orchard in which he had placed him at work
the better to ensure his betrayal. He also adds — after pointing out
the contradictory and erroneous statements of the early chroniclers —
" that no one has remembered the extreme peril of sheltering a traitor,
which would have been punished in that age by loss of life." There
can indeed be little doubt, after a careful review of the whole matter,

history, abounds in subjects of mysterious and romantic interest; it must suffice here to attest to
the fact of Buckingham's speedy capture by Thomas
Mytton, the sheriff of Shropshire[1], and to his delivery into Richard's hands[2] by Sir James Tyler[3],
at Salisbury, on All Souls Day, the 2d November,
1483.

Whatever commiseration may be excited for the
duke, arising from calamities which he could neither
foresee nor control, yet his heartless and unfaithful
conduct to the widowed queen his sister-in-law,
to his nephew Edward V., and to his friend and
kinsman Richard III., proves him to have been so
utterly bereft of principle, and so strongly actuated
by feelings of wild and selfish ambition, that few
will hesitate to admit that his premature death was
well merited, and altogether of his own seeking.
If any doubt prevails on this subject, the last act
contemplated by Buckingham would sufficiently

that Buckingham sought Banastre's protection, too late for any human
being to shelter him; and that Banastre, to save himself and his
family from destruction, was compelled eventually to sanction the
capture of one, too well known to admit of long concealment, and
whose retreat, according to the chronicler of Croyland, was already
tracked, owing to the hospitality of the individual whose life the
Duke had perilled to save his own.

[1] Fabyan, p. 517.; Hall, p. 395.; Grafton, p. 175.
[2] Stafford MSS. (in Blakeway), p. 241.
[3] From the large share of the Duke of Buckingham's wealth
bestowed upon Sir James Tyrrel so immediately after the execution
of the illustrious captive, it is probable that he was the individual
who delivered him into the king's hands; and that the carelessness
of the early writers, who misrepresented the Christian names both
of Banaster and the sheriff, occasioned Sir James Tyrrel's name to
be mis-spelt Tyler, and that he was one " of the two knights of
our lord the king " who were deputed to receive the rebel from the
authorities at Shrewsbury, as shown by the bailiff's accounts for that
year, extracted from the town records by its reverend historian.

expose the deadly malice and spirit of revenge which influenced his conduct to the king. He reached Salisbury on a Sunday; notwithstanding which, Richard, in conformity with the usage of those times, commanded his immediate execution. The duke earnestly besought, as his dying request, a personal interview with his royal master[1], who has been condemned in no measured terms for denying to his captive this last earnest desire. But Richard knew Buckingham too well to doubt that some sinister motive existed for a boon so strenuously urged; and his apparent severity was amply justified by the result, it being admitted in after years by the duke's own son, that his father had secreted a knife about his person, and that he had sought this conference with the king, intending to spring upon his victim[2] when in the act of prostrating himself to sue for pardon, and thus to deprive him by assassination of a crown, which he

[1] Fabyan, p. 517.

[2] " The duke, being by certain of the king's counsel diligently upon interrogatories examined, what things he knew prejudicial to the king's person, opened and declared frankly and freely the conjuration, without dissimulating or glozing, trusting, because he had truly and plainly revealed and confessed all things that were of him required, that he should have licence to speak to the king ; which, whether it were to sue for pardon or grace, or whether he, being brought to his presence, would have sticked him with a dagger, as men then judged, he sore desired and required." — *Grafton*, p. 176. This prevalent belief was fully confirmed in a subsequent reign, by the voluntary admission of Buckingham's heir and successor, the Lord Stafford, — whom, when an infant, his father had so strenuously exerted himself to save from his own perilous position ; for this nobleman, having contemplated similar treachery towards Henry VIII., confessed to the Duke of Buckingham's design, before he, like his unworthy sire, perished in the prime of his days by the hand of the public executioner. — *Herbert's Henry VIII.*, p. 110.

had failed to effect by conspiracy and rebellion. From this act of vindictive deliberate treachery King Richard's sagacity protected him, and Henry of Buckingham, within a few hours of his arrival at Salisbury[1], was beheaded, without trial, and "without speech or sight of the king," on a new scaffold erected for the purpose[2], in the market-place of that city. His remains, deprived of the head and right arm, the customary sentence of rebellion at that period, are said to have been recently disco-

[1] The oft-disputed point as to whether the Duke of Buckingham was executed at Salisbury or Shrewsbury, is set at rest by two important entries in the archives of the latter place, connected with the capture of the rebel, viz. " Money paid for divers costs and expences incurred, touching the custody of the Duke of Buckingham when he was taken and brought to the town, 6s. 4d. and for reward." Also, " Money paid for wine given to two knights of our lord the king, and to other gentlemen by command of the king, at the delivery of the said duke from the town, 16s. 6d." " These entries prove," observes the historian of Shrewsbury (who has published a literal transcript from the original entries), " that the duke was brought hither, but sent away to some other place for execution ; " and he farther adds (after adducing other items from the same roll of accounts, together with strong facts stated in the Stafford MS.), " as it is thus certain that Shrewsbury was not, it is equally certain that Salisbury was, the scene of this execution."—*Blakeway's Shrewsbury*, vol. i. p. 240. The venerable topographer of Wiltshire states, that the similarity of the names of Salisbury and Shrewsbury has led to many historical errors ; and after citing several examples, he traces the origin of the supposition of Buckingham having suffered death at Shrewsbury, to Grafton, who says that King Richard kept his court at that town when the duke was captured. As this chronicler, however, — together with Polydore Virgil and Hall, — agrees with the earlier writers, the Croyland annalist, and Fabyan, in placing his execution at Salisbury, the above statement was probably accidental, the one town being inserted by mistake for the other ; nevertheless it served to mislead Holinshed ; and, after him, Echard and Rapin were induced to represent the execution as having occurred, not at Salisbury, but at Shrewsbury.— *Sir R. C. Hoare's Hist. of Wiltshire*, p. 207.

[2] " Without arraignment or judgment, he was, in the open market-place, on a new scaffold, beheaded and put to death."—*Hall*, p. 395.

vered in digging to some depth on the site of a very ancient inn, which tradition has handed down was built on the spot where the execution took place.[1]

The defeat, capture, and summary punishment of their chief leader, inspired the other insurgents with terror and dismay, the more so as the fearful storms which had led to his destruction had proved equally disastrous to Henry of Richmond. Scarcely had he sailed from Brittany, ere his fleet was scattered and threatened with destruction, and after being himself exposed for many days to the fury of the waves, and narrowly escaping capture from the emissaries of King Richard, he was compelled to seek refuge in France, carrying with him the appalling news of Buckingham's death, and the total defeat of his adherents.[2] But although the

[1] Sir Richard Colt Hoare, in his History of Wiltshire, says, " that a stone is still pointed out in the city of Salisbury as that on which Buckingham suffered. It is in the yard adjoining the house which formerly belonged to the Blue Boar inn." This eminent antiquary and topographer adds, with reference to this subject, " The most remarkable circumstance connected with this locality is the recent discovery of a skeleton, found under the pavement in making some alterations in a kind of kitchen or out-house belonging to the Saracen's Head, which is close to the site of the Blue Boar. It was that of a person apparently above the middle size, and had been deprived of the head and right arm. The workmen by whom it was found omitted to notice whether or not the bones of the neck had been separated by a sharp instrument, but could remember that the bone of the arm appeared to have been cut off, just below the shoulder as if with a saw. These remains were destroyed without proper examination. Of itself the discovery would prove nothing : but if the fact of Buckingham's execution at Salisbury be considered as indisputably established, we shall not be guilty of too great a stretch of imagination in supposing that these were his mutilated remains, interred clandestinely, or at least without ceremony, near the spot where he suffered."—*Sir R. C. Hoare's Hist. of Wiltshire*, p. 207.

[2] Chron. Croy., p. 570.

rebellion had thus received so severe a check, yet Richard felt that the league itself was by no means broken.[1] Remaining, therefore, at Salisbury only sufficiently long to fulfil his pledges to those individuals who had aided him in capturing the deceased Duke of Buckingham[2], and to divide among such of his followers as had most faithfully and zealously supported him in the late perilous emergency, the vast riches of the attainted rebel[3], he broke up his camp, and proceeded towards Exeter, hoping to encounter Richmond if he had effected a landing at Plymouth, or to intercept the numerous detachments which were marching thither to assemble under his banner.

The monarch reached Exeter on the 10th of

[1] Fabyan, p. 517.

[2] King Richard was so well satisfied with the conduct of the burgesses of Shrewsbury on this critical occasion, that he pardoned, remitted, and released for ever twenty marks of the fee-farm yearly. — *Blakeway*, vol. i. p. 239.

[3] To the Lord Stanley he granted " the castle and lordship of Kimbolton, late belonging to the great rebel and traitor Henry Stafford, Duke of Buckingham," on the very day of his execution, being given " at Sarum the 2nd day of November, anno. 1mo."— *Harl. MSS.*, No. 433. p. 120. At the same city, and bearing a corresponding date, is a " commission to the Earl of Huntingdon, Sir James Tyrrel (who is in this instrument styled " the king's full trusty knight for his body "), and Morgan Kidwelly, to enter into all the castles of the Duke of Buckingham and other traitors in North Wales, South Wales, and in the marches, and to seize all his goods." — *Ibid.* p. 121. Corresponding commissions were directed for other counties; and in addition to these, a warrant was issued, commanding all rents belonging to such rebels and traitors as were therein named to be paid " to the king's full trusty squire, Thomas Fowler, gentleman usher of his chamber," whom he appoints to seize, for his use, certain castles, manors, &c. forfeited to the crown, " with the poceeds of which Richard most bountifully remunerated all who had served him faithfully in this conspiracy." — *Ibid.* p. 121.

November, at which city he learnt the extent of his own good fortune, and of the calamities which had befallen his opponents.   The recent tragedy at Salisbury, and the disastrous dispersion of Richmond's fleet and auxiliaries, had utterly dismayed even the most sanguine of his friends; but these dismal tidings being followed up by reports of the rapid advance of the king, supported by a powerful force, and holding out great rewards for the apprehension of the other chief confederates[1], so utterly dispirited them, that ere Richard entered the metropolis of the west, the conspiracy was altogether at an end, its leaders being either in sanctuary, in concealment, or escaped in vessels bound for the Continent.[2]   The few that were captured experienced no mercy.   Richard felt that the stability of his throne depended upon the firmness of his present proceedings.   He was in consequence unrelenting and inexorable, sparing no one who had instigated or headed the revolt; not even the husband of his own sister, who was one of the most violent of his opponents, and for whose life great sums of money were tendered.[3]

[1] A proclamation was issued on the king's departure from Salisbury for the taking of Sir John Guildford and several other of the king's rebels and traitors, offering 300 marcs, or 10*l.* of land, for capturing any of the six first mentioned in the proclamation, and a proportionate reward for any of the remaining individuals there specified; showing the king's intent to administer strict justice to all his subjects, the same instrument forbidding several evil practices under pain of death and other penalties.— *Harl. MSS.*, No. 433. p. 128.

[2] " Then all such gentlemen as had appointed to meet with the said duke were so dismayed, that they knew not what to do, but they that night fled the land, and some took sanctuary places, as they might win unto them." — *Fabyan*, p. 517.

[3] Chron. Croy., p. 569.

Little commiseration, however, can be felt for Sir Thomas St. Leger, in the just retribution which had overtaken him for the ungenerous part he had acted towards the high-minded Henry Holland, Duke of Exeter; whose miseries, when outlawed and proscribed for his fidelity to his lawful sovereign and kinsman Henry VI., were bitterly aggravated by a divorce being sued for and granted to Anne, his unfeeling wife, that she might be united to Sir Thomas St. Leger. She lived not to lament the violent death of her second husband; but King Richard, as shown by a subsequent instrument[1], was no stranger to the heartless depravity of the man who now sought that mercy from him, which, without even a shadow of offence, he had denied to his noble but unfortunate brother-in-law. The most influential of the rebels fled to Brittany[2], amongst whom were the Bishops of Exeter and Salisbury, the Marquis of Dorset, Sir Edward Courtenay, the Lord Wells, and many other noble-men of distinction; but several individuals of high reputation, were apprehended in London, Kent[3], Surrey, and other counties implicated in the revolt, all of whom were immediately executed, as were likewise some of the king's household[4], whom Buck-ingham perfidiously denounced[5] before his death, as traitors to their royal master.[6] The anxiety ex-

---

[1] See Appendix W.
[2] Chron. Croy., p. 569.   [3] Grafton, p. 182.
[4] Fabyan, p. 517.   [5] Pol. Vir., p. 554.
[6] It is somewhat remarkable that, circumstantial as are the details of the Duke of Buckingham's confession, when he hoped by that means to procure an interview with King Richard, and indignant as he is reported to have been after the failure of his dark design, yet

perienced by Richard, from the extent of this formidable league, was pleasingly softened by the
manner in which his prerogative was upheld at
Exeter, and the loyalty with which he was greeted
on entering that city; the authorities of which met
him arrayed in their official robes, the recorder
congratulating him in an eloquent oration, and the
mayor presenting him with a purse containing 200
gold nobles.[1]   The maces and keys of the city gates
were then delivered to him, and he was conducted
with great pomp to the bishop's palace, where he
lodged during his stay, and where he was sumptuously entertained at the cost of the city, as were
also the chief personages of the royal suite in the
dwelling houses of the principal citizens.[2]

A special commission under Lord Scrope having
been held at Great Torrington in the north of
Devon, such rebels as were captured were executed,
and all such as had found means to escape, to the
number of 500, were outlawed, including the bishop
of the diocese, and his brothers Sir Edward and
Walter Courtney.   Thus satisfied that all present
danger was at an end, the monarch disbanded at
Exeter a great portion of his army[3], and sending

he is accused by no chonicler, or even by report, much more on authority, of having certified to the death of the princes, or implicated
their uncle of the murder, although preparing to suffer death upon
the scaffold for striving to dethrone him.

[1] Jenkins' Hist. of Exeter, p. 88.   [2] Ibid.

[3] King Richard visited the chief places of this city, and was
greatly struck with the beauty of its situation, as well as with the
strength and elevated site of the castle.   Chroniclers relate, that on
the king's inquiring the name of this fortress, he was answered
" Rougemont."   This greatly alarmed him, as he had been warned
by a soothsayer that his days would not be long after he had seen

home those who had been summoned from the
north, with substantial recompence for their service,
he quitted the west country in triumph, to pursue
in peace through the southern counties his regal
progress to the metropolis, where he purposed
celebrating the Christmas festivities with marked
solemnity, in gratitude for the success which had
attended his late proceedings.

He reached Winchester on the 26th of November,
as is shown by two remarkable instruments [1] which
received his signature in that city, and which
evince the principle of justice which influenced his
actions even to the humblest of his subjects; it
being a warrant to discharge a chief clerk from the
office of the Privy Seal, who by bribery had been
placed in that position, to the great discouragement
of the under clerks, which, adds the record, "have
long continued therein to have the experience of
the same," and who were greatly mortified to see a
stranger "never brought up in the said office put
them by of their promotion." [2]   The vacancy which
accrued from this mandate was awarded by the
king to the oldest and most diligent of the subordinate clerks " for his experience and long continuance
in the same." [3]   Original memorials such as these,
affording as they do incontestable proofs of King
Richard's genuine sentiments and actions, are invaluable, considering how little contemporary evidence

Richmond; and, mistaking the similarity of sound in the names, he
hastily left Exeter on his return to London: but 'tis likely, adds
the local historian, that this story was invented after his death. —
Jenkins' Exeter, p. 88.

[1] See Appendix X.
[2] Harl. MSS., 433. fol. 123.   [3] Ibid.

exists to refute the mass of fable and mis-statements
from which hasty and wrong conclusions have so
long been drawn to the disadvantage of this
monarch.[1] Certain it is, that the odium in which
he is reputed to have been held is not borne out by
the few well-attested facts which have descended to
posterity. Wherever he went he was welcome, and
the marked respect and affection which were shown
him by the municipal authorities at York, at
Exeter, at Gloucester, and in London, cannot but
lead to the conclusion, either that the dark deeds
imputed to him in after years were not laid to his
charge during his life-time, or, if charged, were not
credited by the respectable portion of his subjects.
As he approached the metropolis, " the mayor and
citizens having knowledge thereof,"[2] made great preparations for receiving him. A body of horsemen,
gorgeously attired in " violet clothing,"[3] were despatched to meet and conduct him in triumph to
the city, which he entered on the 1st of December,
amidst such cordial acclamations as effectually set
at rest all apprehension of danger to himself or his
crown.

Much, however, remained to be done, before

---

[1] Amongst other accusations, Richard is upbraided with cruelty
by the early chroniclers (see *Holinshed*, p. 746.), and stigmatised as
a tyrant for his summary execution of the Duke of Buckingham and
other of the rebels, and for the long list of such as are proscribed as
outlaws. A very brief review of the reigns of his immediate predecessors will show how unfounded is this charge. In executing the
chief conspirators without trial, Richard acted only in accordance
with the practice of those times, and the very small number who
really suffered the penalty of death contrasts strikingly with the
sanguinary proceedings both of Edward IV. and Margaret of Anjou
on similar occasions.

[2] Fabyan, p. 517. [3] Ibid.

Richard could carry out the wise measures which
he had contemplated upon his accession to the
throne. One of his first acts, during this present
period of repose, was to convene a parliament; and
on the 9th of December, the chancellor issued writs
of summons for its meeting at Westminster on the
23d of January "next ensuing."[1] Active measures
were taken for ensuring domestic tranquillity, by
largely recompensing all those who had been chiefly
instrumental in terminating the recent disturbance,
and crushing the remaining power of such of the
exiled leaders as yet retained wealth or authority
in England. The temporalities of the bishopric
of Ely, "now in the king's disposition," together
with the vast possessions of many others who had
fled, were bestowed by Richard on the firmest of
his supporters. To Sir Thomas Mytton, the high
sheriff of Shropshire, who had captured the Duke
of Buckingham, was awarded "to him and his
heirs for ever," one of the princely fortresses appertaining to that peer on the confines of Wales[2]; and
the manor and lordship of Ealding in Kent was
granted to Ralph Banastre, Esq.[3], " in consideration
of the true and faithful service which the said
Ralph hath lately done for and about the taking
and bringing the said rebel unto the king's hands."
This entry effectually implicates Banastre as ac-

[1] Rymer's Add. MSS., 4616. art. 17.
[2] " Grant of the lordship and castle of Cawes, within the county of
Salop and marches of Wales, to Thomas Mittone and his heirs male
for ever. Given the 11th day of Decr. a° primo." —*Harl. MSS*,
433. fol. 130.
[3] " Given at London the 14th day of Decr. a° primo." — *Ibid.*
fol. 133.

cessory to the delivering up to the authorities the person of the Duke of Buckingham, although the fact of his having previously conveyed him to many and distant estates which he enjoyed, for greater concealment, favours the belief that circumstances alone led to his being the unwilling agent of an unavoidable result.[1]

But measures of stern severity to his enemies, or those which common justice required at his hands, were not the only feelings which influenced King Richard at this momentous crisis of his fate. Gratitude for his recent delivery from imminent peril was demonstrated, conformably with the religious custom of his age[2]; and acts of generosity

---

[1] The above-recorded grant affords convincing proof of the Lancastrian origin of many long-received imputations brought by the early chroniclers against King Richard, who is accused of having refused to Banastre the promised reward. " And as for his 1000*l.*, King Richard gave him not one farthing, saying that he which would be untrue to so good a master, would be false to all other ; howbeit some say that he had a small office or a farm to stop his mouth withal."—*Hall*, p. 395. ; *Grafton*, p. 176. This *small office or farm* is shown by one entry in the Harl. MSS. (fol. 130.) to have been a lordship and manor of *value*, part of the forfeited property of the late Duke of Buckingham ; and by another entry in the MSS. the position in life and character of Banastre is rendered apparent by the terms on which he held the estate, viz. " To Ralph Banastre, Esq., the manor of Ealding in the county of Kent, to hold by *knight's service* " (fol. 74.). So little dependence can be placed on chroniclers, who, influenced by party persecution, misrepresented every act of King Richard, to convert them into evidences of his injustice, his tyranny, and his avarice !

[2] On the 16th of December, 1st Richard III. (1483), a writ was issued to the collectors of the customs of Southampton, stating that the king had granted an annuity of 10*l.* to John Bury, clerk, for performing divine service in the chapel of St. George, in the castle of Southampton, for the souls of the king, of Anne his consort, and of Prince Edward their son ; and commanding them to pay the same. — *Rymer's Add. MSS.*, 4616. art. 37.

and mercy were mingled with the harsher decrees that were rendered imperative by the warlike spirit and the stern usage of the times.

On the 19th of December, scarcely six weeks after the Duke of Buckingham had sought openly to hurl him from the throne, and devised clandestinely to deprive him of his life, Richard awarded to the widow of this his treacherous kinsman an annuity of 200 marcs[1]: and, although she was the sister both of the dowager queen and of Lionel the outlawed Bishop of Salisbury,—the chief agents in fomenting the designs of the rebels, — he signed a warrant granting permission for herself, her children, and her servants to come from Wales to London, where her royal sister was abiding in sanctuary.[2] To Florence Cheyney, whose husband and brother had "compassed and imagined the king's death at Salisbury," he evinced a tenderness and chivalrous compassion that contrasts so strongly with the "spiteful, cruel, and malicious feelings" so long imputed to him, that a literal copy of the record is added in justice to his memory. "Safeguard for Florence, wife of Alexander Cheyney, whom, for her good and virtuous disposition, the king hath taken into his protection, and granted to her the custody of her husband's lands, &c.; though, being of late confounded with certain rebels and traitors, he had intended and compassed th' utter destruction of his person, and the subversion of this realm."[3] He paid the Duke of Buckingham's

---

[1] Harl. MSS., 433. fol. 77.   [2] Ibid. fol. 135.
[3] Ibid. fol. 126.

debts[1], gave considerable sums to the distressed
families of many individuals who were outlawed,
and settled annuities even on the relicts of others
who had died openly opposing his regal prerogative.[2] He confirmed charitable grants that had
been made by his father[3], renewed others that had
been conferred by his brother[4], and rewarded with
the most princely munificence those nobles who
had remained faithful to his cause, by bestowing
upon them either important offices or valuable
possessions, forfeited by the attainder of their
former owners. The Lord Stanley, who, it would
appear, had been kept in ignorance (or satisfied the
monarch that such had been the case) of the
coalition which existed between his illustrious
consort and the conspirators, was appointed constable of England for life[5]; and to the Earl of
Northumberland was awarded the great estate of
Lord Powneys, who had joined the Earl of Richmond.[6] The Duke of Norfolk he nominated
master forester, in the room of the Duke of Buckingham deceased.[7] Sir James Tyrrel had the
stewardship of Wales and the adjoining marches[8];
Sir Robert Brackenbury, who had loyally guarded
the Tower during a period of such extreme importance, he appointed receiver-general of all demesnes in the king's hands by reason of attainder

[1] Harl. MSS., 433. fol. 136. 200.
[2] Ibid. ; see various items from fol. 37. to 174.
[3] Ibid. fol. 130.   [4] Ibid. fol. 205.
[5] Fœdera, xii. p. 209.   [6] Harl. MSS., 433. fol. 127.
[7] Ibid. fol. 52.   [8] Ibid.

or forfeiture, being not by the king given[1]; while the Lords Dudley[2], Lincoln[3], Surrey[4], Huntingdon[5], and others of high birth, together with Sir Richard Ratcliffe[6] and Sir William Catesby[7], were proportionably rewarded for their zeal; and Kendale[8], who had been King Richard's private secretary throughout this important period, was made keeper of the princes' wardrobe within the city of London.

It would not be practicable, in the brief limits of this Memoir, to enumerate separately the various edicts, grants, warrants, and rewards which are comprised in the valuable diary that records so circumstantially King Richard's transactions at this period. Sufficient has been adduced to demonstrate the energy, decision, and judgment which characterised this monarch's proceedings. So evenly, indeed, did he balance the claims of justice and friendship, so judiciously mingle acts of clemency with a rigid observance of the laws, that brief as was the period since half the kingdom had been openly arrayed in rebellion against him, yet on the arrival of Christmas, which festival he celebrated with extraordinary pomp and ceremony, Philip de Comines states, " that he was reigning in greater splendour and authority than any king of England for the last hundred years."[9]

So terminated the eventful year 1483! which

---

[1] Harl. MSS., 433. fol. 74.
[2] Ibid. fol. 60.
[3] Ibid. fol. 61.
[4] Ibid. fol. 72.
[5] Ibid. fol. 66.
[6] Ibid. fol. 72.
[7] Ibid. fol. 74.
[8] Ibid. fol. 133.
[9] Philip de Comines, vol. i. p. 514.

had dawned upon Richard as Duke of Gloucester, and whose changeful seasons — a fitting emblem of his own varied career—had successively marked his progress from the position of lord protector to that of monarch of the realm. Its brief cycle chronicles three sovereigns of England, two princes of Wales, two queens-consort, and a double coronation! The same fleeting period commemorates the summary execution of the lordly Hastings, the gifted Rivers, the " deep, revolving, witty " Buckingham, the base and despicable St. Leger! A year so fraught with stirring scenes, with events of wondrous import, can scarcely be paralleled in the life of any individual, or in the regal annals of this or any other land.

CHAP. XVI.

King Richard opens his first parliament. — Confirmation of his title to the throne, and settlement of the crown on his heir, Edward Prince of Wales. — Bill of attainder. — Strong measures adopted by parliament to preserve the peace of the realm. — Convocation of the clergy, and their eulogium of Richard III. — Richard's humane conduct to the female relatives of his opponents. — He prevails on the queen of Edward IV. to quit the sanctuary with her daughters. — The princesses are honourably received at court. — Further proceedings of parliament. — King Richard's beneficial and politic laws. — He founds the Heralds' College. — His character as a sovereign. — Threatening aspect of affairs in Scotland. — The king quits London to quell the disturbances in the north. — He visits the University of Cambridge. — Sudden death of the Prince of Wales. — Grief of his royal parents. — Edward Earl of Warwick declared heir apparent. — The king continues in the north. — The Earl of Lincoln displaces the Earl of Warwick as successor to the crown. — Causes that led to this change. — Richard's embassies to Bretagne. — Negotiation with Scotland. — Letter from the king to his mother. — Other letters from this monarch.

THE opening of 1484 was serene in proportion to the tranquillity which had characterised the close of the eventful preceding year; and King Richard was in consequence enabled to meet the lords and commons of his realm on the day appointed for the assembling of the parliament, well prepared for any discussion bearing on his remarkable position, or having reference to past scenes; whether connected with his deposed nephew, his deceased brother, or the formidable league which had brought forward Henry of Richmond as a competitor for the throne.

The brief interval which elapsed before the time
appointed for the assembly of the legislature was
passed by the king in making a progress into Kent.
He was at Canterbury on the 10th of January [1],
and at Sandwich on the 16th; and, with a celerity
of movement for which he was remarkable, had returned to London by the 22d instant. The parliament, which had been convened for that day, met
at Westminster, and King Richard opened it in
person.[2] The Bishop of Lincoln, as lord chancellor,
made the customary oration, exhorting the assembly
to unity and peace, temperance and moderation:
allusion was made by him to the many distinguished
persons who had perished from evil counsellors, and
the recent fall of the Duke of Buckingham was held
up as a warning against further incitement to rebellion.[3] On the following day the commons elected
Sir William Catesby as their speaker[4], and an act was
forthwith passed for the settlement of the crown
upon the king and his heirs, with a recapitulation of
his title. It recites, that previously to his coronation
a roll containing certain articles was presented to him
on behalf of the three estates of the realm, by many
lords spiritual and temporal, and other nobles and

---

[1] Harl. MSS., 433. fol. 141.   [2] Rot. Parl., vol. vi. p. 237.

[3] " It is too heavy to think and see what care and dangers by
some one person, lately a right and great member of this body,
many other noble members of the same have been brought to. The
example of his fall and righteous punishment should not be forgotten.
Whoso taketh upon him, being a member under the head, with that
to which his office and fidelity appertaineth not, setting the people
into rebellion or commotion against the prince, he never is great or
noble in his estate ; he is, as it were, a rotten member of the body."—
Cott. MSS., Vitel. E. x. p. 139.

[4] Rot. Parl., vi. p. 237.

commons in great multitude, whereunto he " for
the public weal and tranquillity of the land benignly assented[1]; that forasmuch as neither the
said three estates, nor the persons by whom the said
roll was presented, were assembled in form of parliament, by occasion whereof divers doubts, questions, and ambiguities had arisen in the minds of
many persons. It was thereof enacted, that the
tenor of the said roll should be recorded[2], and
should be of the same virtue and force, as if the
said things had been so said, affirmed, specified,
desired, and remembered in a full parliament." The
bill to which the commons gave their assent concludes by the declaration, " that the high and excellent Prince Edward, son of our said sovereign
lord the king, be heir apparent to succeed to him
in the above said crown and royal.dignity, with all
things appertaining thereunto, after the decease of
our said sovereign lord the king, to him and to his
heirs of his body lawfully begotten."[3] This most
important matter being thus definitively settled, the
attention of the legislature was next directed to the
late insurrection, "whereby, as asserted, both the
king's highness and his peace, and also the politic
rule and common weal of this his realm, have been
greatly inquieted and troubled[4]; they [the conspi-
rators] intending thereby — as much as in them
was — the universal subversion and destruction of
the same, and also of the king's most royal person."
An act was forthwith passed[5], in which, after

1 Rot. Parl., vi. p. 240. 2 Appendix Y.
3 Rot. Parl., vi. p. 242. 4 Ibid. p. 244.
5 Ibid. p. 245.

stating that the king, being " moved with benignity
and pity, and laying apart the great rigour of the
law, hath granted to divers persons culpable in the
said offences, his grace and pardon, yet, nevertheless, it being contrary to reason and all policy that
such heinous treason should go utterly unpunished,"
the leaders of the conspiracy (who are therein enumerated [1]) were pronounced rebels and traitors, and
being convicted of high treason, their estates were
forfeited to the crown.

The Earl of Richmond, and his uncle, Jasper
Tudor, Earl of Pembroke, were likewise attainted [2];
but " Margaret Countess of Richmond (mother of
the king's great rebel and traitor, Henry Earl of
Richmond "), by an act which recited that she had
committed treason against the king, by sending
messages, writings, and tokens to the said Henry,
desiring him to come to this realm and make war
against him; and had also raised great sums of
money, as well in London as elsewhere, to be employed for the same purpose; yet, nevertheless,
the king [3], considering the good service which
Thomas Lord Stanley had done, and intended to
do, and for the good trust and love that the king
had in him, for his sake remitted to her the great
punishment of attainder, which was death! She
was, however, declared to be disabled from in-
heriting any estate or dignity, and to have forfeited
her estates to the crown; but a life interest in

[1] Appendix Z.   [2] Parl. Rolls, vol. vi. p. 244.
[3] Rot. Parl., vi. p. 250.

them was given to Lord Stanley, with the reversion to the king.[1]

Similar clemency was extended to the Bishops of Ely, Salisbury, and Exeter; another act of the same date declaring, that although on account of their treason they deserved to lose life, lands, and goods, yet, " considering that they be bishops of great estate in the church of God, and the king preferring mercy and pity before rigour, forbore such rigorous punishment; they were, however, adjudged to be disabled from holding any possessions temporal, or any possessions of their respective sees, so long as they should remain bishops thereof." [2]

The internal peace of the realm being thus effectually secured, by the confirmation of Richard's title, and the stern resolution evinced by the legislature to uphold his power, and put down with the strong arm of justice the rebellious feelings recently shown; parliament next adopted measures for preventing a recurrence of similar evils. This circumspection was the more imperative, as, notwithstanding the calamities which had overwhelmed the insurgents, and the rigid means adopted to crush their league, yet the festival of Christmas, the magnificent solemnisation of which in England was designed to mark the stability of the king's possession of the throne, was selected by his enemies to render yet more sacred the oath they took to compass his deposition, and accelerate the advancement of his rival. The refugees, gradually assembling from all

[1] Rot. Parl., vi. p. 250.   [2] Ibid.

points of the French coast, met Henry of Richmond
at his former place of captivity, Vannes[1], where he
had again fixed his abode, and where, after discussing their recent defeat and congratulating their
chief on his escape from such imminent peril, they
proceeded in solemn state to the Cathedral of
Rennes[2], before the high altar of which, on Christmas day 1483, the Earl of Richmond solemnly
renewed his pledge to marry Elizabeth of York[3];
and the assembled warriors bound themselves with
equal fervour to support him in every emergency,
until they had secured his accession to the English
crown.[4]

In consequence of this re-union of the confederates, the Cinque Ports[5] were ordered to send
out ships to watch the movements of the Bretagne
vessels; and a strong fleet under Sir Thomas
Wentworth was stationed in the Channel to guard
every approach to the English coast, and to be prepared to act on the defensive.[6] The commons
granted a subsidy, " called Tonnage and Pound-
age," for the safeguard and keeping of the sea.[7]
Letters were sent to the magistrates of the chief
towns in the southern counties, charging them not
to suffer any livery, signs, or recognisance whatever, except the king's livery, to be worn or distributed[8]; and commissions were despatched to various parts of the kingdom, empowering the high
sheriffs of their several counties to call before them
" all the temporal inhabitants being between six-

[1] Grafton, p. 180.   [2] Ibid.
[3] Ibid. p. 181.   [4] Ibid.
[5] Harl. MSS., 433. p. 135.   [6] Ibid.
[7] Rot. Parl., vi. p. 238.   [8] Harl. MSS., 433. p. 138.

teen and sixty years of age[1], and there cause them to swear to be true to the king, according to the tenor of the oath of allegiance.[2] The services of John Bramburgh, " a stranger born," who had covenanted with the king to make for him " certain great stuff of gunpowder," were accepted, and warrants were issued[3] for affording him all aid and assistance in the preparation thereof; ships were purchased from the Spaniards to increase the naval force[4] and extend its operations to the coasts of Scotland and France. John Lord Scrope of Bolton was nominated captain and governor of the fleet[5], and commissioners were appointed " to take mariners in the king's name, for the furnishing of the ships, and to do service upon the sea."[6] Equally vigilant were the measures adopted for guarding the coast; orders were issued for the arrest, in the king's name, of artificers and soldiers, with carriages and horses for the convey-

---

[1] Harl. MSS., 433. p. 141.   [2] Appendix AA.

[3] " Warrant to aid and assist John Collingham, yeoman of the crown, whom the king deputed to take in his name all manner of stuff necessary for the making of certain great stuff of gunpowder, which John Bramburgh, a stranger born, had covenanted with the king to make for him, and for the same to agree and make prices with the owners."—*Harl. MSS.*, 433., fol. 145. This early notice of the introduction of gunpowder is very interesting, destined as was that invention to supersede the use of those warlike implements which had gained for the English such high renown in the chivalrous ages to which they belonged.

[4] Harl. MSS., 433. fol. 146.

[5] Rymer's Add. MSS., 4616. art. 62.

[6] This edict constitutes one of the earliest instances of *seamen being pressed* into the king's service : commissioners being appointed to take mariners in the king's name for the furnishing of the ships called the " Andrew," the " Michael," the " Bastion," and the " Tyre," to do service of war upon the sea in the north parts. — *Harl. MSS.*, 433. fol. 168.

ance of the same[1]; and the constable of the Tower
was commanded to deliver from that fortress a
strong supply of cross-bows and long-bows, with
400 sheafs of arrows, 10 gross of bow-strings, and
200 bills.[2]

As far, then, as peaceable possession of the throne
could be secured by the most determined resolution
on the part of the government to uphold the prerogative " of their sovereign lord the king," to preserve him from personal danger, and protect his
dominions from open revolt or secret invasion,
Richard's prospect of a long and flourishing reign
seemed fairer than that which usually falls to the
lot of princes whose accession is effected by civil
or political revolution.   But a convocation of the
clergy, which followed this meeting of parliament,
has greater weight, with reference to his moral
character, than the support thus voluntarily afforded him by the laity.   Not that the petition
addressed to him by the dignitaries of the church,
setting forth the grievances under which they had
long laboured, and their conviction that he would
enforce stricter attention to religious offices, and
restore to them the power of duly and reverently
performing the duties of their sacred calling, could
itself in any degree affect King Richard's reputation ; for the privilege of seeking the protection of

[1] " A commissioner was appointed to arrest, in the king's name,
carpenters called wheelers and cartwrights ; other carpenters, smiths,
plumbers, and other artificers ; also bombards, cannon, culverines,
fowlers, serpents, powder and other munitions, and carriages and
horses for the conveyance of the same." — *Rymer's Add. MSS.*, 4616.
art. 63.
[2] Harl. MSS., fol. 157.

their monarch was alike open to the ecclesiastical as to the civil members of the community. But it is scarcely credible — nay, hardly reconcilable with the most degraded state of society — that the whole body of the English clergy, embracing so many individuals of piety, learning, and independence, could have so far departed from their sacred profession, as to address, in the following language, a monarch whom they considered to be a usurper, and looked upon as the murderer of two innocent children, his unoffending orphan nephews, the only sons of his deceased brother!

" SEEING YOUR MOST NOBLE AND BLESSED DISPOSITION IN ALL OTHER THINGS, we beseech you to take tender respect and consideration unto the premises ; and of yourself, as a most Catholic prince, to see such remedies, that under your most gracious letters patent the liberties of the church may be confirmed and sufficiently authorised by your high court of parliament, — rather enlarged than diminished." [1]

Is it possible to imagine that " Russel," bishop of Lincoln [2], lord chancellor of England, " a wise man and a good ; " [3] " Waynfleet," bishop of Winchester, honoured by the personal regard of King Henry VI., and distinguished for " piety, learning, and prudence ; " [4] or " Fisher," the friend of Erasmus, elected to the bishopric of Rochester by Henry VII. " for his great and singular virtue," and afterwards beheaded by his son and successor

---

[1] Wilk. Concil., vol. iii. p. 614.   [2] More's Rych. III., p. 35.
[3] Chalmers' Oxford, vol. i. p. 192.   [4] Archæologia, vol. xxv. p. 2.

for his uncompromising integrity, virtue, and in-
corruptible morality [1], with many other churchmen
equally eminent and estimable, would have appealed
to the " blessed and noble disposition " of one whose
hands had been imbrued in the blood of his nearest
kindred ? The mind shrinks from such sweeping
condemnation of the whole body of the English
clergy, headed as the convocation was by the aged
Lord Primate, and the venerable Archbishop of
York, both pledged before God and man for the
safety of the royal children! Coupled, however,
as is the remarkable language of their petition with
the absence of all inquiry relative to the position
of the young princes, all allusion to their reported
decease, the confidence reposed in their uncle, by
the lords spiritual and temporal, and by the laity
and clergy in their respective convocations assembled, cannot fail to modify in a great measure the
evil reports of a later period, which seem alike disproved by the conduct as by the language of his
contemporaries.

King Richard acceded to the petition of his
clergy : he confirmed them in their former privileges [2], redressed many of their grievances, and
extended to them the protection which they required, arising from the recent lawless state of
society.

He addressed a letter to the pope [3], extenuating
himself for not having sooner informed him of his
having assumed the crown and government of the
realm ; which he had intended to do, but had been

[1] Fuller's Church History, p. 205.
[2] Harl. MSS., 433. p. 44.   [3] Fœdera, xii. p. 214.

stopped by certain unexpected occurrences (alluding to the insurrection of Buckingham); and he sent the Bishop of St. David's to Rome to do homage to his Holiness.[1] In addition to these ecclesiastical ceremonials, he further gave practical evidence of his sincerity in upholding the church by a munificent grant for the re-building of the Abbey of Fakenham in Norfolk, which had been recently destroyed by fire[2]; by a grant of stone " out of the king's quarry," for building and repairing the steeple church at Towcester[3], in the county of Northampton ; and other works of a similar magnitude. He released the clergy in the north from heavy impositions imposed by Edward IV.[4], and founded at York a college[5] for one hundred priests![6]—acts of piety, the nature of which can be so little appreciated in the present day, arising from the change in manners, customs, and religious observances, that it renders it almost unfair to King Richard merely to record deeds that at the time must have been considered so altogether irreconcilable with alleged depravity of heart, without drawing a comparison between the actions which were then considered indicative of religion and virtue, and those which in after times have succeeded to the more outward formularies observed by our ancestors.

Nevertheless, it is but justice to this monarch to

---

[1] Harl. MSS., 433. fol. 121.

[2] Ibid. p. 153.

[3] Ibid. fol. 165.

[4] Ibid. p. 42.

[5] Ibid. p. 72.

[6] " He founded in the cathedral church of York, a noble chantry of one hundred chaplains, and erected a college at Middleham beyond." —*Rous*, p. 215.

state, that although the historian of his rival and
successor has expressed apprehension that remorse,
not probity[1], led to the acts of piety and wisdom
which influenced these his proceedings ; yet no
foundation exists, beyond the prejudice which gave
rise to that observation, either to justify the surmise
or to bear out the assumption ; while the emphatical
language used by the convocation has descended to
the present day as incontestable and coeval evidence
of the sentiments which were entertained for King
Richard by the dignified representatives of the
whole body of the English clergy, and becomes,
observes Mr. Sharon Turner, " a kind of sacred
testimony to his character."[2]   To quote the strong
language of this able and popular historian, " it
must either have been a phrase of consummate
hypocrisy, or it must be allowed to counterbalance
in no small degree the defamation that has pursued
him."[3]

The last important state question which occupied the attention of the king and the parliament was the withdrawal of the queen and the
princesses from sanctuary. Upwards of six months
they had been strictly watched in their conventual prison, in consequence of reported designs
for conveying the latter out of England, and the
compact afterwards made by their mother for
uniting the royal Elizabeth with Henry of Richmond.   But, all present danger from the latter
source seeming at an end, by the dispersion of the
rebels, and the vigilant efforts of the legislature

[1] Pol. Vir., p. 548.
[2] Turner's Middle Ages, vol. iv. p. 79.   [3] Ibid.

to preserve domestic peace, King Richard yielded
to the humane and generous feelings which on every
occasion marked his conduct towards the gentler
sex, even when their sufferings resulted altogether
from the bitter hostility with which he was pursued by their nearest connections.[1] The daughters
of Edward IV. were just entering upon woman-
hood; they were bound by ties of relationship to
the queen consort as well as to the king; and,
although the same act of parliament which recognised his title to the throne, arising from the illegitimacy of his brother's offspring[2], had of necessity
reduced them from their royal estate to the mere
rank of private gentlewomen, yet their uncle had
no wish to deprive his nieces of their liberty, or to
debar them from advantages suitable to their age.
He well understood the intriguing spirit of their
mother[3]; and that she would detain her daughters
in sanctuary as the most probable means of winning

[1] " The register of his official acts shows many personal civilities
to the ladies of his political enemies, from which, as they have never
been noticed, he has not had his deserved praise."—*Turner*, vol. iv.
p. 81.

[2] After King Richard's election to the throne, Edward V. was
always designated as " Edward bastard, late called King Edward V.,"
or words to the same effect; and a warrant for payment of 14*l.* 11*s.*
5*d.* was issued about the period under present consideration, " for
certain stuff of wild fowl, bought by Sir John Elrington against that
time that the coronation of the bastard son of King Edward should
have been kept and holden."—*Harl. MSS.*, 433. fol. 22. and 138.

[3] " The said pretensed marriage betwixt the above-named King
Edward and Elizabeth Grey was made of great presumption, without
the knowing or assent of the lords of this land, and also by sorcery
and witchcraft committed by the said Elizabeth and her mother,
Jacquetta Duchess of Bedford, as the common opinion of the people
and the public voice and fame is throughout this land."—*Rot. Parl.*,
vi. 240.

back some portion of that authority to which she so tenaciously clung. and had so grievously abused. The calamitous position of the widowed queen, by calling forth those feelings of sympathy and commiseration which are naturally excited for the victims of adverse fortune, has considerably blinded the generality of writers to the true character of Elizabeth Wydville, and to that cold calculating policy which was the incentive to all her actions, and the true cause of her misfortunes. Many years older than Edward IV., she married him clandestinely[1] (and, as asserted, even with the knowledge of his former marriage[2]), not from personal affection, not from attachment to his race or his cause, but from ambition to be queen of England. Callous to all other motives, she sacrificed alike her husband's popularity and the weal of his country to those aspiring views which first led to her own elevation, and subsequently to the aggrandisement of her family[3]; and this at the expense of the honour[4], the integrity, and those just claims of gratitude and

[1] " And here also we consider how that the said pretensed marriage was made privately and secretly, without edition of banns, in a private chamber, a profane place, used not openly in the face of the church, after the law of God's church, but contrary thereunto and the laudable custom of the church of England."—*Rot. Parl.*, vi. p. 240.

[2] Buck, lib. iv. p. 122.

[3] " Her brethren and her first children, although they were not extract of high and noble lineage, took more upon them, and more exalted themselves, by reason of the queen, than did the king's brethren, or any duke in his realm ; which in conclusion turned to their confusion."—*Grafton*, p. 152.

[4] " King Edward himself, albeit he was a man of age and of discretion, yet was he in many things ruled by that bend, more than stood either with his honour or our profit, or with the commodity of any man else, except only the immediate advancement of themselves." —*More*, p. 20.

affection to his kindred and his friends, which ought to have influenced her youthful husband, and, indeed, did influence him until, in an evil hour, at the age of twenty-two, he espoused the widow of a Lancastrian rebel[1], ten years his senior.

Possessed of great personal attractions, which her phlegmatic temperament aided to preserve undiminished from the inroads of time, — too prudent to reproach the king, and too cautious to merit reproach herself,— the queen of Edward IV., notwithstanding the notorious gallantries of that monarch, continued to maintain undiminished that ascendency over her royal consort which first led to his elevating her to the throne. Deprived by his early death of the power she had so fondly prized and had exercised so uncontrolledly, her princely son became the next victim to those arrogant vainglorious views which led to her aiming at a continuance of that sovereign authority which she no longer enjoyed as queen consort. To the machinations indeed of herself and her kindred surreptitiously to obtain possession of the young king's person, and thus set at defiance his father's family, by exercising over him that baneful influence which had gradually weaned from the deceased monarch the affections of his own race, and induced feelings of avowed discontent and hostility in the ancient nobles of the land[2], may be traced those events which led to the

---

[1] " Her husband was Grey, a knight of Groby, who became a very vehement Lancastrian, revolting from the house of York, and therefore the more hateful to those of that family and the well-wishers thereof." — *Buck*, lib. iv. p. 117.

[2] " In effect, every one, as he was nearest of kin unto the queen, so was he planted next about the prince. That drift, by the queen

execution of the Lord Hastings, Lord Rivers, Sir Richard Grey, and Sir Thomas Vaughan, as also the deposition of Edward V. and the election of Richard III.

Secure from molestation in the religious asylum whither, with evident preparations for a long continuance therein[1], she had removed with her children on the arrest of King Edward V., the widowed queen, bereft of both her sons, and full of indignation at hearing they had been, as she must have conceived, supplanted by their uncle, and were closely imprisoned in the Tower, next turned her attention to accomplishing her views through the agency of her daughters, who would in the interim, she well knew, be equally pledges for her own safety as for their uncle's good will, if advantageous overtures were made for their leaving the sanctuary.

Her projects seemed likely to be realised, even earlier, and far more effectually, than she had contemplated, in consequence of the opening afforded by Dr. Lewis's negotiation. It mattered not to Elizabeth that her probable restoration to courtly honours would be brought about by the union of her daughter with Henry of Richmond, the avowed

not unwisely devised, whereby his blood might of youth be rooted in the princes' favour, the Duke of Gloucester turned unto their destruction, and upon that ground set the foundation of all his unhappy building."—*More*, p. 19.

[1] " The archbishop came yet before day unto the queen, about whom he found much heaviness, rumble, haste, and business ; carriage and conveyance of her stuff into sanctuary, chests, coffers, packs, fardells, trusses, all on men's backs, no man unoccupied, some lading, some going, some discharging, some coming for more, some breaking down the walls to bring in the next way, and some yet drew to them that help to carry a wrong way."—*More*, p. 30.

enemy of her race and of her father's house. The summit of her ambition was to be restored to regal state, either as queen-regent or queen-mother. From the first position she was irrecoverably removed by the deposition of her young son, and the revolution which had placed a new monarch on his throne; but the other alternative was now open to her acceptance, and she hesitated not in her decision.[1] The queen's consent was joyfully given to the projected union, and after the young princess was formally affianced to the Earl of Richmond, neither threats nor promises could withdraw her from that abiding place, where she could safely watch the progress of those schemes that bid fair to restore herself and her offspring in some degree to the exalted position they had lost.

But the defeat of the belligerents, and the hopeless prospect of Henry of Richmond, produced a material alteration in " the mutable mind of Queen Elizabeth: "[2] and, notwithstanding her solemn pledge to the exiled earl, to his attainted mother, and to the gallant band who had suffered outlawry and confiscation of lands for her sake and that of her children, she again wavered; and again changing her views[3], with a tergiversation which is as inexplicable as it was certainly indefensible, consented to deliver the daughter whom she had betrothed to

[1] For certain it is she was a busy negotiating woman, and in her *withdrawing-chamber* had the fortunate *conspiracy* for the king [Henry VII.] against King Richard III. been hatched ; which the king knew and remembered perhaps but too well."— *Bacon's Henry VII.*, p. 21.

[2] Grafton, p. 199.

[3] " Surely the inconstancy of this woman were much to be marvelled at."— *Grafton*, p. 199.

Henry of Richmond into the hands of Richard III.; and agreed to quit sanctuary with her and the other princesses, on condition that the safety of herself and her offspring were secured on oath before competent witnesses.[1]

In conformity with this exaction, on the 1st of March 1484, just ten months after they entered the sanctuary, the king solemnly bound himself, in the presence of the " lords spiritual and temporal, and the mayor and aldermen of the city of London," on the word of a king and the security of a written agreement, that if the daughters of Dame Elizabeth Grey, late calling herself Queen of England, would quit their place of refuge and submit to his direction, their lives and honour should be secured to them; that they should not be imprisoned, but be supported in a manner suitable to his kinswomen; and that he would marry them to gentlemen of birth, giving to each an estate in lands of the yearly value of 200 marks; and that he would strictly charge their husbands to treat them as his relations upon pain of his displeasure. He moreover promised to allow their mother 700 marks a-year [466l. 13s. 4d.], and to discountenance any reports circulated to their prejudice."[2]

---

[1] " And so she, putting in oblivion the murder of her innocent children, the infamy and dishonour spoken of the king her husband, the lying in adultery laid to her charge, the bastarding of her daughters; forgetting, also, the faithful promise and open oath made to the Countess of Richmond, mother to the Earl Henry, blinded by avaricious affection, and seduced by flattering words, first delivered into King Richard's hands her five daughters, as lambs once again committed to the custody of the ravenous wolf." — *Grafton*, p. 199.

[2] See Appendix BB.

It is admitted by all parties that Richard honourably and conscientiously fulfilled this pledge. " He caused all his brother's daughters to be conveyed into his palace with solemn receiving, and by " familiar and loving entertainment " strove to efface from their minds their recent adverse position [1]: and the generous treatment both their parent and themselves experienced from King Richard and Queen Anne, together with the marked distinction lavished upon the young and beautiful Elizabeth, justifies the surmise that the king projected a union between her and her cousin, Edward Prince of Wales [2] ; that by so doing the machination of the Lancastrian exiles might be defeated, and peace eventually secured to the divided house of York, as well as to the kingdom at large, upon his decease.

The future aggrandisement of his child seems, indeed, to have been an all-absorbing feeling with Richard III. ; so much so that, notwithstanding the act of settlement recently passed, he again exacted from the nobles, before the offspring of Edward IV. emerged from sanctuary, a solemn oath recognising him as heir-apparent. " It happened one day after midday in February," states the annalist of that period, " that nearly all the lords of the realm spiritual and temporal, and greater knights and esquires of the king's household, the chief of whom was John Howard, who had recently been created by the king, Duke of Norfolk, being assembled by the king's special command, in a certain lower room near

---

[1] Grafton, p. 200.   [2] Lingard, p. 262.

the passage which leads to the queen's chambers, a certain new oath, framed by whom I know not, of adhering to Edward the king's only son as their superior lord, in case ought ill should befall his father, was administered to, and subscribed by them." [1]

Thus ended the momentous proceedings which characterised King Richard's first parliament; the time necessarily occupied in the discussions and considerations connected with which was not fruitlessly spent. Full of energy, mental and bodily; ardently desirous for the prosperity of the kingdom, which now acknowledged him as its ruler; and feelingly alive to the evil consequences of those divisions which had resulted from the indiscretions of Edward IV., the minority of Edward V., and his own iregular accession to the throne; Richard directed his attention earnestly and strenuously to the framing those salutary laws [2], and carrying into execution those useful projects, which, in an interval of tranquillity inconceivably brief, supplied to his subjects the loss which they had sustained in former years. He devised and perfected many regulations for the advancement of trade [3]; and, with the view of rendering more profitable the rich resources of England, he granted to foreign manufacturers of cloth valuable privileges [4], and liberty of settlement in any part of England, Ireland, or Wales. [5] While he protected the industrious English

---

[1] Chron. Croy., p. 570.   [2] Bacon's Henry VII., p. 2.
[3] Harl. MSS., 433. pp. 71. 76. 99. 104.
[4] Buck, lib. v. p. 138.
[5] " To the workers of cloths of strange countries, a confirmation of their liberties, to dwell in Wales, Ireland, or England." — *Harl. MSS.*, 433. p. 64.

artisan by politic and wholesome restrictions [1], he also gave encouragement to the opulent merchants of distant lands to extend their traffic to his shores, inspiring them with confidence by the justice which marked his enactments, and animating them by the liberality which characterised his transactions. [2] Several affluent foreigners settled in the metropolis, were made freemen, that their wealth and lavish expenditure might enrich the land of their adoption [3]; and, with a " love of honour and noble care for the conservation of nobility, chivalry, and gentry,"[4] he founded that most valuable and important establishment the Heralds' College [5]: an act that must for ever immortalise his name, from the benefit it has conferred on posterity. [6] To the industry and erudition, indeed, of

[1] Stat. of Realm, vol. ii.
[2] Harl. MSS., 433. pp. 85. 101.   [3] Ibid., p. 85.
[4] Buck, lib. v. p. 138.   [5] Fœdera, xii. p. 215.
[6] " No one who is conversant in our national history can be ignorant of the high esteem in which noble and illustrious descent was held by our ancestors, and of the strict attention that was paid to the observance of a just and exact distinction between the different ranks or classes of the people. The ignoble never presumed to arrogate a participation in the rights which were incommunicably annexed to eminence of parentage, or to claim honours to which their superiors alone were entitled. On the other hand, the nobility and gentry, cautiously jealous of their dignity and honour, avoided mixing with the vulgar, and were sedulous for the preservation on all public and solemn occasions of that priority of rank and precedence which was due to their birth and stations in life. Family arms becoming the external criterion which distinguished the gentleman from the peasant, and no persons being respected, or suffered to enter the lists to tourney, or exercise any feats of arms, unless they could, to the satisfaction of the heralds, prove themselves to be gentlemen of coat-armour, our ancient gentry took particular care in having their arms embroidered on their common wearing surcoats, and would not bear that any person among the lower class, although gotten rich, should use such tokens of gentilitial distinction ; nay, so

the earlier officers of the College of Arms, succeeding generations have been mainly indebted for authentic memorials of past transactions: and the mere mention of such names as Camden, Dugdale, Vincent, Sandford, Ashmole, and Anstis[1], selected as they are from a host of other learned and celebrated writers belonging to that collegiate body, will alone afford evidence of the invaluable assistance rendered to chronologists, historians, and antiquaries by the society thus incorporated by Richard III. "The genealogical tables and authentic pedigrees by them regularly deduced," states one of their distinguished members[2], "have operated to the detection of frauds, forgeries, and impostures; cleared up doubts and difficulties; established marriages; supported and defended legitimacy of blood; ascertained family alliances; proved and maintained affinity and consanguinity; vindicated and corroborated the titles of lands to their possessors; and been of essential use in settling

jealous were they of any infringements of the armorial rights to which they were entitled, that whenever the arms which they and their families had borne happened to be claimed by any other gentleman, they vindicated their rights even by duel. For these reasons, therefore, and for the guidance of the heralds in the proper and regular discharge of the duties of their functions, it necessarily became incumbent on them to draw out with accuracy and exactness the authentic genealogies of noble and gentilitial families, to continue from time to time and preserve their pedigrees in direct and collateral lines, and to have a perfect knowledge of all hereditary arms, ensigns, armorials, badges of honour, and the outward marks as well of personal as of family rank and distinction." — *Edmondson's Heraldry*, p. 89.

[1] Camden, Clarenceux king-at-arms in 1597. Dugdale, Norroy king-at-arms in 1660. Vincent, Windsor herald in 1624. Sandford, Lancaster herald in 1676. Ashmole, Windsor herald in 1660. Austis, Garter king-at-arms in 1714.

[2] Edmondson, Mowbray herald in 1764.

claims and rights of inheritance by furnishing effectual evidence." " Such," the same writer adds, " hath been, and ever must be, their utility and authority, whilst they are framed with integrity and correctness, and authenticated by references to proper vouchers. Time must indubitably stamp a still further value on such labours, and their value cannot fail of daily increasing more and more."[1]

The royal charter[2] which made the officers of arms a body corporate is dated the 2d of March 1483. It granted them many privileges, freed them from subsidies and tolls, with exemption from all troublesome offices, and empowered them to have and to use a common seal.[3]

King Richard further granted to them and their successors, for the use of the twelve principal officers of the said corporation, a large mansion with its appurtenances, then called " Colde-harbor," " without compte, or any other thing thereof, to us or to our heirs to be given or paid,"[4] wherein the four kings at arms and the rest of the heralds should lodge, live, and common together; where the rolls, muniments, and writings appertaining to the office and art of heraldry and armoury should be kept[5]; giving also lands and tenements for the maintaining of a chaplain, with an annual stipend of 20*l.*, to say and sing service every day, and to pray for the good estate

---

[1] Edmondson, p. 89.

[2] This charter, unabbreviated, may be found in Rymer's Fœdera, vol. xii. p. 215.

[3] Noble's College at Arms, p. 35.

[4] Rot. Parl., 1 Rich. III. p. 3.   [5] Buck, lib. v. p. 139.

of the king, the queen, and Edward their son[1],
during their lives, and for their souls when they
were dead.[2]

How strongly opposed are deeds such as these
to the acts of a tyrant—the conduct of a despot!
How utterly irreconcilable with the heartless, selfish, sanguinary career of a depraved monster, whose
very name has been associated with the subjugation
of the liberties, rather than with the emancipation
and enlightenment, of his subjects. But the reputed
virtues and vices of rulers are far more intimately
connected with the manners, principles, and usages
of their age, than those who pass judgment upon
their actions are apt to consider; and Richard III.
was too great a king, to be also popular with his
nobles as a man.

The period had not then arrived when princes
were to be commended for personally examining
into the comforts of their people, and descending
from their high estate to inquire into the wants of
their subjects. In proportion as Richard III. gave
practical evidence of the enlarged and statesman-
like qualities which proved him "jealous of the
honour of the English nation," and led him to make
laws "for the ease and solace of the common
people,"[3] so did he alienate the affections of the
nobility of the realm, whose haughty independence
could ill-brook the slightest innovation on the unqualified despotism in which they had been nurtured, and which they hoped Richard would have

[1] Buck, lib. v. p. 139.   See also Edmondson, p. 142., and Noble,
p. 55.
[2] See Appendix C C.   [3] Bacon's Henry VII., p. 2.

extended rather than curtailed. They could not appreciate the brilliancy, the strength, and versatility of his talents — the bold, quick, and enterprising genius, which made him so truly great when measured with his compeers. Accustomed to view him only as an able general, and to admire the impetuosity of his physical courage, they comprehended not designs which filled the heart of the patriot, and occupied exclusively the consideration of the sovereign; consequently the calamities which thickened around Richard III. after he was elevated to the throne—which destroyed his peace when living, and blighted his fame when dead—may, in great measure, be summed up in the words of Polydore Virgil, " the disaffection of his nobles:"[1] a disaffection not induced by his assumption of the crown, for that act emanated from and was confirmed by themselves, but disaffection caused by their having elected as their ruler a monarch of principles too liberal and views too enlarged for the comprehension of an aristocracy whose ideas were formed in times when the privileges of their order were upheld with almost sovereign power.

Short however were the periods of repose allotted to this monarch, either to contemplate or to carry into effect the beneficial regulations which promised, at this early stage of his regal career, as much advantage to the real interests of the kingdom as honour to himself. Scarcely had he completed the foundation of his noble work, the College of Arms, and secured to the corporate body by act of parliament

---

[1] Pol. Virg., p. 565.

the immunities and privileges so munificently awarded to them[1], than he was again compelled to turn his attention to warlike preparations, and lay aside the further prosecution of his peaceful projects.

By an instrument dated the 5th of March, it appears that the king had received intimation that divers rebels and foreigners intended to invade various parts of the realm near the coasts with an armed force, and that he was about to proceed to those parts for the defence thereof."[2] Accordingly, on the 6th of March, accompanied by his illustrious consort, he quitted the metropolis, not on a mere regal progress, as on the previous occasion, with all the accompaniments of sovereign state and power, but slowly to wend his way to the disturbed districts, while the commission issued for preserving peace, and more effectually guarding against the threatened evil, was being carried into effect.

Nevertheless on this his second departure from the capital of his kingdom, King Richard gave another and a signal proof of his interest in the welfare and well-being of those great national seminaries of learning, the two Universities; Cambridge being honoured by him on this occasion, as Oxford had been chosen at the period of his former journey, for his first resting-place. Although the particulars of his reception and sojourn at Cambridge are not commemorated with the same minuteness that

---

[1] It was confirmed by the parliament, and dated " 2° die Martii anno regni primo, apud Westmonasterium, Baron ; " and underneath was written, " Per breve di privato sigillo de datu predicto autoritati parliamenti." — *Buck*, lib. v. p. 139.

[2] Rymer's Add. MSS., 4616. art. 63.

records his entrance into and stay at the sister university, yet the charge in the proctor's accounts for " carrying the cross on King Richard's coming," [1] shows him to have been received in procession by the clergy ; and his recorded liberality to the burgesses and commonalty of the town [2] attests his satisfaction generally at the treatment he received. The king entered Cambridge on the 9th inst. [3] He remained there the two following · days; and a decree of the University [4], agreed to at a unanimous assembly " of the regents and non-regents " immediately after his departure, viz. 10th March, acknowledging his liberality and that of his illustrious consort, and decreeing an annual mass during the life of that " most renowned prince and pious king, Richard, after the Conquest, the Third," manifests in the most striking manner the degree of attention he must have given to the interests of the several colleges, and the high estimation in which he was held by the members of the university. He seems to have especially distinguished King's College, " the unparalleled ornament of all England," by his bounty [5] ; for, independent of " founding and erecting buildings there," as perpetuated in the above-named decree, among the entries in his diary [6] are several grants for " churches at King's College,

[1] Cooper's Annals of Cambridge, p. 227.
[2] " King Richard III. remitted for ever to the bailiffs, burgesses, and commonalty of the town of Cambridge, the annual sum of 10l., part of the fee farm payable by them." — *Harl. MSS.*, fol. 63.
[3] Harl. MSS., 433. fol. 251.   [4] See Appendix D D.
[5] " The king appears to have given altogether 700l. towards the completion of King's College Chapel." — *Cooper's Annals of Cambridge*, p. 230.
[6] Harl. MSS., 433. fol. 190. 209. 210.

Cambridge:" and, in addition to his former liberality to Queen's College, — which, as before related, he greatly augmented and endowed on his accession to the throne,— he, on this occasion, "devoutly founded there an exhibition for four priests," and acceded to expressed wishes of his queen that she might further enrich this college with some valuable rents.[1] He ratified the privileges of the university, and, brief as was his sojourn there, spent much money in advancing its interests in various ways.   He bestowed upon Queen's College a seal whereon was engraved his cognisance, the Boar; and the substance of letters patent have been preserved by Rymer[2], dated 25th March 1483, " in favour of Margaret College, Cambridge, founded by Anne the queen consort,"— an act of munificence that proves her worthy to have been associated with her royal partner in the solemn service commanded to be celebrated annually on the 2d of May, " by the whole congregation of regents and non-regents of the aforesaid university, for the happy state of the said most renowned prince and his dearest consort Anne."[3]

By charges which occur in the accounts of the treasurers of the town, for presents connected with

[1] King Richard III., at the request of his queen, gave to Queen's College the manors of Covesgrave and Buckby in Northamptonshire, lands and tenements in several towns in Lincolnshire, the manor of Newton in Suffolk, and of Stanford in Berks, together with 60l. per annum from the fee-farm of Aylesbury in Bucks, and 50l. per annum from the fairs of St. Ives in Huntingdonshire. — Harl. MSS., 433. fol. 68. 87.

[2] Rymer's Add. MSS., 4616. art. 63.

[3] Cooper's Ann. Cam. p. 228.

the royal visit[1], it is apparent that the king was accompanied by the lord chief justice and the Duke of Norfolk : and it is probable that the royal pair were met and received at Cambridge by the Archbishop of York and the Bishop of Durham ; for, independently of the signature of the former ecclesiastic being attached to the above-named decree as chancellor of the university, both these great dignitaries of the Church were munificent benefactors to that seat of learning. The lord primate founded the famed university library[2], and furnished it with choice books[3]; and King Richard's esteem for the latter prelate is evinced by his request to Pope Sextus IV., dated at this period, that his Holiness would confer upon him the dignity of a cardinal.[4] King Richard's visit to this

	£	s.	d.
[1] " For a present to the lord the king, in fishes	6	6	0
In a present given to the chief justice of the lord the king, viz. in wine, spice, fish, and bread - - - -	0	5	0
In a present given to the Bishop of York -	0	8	8
For a present given to the Duke of Norfolk	0	6	8 "

Cooper's Annals of Cambridge, p. 230.

[2] "On the 13th of May, the university, in grateful acknowledgment of the benefaction of their chancellor, Thomas Rotheram, then Bishop of Lincoln (subsequently Archbishop of York), who had completed the new schools, with a library above, which he had enriched with many valuable books, decreed that he should be for ever enrolled amongst their benefactors, and that his name should be for ever recited by the priest who visited each school to pray for the benefactors of the university." — *Cooper's Annals of Cambridge*, p. 221.

[3] " The number of books given by Archbishop Rotheram is said to have been 200. He is considered in the light of a founder of the library (although the university possessed a public library before his time), and his arms, impaled with those of the see of Rochester, which he occupied from 1468 to 1471, appear on the book-plate now used by the university." — *Ibid.* p. 222.

[4] Fœdera, xii. p. 216.

university was preceded by a circular letter, addressed to all the prelates of the realm, calling their attention to the particular duty incumbent upon them to repress vice, however high might be the estate of the offenders : since their evil example induced similar vicious propensities in " persons of lower degree." [1] He expresses his determination to purify the land from the impiety and immorality which had of late prevailed, and to encourage a more virtuous and devotional feeling. " We therefore desire and require you, that, according to the charge of your profession, ye see within the authority of your jurisdiction all such persons as set apart virtue, and promote the execution of sin and vice, to be reformed, repressed, and punished ; not sparing for any love or favour the offender, be he temporal or spiritual." [2]

From Cambridge the king repaired to Nottingham, entering that town on the 20th instant. [3] The castle was a strongly fortified and princely abode, one he had been often in the habit of occupying as lord warden of the north, and its central situation pointed it out as a desirable dwelling-place on the present emergency, from its affording a secure asylum for the queen in the event of open hostilities again compelling Richard in person to take the command of his troops. It was not alone from the shore of Brittany that danger threatened the peace of the realm. True it was, that the most strenuous exertions were making by the friends of Henry of Richmond to

[1] Harl. MSS., 433. fol. 281.   [2] Ibid.   [3] Ibid. fol. 166.

recover from the evil consequences which had so
fatally crushed their former efforts for his advancement; but time was requisite to mature and carry
into execution future and corresponding designs
from that quarter. The great source of uneasiness
to Richard, at this time, arose from his position
with Scotland, and the open warfare which had
commenced on the borders of the two kingdoms.

James was again at enmity with his subjects.
He could neither trust his nobles, nor they their
king; and his brother, the Duke of Albany, ever
ready and willing to fan the flames of discord between the two great estates of the realm, had fled
to England to escape his brother's vengeance,
discomfited, but not subdued. The most friendly
feeling had always subsisted between this latter
prince and Richard: so that, although he did not
openly espouse his cause, he connived at his residence in his dominions; and the perpetual skirmishes by land on the frontiers, the result of this
negative support, and the numerous aggressions
committed at sea in vessels manned by English
seamen, threatened serious results to the peace of
both kingdoms, unless the impending evil could be
quelled by pacific negotiations. Hence the cause
of King Richard's sudden departure from the metropolis, and of his present progress to the north.
Little, however, did Richard anticipate the bitter
domestic trial that was about to overwhelm him,
and in one fatal moment to blight the hopes that
had supported him in all his difficulties, cheered
him in all his trials, and animated him in his
desperate struggles to gain the crown and prove

himself worthy of his election to it. The monarch's stay at Nottingham was marked by the sudden death of the child of his fond affection, his youthful heir, Edward Prince of Wales, whose succession to the throne he had so recently laboured to secure, and whose dissolution severed the ties that bound his afflicted parent to the object he had so earnestly coveted — the sceptre that was now to depart from his house. " How vain is the thought of man, willing to establish his affairs without God!" are the emphatic words of the Chronicler of Croyland, who has left the most explicit account of this calamitous event: " for about the feast of St. Edward in the month of April, 1484, this only son, in whom all hope of royal succession was reposed by so many oaths, died after a short illness at Middleham Castle." . . . . . " Then might you have seen the father and mother, having heard the news at Nottingham, where they then dwelt, almost mad with sudden grief." [1] The anguish of the royal couple indeed appears to have been intense: they were altogether incapable of consolation; and the remarkable words of the other contemporary annalist, when recording the young prince's decease, " he died an unhappy death," [2] induce the supposition that their affliction was rendered doubly severe by its not having arisen from natural causes.

There are, however, circumstances which justify the surmise that the youthful prince was constitutionally fragile and of a weakly frame ; for amongst

[1] Chron. Croy., p. 571.   [2] Rous, p. 216.

other items inserted in his household account is one for the expenses of " my lord prince's chariot from York to Pontefract,"[1] at the time that he accompanied his royal parents thither after the coronation, — a mode of conveyance only then in use for state prisoners, for females, and invalids."[2]

It also appears that he had not been withdrawn from the North, whither he had been sent shortly after his creation as Prince of Wales, even to share in the Christmas festivities which signalised his parents' triumphal return to the metropolis.

Possibly the knowledge of Buckingham's league with the Earl of Richmond, may have determined the monarch to intrust his son to the guardianship of his faithful northern subjects, until the anticipated danger was altogether at an end : certain it is that he finally parted from the young prince at Pontefract shortly after the festivities at York, as the last notice of the personal movements of the illustrious child is conveyed in another entry for the " baiting of the chariot at York " on his progress to Middleham, and likewise charges " for expences of the lord prince's horse "[3] at the same city. That this separation was not caused by any want of affection on King Richard's part is clear from the whole tenor of his conduct. " His parental feelings were pure and kind," observes Mr. Sharon Turner[4] ; and the language used by the monarch in the patents for creating the young Edward, Prince of Wales

---

[1] Harl. MSS., 433. fol. 118.
[2] Bacon's Henry VII., p. 8.   [3] Harl. MSS., fol. 118.
[4] Sharon Turner's Middle Ages, vol. iv. p. 15.

not only justifies this assertion, but exhibits such a
tenderness of feeling and affectionate pride as fully
to explain the depth of anguish which followed the
announcement of the child's decease: " whose excellent wit and remarkable endowments of nature
wherewith (his young age considered) he is singularly furnished, do portend to us great and undoubted hopes, by the favour of God, that he will
make a good man." [1]   But these hopes were not to
be realised. " And if," as forcibly remarks an accomplished writer [2] of the present day, " he was accessory to the murder of his nephews, the blow must
have fallen with additional force, from the suggestions of his conscience that it might have been
directed as an act of retributive justice ; " for, by
a singular coincidence, Edward, the sole heir of
Richard III., breathed his last on the ninth day of
April [3] 1484, the day twelvemonth that chronicled
the decease of King Edward IV., and likewise the
accession of his ill-fated successor, the young and
hapless Edward V.

The lowering clouds which were gradually gather-
ing around King Richard thickened daily ; and after
the first deep burst of agony had passed away, he
felt the necessity of doing violence to his feelings,
by struggling with domestic sorrow, and directing
his energies towards those cares of state which he
had taken upon himself. Grievous as was his afflic-

---

[1] King Richard's Journal penes me. J. S.— Strype's Notes to
Kenneth, p. 525.
[2] Memoir prefixed to the Privy Purse Expenses of Elizabeth of
York, by Sir H. Nicolas, p. 42.
[3] Ibid. p. 42.

tion " the king nevertheless," continues the ecclesiastical historian[1] " attended to the defence of his realm, for it was reported that the exiles, with their leader, the Earl of Richmond, to whom they all, in the hope of his contracting a marriage with King Edward's daughter, swore fealty as their king, would shortly land in England. The Bishop of Ely indeed had never rested, and both himself and the leading nobility who had been attainted and outlawed actively renewed their operations — not alone on the Continent, but by correspondence with their English allies. Yet more threatening was the aspect of affairs in the North. Several English ships were captured by the French near Scarborough, and two of the king's most brave captains, Sir Thos. Everingham and John Nesfield[2], were likewise made prisoners.

To guard against any sudden invasion, either on the southern or northern shores, and also that he might obtain speedy intelligence from the agents employed by him to watch the movements of his enemies, Richard adopted the admirable plan, introduced by Edward IV. during the preceding Scotch war, of placing swift couriers at every twentieth mile, so that by their passing letters from hand to hand he could obtain the news of two hundred miles within two days.[3] Nor was he in want of spies abroad, from whom he learnt almost all the intentions of his rival, to resist whom he was far better prepared than on the former occasion,

[1] Chron. Croy., p. 571.   [2] Ibid.
[3] Ibid.

from the particular grants recently issued and put in force throughout the realm.[1] Thus shielded from immediate personal danger, and strengthened for any great emergencies, Richard prepared to leave Nottingham. By various entries in his register[2], among which is a warrant for the yearly payment of ten marks to a chaplain, whom the king had appointed " to pray for him in a chapel before the holy-rood at Northampton," it appears that he remained at Nottingham from the 20th of March to the 25th of April, when he resumed his progress to the North, and entered York on the 1st day of May. Acute must have been the sufferings of the king and his bereaved consort on re-visiting this scene of their former festivities—the city in which with proud exultation they had seen the brows of their idolised child wreathed with a demi-crown of the heir apparent, and receiving homage as Prince of Wales, but which now, by recalling to remembrance the brief duration of their parental happiness, brought more home to them the irreparable loss they had sustained by the premature death of the object of their tenderest solicitude.

The decease of the young prince made no change in the situation of the offspring of Edward IV.; neither, indeed, could it have done so without nullifying the plea of illegitimacy which had elevated their uncle to the throne: but as it became necessary to appoint an heir to the crown to guard against the event of the king's demise, Richard nominated, as his successor, his nephew, Edward the young Earl

---

[1] Chron. Croy., p. 571.   [2] Harl. MSS., 433. fol. 168. 173.

of Warwick, son of the ill-fated Duke of Clarence, who was the lawful inheritor of the sceptre by male descent, if he had not been debarred from legal claims by reason of his parent's attainder. This selection most thoroughly exonerates the monarch from the unjust charge ordinarily imputed to him of ill-treatment to this prince. His wardship and marriage had been bestowed by Edward IV. on the Marquis Dorset, the queen's son by her former husband[1]; consequently, if the generally-received opinion is well-founded, that the young earl's mind was weakened by cruelty and neglect in childhood[2], the accusation rests on his early guardian, and not upon Richard III., who could have exercised no authority over his unhappy nephew until, by the decease of Edward IV. and the subsequent attainder of the Marquis Dorset, the Earl of Warwick was restored to the surviving members of his father's family. The Marquis was Governor of the Tower, and there he had closely incarcerated the infant earl from the period of his parent's execution until the elevation of Richard to the throne opened his prison gates.

As far as the few memorials of this unfortunate prince admits of an opinion being formed, there appears substantial reason for supposing that he was taken under the kind protection of his maternal aunt[3], the queen consort, immediately after his eman-

[1] Cal. Rot., p. 325.

[2] " He was a child of most unhappy fortunes, having from his cradle been nursed up in prison." — *Sandford,* book v. p. 114.

[3] Anne, the consort of Richard III., was the youngest sister of Isabel Duchess of Clarence. — *Sandford,* book v. p. 414.

cipation from the thraldom of the Wydville connection; for among the noble guests enumerated by
the contemporary historian[1], which graced the
courtly train at Warwick Castle when Queen Anne
rejoined the king at this abode of her ancestors
was " Edward Earl of Warwick[2], then a child in
about his ninth year[3];" and it is evident that
the young prince was abiding with the king and
queen at the time when he was nominated as
successor to the throne, from the particular wording of the account which perpetuates that event.
Not long after the death of the prince, Edward,
the young Earl of Warwick, eldest son of George
Duke of Clarence, was declared heir apparent of
England in court royal; and in services at table
and chamber was served next to the king and
queen." [4]

From York Richard proceeded to his favourite
Middleham, so long his dwelling-place as Duke of
Gloucester, and the scene of his child's last earthly
sufferings, — a spot once endeared to him as the
birth-place of his heir, now doubly fraught with
desolation from his decease having happened within
its walls! No memorial is known to exist relative

[1] Rous, p. 217.

[2] Rous, the historian, is the more to be credited for this fact, as
he saw the young earl in company with Richard at Warwick, on his
progress to York, he being a chauntry priest connected with the
castle, and dwelling at Guy's Cliff, adjoining the town of Warwick.
— *Hist. Doubts*, p. 62.

[3] George Duke of Clarence was put to death in the Tower on the
18th February, 1478, Edward, his son and heir, being at that
time three years of age and upwards (*Dugdale*, vol. ii. p. 162.); and
King Richard and Queen Anne were on a visit at Warwick Castle
8th August 1483. — *Rous*, p. 217.

[4] Rous, p. 217.

to the funeral of the young prince, or denoting his place of interment ; but the strong affection his father bore him when living, united to the magnificence with which the funeral obsequies of the illustrious dead were solemnised in that age, leaves no doubt of the strict observance of the ceremonies suited to the interment of the heir apparent of the throne ; while the touching words, " whom God pardon[1]," added in Richard's own handwriting to one of the grants[2] which awarded payment of the last expenses incurred by the young prince, convey more forcibly than the most laboured monumental inscription the deep sorrow which filled the father's heart for this cherished idol of his affections.

The months of May and June were entirely spent by Richard in visits to the extreme north of his kingdom, in personally surveying the coasts exposed to the inroads of the Scotch and of the French, in examining into the condition of those of his subjects over whom he had formerly ruled, as the viceroy of his brother, and in renewing his connection with his old associates in arms, — striving to ingratiate himself with the people to whom he owed so many obligations, both at an early

---

[1] " Warrant for payment of 139*l.* 10*s.* to John Dawney, late the king's treasurer of Pountfreit, due to him for divers provisions and emptions by him made for the expense of the king's most dear son, *whom God pardon.*

"Given at York, 21st July, An°. 2ᵈᵒ."

Harl. MSS., 433. p. 183.

[2] " Warrant for payment of 73*l.* 13*s.* 4*d.* unto John Dawney, late treasurer of the household, with the king's dearest son the prince.

" Given at the Castle of Pountfreit, 23d July, An°. 2ᵈᵒ."

Harl. MSS., fol. 124.

period of his life and during the late formidable insurrection, when the fidelity of the Northern men formed so striking a contrast with the contumacious and turbulent spirit evinced in the southern division of the kingdom.

Durham, Scarborough, and York appear to have been his chief abiding places during this military survey. He was sojourning at the first-named city on the 15th of May, at Scarborough on the 22d, and at York on the 27th inst.[1], on which latter day he signed a warrant for " the payment of twelve marks to the friars of Richmond for the saying of 1000 masses for the soul of King Edward IV.[2];" another instance of his attachment to his brother's memory, however little he may have shared the same feeling for Elizabeth and her offspring. After a brief sojourn at York, Richard departed for Pontefract; and remaining there, from the 30th of May to the 13th of June, he again returned to York: at the regal palace of which city circumstances render it probable that the queen and the youthful Earl of Warwick dwelt, surrounded by the court, during the period occupied by King Richard in his various and rapid journeys, and where the monarch was himself stationary from the 14th to the 25th of June.[3] Thence he once more bent his steps northward, resting at Scarborough from the 30th[4] of

---

[1] Harl. MSS., 433. pp. 165. 195.   [2] Ibid. fol. 176.

[3] Ibid. fol. 165. 195.

[4] The sign manual is affixed to a document issued from this town on the 30th, commanding "mariners, soldiers, &c. to be taken up at the king's price, to do the king service in certain of his ships; and victual and other things behoveful for the same.

" Dated at Scarborough, 30th June, 1484."

Harl. MSS., 433. fol. 179.

June to the 11th of July, and returning to York on the 20th of that month. By this time his activity and unwearied exertions had been rewarded by a success that, in great measure, compensated for the inauspicious appearance of public affairs, which threatened such evil consequences at the spring of the year. He had gained many and signal advantages over the Scotch by sea[1]; and after several skirmishes by land, which were all attended with advantage to the English, a decisive battle was fought on the West March[2], in which although the loss was nearly equal in both armies, yet the Duke of Albany, who, fighting on the English side, had recently been captured[3] with the Earl of Douglas[4], was retaken; and it was forthwith intimated that preparations were making by the Scottish monarch for sending ambassadors to England, to negotiate a peace between the two kingdoms.[5]

The king's object in removing his court to the North being thus fully accomplished, he felt the necessity of returning to his city of London; things having assumed a more serious aspect as regarded the movements and intentions of the Earl of Richmond, not alone from his own immediate operations, but by strong symptoms of insubordination among the disaffected in the metropolis. Before quitting

---

[1] Chron. Croy., p. 571.

[2] Marches signify the bounds and limits between us and Wales, or between us and Scotland. The word is used generally for the precincts of the king's dominions in the statute 24 Hen. VIII. cap. 8.

[3] Chron. Croy., p. 571.   [4] Lingard, p. 263.

[5] Ibid.

York, however, a material change was made in the succession to the crown, the name of the young Earl of Warwick being withdrawn, and that of his cousin the gallant and chivalrous Earl of Lincoln, eldest son of King Richard's eldest surviving sister, the Duchess of Suffolk, being substituted in its place.[1] The general rumour of the weakness of intellect, which has always prevailed, and rendered the unfortunate heir of the house of Clarence[2] so much an object of compassion, had, in all probability (judging from this sudden and decisive step), become but too apparent to his uncle : and if, indeed, symptoms of hopeless imbecility displayed itself at so tender an age, undoubtedly it afforded but little prospect of comfort to the young prince or advantage to the kingdom, should any unlooked-for casualty early call him to a contested throne.

With that decision of purpose which invariably led Richard to carry into immediate execution measures which he had seen the wisdom of adopting, he nominated[3] his sister's accomplished son to fill that exalted position which after events proved his brother's child would have been unfitted to occupy.[4]

[1] Rous, p. 217.

[2] " He had been kept in the Tower from his very infancy, out of all company of men, and sight of beasts, so as he scarcely knew a hen from a goose, nor one beast from another." — *Baker's Chron.,* p. 225.

[3] Rous, p. 217.

[4] Nearly the whole of the Tudor chroniclers coincide with Hall (p. 55.) in his description of the deficiency of intellect which was apparent in the young prince's conversation, when in after-years he was conveyed to the royal palace at Shene, to establish the fact of Lambert Simnell's imposture. How far this weakness of mind may have been induced by early severity and constant imprisonment, it is hard to decide; but as the contemporary evidence of Rous (p. 217.)

The abilities of the Earl of Lincoln were well known to his uncle, for they had been tried and proved on many important occasions; moreover he was of an age and of a temperament to take an ardent part in the stirring scenes of these mutable times, and was equally by nature as by education suited for the high post he might one day be called upon to fill, could the legitimate claims of the youthful Warwick be overlooked in the more active habits and brilliant acquirements of his cousin of Lincoln.[1]

Whatever may have been the exciting cause that induced the change of succession to the crown, yet none among the many calumnies so unjustly laid to Richard's charge are more unfounded than the accusation of his having harshly treated and cruelly imprisoned his unfortunate nephew.[2] He sent him at this time, it is true, to Sheriff Hutton Castle, but not as a prisoner[3]: it had been the home of young

proves that during one portion of his life, at least, he was admitted to the dignities and enjoyments of his high birth, when residing at the court of Richard III., it adds force to the attestation of Cardinal Pole, his nephew, and the inheritor of his possessions (*Phillips' Life of Cardinal Pole*, p. 228.), that the mental powers of the unfortunate Warwick never advanced beyond that of the earliest childhood.

[1] " This earl was a man ot great wit and courage." — *Bacon*, p. 28.

[2] Horace Walpole states, that the king had an affection for his nephew, in proof of which he instances his proclaiming him heir to the crown, after the decease of his son, and ordering him to be served next to himself and the queen; although he adds, he afterwards set him aside, and confined him in the Castle of Sheriff Hutton, on account of the plots of his enemies thickening, so that he found it necessary to secure such as had any pretension to the crown. — *Hist. Doubts*, p. 62.

[3] The prince was kept here during the whole of Richard's reign, but he was not treated harshly. — *Castel. Hutton.*, p. 17.

Warwick's ancestors[1], and was at this identical period occupied by his immediate kindred the Nevilles. The king had himself visited the castle to examine into its fitness for his nephew's abode[2]: and the extreme beauty of the situation, together with the attention he had some years previously bestowed in renovating and embellishing this noble demesne, had, it will be remembered, tempted Edward IV. to purchase back, at a high price, the lordly pile, which he, of free gift, had bestowed in his youth on Richard of Gloucester.

" I saw no house in the North so like a princely lodging," is the language of Leland[3]; and Camden bears testimony to " the stately mansion[4]" allotted for the dwelling of young Edward of Warwick. If, then, during his abode at Sheriff Hutton the earl was guarded as a kind of state-prisoner, it arose from the disorganised state of the realm, and the necessity of protecting all of the blood royal from falling into the hands of their enemies, and

[1] Sheriff Hutton descended by marriage to the noble family of the Nevilles, and continued in their possession upwards of 300 years, through a regular series of reigns, until seized by Edward IV. in 1471, who soon after gave the castle and manor to his brother, the Duke of Gloucester, afterwards Richard III. On the Wardens' Tower four shields of arms are placed, exhibiting the achievements of the Nevilles ; the third shield is quartered with the royal arms, one of the Nevilles having married a daughter of John of Gaunt. — *Castel. Hutton.*, p. 4. 9.

[2] " It appears from some coeval records connected with this princely fabric, that King Richard occasionally visited the castle during his progresses in Yorkshire ; and likewise that there are letters preserved to this very day in Richard's own handwriting, dated Sheriff Hutton Castle." From the same source is derived the knowledge of the fact that " the king had gone over to Sheriff Hutton Castle to examine its strength previous to assigning it as the future dwelling-place of the Earl of Warwick."—*Castel. Hutton.*, pp. 2. 15.

[3] Leland's Itin., vol. i. p. 73.   [4] Camden's Brit., p. 588.

revolt : but the " strict confinement " named by
Rous [1] was by no means imposed from harshness
or severity. It was absolutely essential for the
young prince's safety, recently nominated as he
had been heir apparent to the throne, and notori-
ously the last male heir of the line of Plantagenet.
Admitting then that the dwelling-place selected
for him was one of strength and security, and that
limits were set to his walks, as is traditionally reported [2], yet these precautionary measures obviously were the consequences of the turbulent age,
rather than the result of unworthy or cruel motives on the part of the king. To whose particular
care Richard entrusted the custody and education
of his nephew is not known ; but the historian of
York states [3], that " the castle of Sheriff Hutton was
then in the possession of the Nevilles [4] ", and he instances its selection for the future dwelling of the
Earl of Warwick as another instance of the trust
which the king reposed in the northern rather than
thus being made a fresh tool for insurrection and

[1] Rous, p. 217.

[2] Around Sheriff Hutton Park, states its historian, were many fine
oaks of ancient growth and venerable appearance. One of these
trees, which was blown down many years since, is said to have been
standing in the reign of Richard III. : it was called the " Warwick
Oak," from having been, according to the tradition of the neighbourhood, the limit to which the unfortunate Earl of Warwick was
permitted to extend his walks during the period of his confinement
in the castle of Sheriff Hutton. — *Castel. Hutton.*, p. 40.

[3] Drake's Ebor., p. 124.

[4] The Harl. MSS., No. 433., perpetuates many grants and marks
of liberality shown by Richard to different members of this family,
especially to Ralph Lord Neville, to Sir John Neville, and to Dame
Alice Neville, all the near kindred of his queen. Sir John Neville
was at this time governor of Pomfret Castle ; it is therefore probable
that Sheriff Hutton Castle was under the charge of the Lord
Neville. — *Harl. MSS.*, fol. 57. 193.

the southern parts of the kingdom.   And, truly,
he had sufficient cause for this preference, for
two distinct principalities could scarcely be more
opposed in sentiment and action than were these
two extremes of the realm.

Although the insurgents had been wholly defeated in the recent rebellion, it had neither lessened
their enmity to Richard nor changed their zeal
for Richmond; and the oath by which the leading members of the rebellious compact had bound
themselves to succeed or fall in his cause raised by
degrees the drooping spirits of their adherents in
England, and encouraged them to labour stealthily,
but unceasingly, to further some future re-union.
These designs were made known to the king through
the vigilance of his spies; and no expense was
spared to procure unceasingly the most explicit
accounts from Brittany.   Experience had shown
him that neither severe enactments at home nor
strict watchfulness abroad could control or counteract the threatened danger to his crown; and
although well-disposed to have recourse to negotiation, and again to try the effect of bribes and
costly gifts, it seemed probable that these politic
essays would be as little crowned with ultimate
success as had been the similar attempts of himself and his deceased brother.   Nevertheless fortune once more smiled on Richard ! more faintly,
it is true, than heretofore, but sufficiently to inspire a hope that his rival, like Buckingham, might
be entrapped into his hands, and peace thus be
effectually secured to the disturbed kingdom.[1]

[1] Grafton, p. 188.

Francis of Brittany was now advanced in years, and recent severe illness had greatly weakened his faculties, so that the measures of his government had devolved almost entirely on his confidential minister Peter Landois.[1] This individual, as is common with favourites at court, had become so obnoxious to his compeers, that the circumstance afforded an unlooked-for prospect of success to Richard.[2] The alliance and support of the powerful English monarch was of greater value to the unpopular Landois than the friendship of the exiled and attainted Earl of Richmond; and under the influence of munificent presents sent ostensibly to his afflicted sovereign, but judiciously made over to the minister[3], in addition to a promise that the revenues of the earldom of Richmond[4], which had anciently belonged to the dukes of Brittany[5], should be restored to that principality, Francis was

[1] The English ambassadors came to the duke's house, where with him they could have no manner of communication concerning their weighty affairs, by reason that he, being faint and weakened by a long and daily infirmity, began a little to wax idle and weak in his wit and remembrance. For which cause, Peter Landoyse, his chief treasurer, a man both of pregnant wit and great authority, ruled and adjudged all things at his pleasure and commandment. — *Grafton,* p. 189.

[2] Grafton, p. 189.   [3] Ibid. p. 190.

[4] Ibid.

[5] The honour of Richmond appears to have been considered as extending into various counties, comprising the whole of the possessions of the family of Brittany in England. The lands in Yorkshire formed only part of what was afterwards called the honour of Richmond,—and in early times the honour of Brittany, or the honour of the Earl of Brittany,—which extended into various counties. The title of Earl of Richmond was of much later date, and probably assumed in consequence of the Castle of Richmond being the principal seat of the property. — *Report of the Lords' Committee on the Dignity of the Peerage,* vol. ix. p. 132.

made to promise, through the medium of his official
adviser Landois, that he would again clandestinely
capture and imprison the earl; an underplot being
secretly formed by the treacherous courtier to seize
and deliver him into the hands of the English
ambassadors. [1]

But the vigilance of Richard's deadly enemy,
Bishop Morton, again preserved Richmond and defeated the well-laid plans of the king. This prelate
had discovered the nefarious design of Landois, and
despatching the trusty Urswick to the Earl of
Richmond, that ecclesiastic disclosed to him his
danger in sufficient time to enable him to escape
from the traps of his crafty adversaries.[2]

Scrupulously concealing his secret, even from his
intimate and staunch friends, Richmond, attended
by five trusty followers only, proceeded ostensibly to
visit one of his adherents in an adjoining village;
and thus having eluded suspicion by his seeming
openness, the earl suddenly entered a thick wood,
and assuming the garb of a humble page[3], fled to
the confines of Brittany, and by dint of great exertions reached the frontiers of France[4] before Landois
had even sufficiently matured his scheme to carry it
into effect.[5] The anger and rage of the defeated

[1] Grafton, p. 192.   [2] Ibid. p. 191.
[3] Ibid. p. 192.   [4] Pol. Virg., 555.
[5] The stratagem by which Landois had hoped to secure the
person of Henry of Richmond was to have been carried into
execution through the medium of certain trusty captains, a band of
whom he had hired under the pretext of aiding the earl in his
designs upon England, but who were secretly instructed to seize their
victim, and likewise at the same time the most influential of the
exiled nobles. It was not until the fourth day of his departure that
Richmond's flight was discovered. Couriers and horsemen were

and wily minister could only be equalled by the disappointment of the English monarch[1], whose mortification was increased in consequence of the unfriendly feelings which subsisted between himself and the French king. This very circumstance, however, secured for Richmond a more flattering reception than he might otherwise have met with from Charles VIII., who, being also at enmity with the court of Bretagne, received the princely exile with marked respect, invited him to his court, and conducted him in person to Paris, which city henceforth became the point of re-union to the exiled English. The malady which had attacked the Duke of Brittany having subsided, and his mind becoming to a certain degree restored, his indignation was aroused upon hearing of the treachery designed by his minister[2], and he strove to compensate for the deception by furnishing the English refugees with money to enable them to join their prince.[3] He did not, however, give Richmond any encouragement to return to Brittany.

Wearied with the difficulties that had so often threatened his peace in consequence of the asylum afforded to the earl in his principality, Francis renounced all further connection with the confederates, and concluded a friendly alliance with Richard. This important arrangement was completed during

then despatched to the coast and to the frontier towns in all haste, and with such celerity did they proceed, that the fugitive " was not entered into the realm of France scarce one hour " when his pursuers reached the point which marked the boundaries of Bretagne.— *Grafton*, p. 193.

[1] Grafton, p. 193.   [2] Ibid., p. 195.
[3] Ibid.

the king's stay at Pontefract, from the castle of which place a proclamation was issued[1], announcing that the king had entered into a truce with Francis Duke of Brittany from the 1st of July to the 24th of August next ensuing. That period was now fast approaching, and the king was the more desirous to negotiate peace with Scotland, that he might be free to quit the North and be nearer to the new point of danger, — the dominions of the French sovereign, — in which his rival was not only lodged in safety, but succoured with a display of warmth and generosity that caused Richard as much alarm as it excited in him anger and indignation. He quitted York on the 21st July, rested at Pontefract on the 23rd, and entered Nottingham on the 30th, where he again sojourned for some weeks, and where he was greeted with the anticipated letter from the Scottish monarch, desiring safe conduct for his ambassadors coming to England to treat respecting a peace.[2]

It was with no small degree of satisfaction that Richard, on the 6th of August, affixed his signature to the required instrument[3], enabling him as it did to direct his attention exclusively to the policy of Charles VIII. Little time was allowed him for doubt on that subject; and his annoyance at the escape of his rival from the plot of Landois was aggravated by reports that it was the intention of the French to take from the English the Castle of Guisnes.[4] Immediate provision was made for the

---

[1] Fœdera, xii. p. 226.　　[2] Ibid., p. 230.
[3] Harl. MSS. 433. fol. 263.　　[4] Fœdera, xii. p. 232.

defence of this fortress, but conviction was brought home to Richard's mind that circumspection abroad would avail little in counteracting the designs of his rival, unless by well-timed severity at home a check could be put to the hopes inspired by his own rebellious subjects. Consequently many persons of wealth and family who were ascertained to be in correspondence with the exiles were imprisoned, and an example made by the execution on Tower Hill of one of the most seditious of the ringleaders, William Collingbourne. He had been arrested some weeks previously with a gentleman by the name of Turberville, on manifest proofs of treasonable practices, notwithstanding which he had renewed his communication with Richmond; and although he had received from Richard's bounty places and emoluments of such import[1] that the highest nobles in the realm coveted the reversion upon his arrest, he, during his imprisonment, proffered substantial sums to any individual who would join Richmond and Dorset, and urge them to invade the English coasts, so as to secure the revenues due to the crown at Michaelmas, assuring them that he and others would cause the people to rise in arms for Richmond.[2] Perhaps no more striking instance could be adduced from Richard's life or reign of the unfairness with which he has been treated, or the unjustness with which his every action has been perverted and condemned, than the report so universally

---

[1] Among the innumerable grants preserved in the Tower records is one from Richard III. of the manor of Clofert to William Collyngbourne, whom the king styles " Sergeant of our Pantry."

[2] See Collingbourne's indictment, in Holinshed, p. 746.

believed that Collingbourne was executed merely
for a political sarcasm on the king and his three
chief advisers, the Lord Lovell, Sir Richard Ratcliffe,
and Sir William Catesby.

> " The Ratte, the Cat, and Lovell our dogge,
> Rule all England under the Hogge." [1]

True it is that he did make and disseminate the
distich ; and it is by no means improbable that these
doggrels were devised and circulated for a seditious
purpose : but it was not alone for so simple a transaction that Collingbourne was condemned to suffer
death ; it was for open and avowed treason, as is
clear from the indictment, which charges him, in
addition to the accusations above named, with
striving to bring the king and his government into
contempt through the medium of rhymes stuck on
the doors of St. Paul's church [2], and with infusing
groundless suspicions into the French king's mind,
so as to induce him to aid Richmond in expelling
Richard from the throne. He sought, and merited,
the condemnation he received—that of the death of
a traitor ; and if, in the execution of his sentence,
unnecessary cruelty was exercised [3], the odium rested
with the civil authorities who carried it into effect,

---

[1] " Meaning, by the hog, the dreadful wild boar, which was the
king's cognizance : but because the first line ended in dog, the
metrician could not — observing the regiments of metre — end the
second verse in boar, but called the boar an hog.   This partial
schoolmaster of breves and songs, caused Collingbourne to be abbre-
viated shorter by the head, and to be divided into four quarters."

[2] Holinsh., Chron. p. 746.

[3] Fabyan states, when recording the harrowing details of his
death, that he " died to the compassion of much people." — *Fabyan*,
p. 518.

and neither with the judge who found him guilty nor with the king, who, though he sanctioned his execution, was at the time in a distant part of his kingdom. The precise date of Collingbourne's death does not plainly appear, but he was arraigned on the 18th July, and his previous suspension from office is made apparent by a letter from the king to his venerable mother, bearing date the 3d of June 1483[1]; a document of so much interest and value, as portraying the unabated affection which still subsisted between Richard and his now aged parent, that the mind turns with satisfaction from scenes of bloodshed and acts of violence to rest on one genuine record of those kindly feelings which contrast so strikingly with the selfishness, ingratitude, and avarice that were the prevalent incentives to action at this unsatisfactory period of English history. It would seem that Collingbourne held some lucrative and responsible situation connected with the Lady Cecily's rich demesnes—an office that the king was desirous of bestowing upon one of his own household. The style of this letter, couched as it is in such respectful terms, and breathing such filial deference, will better substantiate than could any conclusion drawn from it the confiding tenderness and reverential affection which subsisted between King Richard and his mother : —

" Madam, — I recommend me to you as heartily as is to me possible. Beseeching you in my most humble and affectuous wise of your daily blessing to my singular comfort and defence in my need.

[1] Harl. MSS. 433. fol. 2.

And, Madam, I heartily beseech you that I may often hear from you to my comfort. And such news as be here my servant Thomas Bryan, this bearer, shall show you to whom, please it you, to give credence unto. And, Madam, I beseech you to be good and gracious, Lady, to my Lord my chamberlain, to be your officer in Wiltshire in such as Collingbourne had. I trust he shall therein do you good service. And that it please you that by this bearer I may understand your pleasure in this behalf. And I pray God to send you the accomplishment of your noble desires. Written at Pomfret the 3d day of June 1484, with the hand of

" Your most humble son,

" RICARDUS REX."

It is apparent, from the king's expressed wish " of often hearing " from his mother, that himself and the Lady Cecily were in frequent correspondence, and living on the most amicable terms ; and it cannot but be remarked, that if the style of the above letter helps to weaken the prevalent belief in Richard's despotic and overbearing disposition, it is equally characterised by the absence of that obsequiousness and fawning servility which is invariably ascribed to this monarch in the character of hypocrite and tyrant.[1]

There are no materials for biography so satisfactory as letters — none that so effectually portray the sentiments of the individual, who, in his confi-

---

[1] " Look when he fawns he bites ; and when he bites,
His venom tooth will rankle to the death."
Shakspeare's Rich. III., act i. sc. 3.

dential intercourse with relatives and friends, lays bare, as it were, the feelings of his heart, and depicts unwittingly the bent of his mind and inclinations. " In autographs," it has been effectively observed[1], " we contemplate the identical lines traced by the great and good of former days ; we may place our hands on the spot where theirs once rested, and in the studied or hasty letter may peruse their very thoughts and feelings." Perhaps, then, no more fitting opportunity could be selected than the present for inserting another letter from Richard III., which even beyond the one addressed to the Lady Cecily displays the absence of harsh and unrelenting severity, in a monarch whose character has been considered as altogether devoid of compassionate or merciful feelings.

The epistle alluded to is one relative to the proposed re-marriage of Jane Shore, whose beauty or sweetness of manners, in spite of her frailties, had so captivated Thomas Lynom, the king's solicitor-general, that he was at this time desirous of making her his wife. It would appear that Richard was grieved and astonished at the contemplated union. She had been faithless to her own husband, and the avowed mistress of his deceased brother; moreover, in addition to the ordinary report of her having afterwards resided with the Lord Hastings up to the period of his execution, she was accused by King Richard himself, in his official proclamation, of an equally disreputable connection with the Marquis

---

[1] See the " Retrospective Review " on " Nichol's Autographs of noble and remarkable Personages."

of Dorset. How far either of these last imputations
is well founded it were hard to say, in consequence
of the contradictory reports which envelope the fate
of Jane Shore in the same veil of mystery that
shrouds the career of almost all the prominent personages connected with her time. But this much
is certain : she was the paramour of Edward IV. for
many years, she did penance for her irregular life
after his decease, and she is shown to be a prisoner
in Ludgate for treasonable practices[1] at the identical
period that so important a functionary as the solicitor-general sought her in marriage.

And what was the conduct pursued by the
monarch in this emergency ? Not that of a tyrant,
not that of a persecutor, but of a kind and indulgent
master, anxious to arrest a faithful servant in the
commission of an act injurious to his interests,
but willing to yield to his wishes, if remonstrance
failed to open his eyes to the unfortunate alliance
which he desired to form. With this view Richard
addressed the following remarkable letter[2] to Dr.
Russell, Bishop of Lincoln, then Lord Chancellor,
and to whom, as has been before observed, was applied the eulogy of " the learned and the good."[3]

---

[1] It is probable that Jane Shore was re-committed to Ludgate
after the reward offered for the Marquis of Dorset's apprehension,
and by no means unlikely that the charge of her unlawful connection
with that nobleman may have originated from her having aided his
departure from sanctuary, and either concealed him in her apartments,
or sanctioned her dwelling being used as the point of reunion for the
insurgents in Buckingham's revolt, as it had previously been, there is
reason to believe, in Hastings' conspiracy.

[2] Harl. MSS., No. 2378.

[3] More, p. 35.

" By the King.

" Right Reverend Father in God, &c., signifying
unto you that it is showed unto us, that our
servant and solicitor, Thos. Lynom, marvellously
blinded and abused with the late wife of William
Shore, now being in Ludgate by our commandment, hath made contract of matrimony with her,
as it is said, and intendeth, to our full great marvel,
to proceed to effect the same. We, for many
causes, would be sorry that he so should be disposed, pray you therefore to send for him, and in
that ye godly may exhort and stir him to the contrary. And if ye find him utterly set for to marry
her, and none otherwise would be advertised, then,
if it may stand with the law of the church, we be
content (the time of marriage being deferred to our
coming next to London), that upon sufficient surety
found of her good abearing [behaviour] ye do send
for her keeper and discharge him of our commandment by warrant of these, committing her to the
rule and guiding of her father or any other, by your
discretion, in the mean season.[1]

" Given, &c.

" To the Right Rev. Father in God the
Bishop of Lincoln our Chancellor."[2]

There is no compulsion enjoined in this epistle,
no stretch of regal power, no threats, no stipulated
resignation of office, but simply exhortation en-

[1] There is no date given to this curious document; but it was
probably written about this period — that is to say, during Richard's
second absence from the metropolis, judging from the king's expression, "our coming next to London."

[2] Preserved among Lord Hardwicke's state papers in the Harleian
Library, No. 2378.

joined from the highest dignitary in the state, himself a prelate of unblemished reputation and virtue. The chancellor was empowered to release the frail but fascinating Jane from prison, to deliver her into the charge of the person most fitting to succour her—her own father, and even to sanction the marriage provided it held good " with the law of the church." Is this conduct indicative of cruelty? Does this letter exemplify the arbitrary, imperious, selfish destroyer of his people's comforts and happiness? Surely not! And when it is remembered that in Richard's days letters were neither designed for, nor liable to, publication, as in later times, but were the secret deposits of the unbiassed sentiments of the individual who penned them, it must be admitted that the letters above given are satisfactory indications of the king's frame of mind, and tend materially to redeem his character from many of the harsh traits ordinarily affixed to him by historians.

It also completely exonerates him from the tradition of having caused Jane Shore's decease by starvation, from his merciless prohibition of all assistance being afforded her in her misery. She survived the monarch many years[1]; and the very circumstance of her dying in advanced age, and so decrepit that she was " but shrivelled skin and hard bone," removes her death to a period long

---

[1] Jane Shore was living at the time that Sir Thomas More wrote, which was nearly thirty years after Richard's decease ; for, in his history of that monarch, he says, " Thus say they that knew her in her youth. Albeit some that now see her, *for she yet liveth*, deem her never to have been well visaged."—*Sir Thomas More*, p. 84.

subsequent to King Richard's reign, when her attractions,

> —— " A pretty foot,
> A cherry lip,
> A bonny eye, a passing pleasing tongue," [1]

were sufficiently remarkable to attract the young
Marquis of Dorset, and after his attainder to win
the king's solicitor-general.

Many more letters might be adduced illustrative
of King Richard's lenity, forbearance, and kindness
of heart; for notwithstanding the rarity of epistolary
communication at this early period of English history [2], yet the letters of this monarch are abundant:
they are mostly, it is true, on matters of state, but
whether official or private, or of courtesy to crowned
heads, the " chief are the king's own." [3]   The subjoined autograph letter hitherto unpublished is now
given under the impression that a fac-simile of one
altogether in Richard's hand-writing was indispensable in a memoir of his life ; but the mass of facts
connected with his remarkable career equally precludes the possibility of introducing the whole of
his correspondence, as of making copious extracts
from the invaluable register which has been so frequently referred to in this work. " I made the
attempt," states Mr. Sharon Turner, when speaking
on the latter point, " but I found the entries too
numerous for insertion: it contains from 2000 to
2500 official documents, most of which are the king's
beneficial grants." [4]   Had the reign of Richard III.

[1] Shakspeare's Richard III., act. i. sc. 1.   [2] More, p. 84.
[3] Ellis's Orig. Lett., 2d series, p. 147.
[4] Turner's Middle Ages, vol. iv. p 58.

Fac-simile of an Autograph Letter

FROM

KING RICHARD III. TO THE LORD CHANCELLOR.

COPIED FROM THE ORIGINAL, PRESERVED AMONGST THE RECORDS IN THE TOWER OF LONDON.

In modern English, thus:—

My lorde Chaunceler.—We pray you, in all haste, to send to us a pardon under our Great Seal to Sir Harry Wode, priest, &c., and this shall be your warrant.

RICARDUS REX.

Master Skipton, speed this forth with expedition.

JO. OMCOTS.*

* Perhaps the Chancellor's secretary.

extended over as many years as it is now numbered by months, the above well-authenticated fact,
and the probable results of so vigorous and active a
mind—a mind devoted to the interests of his country
and to the well-being of his subjects—would, in all
probability, have conduced to the life and character
of this monarch being perpetuated in a far different
and truer light to that in which it has hitherto been
depicted.

CHAP. XVII.

THE month of August had commenced before King Richard could put in execution his earnest desire of returning to the capital of his kingdom. Six stormy months had marked the period since he had abruptly quitted the scene of his former triumph, — that city which had witnessed his accession, his coronation, and the ratification of his election to the crown. Threatening as the aspect of affairs then appeared, he yet quitted his capital sustained by hope, undaunted by fear, for he had attained the summit of his ambition. Not alone was his own brow encircled with the much-coveted diadem, but the sceptre seemed irrevocably fixed in his house by the act of settlement which had made the succession of his son the law of the land. How fragile is the slight tenure of earthly prosperity! The toil and the labour of years are crushed in a moment, and the littleness of man, at the height of his greatness, is often brought fearfully home to him by one of those immutable decrees from which there is no appeal. Although successful in arms, in political negociation, and in the happy result of his own personal exertions, the king returned to his metropolis subdued in spirit and desolate in heart, for he was now childless. His youthful heir had been taken from him suddenly, and without warning. Before one anniversary had celebrated his parent's accession to the throne, or commemorated his own exalted position as Prince of Wales, young Edward of Gloucester slept in his tranquil grave. Disaffection, too, was overspreading the land; the regal treasury had become fearfully diminished, owing to the precautions requisite for frustrating the designs of Henry Earl of Richmond; and internal discord foreboded as much cause for anxiety within the realm as had already been created by avowed hostility from foreign enemies. These accumulated difficulties had made the king yet more earnest to return to his capital. He was well acquainted with the seditious spirit which there prevailed, and he was not ignorant that his popularity was waning. The citizens of London had been too long accustomed to, and had too fully revelled in, the

pleasurable and luxurious habits promoted by
Edward IV.[1] not to feel keenly their changed
position under the severe rule of his successor.
Edward, that gay and gallant monarch, had sacrificed health, fame, dignity, even his love of glory,
to his still greater love of ease. " But," observes
Sir Thomas More[2], " this fault not greatly grieved
the people," although it irritated his warlike nobles,
and weaned from him their respect and affection ;
for the community at large had imperceptibly
reaped the benefit of that commercial prosperity[3]
which resulted from " the realm being in quiet and
prosperous estate," — no fear of outward enemies,
and among themselves " the commons in good
peace."[4] Richard, on the contrary, notwithstanding
his desire of pursuing a similar course of domestic
policy, — one which was altogether in accordance
with his own enlightened views, and to perfect a
system which had produced such beneficial results,
was, from the distracted state of the country, which
led to his elevation to the throne, speedily called upon
to withdraw his attention from pacific and tran-
quillising measures, and, from the time of his accession, to make warlike and martial preparations
the leading object of his government.   The caprice
and instability of many of his nobles being the

[1] " In the summer, the last that ever he saw, his highness being
at Windsor, hunting, sent for the mayor and aldermen of London
to him, for none other errand than to hunt and make merry with
him." —*More*, p. 5.

[2] More's Rich. III., p. 5.

[3] The twelve years succeeding the restoration of Edward IV. are
reckoned by political economists the most prosperous ever enjoyed
by the English people.

[4] More, p. 5.

existing cause of the renewal of civil discord,
Richard had not the advantage of their undivided
support to counterbalance the spirit of insubordination which generally prevailed among the middling
classes, or the satisfaction of acting in concert with
this powerful body of his subjects ; while the discomfort which had resulted from the revival of
internal feuds, united to the total cessation of commercial intercourse with France and Scotland, and
the heavy cost of keeping up armaments by sea
and land, had gradually fostered in the citizens of
London a spirit of tumult and disorder very unfavourable to the views of the monarch, and very
distressing to himself individually.   Various causes
of less import tended to increase this feeling of discontent. The court had been stationary at York
for six months; and the evident partiality which
Richard publicly testified for his northern subjects,
added to the extensive repairs and embellishments
which he had commanded at the royal palace in
that city[1], made the inhabitants of the southern
portion of the island fear the possibility of the
regal abode being eventually removed to the scene
of the new king's second coronation, and of his
early popular rule, or, to say the least, that he
might be induced to divide, between his northern
and southern capitals, those great privileges which
had hitherto been exclusively enjoyed by the
ancient seat of government. But King Richard
was too able a statesman, too wise a ruler, to be
ignorant of the fatal consequences which must

[1] Harl. MSS., 433. fol. 183.

ensue to the governor of a divided kingdom, and
he was proportionably desirous to return to London,
that by his presence among his former supporters
he might allay their apprehension, and inspire them
with renewed confidence towards himself. The
monarch quitted Nottingham[1] on the 1st of August,
and appears to have reached the palace at Westminster about the 6th instant, as, on that day,
" letters of safe conduct " were granted to the
ambassadors from Scotland[2], appointing the 7th of
September for a desired conference, and fixing
Nottingham, from its central position, as the place
in which the king would receive them. A letter,
also, was delivered from James III. to Richard,
expressing his intention of sending commissioners
to England, to treat not only " of truce and ab-
stinence from war, but likewise of marriage, between those of the blood of both kings."[3] To this
letter an official answer was returned, which fixes
King Richard at Westminster on the 7th of August, 1484.[4] He continued there during the remainder of the month, which was characterised by
one of the most interesting ceremonies connected
with his reign — that of the removal of the
body of Henry VI. from his place of interment
at Chertsey Abbey to the collegiate church of

[1] The document which fixes King Richard at Nottingham on the
30th of July is sufficiently curious to merit insertion. " Commission to Thomas Fowler, squire for the body, John Whitelocke,
William Lok, and Richard Austin, to make search for certain
treasure, which, as the king was credibly informed, is hid in a
ground called Sudbury, or nigh thereabouts, within the county of
Bedford." — *Harl. MSS.*, 433. fol. 186.

[2] Fœdera, xii. p. 230.

[3] Harl. MSS., 433. fol. 263.   [4] Ibid.

Windsor, in order that the ashes of the deposed monarch might be placed beside those of his royal predecessors. Richard's every action has been so suspiciously viewed, all his measures, whether prompted by policy or generosity, have been so perverted and misrepresented, that it can scarcely excite surprise that this act of respect to the memory of the amiable but unfortunate rival of the house of York should be reported to Richard's disadvantage, after he himself became the sport of adverse fortune and political contumely. " He envied," it is stated by the partisans of the house of Tudor, " the sanctity of King Henry," and translated him from Chertsey " to arrest the number of pilgrimages made to his tomb,"[1]—a tomb admitted by the same authority to have been unfitting for the resting-place of a crowned head, and situated in so retired a spot[2] that the few devotees who there resorted could never have procured for the deceased king that revival of compassionate feeling which was called forth by his public disinterment, and the removal of his body to the regal mausoleum of his ancestors. If any positive fact could weaken the mere report of King Richard having himself assassinated the Lancastrian monarch, this proceeding might well be cited in his favour. The mortal remains of the hapless prince had reposed in their last resting-place upwards of thirteen years. His exhumation was neither caused by the murmurs of the populace, nor required as an act of justice for

[1] Wilk. Concil., iii. p. 635.   [2] Ibid.

any former absence of accustomed ceremonial.[1] The people flocked to King Henry's tomb because his saintlike habits during life, united to the severity of his sufferings, had gradually invested his memory with superstitious veneration; yet did Richard voluntarily, openly, without fear of any popular ebullition of feeling for the unfortunate Henry, or the dread of evil consequences to himself, which a consciousness of guilt invariably produces, transfer the relics of the deceased sovereign to a more fitting place of interment — one of such distinction and notoriety, that visits to his tomb, if offensive to the reigning house, would thereby have been rather increased than diminished.

The words of the historian Rous[2], through whom the event has been recorded, and whose political enmity to King Richard exonerates him from all supposition of undue praise, will better tend to place the act itself in its true light than any arguments that can result from a mere review of it: " And in the month of August following the body of King Henry was dug up, and translated to the new collegiate church of Windsor, where it was *honourably received*, and again buried with *the greatest solemnity* on the south side of the high altar."

This simple detail, by a contemporary writer of

---

[1] " Many writers have committed the error of affirming that Henry VI. was buried without honours," observes the editor of Warkworth's Chronicles (p. 67.) ; but reference to Devon's Issue Rolls of the Exchequer (p. 491.), wherein are specified sums paid for the expenses of that monarch's interment, will, he further observes, " prove that every respect was paid to his funeral obsequies."

[2] Rous, p. 217.

acknowledged Lancastrian prejudices, an ecclesiastic by profession, and a warm partisan of Henry VI., joined to the fact that King Richard's motives were not impugned on this head until that monarch had been dead for many years, and not until it was in contemplation " to canonise King Henry VI. for a saint"[1] arising from miracles reputed to be performed at his tomb, fully exposes the malignity with which Richard has been, on all points, defamed. The very document, indeed, which impugns his motives, and charges him with envying King Henry the fame that attached to him after death, assists in exculpating Richard from the unsupported tradition of having deprived the Lancastrian sovereign of his life. " He had yielded to a pitiable death by the order of Edward, who was then king of England," are the words used by the English clergy in an address to the see of Rome. This address was written long after Richard's death, and at a time when King Edward's daughter was the reigning queen.[2]

Had there been solid foundation for the rumour that afterwards prevailed of Henry of Lancaster having been murdered by Richard, who can doubt that these ecclesiastics would unhesitatingly have substituted the words " by the hands of the Duke of Gloucester," when no reason existed for sparing the memory of one so maligned, and which would have saved them the necessity of fixing the crime

[1] Bacon's Henry VII., p. 227.
[2] A petition was presented to Pope Alexander VI., in the year 1499, praying that the remains of King Henry VI. might be removed to Westminster Abbey. — *Wilk. Concil.*, iii. p. 635.

on the sire and grandsire of the queen consort and
the heir apparent of the throne ?

Brief as was King Richard's stay in London, it
was characterised by acts of bounty and munificence similar to those which had marked his
former sojourn there. He then commenced many
public works of , great importance; those he now
continued, and also carried out other designs, which
had been interrupted by his sudden departure for
the North. He founded a college of priests in
Tower Street, near the church called " Our Lady
of Barking."[1] He commanded the erection of a
high stone tower at Westminster,—" a work," states
Sir George Buck, " of good use, even at this day."[2]
He caused substantial repairs to be commenced at
the Tower of London, erecting new buildings, and
renovating the older portions; "in memory whereof,"
narrates the above quoted historian, " there be yet
his arms, impaled with those of the queen, his wife,
standing upon the arch adjoining the sluice gate :"[3]
and both Windsor Castle[4], the Palace at Westminster[5], Baynard's Castle[6], and the Erber, or King's
Palace[7], as it was then designated, evince, by the
additions and improvements undertaken by his
command, the desire which Richard entertained of
giving employment to the industrious portion of
the community, and of exciting the more wealthy
citizens, by his own example, to undertake works
of useful design. He desired thus to divert their

---

[1] Rous, p. 215. ; Buck, lib. v. p. 138.   [2] Ibid.
[3] Buck, lib. v. p. 139.   [4] Harl. MSS., 433. fol. 211.
[5] Ibid., fol. 204.   [6] Ibid., fol. 175.   [7] Ibid., fol. 187.

minds from sedition and insurrection to the encouragement of peaceful occupations, and the promotion of acts that would reflect honour on themselves, and confer lasting benefit upon their country.[1]
Most opportunely for the king, as affording him
additional means for checking the growing discontent, messengers arrived in London from the
French monarch, craving letters of protection for
ambassadors appointed to treat for peace.[2] The
required letters were issued by Richard on the 1st
of September; and this important step towards the
procurement of that peace so much desired by the
citizens was rendered more effective by its having
so immediately succeeded a corresponding application from Scotland, with which country an amicable league was on the eve of being cemented.
An opening was thus afforded for a renewal of
commercial intercourse with both kingdoms.

The immediate causes of his unpopularity, or at
least a portion of them, being in some degree modified, the monarch again departed for Nottingham,
which he reached on the 12th of September[3], and
on the 16th he gave audience to the deputies from
Scotland, who were there most honourably received
in the great chamber of the castle[4], the king
being seated under a royal canopy, and surrounded
by his court and the chief officers of state. The
noble commissioners[5] sent by James III. were ac-

---

[1] " This King Richard is to be praised for his buildings at
Westminster, Nottingham, Warwick, York, Middleham ; and many
other places will manifest." — *Rous*, p. 215.

[2] Fœdera, xii. p. 235.

[3] Harl. MSS., 433. fol. 187.   [4] Buck, lib. i. p. 33.

[5] " The embassy consisted of the Earl of Argyle, chancellor of

companied by his secretary and orator, " Master Archibald Quhitlaw," who, stepping before the rest, addressed an eloquent oration to the English sovereign in Latin, panegyrising his high renown, noble qualities, great wisdom, virtue, and prudence. " In you, most serene prince, all the excellent qualities of a good king and great commander are happily united, insomuch that to the perfection of your military and civil accomplishments nothing could be added by the highest rhetorical flights of a most consummate orator."[1]

This address, although couched in the extravagant language of the times, confirms three facts connected with King Richard of no small importance, viz., his mildness of disposition : " You show yourself gentle to all, and affable even to the meanest of your people." His beauty of feature—" In your face, a princely majesty and authority royal, sparkling with the illustrious beams of all moral and heroical virtues ; " and lastly, that his stature, though small, was unaccompanied by deformity, since the Scottish orator made it the vehicle of his chief eulogy : " To you may not be unfitly applied what was said by the poet of a most renowned prince of the Thebans[2], that Nature never united to a small frame a greater soul, or a more powerful

Scotland, the Bishop of Aberdeen, the Lord Lisle, the Lord Dramonde of Stobhall, Master Archibald Quhitlaw Archdeacon of Lothian and secretary to the king, Lion King-at-Arms, and Duncan of Dundas."—*Buck*, lib. i. p. 33.

[1] Buck, lib. v. p. 140.

[2] " So great a soul, such strength of mind,
   Sage Nature ne'er to a less body joyn'd."
                              Translation in Kennet, p. 573.

mind."[1] The conference ended, the ambassadors
delivered to King Richard a letter from their sovereign, to which the English monarch returned a
brief but dignified reply.[2] They likewise inquired
his pleasure relative to the reception of commissioners, then on their progress from Scotland to
negociate a marriage between the Duke of Rothesay,
eldest son of King James, and the Lady Anne de
la Pole, daughter of the Duke of Suffolk, and sister
of the Earl of Lincoln, whom the English monarch
had nominated his successor to the throne.

This important proposition, intended as a means
of establishing peace between the two countries[3],
was finally decided upon on the 20th of September[4],
when the contract of marriage between the heir of
the Scottish crown and King Richard's niece was
signed by the Scotch commissioners and the great
officers of state attached to the English government[5];
and on the same day a truce with Scotland for
three years was concluded[6], and duly ratified by
commissioners nominated for that purpose by their
respective sovereigns.[7] It will be fresh in the mind
of the reader, that the faithless performance of a
corresponding matrimonial engagement entered into
some years previously between the above-named
Duke of Rothesay and the Princess Cecily was the

[1] " If Richard had not been short," observes Mr. Sharon Turner,
" the prelate who came ambassador to him from Scotland would not,
in his complimentary address delivered to him on his throne, have
quoted these lines ; nor would he have made such an allusion, if it
had not been well known that Richard cared not about it."—*Middle
Ages*, vol. iii. p. 476.

[2] See Appendix EE.

[3] Fœdera, xii. p. 232.

[4] Fœdera, xii. p. 244.

[5] Buck, lib. i. p. 33.

[6] Fœdera, xii. p. 235.

[7] Buck, lib. i. p. 33.

origin of the war in which King Richard, before his accession to the throne, acquired such high military reputation; and it is somewhat remarkable, as a proof of the vicissitudes consequent on those mutable times, that this second contract with the line of York, now entered into as the means of terminating warfare, and cementing peace and amity between the two kingdoms, was destined to terminate in a manner similar to the former betrothment, and to entail equal mortification on another of Richard's nieces.

The Lady Anne de la Pole, like her fair cousin Cecily, became the victim of the inconstancy of the age. The pledge solemnly plighted at Nottingham was but lightly regarded in after-years. " Upon the breach thereof," states Sir George Buck, " the young affianced, resolving to accept no other motion, embraced a conventual life, and ended her days a nun in the monastery of Sion [1]," while the Scottish prince was reserved for marriage with the daughter of the rival and enemy of their house and race, Henry of Richmond [2]; although, as the daughter of his consort, Elizabeth of York, the Princess Margaret of Tudor was the niece of his first betrothed, and the cousin of the Lady Anne, whose marriage has been just detailed.

The aspect of political affairs continued to brighten during Richard's prolonged stay at Nottingham; another treaty of peace and amity was

---

[1] Buck, lib. i. p. 33.

[2] James IV. of Scotland was united to the Princess Margaret, the eldest daughter of King Henry VII. and of his Queen Elizabeth of York, on the 8th of August 1503. — *Lel. Coll.*, iv. fol. 205.

sought for by Francis Duke of Brittany, or, rather, a ratification of former negociations; and as soon as the Scotch ambassadors had fairly departed shipping was ordered to convey an English mission[1] to that principality, which sailed[2] on the 13th of October, and succeeded in establishing so friendly an alliance between the two countries[3] that all apprehension of Richmond's receiving aid from that quarter was entirely set at rest. Architectural improvements on an enlarged scale at Nottingham Castle[4], and at the royal palace at York[5], a warrant for rebuilding, at the king's cost, a chapel at Pontefract, and the house adjoining of Dame Margaret Multon, an anchorite[6], together with other of those acts of piety and munificence[7] which so endeared King Richard to his northern subjects, attest the fact of this monarch's sojourn at Nottingham for the remainder of the autumn, with the exception of a brief visit from thence at the close of October to his lordship and castle at Tutbury.[8] Having, at length, restored peace within the realm, and cemented amicable leagues with Scotland, France, and Brittany, Richard made preparations for returning to London for the winter, where he was welcomed by the citizens with demonstrations of popularity and joy, fully as great, if not greater than those which had characterized his triumphant entry into the metropolis at the

[1] Harl. MSS., 433. fol. 189. [2] Ibid., fol. 192.
[3] Fœdera, xii. p. 255.
[4] Harl. MSS., 433. fol. 193.; see also Leland's Itin.
[5] Harl. MSS., 433. fol. 187. 218.
[6] Ibid., fol. 193. [7] Ibid., fol. 191.
[8] Ibid., fol. 193.

same period a twelvemonth before. " In the beginning of this mayor's year, and the second year
of King Richard," retails the city chronicler [1],
" that is to mean the 11th day of the month of November, 1484, the mayor and his brethren, being
clad in scarlet, and the citizens, to the number of
five hundred or more, in violet, met the king beyond Kingston, in Southwark, and so brought him
through the city to the Wardrobe [2], beside the
Black Friars, where for that time he was lodged."

Thus, reinstated in public favour, and bemoaning
the demoralizing effects which had resulted from
the disturbed state of the kingdom since his accession, the king essayed to promote kindlier and
gentler feelings amongst all classes of his subjects,
by encouraging and patronising such sports and
pastimes as were consonant with the spirit and
habits of the age. Falconry and hawking especially engaged his attention. He had nominated
John Grey of Wilton to the office of master of the
king's hawks, and the keeping of a place called the
Mews [3], near Charing Cross [4], in the preceding

[1] Fabyan, p. 518.

[2] On Bennet Hill, in the neighbourhood of the Herald's College,
a little to the west, anciently stood the royal wardrobe, kept in a
house built by Sir John Beauchamp, who made it his residence. It
was sold to King Edward III., and in the fifth year of Edward IV.
it was given to William Lord Hastings; it was afterwards called
Huntingdon House, and became the lodging of Richard III. in the
second year of his reign.— *Pennant's London*, p, 356.

[3] The term " Mew " signified moulting; and the range of buildings which once stood near Charing Cross, called the King's Mews,
and which were converted into stables by King Henry VIII., derived
the appellation from the royal hawks being kept there during the
time of their moulting.— *Old Sports of England*, p. 28.

[4] Harl. MSS., 433. fol. 53.

year; and he now issued warrants for securing, at
a reasonable price, such hawks and falcons as should
be necessary for the " king's disport," following
up this command by the appointment of a serjeant
of falcons for England, and a purveyor of hawks
for parts beyond the seas. [1] Hunting also, the
sport to partake of which King Edward had so
frequently invited the civic authorities of London,
a condescension which had told so much in his
favour, was not overlooked by his politic brother.
It was an amusement to which Richard had been
early inured, and to which he was much attached:
and the minute particulars in his register of the
payments awarded to the chief officers of the royal
establishment, as well as the distinct enumeration
of the several appointments connected with the inferior departments [2], together with the provision allotted to the horses and dogs, evince his determination to uphold a recreation which the disturbed state
of the kingdom had, for a time, interrupted. Nor
were the amusements of the humbler classes forgotten by the monarch; the exploits of the bear-
ward, the appellation given to the keeper of dancing
bears, together with the grotesque antics of apes
and monkies, by which the former animals were
usually accompanied, was a rude pastime greatly
estimated at this period by all ranks; and the king,
shortly after his accession, had appointed a " master guider and ruler of all our bears and apes
within England and Wales " [3] — the greater part

---

[1] Harl. MSS., 433. fol. 103. 214.
[2] Ibid., 433. fol. 49. 175. 195.   [3] Ibid., 433. fol. 139.

of the animals thus exhibited being the property of the crown; and letters were sent to the several mayors and sheriffs throughout the kingdom, requiring them to protect the " said game," as well as the master and subordinate keepers whom the king licensed, " reasonable money paying," to travel through the country with them. But the recreation to which Richard himself seemed most devoted was that of music. Innumerable grants to minstrels [1] were bestowed from the royal funds, and foreign musicians received from him the greatest encouragement. [2] He kept a band of trumpeters at a yearly payment [3], and promoted a royal choral assemblage upon a very enlarged scale, having empowered " John Melynek, one of the gentlemen of the chapel royal, to take and seize for the king all such singing men and children, being expert in the science of music, as he can find, and think able to do the king's service within all places in the realm, as well cathedral churches, colleges, chapels, houses of religion, and all other franchised and exempt places or elsewhere, the college royal of Windsor excepted [4]; " an act which singularly illustrated the despotism of the period, and the little personal freedom enjoyed by the people of England, but which might have been highly beneficial in advancing the art of music in this country, had King Richard been permitted sufficient leisure and tranquillity to carry into effect the enlarged views which he entertained on all matters connected with the improvement or benefit of his country.

[1] Harl. MSS., 433. fol 46.
[2] Ibid., fol. 190. 210.
[3] Ibid., 78. 96. 104.
[4] Ibid., 189.

But Richard's peaceful days were few in number and of short duration. His earnest desire was to quell discord, and to ensure a period of repose by exertions the most praiseworthy and unceasing. Nevertheless he was too wise to slumber or to be lulled into security while any symptom existed for alarm; and so long as Richmond was at large, and his supporters unsubdued, just cause for apprehension remained that peace was by no means settled.

The treaties with France, Brittany, and Scotland had, indeed, tempered any present suspicion of danger; nevertheless rumours and reports reached King's Richard's ears from time to time which induced him to fix his attention warily upon the movements of his enemies, even when seemingly engaged in promoting such amusements and recreations as were fitted for a season of tranquillity. So early after his return to London as the 6th of December[1] intelligence was communicated which led him to doubt the good faith of the French nation, and to compel him to issue a strong proclamation to that effect. " Forasmuch as we be credibly informed that our ancient enemies of France, by many and sundry ways, conspire and study the means to the subversion of this our realm, and of unity amongst our subjects, as in sending writings by seditious persons with counterfeit tokens, and contrive false inventions, tidings, and rumours, to the intent to provoke and stir discord and disunion betwixt us and our lords, which be as faithfully disposed as any subjects can suffice. We therefore

---

[1] Harl. MSS., 787. fol. 2.

will and command you strictly, that in eschewing
the inconveniences aforesaid you put you in your
uttermost devoir of any such rumours, or writings
come amongst you, to search and inquire of the first
showers or utterers thereof; and them that ye shall
so find ye do commit unto sure ward, and after
proceed to their sharp punishment, in example and
fear of all other, not failing hereof in any wise, as
ye intend to please us, and will answer to us at
your perils."[1]   The result of this strong edict was
the arrest of Sir Robert Clifford at Southampton,
who, being sent to the Tower of London, was arraigned and tried at Westminster, and being found
guilty was from thence drawn unto the Tower Hill
upon " a hurdle," where he suffered the death of a
traitor.[2]

Whether he was the bearer of private instructions to his accomplices in England, or whether
King Richard obtained by means of his own emissaries more direct information respecting the views
of the rebels in France, does not plainly appear;

---

[1] Harl. MSS., 787. fol. 2.

[2] That Sir Robert Clifford was strongly and strenuously supported
by the disaffected party in London is evident from the measures
taken to prevent his execution, the detail of which is thus quaintly
given by the city historian. " But when he came fore St. Martin-
le-grand, by the help of a friar which was his confessor, and one of
them that was next about him, his cords were so lowered or cut,
that he put him in devoir to have entered the sanctuary ; and likely
it had been that he should have so done, had it not been for the
quick help and rescue of the sheriffs and their officers, the which
constrained him to lie down upon the hurdle, and new bound him,
and so hurried to the said place of execution, where he was divided
into two pieces, and after his body, with the head, was conveyed to
the Augustine Friars, and there buried before St. Katharine's Altar."
—*Fabyan*, 518.

but the fact was speedily ascertained that Harwich was the point where the insurgents intended to land, and measures for resisting their attempts were instantly adopted. Instructions were issued on the 18th of the same month to the commissioner of array for the counties of Surrey, Middlesex, and Hertford, " to call before them all the knights, squires, and gentlemen within the said counties, and know from them what number of people, defensibly arrayed, every of them severally will bring at half a days' warning, if any sudden arrival fortune of the king's rebels and traitors."[1]   Sir Gilbert Debenham and Sir Philip Bothe were despatched with a strong force to the protection of Harwich, a commission being sent to the bailiffs, constables, and inhabitants to assist them in keeping the said town, and to resist the king's rebels if they should arrive there.   These precautions had the desired effect. The conspirators were either intimidated by the resistance which they understood would await them, or their projects were defeated by finding that the king was not thrown off his guard by the recent truce with France, and was well acquainted with their designs, and fully prepared to subvert them.

Whatever occasioned the delay, the threatened danger was again dispelled, and King Richard was left to celebrate his Christmas in undisturbed tranquillity.   He solemnised this festival with pomp and splendour, corresponding to that which had characterised its anniversary in the preceding year, encouraging the recreations usual at the season, presiding

---

[1] Harl. MSS., 433. fol. 198.

himself at the customary feasts, and so attentively
observing even the most trivial customs, that a warrant is entered for the payment of " 200 marks for
certain new-year's gifts, bought against the feast of
Christmas."[1]   The festivities continued without interruption until the day of the Epiphany, when they
appear to have terminated with an entertainment
of extraordinary magnificence, given by the monarch
to his nobles in Westminster Hall,—" the king himself wearing his crown," are the words of the Croyland historian[2], " and holding a splendid feast in the
great hall similar to that at his coronation."

Widely different, however, were the results of the
two entertainments — the one giving promise of a
peaceful and popular reign, from the seeming unanimity which then prevailed, the other being destined to usher in that period of anarchy and feud
which was alike to deprive Richard of his crown and
of his life ; for, " on the same day," continues the
chronicler[3], " tidings were brought to him by his
seafaring intelligencers that, in spite of all the
power and splendour of his royal estate, his enemies
would, beyond all doubt, enter, or attempt to enter,
the kingdom during the approaching summer."
Little did Richard imagine that this would be the
last feast at which he would preside—the last time
he would display his crown in peace before his assembled peers ! Strongly imbued with the innate
valour of his race, he hailed with satisfaction the
prospect of terminating a system of petty warfare,

[1] Harl. MSS., 433. fol. 148.
[2] Chron. Croy., p. 571.   [3] Ibid.

which ill suited the daring and determined spirit of a prince of the line of York; he ardently longed for the period when he should encounter his rival hand to hand, and, by one decisive blow, crush his aspiring views, and relieve himself from those threatened invasions, the guarding against which were more harassing to a mind constituted like his than the most desperate conflicts on the field of battle. Measures were forthwith taken to provide for the defence of the town and marches of Calais, and a warrant was sent to the collectors of customs at the port of Sandwich[1], commanding them to pay the mayors and bailiffs of the Cinque Ports, whereat they should take shipping, for the expenses which they might incur for the same.[2]

Similar precautions were taken for the preservation of the castle and county of Guisnes, of which Sir James Tyrell was appointed governor, " to have

---

[1] This document contains, amongst other items, an article that is somewhat remarkable, and one which cannot fail of interesting those who consider that Perkin Warbeck was indeed the true Duke of York, and conveyed secretly into Flanders by the friends and supporters of his family, and not surreptitiously by command of King Richard III., viz., " Warrant to the Privy Seal in order towards the repaying the mayor, &c. of Dover four marks, by them advanced for defraying the passage, &c. of Sir James Tyrell, the king's councillor, and knight of his body, who was of late sent over the sea, into the parties of Flanders, for divers matters concerning greatly the king's weal." If one or both of the young princes were privately conveyed to Flanders, as both Sir Thomas More and Lord Bacon assert was currently reported at the accession of Henry VII., there can scarcely be a doubt that their uncle would strive to discover their retreat ; and Sir James Tyrell, though by no means likely to have been " their employed murderer," would, as the king's councillor and " squire of the body," be a fitting agent for despatching to the Continent on so delicate and important a mission as seeking out the princes, if alive.

[2] Harl. MSS., 433. fol. 200.

the charge, rule, and guidance of the same during the absence of the Lord Mountjoy, the king's lieutenant there."[1] The knights, squires, gentlemen, &c. of the county of Chester were commanded by an edict " to obey the Lord Stanley, the Lord Strange, and Sir William Stanley, who had the rule and leading of all persons appointed to do the king service, when they shall be warned against the king's rebels[2];" and a like commission to the knights of other counties were issued, " to do the king's grace service, against his rebels, in whatsoever place within the realm they fortune to arrive."[3] Richard, in fact, neglected no precaution that could secure his personal safety, or ensure tranquillity to his kingdom; but such a continual system of warfare, or rather provision against its anticipated occurrence, could not be met by the ordinary resources of the country in those troubled times; and the enormous expenditure to which he had been subjected almost from the period when he ascended the throne had so exhausted the Treasury, and dissipated the funds amassed by King Edward IV.[4], that Richard, in spite of his repugnance to adopt, by compulsion, a measure he had resolutely refused when it was voluntarily offered to him[5], was necessitated at length to fall back upon the despotic and unpopular system entitled " Benevolences[6]," — a mode of taxation which

---

[1] Harl. MSS., 433. fol. 201.
[2] Ibid. fol. 202.   [3] Ibid. fol. 203. 205.
[4] Chron. Croy., p. 571.   [5] Rous, p. 215.
[6] " This tax, called a Benevolence, was devised by Edward IV., for which he sustained much envy. It was abolished by Richard III., by act of parliament, to ingratiate himself with the people, and it was now revised by King Henry VII., but with consent of par-

he had not only condemned at his accession, but had afterwards abolished by act of parliament; one which excited so much anger against his brother, by whom it was first devised[1], and one to which Richard had proved he never would have had recourse but from a necessity which admitted of no alternative. To this obnoxious proceeding, indeed, there can exist little doubt, may be traced those accumulated evils, and the origin of most of those malignant accusations which have cast so deep a shade over the latter part of this monarch's reign, that even time itself has failed to soften its ill effects, and justice has been powerless in withdrawing the veil which anger, discontent, and popular excitement at so odious a measure cast over every subsequent act undertaken by this sovereign.

Tumult and insurrection speedily followed[2], when Edward IV., in all the fulness of prosperity, had descended from his high estate to distrain his subjects, under this misapplied term of " Benevolence," for bounty despotically extorted from them.[3] King Richard had not only despised such regal beggary, but had rendered a renewal of similar exactions illegal by act of parliament.[4] Tenfold, therefore, was the public indignation increased against him, when, unsupported by his brother's more favoured position, and with the partisans of that brother's offspring arrayed in hostility against him, he revived a measure which even King Ed-

liament, for so it was not in the time of King Edward IV."— *Bacon's Henry VII.*, p. 100.

[1] See vol. i. ch. 10. p. 372.   [2] Lingard, vol. v. pp. 221. 225.
[3] Buck, lib. v. p. 134.   [4] Stat. of Realm, vol. ii. p. 478.

ward's popular manners, united to his stern and unrelenting rule, could with difficulty carry into effect.[1]

It was, indeed, the death-blow to Richard's
waning popularity; and reference to the strong
language of the Croyland historian, and Fabyan,
the city annalist, will sufficiently prove that, from
the time this king sanctioned the imposts, religious
and secular, to which he was driven, in this his
great strait (for the sum was specified which the
clergy as well as laymen were required to give [2]),
he was subjected to the united enmity of the
church, which had recently lauded him to the skies,
of the citizens of London, who had conducted him
twice in triumph to their city, and of the many
wealthy and richly-endowed commoners, who had
hitherto remained neuter amidst the political dis-
tractions which had terminated one dynasty and
elevated another to the throne.

The ecclesiastical writer, after detailing the immediate cause that led to this mode of replenishing
the royal coffers, viz. the impending invasion of the
Earl of Richmond, says [3] : " Herewith he (King
Richard) was not displeased, thinking it would put
an end to all his doubts and troubles;" " cunningly,
however, remembering that money, of which he
had now so little, was the nerve of war, he resorted
to the exactions of King Edward [4], which he con-

---

[1] Hab. Edw. IV. p. 131.   [2] Harl. MSS., 433. fol. 275.
[3] Chron. Croy., p. 571.

[4] Fabyan (p. 664.) states that King Edward demanded from the
wealthiest of his commoners " the wages of half a man for the year,"
or 4l. 11s. 3d., and that he got from the lord mayor 30l., and from
each alderman 20 marks, or at least 10l. Before exacting these
contributions, as " a present for the relief of his wants," the clergy,

demned in full parliament benevolences — a word hated by all: and he sent chosen men, sons of this age, more prudent in their generations than the sons of light, who, by prayers and threats, extorted from the chests of almost all ranks very large sums of money."[1]

Fabyan not only corroborates this account, but so forcibly depicts the distressed state of mind to which the king was reduced before having recourse to the measure, that his emphatic description of the treachery and ingratitude which evidently aggravated the king's most trying position at this crisis affords a melancholy picture of the degenerate state of the nobility at this most important period of English history. "And in the month of February following," he writes, "King Richard, then leading his life in great agony and doubt, trusting few of such as were about him, spared not to spend the great treasure which before King Edward gathered in, giving of great and large gifts. By means whereof he alone wasted, not the great treasure, but also he was in such danger that he borrowed many notable sums of money of the rich men of this realm, and especially of the citizens of London, whereof the least sum was forty pounds, for surety whereof he delivered to them good and sufficient pledges."[2]

With such guarantee for repayment, and it is well-known that Richard pledged even his plate[3]

---

the lords, and the commons had separately granted this monarch a tenth of their income. — *Lingard,* vol. v. p. 220.

[1] Chron. Croy., p. 571. [2] Fabyan, p. 518.

[3] His want of money appears from the warrants in the Harl.

and jewels to raise money in this emergency, it can scarcely be said that he revived in its extreme sense the obnoxious system of " Benevolences;" the tax so designated being absolutely required as a gift by King Edward. " The name it bore," observes that monarch's biographer[1], " was a Benevolence, though many disproved the signification of the word by their unwillingness to the gift." Whereas King Richard is allowed by one of the citizens of London, who was contemporary with him[2], to have given " good and sufficient pledges," as surety for the sums which he sought as a temporary loan. The official record, which perpetuates the tax, yet further certifies to this fact: " Commissioners were appointed to borrow money for the king's use[3];" and the same register demonstrates also, most conclusively, the cause for which these loans were made, viz. " for such great and excessive costs and charges as we must hastily bear and sustain, as well for the keeping of the sea as otherwise for the defence of the realm."[4] Although no mention is made of the assembling of parliament during this second year of his reign, yet the letters delivered by the above-named commissioners afford undeniable proof that Richard adopted this strong measure by the consent and sanction of his Privy Council; and these credentials[5] being prefaced with the words — " to be delivered to those from whom

---

MSS., " for pledging and sale of his plate." — *Turner's Middle Ages,* vol. iv. p. 29.

[1] Hab., Edw. IV. p. 131.   [2] Fabyan, 518.
[3] Harl. MSS., 433. fol. 276.   [4] Ibid.
[5] See Appendix FF.

the commons requested loans in the king's name,"
together with their embracing also this strong
expression—"for that intent his grace *and all his
lords* thinking that every true Englishman will
help him in that behalf," it justifies the inference
that King Richard neither acted tyrannically nor
unadvisedly in this important matter, but rather
followed the advice of certain leading members of
both houses, whom he had probably summoned to
aid him with their counsel in so momentous a crisis.

But vain were his efforts to stem the tide of adverse
fortune! Domestic trials, mingled with the cares
of state; and the hand of death was already pressing
heavily on another of his house, threatening to
sever the only remaining tie of home affection
which had soothed and softened the anxious cares
of Richard's regal career. His gentle consort, the
companion of his childhood, and the loved one of
maturer years, had never recovered the shock which
she sustained from the sudden death of her only
child. The king was indeed compelled to struggle
with his grief, being speedily called upon to take
part in stirring scenes, which afforded little time or
opportunity for indulging in that anguish which
the chronicler of Croyland graphically paints as
approaching almost to insanity[1]: not so the afflicted
and distressed queen; she had both time and leisure
to dwell upon her irreparable loss.[2] To all the

[1] Chron. Croy., p. 570.
[2] "The queen could not hold so proportioned a temper over her
grief, the tenderness of her sex letting it break upon her in a more
passionate manner, and with such an impression, that it became her
sickness past recovery, languishing in weakness and extremity of

tenderness of the fondest parent she united that
pride of ancestry which was inherent in her lofty
race, and which was so strikingly exhibited at York
as she led by the hand in triumph her princely
child, his fair young forehead graced with the
golden circlet of heir apparent to the throne.
The anguish of the bereaved mother, the blight
which had prematurely withered her fondest hopes,
and left her childless at the very period when maternal love and maternal pride most exultingly
filled her heart, produced so disastrous an effect on
a frame which was never robust, and of late had
been subjected to excitement of no ordinary kind,
that it gradually produced symptoms which pre-
saged a dissolution as premature, arising from a
disease similar in its nature to that which had consigned her sister, the Duchess of Clarence, to an
early grave.[1]   Consumption[2], there seems little
doubt, was the true cause of the " gradual decay "
which is stated, in both instances, to have wasted
the strength of the daughters of the Earl of
Warwick.   If, however, the state of debility consequent on that incurable disease, and into which the
Lady Isabel fell for two months preceding her death,
was publicly imputed to poison[3], and if the im-

---

sorrow, until she seemed rather to overtake death than death her."
— *Buck*, lib. 2., p. 43.

[1] Isabel Duchess of Clarence, only sister of Anne queen-consort
of Richard III., died of a deep decline, the 12th of December, 1746,
in the twenty-fourth year of her age, having been born September
5th, 1451." — *Sandford*, book v. p. 412.

[2] " A consumption, and past hopes of recovery." — *Buck*, lib. 4.
p. 128.

[3] Rot. Parl., vi. p. 173.

petuous Clarence not only procured the execution
of one of her attendant gentlewomen on that charge,
but even accused King Edward's queen of accelerating the dissolution of his duchess by means of
necromancy[1], it can scarcely be wondered at that
Richard, accused of the murder of his nephews, and
to whom even the death of his royal brother by
poison had been imputed by the malice of his
enemies[2], although he was widely separated from him
at the time the event occurred, it can scarcely, I
repeat, excite astonishment that motives were in-
dustriously sought for to account for Queen Anne's
declining health, or that her death, following so immediately as it did upon that of the young Prince
of Wales, was imputed to the king's desire of ridding
himself of a consort, now weak in health and subdued in spirit.[3] Poison was the vague instrument
to which it was the custom of the times to attribute
all cases of sudden or unexpected death, and the
accusers of Richard acted upon a custom at once
so common and so convenient.

But nothing can be more cruel or more unrea-
sonable than this base insinuation, for which there
exists no sort of foundation, even on the ground of
expediency, as in the case of the murder of the
young princes. From infancy the cousins had
lived on terms of amity and affection. No record
exists, either positive or implied, as in the preceding

[1] Rot. Parl., vi. p. 174.

[2] " They who ascribe it to poison are the passionate enemies of
Richard Duke of Gloucester's memory."—*Hab. Edw. IV.*, p. 222.

[3] " Either by inward thought and pensiveness of heart, or by infection of poison,—which is affirmed to be most likely,—the queen
departed out of this transitory life."—*Cont. More by Grafton,* p. 201.

and succeeding reigns, to intimate that the royal
pair, after their union in marriage, were unhappy,
or led a life of cold indifference. In every public
ceremony, in every state banquet, on every momentous occasion, Richard III. was accompanied by
Queen Anne. She is to be found supporting her
part with becoming splendour and dignity at both
his coronations; she was the companion alike of his
regal progress and of his sojourn in more troubled
times in the North; and it was the queen, and not
the king, who exhibited to the delighted multitude
at York young Edward of Gloucester as the future
monarch of England. They were resting together
at Nottingham Castle when intelligence arrived of
his death; and the harmony and affection in which
they were living at the time that this fearful stroke
of domestic bereavement fell upon them can scarcely
be better illustrated than by the fact that the contemporary annalist, in his forcible description of
the bitterness of heart which overwhelmed both
parents, sinks the dignity of their regal state in the
appellation which most pathetically painted the
union of home affections thus severed and broken:
" Then might you have seen the father and mother,
having heard the news at Nottingham, where they
then dwelt, almost mad with sudden grief." [1]

There is not, in fact, the slightest basis for imputing to Richard a crime as far exceeding all
charitable belief as it was unnatural and uncalled
for; nor, indeed, have his calumniators advanced
any stronger proof to convict him of the monstrous

[1] Chron. Croy., p. 570.

charge than that inferred from suspicions excited
by the simple fact that the youthful Princess
Elizabeth, who, after the reconciliation of her uncle
and her mother, was placed about the person of her
aunt, the queen consort, appeared in robes of a similar form and texture to those worn by Queen
Anne. On this interpretation of a circumstance,
in itself so unimportant that the " only rational
conclusion to be drawn from the coincidence," justly
observes one of the ablest writers of the present
day[1], is the proof it affords that Richard strictly
fulfilled his engagement, that his nieces should be
supported as became his kinswomen, has this last
and most appalling of this monarch's reputed crimes
been fastened upon him; and, to heighten the fearful picture, his object in destroying the wife whom
he had struggled to obtain in youth amidst the
severest difficulties is inferred to have arisen from
the desire of elevating to the throne his own niece!
the sister of the young princes whom he is reputed to have slain, the daughter of his own
brother, and, as surmised, the destined spouse of
his deceased child. It is too monstrous to be credited; and the insinuation is rendered more doubtful from the prejudiced source from whence it
springs.

This most heinous and revolting crime is not
hinted at by the ecclesiastical historian, who has
perpetuated the report, until Richard had incurred
the anger of the church by his renewal of " Benevo-

[1] See Sir Harris Nicolas' Memoir prefixed to the " Privy Purse
Expenses of Elizabeth of York," fol. 42.

lences," which tax,—from their great wealth,—fell
with peculiar severity on the religious fraternities of
which this writer was a member; and because the
amusements and festivities which immediately preceded the levying of that tax, and with which the
king had thought fitting to modify the discomfort
that had hitherto characterised his reign, afforded
them an opening for ascribing the king's pecuniary
wants to unnecessary profuseness. " It is not to
be concealed, that during the feast of the Nativity
he was over much intent upon singing and dancing
and vain changes of dress," is the strong language of the ecclesiastical chronicler[1], " which were
given of the same colour and form to Queen Anne
and to the Lady Elizabeth, daughter of the deceased
king, whereat the people were scandalized, and the
peers and prelates marvellously wondered; for it
was said by many, that the king, either in expect-
ation of the queen's death, or by divorce, for the
procuring of which it was conjectured that he had
sufficient cause, applied his mind in all ways to
contracting a marriage with the said Elizabeth;
he did not otherwise see that the realm would be
confirmed to him, or his competitor deprived of
hope."

That King Richard should strive to the utmost
of his power to cancel the betrothment between
Henry of Richmond and the Princess Elizabeth,
whose stipulated marriage was alike the condition,
as it formed the sole ground of hope, for his rival
being supported in his attempts upon the crown, is

[1] Chron. Croy., p. 572.

a conclusion not only reasonable in itself, but one which can admit of no doubt.

Far different, however, is the surmise that Richard's own union with his niece could confirm to him the realm, or in the remotest degree strengthen his regal position. To have elevated her to the throne, in virtue of her illustrious descent, as King Edward's eldest daughter, in which position alone she could have given weight to his disputed title, would at once have impeached his own right to the throne, would have impugned the validity of the decree of parliament which confirmed that assumed right, and would have made him a self-convicted usurper, by disproving not alone the charge of Queen Elizabeth's marriage being invalid, but rendering informal also the Act of Settlement by which her offspring were declared illegitimate, and himself the true, just, and rightful heir to the throne, arising from the stigma attached to the birth of young Edward V., and the legal impediments which excluded the offspring of the Duke of Clarence from the throne, by reason of their parents' attainder, which had never been reversed. The learned biographer of Elizabeth of York, in his most interesting memoir of that Princess [1], has devoted so much attention, and evinced such ability in his keen and searching examination into this disputed, and, as it would appear, most groundless accusation, that little opening is left for any more conclusive arguments than those which that eminent writer advances, after

[1] Privy Purse Expenses of Elizabeth of York, fol. 42. 46.

testing the charge insinuated by Richard's political
enemies, and weighing their evidence by other and
more valid documents.[1] Convincing, however, as
are the reasons which Sir Harris Nicolas brings
forward to invalidate a charge which rests, as he
most distinctly proves, on no more solid basis than
surmise, yet being there advanced with a view of
exculpating the youthful daughter of Edward IV.,
and not King Richard III., they can only be
referred to in this memoir. Nevertheless the
learned writer, in defence of the niece, has adduced
causes that equally tend to exonerate the uncle
from a project in which both parties are alike implicated : for it is beyond all credibility to suppose
that this young and singularly exemplary princess,
who had not attained her nineteenth [2] year, and
had been subdued by trials and mortifications [3],
more than sufficient to blunt the most buoyant and
elastic spirit, could calmly insult the feelings of the
reigning queen by appearing publicly in the character of her successor [4], could unblushingly present herself to the assembled multitude as the
affianced of their sovereign during the lifetime of
his wife [5], or that she should eagerly watch, as

---

[1] See Appendix GG.

[2] Elizabeth of York, eldest daughter of King Edward IV., was
born at Westminster, 11th of February, 1466. — *Sandford*, book v.
p. 395.

[3] This young princess had early been promised in marriage to the
Dauphin of France, and in the court of France was called Madame
la Dauphine ; but Louis, the reigning sovereign of that kingdom,
broke his solemn pledge to Edward IV. : indignation at which, not
only led to the death of that king, but was the exciting cause of the
severe misfortunes which afterwards overwhelmed his offspring.

[4] Chron. Croy., p. 572.   [5] Ibid.

asserted [1], for the decease of her aunt, which,
whether resulting from natural causes [2], or from
poison said to be administered by her husband [3],
was to be the means of raising her kinswoman to
the throne as the consort of her own uncle, and
that too the same person who was accused of
having murdered her brothers! for by admitting
the certainty of their deaths only could she have
been the heiress of Edward IV., or have possessed
any claim to that inheritance, the admitted title to
which, as giving stability to Richard's alleged unlawful seizure of it, was the cause assigned by his
contemporary [4] for his selecting Elizabeth of York
as his future consort. The supposition is indeed
too monstrous for belief, and justifies the conclusion
of the above-quoted most able historian, that King
Richard "never contemplated a marriage with his
niece," but "that the whole tale was invented with
the view of blackening his character, to gratify the
monarch in whose reign [5] all the contemporary
writers who relate it flourished." [6] This conclusion
is also strengthened by the fact, that all these writers agree in exculpating the princess (then the
royal consort of Henry VII.) from all participation
in the scheme, whereas those who were contemporary with the rumour, and give it as such only [7],

---

[1] Buck, lib. iv. p. 123.　　　　[2] Ibid.
[3] Rous, p. 218.　　　　[4] Chron. Croy., p. 572.
[5] Grafton, Hall, and Hollingshed, with other chroniclers who perpetuate the rumour, or rather record it as an acknowledged fact,
not only penned their works during the Tudor dynasty, but commenced them very many years after King Richard's death.
[6] Memoir of Elizabeth of York, p. 46.
[7] Chron. Croy., p. 572.

make no reservation, but, on the contrary, assign as the foundation for the surmise a circumstance which, if true, implicates her fully as much as her uncle; if false, exculpates both, and invalidates the report altogether. In addition to the arguments thus drawn from the untenable and unsatisfactory character of the rumour itself there exist many positive facts, which tend still further to weaken this aspersion of King Richard.

These ought to have their due weight in rescuing that monarch from an imputation which, it has been shown, originated with unscrupulous political assailants, but which has since too long passed and been received as an historical fact. It appears that after the widow and children of King Edward IV. were induced to leave the sanctuary at Westminster they were received " with honourable courtesie [1] " by Richard and his royal consort, especially the Lady Elizabeth, who " ranked most familiarly in the queen's favour, and with as little distinction as sisters." [2] This admission alone would satisfactorily account for any coincidence in the form or texture of their dresses. [3] The young princess was placed by the queen on an equality with her-

---

[1] Buck, lib. iv. p. 127.   [2] Chron. Croy., p. 571.

[3] It was not until a later period of history that sumptuary regulations were issued for the " reformation of apparel for great estates or princesses, with other ladies and gentlemen." These statutes, with the " orders for precedence," yet extant in the Heralds' College, were drawn out by the Countess of Richmond, by command of her son Henry VII., in the eighth year of his reign. It is therefore evident that at this time there existed no impediment to preclude the queen and the princess from wearing corresponding dresses on general occasions. Had such an edict prevailed, subsequent laws would not have been required.

self; and since no statement is made of Elizabeth being arrayed in the vestments of royalty, but simply that at feasts, in which " dancing and singing and vain changes of dress" were made a reproach to her uncle, she was attired in robes similar to those of her aunt, nothing can be more reasonable than the supposition that the queen should soften the painful position in which her young relative now appeared at court, as the daughter of Dame Elizabeth Grey, instead of, as heretofore, the Princess Royal of the line of York, by attiring her as became the niece of the reigning monarch, and one whom the queen loved and distinguished " as a sister." Moreover, the peculiar degree of favour which was quickly lavished upon the Lady Elizabeth gave occasion for the surmise that she was destined to be the bride of the young Prince of Wales." [1] If such were indeed the case, she would become yet more an object of interest to her afflicted aunt ; and the similarity in their dresses would be still more satisfactorily accounted for from the pleasure, melancholy but natural, which the queen would feel in arraying the contemplated bride of her deceased child as befitted the exalted station which she would probably have filled had his life been spared. The words which follow the passage recently quoted from the contemporary chronicler, for the purpose of demonstrating the terms of familiarity on which the queen and the princess lived, seem to imply that it bore some connection to the deceased prince; " but

---

[1] Lingard, p. 262.

neither society that she loved, nor all the pomp
and festivity of royalty, could cure the languor or
heal the wound in the queen's breast for the loss
of her son." [1]   As the consort of the Prince of
Wales Elizabeth would indeed have destroyed all
hope of Richmond's attaining the crown; equally
expedient also, in regard to policy, would have
been the alliance between the two cousins, with
reference to its strengthening the position of King
Richard: since, without in any degree compromising the justice of the plea by which he was
elected to the throne, or repealing the act that
made his brother's offspring illegitimate, the union
of a daughter of Edward IV. with the heir of
Richard III. would have softened the resentment
of the opposing party, by the prospect which it
held out of restoring the sceptre to King Edward's
race in the person of his eldest child.   But the
demise of the Prince of Wales occurring so immediately after the reception of Elizabeth and
her sisters at court, and before any such measure, if it were contemplated, could be adopted
by the king for carrying into effect a scheme so
desirable for restoring peace to the realm, this circumstance left his niece still the betrothed of Henry
of Richmond, and, as such, an object of anxious
and unceasing solicitude to her uncle.   Hence arose
the real cause of her close companionship with the
queen, by being placed in personal attendance upon
whom the young Elizabeth was kept in real though
honourable captivity. [2]   As far as the investigation

---

[1] Chron. Croy., p. 571.   [2] Lingard, vol. v. p. 262.

of this, the darkest of King Richard's reputed crimes, has yet been pursued, the imputation has rested on conjecture alone; but as the question of whether he did actually wish to marry his niece is as important to his character as the allegation that he hastened the death of his wife to further that intention is altogether destructive of it, it is requisite to state, that Sir George Buck gives the substance of a letter said to have been written by the Lady Elizabeth to the Duke of Norfolk, which, if the fact could be substantiated, would fully support the injurious accusation as regards the king, and implicate his niece in the heinous charge of seeking to further her uncle's unhallowed and most criminal design. The Croyland writer unhesitatingly asserts that Richard contemplated a union with the Princess Elizabeth; but this assumption, it has been shown, was gratuitous, and based only on common rumour. Fabyan, another contemporary writer, is altogether silent on the subject; so likewise is Rous, the only remaining historian coeval with the monarch, although, in summing up the catalogue of his imputed crimes, he includes the poisoning of his wife.[1] This catalogue, it may be necessary to remark, is compiled with such an evident party feeling towards the house of Lancaster, and so unreservedly includes every accusation advanced against King Richard without adducing proof in support of any single allegation, that it cannot be regarded as possessing a shadow of historical authority. Nothing, indeed, approaching to evidence has ever been

---

[1] Rous, p. 215.

adduced, with the exception of the letter above
named, as cited by Buck; and his notice of so important a document appears in so questionable a
form, that it goes but very little way towards establishing the point.

" When the midst and last of February was past,"
writes Sir George Buck[1], " the Lady Elizabeth,
being more impatient and jealous of the success
than every one knew or conceived, wrote a letter
to the Duke of Norfolk, intimating, first, that he
was the man in whom she most affied, in respect
of that love her father had ever bore him. Then
she congratulates his many courtesies, in continuance of which she desires him to be a mediator
with her to the king in behalf of the marriage pro-
pounded between them, who, as she wrote, was her
only joy and maker in this world; and that she was
his in heart and thought: withal insinuating that
the better part of February was passed, and that
she feared the queen would never die." " All these
be her own words, written with her own hand; and
this is the sum of her letter," continues the historian[2], " which remains in the autograph or original draft, under her own hand, in the magnificent
cabinet of Thomas Earl of Arundel and Surrey." [3]

If Sir George Buck had himself seen the letter,
and spoken of its contents from his own knowledge, — if either himself or any other writer
had inserted a copy of it, or even a transcript

---

[1] Lib. iv. p. 128.   [2] Buck, lib. i. p. 128.
[3] The valuable collection of MSS. made by Thomas Earl of
Arundel, now termed " The Arundelian Library," has been most
carefully examined, with reference to the present work, but no trace
appears of this extraordinary letter.

from the " original draft," then, indeed, it would have been difficult to set aside such testimony. But considering that every search has been made for the alleged autograph,—that no trace of such a document has ever been discovered, or even known to have existed,—that no person is named as having seen it, or is instanced in support of its validity,—and moreover that Sir George Buck throughout his history of Richard III. inserts at full length copies[1] of almost every other instrument to which he refers, or gives marginal references to the source whence his authority was derived, but, in this instance, contents himself with merely stating the fact, and giving the substance of a letter which he appears to have received from rumour or hearsay information, the conviction cannot but arise that the letter in question was either not the production of Elizabeth of York, or, if so, that the insinuations referred to in it were misconstrued, and that its contents had reference to some other individual, and not, as was supposed, to her uncle.[2]

Although Richard III. is described by his enemies

---

[1] See pp. 23. 31. 48. 119. 121. 137. 139.

[2] " If the letter cited by Buck really existed, its purport may perhaps be reconciled with other facts by supposing that he mistook, or assigned to it a wrong date, and that, in fact, the person for whom she expressed so eager a desire to marry was Henry instead of Richard. Many parts of the abstract would agree with this hypothesis, for the allusion to February and Queen Anne, Buck calls an ' insinuation ;' and a passage of doubtful import becomes doubly so when construed by so suspicious a reporter. The only thing which renders this surmise unlikely is, that the letter is said to have been addressed by the Duke of Norfolk, who perished at Bosworth Field : but may not its address, too, have been only inferred, arising from its being in the possession of the duke's descendant?"—*Memoirs of Elizabeth of York*, fol. xlix.

as being destitute of all principle, moral and religious,
it was not so with his gentle niece; and the piety
and virtue for which she was so pre-eminently distinguished throughout a life of peculiar trial and
vicissitude[1] materially lessens the effect of the
slight evidence just produced, though it sufficiently
accounts for the " sisterly " affection with which she
was beloved by the queen, her intimate companionship with whom was, in all likelihood, the cause of
the injurious rumour which has alike darkened her
own fame and that of the king. Her widowed parent
likewise shared in the odium which attaches to all
the parties concerned in promoting this unnatural
union, it being stated that she was so overjoyed at
the proposed alliance of King Richard with her
daughter that she sent over to France to withdraw
her son, the Marquis of Dorset, from attendance
on the Earl of Richmond[2], soliciting his return to
England to participate in the advancement and
favour which Richard had promised to show him.
Considering that Queen Anne was living at the time
the alleged union was proposed, and that some length
of period must have elapsed before the dispensation
could be procured from Rome, which was necessary
to legalise the marriage of an uncle with his niece,
it is very improbable that so circumspect and politic
a woman as the widowed queen of Edward IV.
would risk the life of her only surviving son, by

[1] " From her youth, her veneration for the Supreme Being and
devotion to Him were admirable.   Her love to her brothers and sisters
was unbounded.   Her affection and respect to the poor and to religious
ministers were singularly great.' — Bern. Andreas, Cotton MS., Dom.
xviii.
[2] Buck, p. 127.

withdrawing him from the service of the prince, who was the betrothed of his sister, to place him in the power of a monarch who was reported to have slain his brothers. It is, indeed, altogether beyond belief that a mother should promote the marriage of her daughter with the reputed murderer of her other children, — the uncle who had deprived her sons of their birthright, and degraded herself and her daughters from their high estate to the rank of private gentlewomen, in order to possess himself of their inheritance. One of the charges must be false ; and either the widowed Elizabeth was satisfied that King Richard had not destroyed her offspring, or otherwise she must, in common with her daughter and the king, have suffered unjustly from rumours based on shallow foundations, or inferences drawn from false premises to suit the degraded and deceitful policy of the times. It is, nevertheless, due to her to state, that the chroniclers who narrate the circumstances of her endeavouring to detach the Marquis of Dorset from Richmond's interest place it as occurring at the time when she quitted sanctuary[1] with her daughters, and, consequently, before the queen's illness or the death of the young prince gave an opening for Richard to propose an alliance with the youthful Elizabeth. If then, amidst such

---

[1] " Wherefore the king sent to the queen, being in sanctuary, divers and often messengers, which first should excuse and purge him of all things before against her attempted or procured, and afterwards should so largely promise promotions innumerable and benefices, not only to her, but also to her son Lord Thomas Marquis Dorset, that they should bring her if it were possible into some wanhope, or, as men say, into a fool's paradise." — *Grafton, Cont. More*, p. 198.

contradictory accounts, any opinion can be hazarded on the probability of a fact so involved in mystery, the natural conclusion to be drawn from this last statement would be that the Queen Dowager was induced to quit the sanctuary from the prospect of her daughter being allied to King Richard's heir, and that she wished, from this circumstance, to detach her son from the Earl of Richmond, and in consequence made the attempt at the period mentioned, it being a proposition under her peculiar and very trying circumstances that would justify her saying, without compromising her own or her daughter's honour, " that all offences were forgotten and forgiven," and that she was "highly incorporate in the king's heart."[1]

It appears that the severe illness which threatened the life of Queen Anne occurred a few days after the Christmas festivities. From the period of her child's decease a report certainly prevailed of her languid and precarious state of health[2]; and the fatigue resulting from the entertainments which ushered in the new year of 1485 may, very possibly, have increased the disease which originated in " pining grief" and desponding of heart at her severe domestic bereavement. But the charge of King Richard having poisoned his wife, which fills up the measure of this monarch's alleged crimes, is not only negatived by the fact of her slow but gradual decline, and the duration of her illness for a period infinitely too long to have seemed likely to result from sinister means or violent measures, but

[1] Grafton, p. 199.'   [2] Buck, lib. ii. p. 44.

is still further disproved by the testimony of the
Croyland historian, who expressly avers that from the
commencement of her attack the queen was under
the care and control of physicians ; and that the
king abided so implicitly by their advice that he
withdrew from the society of his consort[1] when this
separation was rendered necessary in consequence
of her increasing illness.   Even this act, however,
which was the result, and not the cause, of her
sufferings, has been made a further cause of reproach to her husband, who by the Tudor chroniclers[2], has been accused of hastening her death by
neglect and unkindness, nay of even spreading a
report that she was actually dead, in the hope that
indignation at such heartless indifference for her
fate would more speedily terminate her existence.
If, indeed, King Richard had recourse to such an
expedient, and if the rumour designed for the
queen's ears was rendered more painful to a wife's
feelings by being accompanied by the most harsh
and inhuman reflections on her enfeebled state[3],
his behaviour, as detailed by the same writer to his
declining queen, when with tearful eyes, and in
sorrowful agony, she repaired to his presence to
inquire " why he had judged her worthy to die[4],"
is very singularly opposed to the merciless conduct
which led to so affecting an interview.   " The king
answered her with fair words," he soothed her
grief, comforted her with smiling and tender
caresses, " bidding her be of good cheer, for to his

[1] Chron. Croy., p. 570.
[2] Pol. Vir., p. 557. ; Grafton, p. 201. ; Hall, p. 407.
[3] Ibid.   [4] Ibid.

knowledge she should have no other cause." [1]　Nor
is there, indeed, the slightest proof on record to
show that Queen Anne had other cause for death
than the gradual but certain effects of the linger-
ing consumption, which was surely, but slowly,
consuming her.　From the fact of the court removing to Windsor [2] on the 12th of January, shortly
after the first symptoms of danger appeared, it
would seem as if every means was adopted that
human skill could devise for checking the progress
of the disease, and such as were consistent with the
assertion that Richard was " affectionately inclined
to his wife [3]," and had the commendation of a
"loving and indulgent husband." [4]　But, in truth,
from the very commencement of her seizure the
physicians had pronounced the queen's case to be
hopeless, and even considered it unlikely that she
would survive the month of February. [5]　She lingered, however, until March, " about the middle of
which month," says the Croyland writer, " on the
day of the great eclipse of the sun, she died, and
was buried at Westminster, with all honour befitting a queen." [6]

So terminated, in the spring of the year 1485,
the life of Queen Anne, the only surviving daughter
of the Earl of Warwick, and the partner for
twelve years of the last monarch of the princely
race of York; the accession of which dynasty
to the throne, and its subsequent deposition, had

---

[1] Grafton, p. 201.
[2] Harl. MSS., 433. pp. 200, 201.
[3] Buck, lib. iv. p. 129.　　[4] Ibid., p. 130.
[5] Ibid., p. 128.　　　　　　[6] Cron. Croy., p. 571.

mainly contributed to fix upon her father his title of "the king-maker." She sank to rest in the thirty-first year of her age, after wearing the crown as queen consort for the limited space of twenty months — a period, notwithstanding its short duration, that commemorates her as the only instance in our regal annals of a twice crowned and twice enthroned queen, a period which was characterised by the elevation of her husband to the throne, although at the time far removed from the direct line of succession, and which chronicles her child as bearing the title of Prince of Wales, — which had been so ominous to his race[1], — for an interval as brief as that which commemorates her own betrothment to the heir apparent of the house of Lancaster; by virtue of which political contract she forms one out of the six[2] illustrious individuals who alone have borne the high and ancient appellation of Princess of Wales. This early and transient prospect of succeeding to the exalted rank to which she eventually attained, and which Rous her contemporary has perpetuated by surmounting her portrait with two mystic hands, the one tendering to her the crown of Lancaster, the other that of York[3], adds another to the many remarkable events

[1] Richard Duke of York, the father of Richard III. (created prince by the parliament, which admitted his claim to the throne), was killed at Wakefield ; Edward Prince of Wales, the heir of King Henry VI., was slain at Tewkesbury ; Edward Prince of Wales, eldest son of Edward IV. (and who for a few months bore the title of King Edward V.), is reputed to have been murdered in the Tower ; and Edward Prince of Wales, the only child of Richard III., died suddenly a few months after he was advanced to the title.

[2] Strickland's Lives of the Queens of England, vol. iii. p. 362.

[3] See the frontispiece prefixed to the second volume of this work, in which Queen Anne is represented as standing between the rival

which procured for her the epithet of " the pageant queen[1]," that of receiving homage as Princess of Wales from one branch of the race of Plantagenet, although the one which was never destined to elevate her to the throne,—and attaining the dignity of queen through a union with the youngest member of the rival house, him in whom the race as well as the dynasty became altogether extinct, but who, as neither heir apparent nor heir presumptive, could hold out no prospect at the time of bestowing upon her that regal coronet which, wreathed with the red rose, she had indeed once been led to expect as her marriage portion. Its after-possession brought with it but little of peace, and still less of happiness, arising from the rival broils and domestic trials which marked the brief interval that elapsed before the white rose of York withered on the brows of the last of the Plantagenet queens, the gentle and amiable consort of Richard III.

Her decease, occurring on a day rendered remarkable by a total eclipse of the sun, an event viewed with superstitious feelings and gloomy fore-

crowns, extending her hand to King Richard ; beneath her feet rests, muzzled, the bear, the badge of the noble house of which she was the co-heiress. The monarch, as likewise the young prince their son, are both in armour, having surcoats of the royal arms. The former wears his crown on his head, and holds his sceptre in his right hand ; the brow of the latter is encircled with the coronet of heir apparent. The father and son are each represented as standing on the boar, the usual cognizance of King Richard III. These portraitures were drawn by the antiquary's own hand, to complete a pictorial history of the Earls of Warwick, who are most curiously depicted on a roll of vellum nearly eight yards long ; and the engraving now presented to the public has been faithfully copied from the original illuminated MS., still preserved in the College of Arms.

[1] Lawrence's Mem. of the Queens of England, p. 440.

bodings at this early period of history, doubtless
added force to the rumours which had long prevailed to the disadvantage of the king, and contributed to raise fresh reports, which, being based
on compassion for the deceased queen, were eagerly
adopted as facts by Richard's political enemies, and
thence found their way into the pages of history
by succeeding prejudiced annalists. The gorgeous
manner, however, in which the obsequies of the
deceased queen were solemnised, the magnificence[1]
of the funeral, the solemnity[2] by which it was
characterised, the tears[3] which her husband is
allowed to have shed when personally attending
her remains to St. Peter's, Westminster[4], near the
high altar of which she was interred, with all honour befitting a queen[5] — not only give proof that
her decease "added not a little to the king's sufferings and sorrows[6]," but fully justify the biographer of her reputed rival in stating (after defending
Richard from the calumnious accusation of poisoning his wife to espouse his niece), that it is a
charge which is deserving of attention for no other
reason than as it affords a remarkable example of
the manner in which ignorance and prejudice sometimes render what is called history little better than
a romance.[7]

[1] Buck, lib. iv. p. 129.   [2] Grafton, p. 201.
[3] Baker's Chron., p. 232.   [4] Grafton, p. 201.
[5] Chron. Croy., p. 571.   [6] Buck, lib. ii. p. 44.
[7] Memoirs of Elizabeth of York, p. 46.

CHAPTER XVIII.

IF the exigencies of the state at the period of his
son's decease allowed King Richard but little leisure
to indulge in the anguish consequent upon a stroke
as poignant as it was irreparable, still less time or
opportunity was permitted him to brood over the
loss of that gentle consort who from childhood was
associated in the vicissitudes that characterised the

fortunes of his race. The kingdom, indeed, was on the eve of a rebellion [1]; perfidy within his household [2] had destroyed Richard's confidence in those that surrounded him [3]; and rumour from without, with her hundred tongues, by rendering him odious to his subjects at large, had completed the measure of his misfortune. Little is it then to be marvelled at that the monarch was altogether subdued by a state of things so disheartening, or that he felt keenly the loss of that faithful partner with the remembrance of whom must have been associated the recollection of days of unmingled happiness and prosperity. Many trifling anecdotes, indeed, although in themselves unimportant, demonstrate the affection which Richard III. entertained for the companion of his youth. One of his last acts prior to the queen's decease, and at the time when her dissolution was hourly expected, was a grant of 300l. to that university which in the preceding year had decreed an annual mass for " the happy state " of the king and "his dearest consort, Anne [4];" and one of the first instruments which bears his signature after her demise affords proof also of the disinclination which he felt to take part in those pageants which heretofore he had considered it a duty to promote, and in the celebration of which he had invariably been accompanied and assisted by his queen. The document here alluded to is a com-

[1] Fabyan, p. 518.
[2] See Sharon Turner's Middle Ages, vol. iv. p. 57.
[3] Fabyan, p. 518.
[4] Cott. MS. Faustina, c. iii. 405.; see also Cooper's Ann. of Cambridge, p. 229.

mission addressed to Lord Maltravers, appointing him his deputy at the approaching festival " of the glorious martyr, and patron of England, St. George," which solemn feast the king could not at this time, " in his own person, conveniently keep." [1]

There can be little doubt, indeed, from the superstition which characterised those times, that the astronomical phenomenon which marked the day of Queen Anne's decease was pregnant with evil consequences to her husband. The ignorance of the age, which construed even the most natural events into good or evil omens[2], considered the eclipse of the sun to be an unequivocal proof that some unhallowed means had been used to accelerate her dissolution, and regarded it as affording additional evidence of the truth of the rumour that her illness had originated in the king's desire of elevating his niece to the throne.

In vain was every pains taken by the monarch to prove the groundlessness of such a charge, in vain his efforts to show, by his actions, that whatever seeming foundation there might have been for the report, arising from the coincidence in the dresses of the aunt and the niece, yet that it was

---

[1] Harl. MSS., 433. fol. 213.

[2] See Warkworth's Chronicle for an account of the comet, — " the most marvellous blazing star," — that appeared in the eleventh year of the reign of King Edward IV. ; and also for many examples of the superstition which characterised that age — "tokens of death, of pestilence, of great battle, of war, and of many other divers tokens " which have been showed in England " for amending of men's living," the which " note of prognosticating prodigies " are the more valuable from being penned in the same year in which they happened.— *Warkworth's Chronicle, printed by the Camden Society*, pp. 22. 24. 70.

so judged of by others on the ground of political expediency alone. It was sufficient for his enemies that he carefully guarded the young Elizabeth from collision with the partizans of Henry of Richmond, and that his queen, shortly after she was left childless, followed her offspring to the tomb, and left an opening for King Richard to elevate to the throne the affianced of his much-hated rival.

Whatever may have been the nature of King Richard's views with reference to the Lady Elizabeth, — whether, in accordance with the dissembling policy of the age, he tacitly permitted the report to gain ground from the wish to mortify and thwart the hopes and expectations of the Earl of Richmond, — yet this one fact is incontrovertible, Richard neither sought a divorce during the life of the queen, notwithstanding his niece was betrothed to Henry of Richmond long before apprehensions were excited for the safety of his royal consort, neither did he profess himself the suitor of his young kinswoman, or give any pretence for asserting that he entertained so unnatural a design after death had severed the only tie that interposed against its accomplishment: on the contrary, the king promptly adopted measures to exculpate himself from a charge equally at variance with policy and religion.

Immediately after the remains of the deceased queen were " honourably " laid at rest Richard summoned a council of state for the express purpose of distinctly repelling the calumnious report relative to his proposed union with his niece.

He solemnly protested, " with many words, that

such a thing had never entered into his mind[1];"
and it must be admitted that if he were guiltless of
the charge he could not have adopted a more
manly course than this speedy denouncement of an
act of which he felt himself unjustly accused. Not
satisfied, however, with this explicit denial before
his great officers of state, the king further resolved
on making his abjuration yet more public and decisive. Accordingly, " a little before Easter," in
the great hall of St. John's Priory, Clerkenwell,
Richard, " in the presence of the mayor and citizens
of London, with a clear and a loud voice, repeated
the aforesaid disavowal[2]," contradicting most unreservedly the invidious rumour before the assembled multitude, and protesting his innocence of
having ever contemplated a marriage so repugnant
to the habits and usages of the English nation.
The promptitude with which the king executed
the strong measures he had thus resolved upon,
cannot but add considerable weight to his distinct
and emphatic refutation of the charge. He allowed
himself no time for considering the possible advantages that might result from a union with his niece,
or even of ascertaining the probability of reconciling his subjects to such an alliance, in case, " as
a disciple of the church of Rome, he had sought to
fortify his throne, and prevent a civil war, by
availing himself of an indulgence[3] which then, as

---

[1] Chron. Croy., p. 572. [2] Ibid.

[3] The legality or illegality of a marriage of relations must depend
upon the rules of the church to which the parties belong. It was
undoubtedly forbidden by the canon law ; but the same law forbade
a marriage between persons within the fourth degree of kindred.
The pope was however considered to possess a dispensing power ;

now, is tolerated in Roman Catholic countries as legal[1];" but as soon as he was at liberty to select a fresh partner to his throne he summoned a council of state to negative a report so offensive; and within the shortest possible period that decency admitted after this more private adjuration he called before him, not only the civic authorities of London, but " the most sad and discreet persons of the same city in great number, being present many of the lords spiritual and temporal of our land, and the substance of all our household[2]," to reiterate his denial of having ever contemplated— for such are his own words—" acting otherwise than is according to honour, truth, and the peace and rightfulness of this our land." [3]

Such, in effect, is the testimony of the Croyland chronicler, who, after stating that the queen expired about " the middle of March," specifies the king's interview in the great hall of St. John, as occurring " a little before Easter," seasons so closely approximating that the ceremonial of the queen's funeral obsequies could scarcely have terminated ere the king presented himself before the citizens of London, publicly to refute an accusation eagerly seized upon by his opponents to render him yet more unpopular with the great mass of

and though, as a matter of feeling, there is a material difference between the union of first or second cousins and the marriage of a niece to her uncle, each alliance was illegal without the exercise of that power. The pontiff not only might, but often did, authorize the marriage of uncles and nieces. — *Memoir of Elizabeth of York,* p. 42.

[1] Memoir of Elizabeth of York, p. 42.
[2] Drake's Ebor., p. 119.   [3] Ibid.

the people. But words and deeds were alike in-
effectual towards reinstating the king in the
affections of his subjects. The rumours that took
their rise in those festivities, the alleged profuseness attending which, was considered as the immediate cause of the hated tax he had been compelled
to levy, fell in too well with the discontent of the
multitude to afford due chance of belief in an
asseveration which was imputed, not to choice, but
to necessity. " The king was compelled to excuse
himself," says the before-named chronicler[1], " because his proposed marriage had become known to
those who would not that it should occur."

And again, " Sir Richard Ratcliffe and Sir
William Catesby, whose opinions he scarcely ever
dare resist, brought forward twelve doctors in
theology, who asserted that the pope could not
grant a dispensation on such a degree of consanguinity."[2] That the supreme head of the Romish
church could, and frequently has, exercised that
power, and that he continues up to the present
day to sanction corresponding alliances in kingdoms under his immediate ecclesiastical control, is
an historical fact that cannot be denied or re-
futed[3]; but that Richard would attempt by such
an extreme measure to accomplish a purpose which
would bring him in collision with his subjects of
all ranks, by setting at defiance the usages of his

---

[1] Chron. Croy., p. 572.   [2] Ibid.

[3] Marriages between uncles and nieces have been very frequent,
and allowed in other countries by the church. In the house of
Austria marriages of this kind have been very usual, the pope dispensing with them. — *Buck*, lib. iv. p. 129.

country, and striking at the root of its prejudices, both civil and religious, is too improbable to admit of its being placed in opposition with the recorded fact of his fervent and solemn denial of the charge, even if the ecclesiastical chronicler himself had not summed up his account by the admission, that "it was thought by many that the king's advisers, alarmed lest there should be foundation for the rumour, had started these objections, from fear that if the Princess Elizabeth attained the royal dignity she would avenge the death of her relatives, the Lord Rivers and Sir Richard Grey, upon such as had counselled the deed."[1]

Most justly has it been observed, with reference to this occurrence, that "if a statement which stands on very dubious authority cannot be believed without assigning to him to whom it relates conduct directly at variance with that which the public records show he pursued, and if credence on that statement can only be given by imputing to the person an inconsistency so great, and a change of opinion so flagrant, that his political existence must have been endangered, there is just cause for rejecting every thing short of positive proof."[2]

It is very clear that King Richard left no legitimate means untried to stem the torrent of undeserved calumny, and to testify, by his actions, how grievously he had been defamed. He addressed a letter[3] to the citizens of York on the 11th of April, bitterly complaining of the " false and abominable

[1] Chron. Croy., p. 572.
[2] Memoir of Elizabeth of York, p. 46.
[3] See Appendix HH.

language and lies," the "bold and presumptuous open speeches[1]," spread abroad to his disadvantage, requiring the magistrates of that city to repress " all such slanders, and to take up the spreaders of it:" but the strongest proof that he gave of his wish to discountenance so injurious a rumour was his removing the Princess Elizabeth to an asylum far distant from himself or his court. The regal palace, indeed, was no fitting abode for his young niece, now that her aunt was no longer an occupant of its silent halls. To place her again under the care of her mother was at once to give her into the hands of his rival. Richard, therefore, chose a middle path, and sent her to share the nominal captivity of the youthful Earl of Warwick at Sheriff Hutton, " a goodly and a pleasant house of his own in Yorkshire, where he had liberty, large diet, all pleasure, and safety."[2] The monarch neither imprisoned the young Elizabeth, nor acted with cruelty towards her; he neither committed her to a solitary dungeon, nor concealed her place of abode from her friends or from the world: he kept her still in "honourable " captivity[3], although the evil reports which prevailed, no longer permitted him to do so under his own immediate eye. But if that were imprisonment which she shared with young Edward of Warwick, then indeed it was " a prison courteous," as John Froisard saith[4], for every latitude and indulgence was permitted consistent with the vigilant watch that was of ne-

[1] Drake's Ebor., p. 119.   [2] Buck, lib. v. p. 135.
[3] Lingard, vol. v. p. 262.   [4] Buck, lib. v. p. 135.

cessity kept over the two members of his family, whom faction would gladly have seized upon as the individuals best suited to further the ends of the disaffected, and to insure the downfal of their uncle.

There is nothing, however, so hard to disabuse as the public mind—nothing so difficult to overcome as popular prejudice. Perhaps no stronger instance of this can be adduced than the degree of credit which has been attached for ages to every idle and vague rumour propagated to the disadvantage of Richard III., and the slight attention which has been directed to those really excellent and imperishable acts, which rest not on report alone, but are indelibly connected with his name. His just and equitable laws[1], his wise and useful statutes, his provident edicts, and bold enactments, have, indeed, been eulogised by the soundest lawyers[2], and called forth the admiration of the most profound politicians.[3]

Brief as was the period during which he was permitted to rectify the abuses, and meet the exigencies, of those troubled times, he not only revived the substance of many obsolete Saxon laws in all their original purity, but he instituted fresh ones, based on such solid ground, and framed with such legislative wisdom and ability, that to this day many of the statutes of Richard III. remain in full force, and justify the encomiums which his enemies have passed upon them. " In no king's reign," states Sir Richard Baker, the chronicler of the English mon-

[1] Bacon, pp. 2, 3.   [2] See Sharon Turner, vol. iii. p. 72.
[3] Buck, lib. v. p. 136.

archs, " were better laws made than in the reign of
this man: " " he took the ways of being a good king
if he had come to be king by ways that had been
good."[1] Even Lord Bacon, the biographer of his
rival, bears testimony to " his politic and wholesome
laws[2]," an admission of no small importance, as
emanating from the highest legal authority in the
realm, and from one of the most learned men who
are numbered amongst the lord chancellors of
England; notwithstanding which, so firmly established was the belief in this sovereign's mal-practices
that Lord Bacon felt himself obliged to modify (in
accordance with the prejudices of the age) the statement which his own sense of justice drew forth, by
adding that " these laws were interpreted to be but
the brocage of a usurper, thereby to woo and to
win the hearts of the people."[3] " He was a good
law-maker for the ease and solace of the common
people," further testifies this profound philosopher
and statesman ; yet in summing up the " virtues
and merits " of King Richard, he could not forbear
adding that " even those virtues themselves were
conceived to be feigned[4] : " so hard is it to banish
early impressions, so difficult to remove prejudices
which have been long and steadily rooted in the
minds even of the most discerning and erudite
judges. Richard III. did indeed merit more generous
treatment from his subjects, for amidst the turmoils
and vexations, the mortifications and disappoint-
ments, which fell so thickly and so heavily upon

[1] Chron. of Kings of England, p. 234.
[2] Bacon's Henry VII., p. 3.
[3] Ibid.   [4] Ibid. p. 2.

him, his attention was unceasingly directed to one
point—that of emancipating the great body of the
people from the many oppressions under which they
had so long and so painfully laboured, and diffusing
a nobler and better spirit among all ranks, by the
soundness of his edicts, and the high principles of
justice, religion, and morality, on which they were
based. " The king's highness is fully determined
to see administration of justice to be had throughout
his realm, and to reform and punish all extortion
and oppression," were the words of the proclamation
in which, during a brief progress into Kent, Richard
invited the humblest of his people, who had been
unlawfully wronged, to make his petition " to his
highness; and he shall be heard, and without delay
have such convenient remedy as shall accord with
the laws:" for, finally concludes this important document, " his grace is utterly purposed that all his
true subjects shall live in rest and quiet, and
peaceably enjoy their lands and goods according to
the laws."[1] As a means of checking the unjust
verdicts which had of late years prevailed, bringing
the courts of law into contempt, and frustrating
the benefit designed by that noblest of our institu-
tions—trial by jury, he struck at the root of the
evil by decreeing that no individual but such as
possessed freehold property to the amount of forty
shillings a year should be deemed eligible to be
chosen a juror[2]; he also granted to every justice
of the peace power to bail such persons as were ar-

---

[1] Harl. MSS., 433. fol. 128.
[2] Stat. of Realm, vol. ii. p. 479.

rested for felony on suspicion alone[1] : but the most
beneficial of his enactments, and that which afforded
the greatest relief to the community at large, was
a law prohibiting the seizure of property belonging
to persons imprisoned on a charge of felony before
conviction[2]—a measure which was loudly called for
in consequence of the opening which a contrary
usage had long afforded to the powerful to oppress
the poor, their weaker opponents, and by false indictment to set at defiance all principles of justice
and humanity. He framed most admirable laws for
the better regulation of the temporary courts held
during fairs[3]—courts which in themselves, indeed,
were insignificant[4], but which, as instituted to do
justice to buyers and sellers, and summarily to
redress disorders committed during these chartered
meetings, were invested at this time with very considerable power, arising from the importance that
attached, in the middle ages, to those periodical
marts, which were founded as the only medium of
bartering with the merchants of other lands, and
diffusing generally throughout the kingdom the
various manufactures and staple commodities of its
most distant provinces. The protection, indeed,
which was afforded by King Richard to commerce
and trade has been already partially detailed; it may,
however, be further observed, that although he had
reigned but twenty months up to the period under
consideration, yet the nation had already extended

---

[1] Stat. of Realm, vol. ii. p. 478.
[2] Ibid. p. 479.   [3] Ibid. p. 480.
[4] These courts were entitled " Pie-poudre," a corruption of pied-
poudre, dusty-foot.

its commerce towards the North Pole as far as Ice-land[1], and was peaceably trafficking with Denmark[2], Germany, Flanders, and the Netherlands[3], as also those rich republics in the south of Europe, Genoa[4], and Venice[5], which were then in the zenith of their prosperity. His attention to the maritime interests of the country are abundantly shown by edicts tending to the safety and protection[6] of those whose enterprising spirit led them to brave the perils which, in these early days of navigation, were in-separable from long and distant voyages ; while the permission which he at this time granted for English wool being transported beyond the Straits of Morocco[7] was scarcely less beneficial to the realm than the restriction which was judiciously imposed on the importers of foreign products, to dispose of their commodities wholesale, or otherwise to take them back within a given and limited period.[8] The register, in short, which so minutely details the public acts of this monarch affords innumerable examples of the salutary results of his legislative ability, if deduced only from the vast sums which in an incredibly brief space of time enriched the country, arising from money received on imports from Spain alone[9]; while the abuses which he rectified in fines, feoffments, and tenures, and the admirable regulations which he introduced on these and other

1 Harl. MSS., 433. fol. 88. 159.
2 Buck, lib. i. p. 33.   3 Harl. MSS., 433. fol. 86.
4 Ibid. fol. 30.   5 Ibid. fol. 71.
6 Ibid. fol. 159. 180.   7 Ibid. fol. 104.
8 Stat. of Realm, vol. ii. p. 508.
9 Harl. MSS., 433. p. 99. 100.

modes of transferring landed property, together
with his edicts against gambling[1], and his encouragement of the truly English pastimes of archery
and shooting, when legally exercised[2], justify the
observation[3], that " the proclamation of Perkin
Warbeck in the ensuing reign, being addressed to
popular feeling, may be considered as expressing
the general estimate of Richard's reign : although
desire of rule did blind him, yet in his other actions
he was noble, and loved the honour of the realm,
and the contentment and comfort of his nobles and
people."[4]   In carrying out and perfecting measures
thus worthy of a great monarch, one who coveted
the affection of his people, and sought to obtain it
by devoting the energies of a powerful mind
towards redressing their grievances, and correcting
abuses so detrimental to the welfare and peace of
the realm, did Richard III. pass the period that
elapsed after the decease of his queen, and while
anticipating the threatened invasion of the Earl of
Richmond—a period the beneficial occupation of
which procured for him the ungracious admission,
in after-years, of " beginning to counterfeit the
image of a good and well-disposed person[5]," but
which bid fair, had he lived sufficiently long to reap
the fruits of a soil so judiciously cultivated, to have
secured lasting advantages to his country, and proportionate renown to himself.

These pacific occupations did not, however, lessen
the king's watchfulness over the motives of the insur-

---

[1] Harl. MSS., 433. fol. 219.   [2] Ibid.
[3] Turner's Middle Ages, vol. iv. p. 93.
[4] Bacon, p. 155.   [5] Grafton, p. 200.

gents, or lead him to relax in his vigilance against
the threatened invasion. Various reports had
reached him from time to time relative to the intentions of the rebels, but the movements of their
leader were enveloped in a degree of mystery and
uncertainty that caused the king considerable anxiety. From the time that Henry of Richmond had
been so courteously received by the French monarch after the earl's flight from the principality of
Bretagne, or rather from the period when a truce
had been sought for by Charles VIII., and a league
of amity been agreed to by Richard III., no satisfactory information had been received respecting
his rival. Under the plea of strengthening his
cause, by seeking out the exiled supporters of the
house of Lancaster, the representative of that fallen
dynasty had abruptly quitted Paris and the asylum
there afforded to himself and his partizans, and
had subsequently eluded the vigilance of King
Richard's spies to ascertain or gain intimation of
his retreat. Respecting his subsequent movements
the continental historians, together with the English chroniclers, are altogether silent; not so, however, the Welsh bards: their contemporary metrical lays abound with such marked allusions to
the Earl of Richmond and to King Richard, under
the emblems of the eagle and the lion, in conformity with the allegorical style of the poetry of
that age, that there is every reason to believe that
Richmond passed privately from France into Wales[1];
and that many wild and allegorical compositions

[1] Pennant's Tour in Wales, vol. i. p. 9.

which are yet extant refer to his perilous adventures when concealed for many months among the fastnesses of his native Cambria, wandering in various disguises among the haunts of his youth, partly to ascertain the sentiments of the populace as regards King Richard, and partly to judge how far he himself might venture to renew an invasion which, on the former occasion, had terminated so disastrously for himself and his supporters.

By what means the king's suspicions were excited it is not possible to say; but the fact of some intimation having been made of the probability of his rival being concealed in Wales is evident from the circumstance of a tradition having been handed down in the Mostyn family, that the earl's retreat was actually discovered by Richard's emissaries, and that, while sojourning with the chief of that ancient race, the house was surrounded by soldiers, and Richmond, escaping with difficulty through an open window in the rear of the house, lay concealed in an obscure spot, which, under the epithet of the " King's Hole[1]," yet perpetuates the romantic tale, and favours the belief that the future fortunes of the Tudor dynasty were greatly influenced by personal communication with his correspondents and allies in the West. It is certain Richmond was in full possession of all that was passing at the English court ; he had both heard, and gave credit to, the rumour of King Richard's design of espousing the Princess Elizabeth: and if the reputed report of the alliance

[1] Pennant's Tour in Wales, vol. i. p. 9.

was really propagated from political views, and with the design of counteracting the schemes of the disaffected party, the device had well nigh succeeded, for the earl, trusting to the indignation which he foresaw would be excited against so unpopular a measure, resolved on strengthening his own cause by seeking to ally himself in marriage with one of the most powerful and influential families in Wales, that of Sir Walter Herbert [1], whose parents had been entrusted with his guardianship in childhood, and to whom they had hoped to have united their eldest daughter.[2]

The Earl of Northumberland, firmly attached to King Richard's service, had married this lady; and it was a stroke of consummate policy that led Richmond to decide on making, at this crisis of his fate, proposals to her sister, and thus possibly to pave the way by a renewal of early ties for interesting in his cause two chiefs now openly opposed to his schemes, but whose overwhelming influence in the North and in the West would give such weight to his future movements.

The re-appearance of the Earl of Richmond amongst his exiled friends was as abrupt as had been his disappearance. Full of hope, and confident of success, bringing with him vast sums of money, and captains of known experience to aid him with their councils, he did not present himself either to his partizans or at the French court until measures were sufficiently matured to admit of his being welcomed by the former with enthusiasm,

[1] Grafton, p. 208.   [2] Life of Margaret Beaufort, p. 73.

and received by the latter with that courteousness which is generally extended to those on whom fortune smiles, and over whose prospects the sun of prosperity is shining.[1] Keen and observant as was the English monarch on all points connected with his own interest, or the safety of the realm, it may be supposed that he was not slow to observe the increasing strength and well-organised schemes of the rebels, notwithstanding the mystery that veiled the individual movements of their leader. Had he, however, been lulled into fancied security by the seeming inactivity of his opponent, the uncertainty of his own position could not but be painfully forced upon him by the continual defection of many wealthy commoners and influential men in all ranks of society, who, despite his vigilance and conciliatory measures, were perpetually reported to him as having passed over to the enemy.[2] Still no positive imminent danger appeared to menace the kingdom, and Richard continued to reside at Westminster for the remainder of the spring, 1485, exerting himself to ameliorate the condition of his people, and bestowing earnest attention upon all works of charity and beneficence, as is instanced by the last document which received his signature prior to quitting the metropolis — that of empowering the " Hermit of Reculver," by royal commission, to collect alms for the purpose

[1] " When the earl was thus furnished and appointed with his trusty company, and was escaped all the dangers, labyrinths, and snares that were set for him, no marvel though he was jocund and glad of the prosperous success that happened in his affairs." — *Grafton*, p. 194.

[2] Fabyan, p. 218.

of restoring an ancient church " consecrated to the
sepulture of shipwrecked mariners, and those who
have perished by casualty of storms."[1]

But the crisis which was to decide the destinies
of England as well as the fate of her monarch, was
fast approaching.   Sir James Blount, the governor
of Hammes, a veteran soldier in whom Richard
had reposed the greatest confidence, not only
abandoned his trust and deserted to the Earl of
Richmond, but released from captivity the Earl of
Oxford[2], a state prisoner of known experience in
martial acquirements, and who had been placed
under his charge as a determined enemy of the
house of York.

This dereliction, it is considered, was owing to
the machinations of Bishop Morton; but the act
itself was rendered more mortifying to Richard by
its being accompanied by the information that
Richmond's re-appearance had been concomitant
with this most important addition to his forces.[3]
It is true that prompt measures were forthwith
taken for recapturing the castle and town of
Hammes, and that the success which attended
them, in some degree reassured the English monarch[4]; nevertheless, the fact itself, and the desertion of Sir John Fortescue and some of the
garrison at Calais, which immediately followed,
could not fail to convince him that some powerful
agent was tampering with the troops of his most

---

[1] Harl. MSS., No. 433. fol. 213.   [2] Fabyan, p. 518.
[3] Buck, lib. ii. p. 58.   [4] Hall, p. 408. ; Grafton, p. 203.

important strongholds. It must also have impressed upon him the conviction that repose no longer befitted him, but that his personal presence had become imperatively necessary to check the tendency to revolt which was thus fearfully apparent, and to nullify the seditious spirit which it was the object of his enemies to excite throughout his dominions. Accordingly, " a little before Pentecost," King Richard once more quitted the metropolis, and " proceeded to the north."[1]

Each day added strength to the current rumour that the rebels were hastening their approach to England, yet Richard could obtain no decisive information as to where they intended to land[2]; and as he slowly but steadily passed on from town to town, he perceived little indication of internal revolt, or of those symptoms of disaffection and anarchy which generally presage civil war. He reached Coventry towards the end of May[3], and there rested for many days, when he departed for Kenilworth, at which castle he appears to have been sojourning on the 6th of June."[4] He finally fixed his temporary abode at Nottingham[5], the strength of its fortress rendering it a desirable post in the event of any sudden outbreak, while the central situation of the country made its capital a convenient spot from whence Richard without delay could direct his steps to encounter his enemies as soon as decisive information was obtained of the point where they purposed landing.

[1] Chron. Croy., 572. [2] Ibid.
[3] Harl. MSS., No. 433. fol. 200. [4] Ibid. 219.
[5] Ibid. 220.

To his faithful chamberlain and devoted follower, Francis Lord Lovell, the companion and friend of his youth, he committed the charge of his naval forces, leaving him at Southampton in command of the fleet[1] which was there stationed to resist any invasion of the southern coasts.

Before quitting London, Richard had adopted all available and politic measures for securing the peace and safety of the capital; and immediately upon his arrival at Nottingham, he followed up these salutary precautions, by apprising the authorities in his northern metropolis of the impending invasion, demanding assistance from the loyal citizens of York, and soliciting from them substantial aid in the forthcoming crisis.[2]

Corresponding intelligence was sent to the commissioners of array in every county throughout England, accompanied by " instructions[3] " so explicit as regards reviewing the soldiers, and seeing " that they be able persons, well horsed and harnessed" — so decided in commands that their captains, " lords, and noblemen, do lay apart all ancient grudges, quarrels, rancours, and unkindness" — and so peremptory, with reference to the frequent muster of " all knights, esquires, and gentlemen," that they, " in their proper persons," may be prepared to do the king service " upon an hour's warning, whenever, by proclamation or otherwise, they shall be thereunto commanded," that Richard, although fully alive to the forthcoming storm, was

---

[1] Chron. Croy., p. 572.   [2] See Appendix II.
[3] Appendix KK.

equally prepared to encounter its evil consequences,
and enabled calmly to await the result of the en-
quiries he had set on foot, and to pass the remainder of June and the greater part of the month
of July in comparative tranquillity.   The castle of
Nottingham had always ranked high in favour with
the princes of the house of York.

Apart from its commanding situation, its natural
advantages rendered it a station of vast importance
during the sanguinary wars of the Roses; and
many are the notices in its local history of times
when the banner of England waved proudly from
its castellated battlements.   Under the direction
of King Edward IV., this ancient fortress, which
had sheltered him in some of the most remarkable
vicissitudes of his reign, received many additions,
important as regards strength, and admirable as
specimens of architectural taste.   Richard III.,
who yielded to none of his race in natural genius,
or in the patronage of science and art, not only
carried out the noble works commenced by his
royal brother, but yet further enlarged and beautified this princely structure, " so that surely,"
writes Leland in his interesting description of it,
" that north part is an exceeding piece of work; "
indeed, to this very day, the site of its principal
bulwark — the sole remnant of its former magnificence — bears the appellation of " Richard's
Tower," in consequence of its having been erected
by Richard III.

The castle of Nottingham is in fact associated
intimately and inseparably with almost all the

leading events of that monarch's remarkable career. It was his frequent abode during his wardenship of the north ; there he rested on his bridal progress to Middleham, and there he took upon himself the custody of young Edward V.; assumed the office of lord protector, and made that compact with the unstable Buckingham, which led to Richard's subsequent elevation to the throne.   It was within its walls that he issued commands for his second coronation, and there also were his brightest and fondest hopes laid prostrate by the announcement of the decease of his son; there he passed the last days of healthful companionship with his departed queen, and thither he now returned preparatory to renewed struggles for that crown, which had yielded him so little of peace or enjoyment.

The nature of King Richard's feelings with reference to this favoured provincial palace of the monarchs of the house of York, may be estimated by the appellation which he bestowed upon it; he called it the " Castle of Care." [1]

Nevertheless at this crisis, having secured himself against immediate danger, and adopted the most strenuous measures for the defence of the realm, the king kept his court within its walls with his usual magnificence and liberality; and so sedulously cultivated the friendship of the surrounding gentry, that he won many over to his cause, amongst whom was Sir Gervoise Clifton, whom at his coronation he had created a knight of the Bath [2], and whose devotion to Richard, even unto death, has

---

[1] Hutton's Bosworth, p. 40.   [2] Buck, lib. i. p. 26.

been made the subject of historical record.[1]   The
edicts which the king had issued, and the ordinances that had been circulated requiring each
shire to furnish its contribution of troops at an
hour's notice[2], was·followed up by strong letters
addressed to the sheriffs[3] of every county, furnishing them with copies of the instructions sent
to the commissioners of array, and enjoining their
" continual abode within the shire town of their
office," to the intent that it might be openly known
" where they might be found," in the event of increased danger.

To prove the necessity of these precautions, and
still farther to secure the co-operation of his subjects in resisting the invaders, Richard summed up
his various manifestos by a proclamation[4] of considerable length, denouncing " Henry Tudor " as a
traitor, his supporters as exiles and outlaws, " enemies to their country, and subverters of the peace

[1] Sir Gervoise Clifton and Sir John Byron were friends and
neighbours in Nottinghamshire ; the former joined King Richard's
standard, the latter fought with the Earl of Richmond.   They had
mutually agreed, that whichever party conquered, the supporter of
the victor should intercede for his friend's life, and procure the
estate for the benefit of their family.   In the heat of the conflict
at Bosworth, Sir John Byron saw Clifton fall, and rushing to the
enemy's ranks, came to his friend, supported him on his shield, and
life not being extinct implored him to surrender.   But the wound
was mortal.   Sir Gervoise faintly exclaimed, " All is over," and expired while reminding Byron of his pledge, that he would use his
utmost efforts to procure the restitution of his land to his children,
in the event of Richmond's party gaining the day.   Sir John Byron
gave the promise and fulfilled his pledge ; the estate was preserved
to the Clifton family.— *Hutton's Bosworth,* p. 117.

[2] Harl. MSS., fol. 221.   [3] Appendix LL.
[4] See Appendix MM.

of the realm." The assumed pretensions of Richmond were fully detailed, to prove that his illegitimate descent gave him no lawful claim to the throne, or justified his invasion of the realm to contest it; and that his league with the ancient enemies of England was purchased by a pledge, " to give and release to the crown of France such continental possessions as appertained to the English nation, and all right, title, and claims that her monarchs have, and ought to have, to the sovereignty of that kingdom." The miseries that must ensue from open rebellion, and from the admission of mercenary troops into the country, were depicted in strong language; and an earnest and energetic appeal made to the feelings of all classes, that, " like good and true Englishmen, for the defence of their wives, children, goods, and inheritance, they furnish themselves with all their powers ;" promising in requital that their sovereign lord, " as a well-willed, diligent, and courageous prince, will put his royal person in all labour and pain necessary in their behalf, for the resistance and subduing of his said enemies, rebels, and traitors."[1]

Thus nothing was left undone that policy, foresight, and courage could devise, to prevent a recurrence of domestic feud, or to save the already impoverished land from the evils attendant on the substitution of martial for civil law.

This determined resolution and statesmanlike vigilance on the part of King Richard, urged on the progress of the Earl of Richmond and those

[1] Paston Letters, vol. ii. p. 319.

who had sworn to depose the reigning sovereign; it served to bring matters to a crisis, by showing the necessity of the most prompt measures. Richmond's purposed attempt upon the English crown was too widely promulgated, and had been too fully matured to be abandoned, and both the insurgents and their leader felt that prolonged delay might possibly frustrate their schemes, and lead, as upon the former occasion, to unlooked-for defeat and ruin.

The proclamation issued by the English monarch was met by a decisive and powerful reply from the earl.[1] He avowed his intention of contesting the throne, and branded King Richard as a "homicide and unnatural tyrant;" pledging himself to pass over the seas with such forces as his friends were preparing for him, "so soon as he was advertised of the names of the leaders who would co-operate with him on his arrival in England."

Courteously, however, as Henry of Richmond had been received by Charles VIII. on his re-appearance at Paris, he failed in obtaining from him the full and efficient aid on which he calculated.[2] Political dissensions at the court of France[3] had greatly curtailed the power of its monarch, who consequently was in no position to break his faith with Richard, although otherwise well disposed to lend a helping hand to his rival. He

[1] Appendix NN.
[2] "The Earl of Richmond was with his suite in the court of France sore wearied, and desiring great aid could obtain small relief." — *Grafton*, p. 204.
[3] Grafton, p. 206.

welcomed him with professions of regard, but shrank from openly committing himself to the encouragement of attempts upon the British sceptre.

This cautious policy was a source of considerable exultation to Richard[1], although but of short duration; for the security which it seemed to promise was quickly dispelled by information, that the earl had obtained as a loan those succours which were refused on the score of friendship, or as the compact of a political alliance, the advantages to result from which rested on such uncertain grounds. Nevertheless Charles VIII. yielded at last to the importunate Richmond, and advanced him a considerable sum of money, besides furnishing him with 3000 men[2], an accession of strength which speedily enabled him to quit Paris, and proceed towards Harfleur, the present rendezvous of his troops.[3] Bidding farewell to his friends at the French court, he left there as hostages for repayment of the assistance which had been afforded him, Sir John Bourchier and the renegade Marquis of Dorset[4]; who, doubting the success of the earl's application to Charles, had suddenly abandoned the cause of the insurgents from considering their prospects as hopeless, and fleeing to Flanders was overtaken at Campeigne, in his progress to ally himself with King Richard.

To give time for mustering his forces and provision his shipping, the Earl of Richmond rested for a brief period at Rouen: there he was joined by his chief commanders, whose indignation at the

[1] Grafton, p. 206. [2] Buck, lib. ii. p. 57.
[3] Ibid. p. 78. [4] Grafton, 207.

rumour, now universally spread, of Richard's determination to espouse the Princess Elizabeth, decided
him on carrying into effect, although without their
knowledge, his project of a Welsh alliance, and of
privately dispatching messengers to Sir Walter
Herbert, with proposals of marriage to his sister[1],
and likewise to the Earl of Northumberland, hoping
to prevail upon him to advocate his views.

Here also, to his surprise and joy, he received a
considerable reinforcement of troops from Francis
Duke of Brittany[2], who, repenting his former refusal, now sent unsolicited the seasonable and efficient aid of 2000 Bretons; so that no obstacle
remained to prevent the earl from carrying into
immediate execution his long threatened and projected invasion. It is true that, judging from Philip
de Comines, few auxiliary forces could have been
more contemptible than the band of soldiers furnished by France[3], but their inefficiency in military
skill was more than counterbalanced by their reck-
less hardihood, while the prospect of advancement
and of requital for services which stimulated them
to zealous exertions, rendered these children of desperate fortune more valuable as a body than the
better disciplined troops of the English monarch,
commanded by time-serving courtiers, who after
having been enriched and ennobled by the bounty
of the prince, whom two years previously with
shouts and joyful acclamations they had elevated
to the throne, were now ripe to betray him. The

[1] Grafton, p. 208.   [2] Buck, lib. ii. p. 58.
[3] Philip de Comines, p. 356.

great secret, indeed, of King Richard's downfall was the defection of his miscalled friends, and the duplicity of those who, for more selfish purposes, had insinuated themselves into his confidence, the more readily to carry on that system of complicated intrigue, which was designed to throw him off his guard, that he might the more surely be entangled in the snares which were laid for his destruction. Most justly did Sir Thomas More depict this fact, when, after admitting the generosity which formed so striking a feature in his character[1], " he was above his power liberal[2]," he further added, " with large gifts he gat him unsteadfast friendship, for which he was fain to pil and spoil in other places, which gat him steadfast hatred."[3] This was indeed unhappily the case.   Had Richard been more ava- ricious and mercenary, had he been less frank and generous, more tyrannical, more suspicious of those that surrounded him, less chivalrous and gallant in the treatment of his nobles, neither Henry of Rich- mond nor the combined tributaries of France and Brittany could have vanquished him.   One of the ablest generals and wisest legislators of his age was the victim of the stealthy and systematic treachery, which peculiarly marked this era in other Euro- pean courts; and although forming, comparatively speaking, a new feature in English policy, the monarch had been too early initiated into the crafty proceedings of Louis XI. and the wily counsellors of Francis of Brittany, to be altogether blind to the true cause that was gradually accelerating his own

[1] More, p. 9.   [2] Ibid.   [3] Ibid.

ruin. Many members of his court pierced him to
the heart by their open ingratitude; but foremost
amongst those whose concealed perfidy contributed
to his destruction was Morgan Kydwelly[1], the attorney-general[2]; who, ranking high in the king's
favour[3], was not only in a position to watch the
arrangements of his sovereign, but in virtue of his
high office could contrive the means of conveying
clandestinely to the enemy that intelligence, which
alike counteracted the designs of the English
monarch and strengthened the projects of his rival.[4]
He it was who warned the Earl of Richmond to
avoid a landing on the southern coasts, which were
so carefully watched by sea, and vigilantly guarded
on shore by the trusty Lovell.[5] He also advised
him to direct his course to Wales[6], and to " hasten
his departure " while that portion of the kingdom
was less rigidly watched, although most ripe for
the furtherance of his scheme. It was Kydwelly
who placed Richmond in possession of the names of
those powerful chieftains[7] who were disposed to
abandon King Richard, and espouse the cause of
his opponent; he who informed him that Reginald
Bray awaited his landing, with vast sums of money
collected for the payment of " his mariners and

[1] Grafton, p. 209.
[2] See the Harl. MSS., No. 433. p. 79.
[3] King Richard's liberality to Morgan Kydwelly is shown by the
various entries in the Harl. MSS., which contain the grants of
several rich manors, the stewardship of the lordships in the duchy of
Lancaster, and other acts of bounty of a similar nature.— *Harl.
MSS.*, No. 433. fol. 49. 69. 73. 79.
[4] Grafton, p. 209.   [5] Ibid.; Pol. Virg., p. 559.; Hall, p. 410.
[6] Ibid.   [7] Ibid.

soldiers[1]" out of the rich possessions in England
and Wales belonging to the earl's mother the
Countess of Richmond, which Richard generously
forbore to confiscate[2] when applied to a similar
purpose under Buckingham's rebellion. But the
treacherous Kydwelly being unsuspected, caused
his royal master no uneasiness. There was, however, one illustrious member of his household, high
in his confidence, and possessing powerful influence
in the west, whose ambiguous and suspicious conduct occasioned the king deep and unceasing anxiety,
and that was the Lord Stanley.[3] Nor was this
without reason, for as the head of one of the most
powerful families in the west of England, his extensive connections, vast resources, and unbounded
influence over his vassals and retainers could not
but impress Richard with the conviction, that on
his fidelity would greatly depend the probable issue
of the approaching contest. Although decidedly
opposed to him when lord protector, yet Richard
as king had acted most generously to this nobleman.
He had released him from prison, had pardoned his
reputed connection with Lord Hasting's conspiracy,
had advanced him to the highest offices in the
government, as well as the most trustworthy places
about his royal person ; and on the discovery of
the agency of his wife in fomenting the Duke of
Buckingham's rebellion, had abstained from involving him in the consequences of her known dereliction of fidelity, nay, had even softened the

---

[1] Grafton, p. 209.   [2] Rot. Parl., vi. p. 240. 251.
[3] Grafton, p. 202.

severity of the sentence so justly her due, in consideration of her husband's integrity.[1] It is but just to add, that, up to the present crisis, the Lord Stanley had continued faithful to the trust reposed in him; but whether in accordance with the dissembling policy of those degenerate times, he merely temporised until the fitting period arrived for a counter-revolution—whether the anticipated elevation to the throne of his son-in-law, joined to his proposed alliance with King Edward's daughter, had weakened his loyalty to King Richard—or that the influence of his illustrious consort, which is asserted by the contemporary chronicler[2], had overcome the nobler feelings inherent in his race, and tempted him to desert his post and swerve from the oath of allegiance twice vowed to the reigning sovereign, cannot of course be determined.

Thus much, however, is very certain, that King Richard for some time had entertained just reason to doubt the stability of this nobleman, the "lord steward of his household" and the "high constable of the realm;" and a request preferred at this momentous crisis for leave to quit the presence of his sovereign, and to return to "his country to visit his family and to recreate his spirits[3]," not only confirmed his royal master in the belief of his wavering policy, but so convinced him, that his departure was to the intent to be in perfect readiness to receive the Earl of Richmond[4], that although Richard was too wise to accelerate

---

[1] Rot. Parl., vi. pp. 240. 251.   [2] Chron. Croy., p. 573.
[3] Ibid.   [4] Grafton, p. 203.

disaffection by premature and possibly uncalled-for suspicion, he would in no wise suffer him to depart until he consented to send[1] as an hostage the Lord Strange, his "first begotten son and heir." The result proved the monarch's discretion on this point, and removes likewise all doubt as to the fact, that the attorney-general and the Lord Stanley were certainly leagued together—the one as the organ of communication with the rebels in France, and the other as carrying into effect the well-concerted plan that was to end in the junction of the exiles with their English supporters. For about the same period that the Lord Stanley left the court the Earl of Richmond hoisted his standard at Harfleur, and was admonished by the crafty Kydwelly "to make quick expedition, and shape his course directly for Wales;" in the north part of which principality Sir William Stanley held the responsible situation of chamberlain[2]; and consequently, in virtue of his office, could leave any portion of the coast unguarded, and prevent even all hostile opposition to the invaders from the royal forces there stationed by King Richard, and which in the preceding winter had been placed by that monarch under the sole command of himself and his brother for the protection of the west country.[3] By no possibility, indeed, could Kydwelly otherwise have communicated to the earl matter so intimately connected with the domestic policy of the Stanleys, or have known

---

[1] Chron. Croy., p. 573.   [2] Ibid. p. 575.
[3] Harl. MSS., No. 433. fol. 200.

the sums of money that awaited him from his
mother (the Lord Stanley's consort), or have
been in a position to have intimated the propitious
moment for Richmond's departure, or the unsuspected point at which to direct his course.   And
equally too does the result prove, that this league
was well understood and responded to by the earl ;
for in strict conformity with the instructions sent
he made "all convenient haste," set forward and
carried to his ships armour, weapons, victual, and
all other ordinances expedient for war[1]," and
exerted himself so strenuously, that he was in a
position to embark on the 26th of July[2], and had
actually sailed from Harfleur before King Richard
could obtain any farther knowledge of his movements, than that his fleet had assembled at the
mouth of the Seine.   This information, however,
was made known to the king within so brief a
period after the departure of the Lord Stanley,
that it added considerably to the misgivings which
had been before excited by his absenting himself
from the court at so critical a period.   He, therefore, quickly dispatched fresh precautionary instructions to those who were engaged in guarding
the sea ports, and established relays of cavalry on
all the high roads for the more rapid communication of intelligence.

He sent also to the lord chancellor " for the great
seal," as on the previous insurrection of Buckingham ; the which, in consequence of the king's mandate, " was surrendered to him by the Bishop of

---

[1] Grafton, p. 209.   [2] Blakeway's Shrewsbury, vol. i. p. 242.

Lincoln in the Old Temple, London, on the 29th July."[1]

But Richard's vigilance was vain! So prosperous was the wind[2], so favourable the weather, that the earl reached the Welsh coast on the seventh day after his departure from France; and having been apprised that a garrison which was unfavourable to his cause, and which had been awaiting him at Milford Haven throughout the winter, was removed, he made direct for that port[3], and there disembarked, without opposition, on the evening of the 1st August, 1485.[4] He forthwith commenced his march, and before sun-rising the following day had reached the town of Haverfordwest, to the great astonishment of the inhabitants. They welcomed him with joy, his descent from their native princes seeming to realise a prediction that had long prevailed, and was superstitiously believed, viz. that the sceptre which had been usurped from the ancient British kings by the Saxons, the Danes, and the Normans, would be restored to them by a native of Wales, a descendant of the renowned Prince Arthur.[5] Availing himself of a tradition so well calculated to advance his interests, he caused a banner, displaying the insignia of Cadwallader, the last of their kings, to be carried in front of his troops; and marching direct to Cardigan, he passed through Wales by rough and indirect paths.[6] Choosing the most unfrequented tracks, and the wildest

[1] Fœdera, xii. p. 271.
[3] Ibid.
[5] Baker's Chron., p. 252.
[2] Grafton, p. 209.
[4] Chron. Croy., p. 573.
[6] Chron. Croy., p. 573.

mountain passes, he bent his course to the northern
part of the province, hoping to increase his strength,
by winning to his cause many of the Welsh chieftains, and to join Sir William Stanley before the
fact of his landing became generally known.   Thus
the Earl of Richmond was in the heart of the kingdom before Richard knew of his having sailed from
Harfleur ; and his landing being effected at a point
where no regular communication had been established with the court, he had made considerable
progress before the fact even of his disembarkation
could be known to the king.   His central position,
however, as he had foreseen, was singularly favourable to the promptitude which ever characterised
his movements.   The Duke of Norfolk, who had
been guarding the eastern counties, was commanded
forthwith to join the monarch with his full strength
at Nottingham.[1]   The Earl of Northumberland was
summoned from the north, and the Lord Lovell
and the Lord Stanley from the south and from the
west, were also required to repair to his presence
with their respective forces.[2]

Mandates were sent to the Tower, enjoining the
attendance of the faithful Brackenbury[3], and placing
under his command " divers other knights and
esquires, in whom the king placed less confidence[4]; "
while letters were dispatched to every county,
" forbidding all who were born to any inheritance
in the realm to withdraw from the ensuing conflict

---

[1] Grafton, p. 204.   [2] Ibid.
[3] Ibid.   [4] Ibid.

on pain of forfeiture of life, and goods, and possessions."[1]

Prompt was the obedience of the Lords of Norfolk, Northumberland, and Lovell, but not such that
of Lord Stanley; he excused himself on the plea of
sickness[2]; but the pretence was too shallow, too
customary at this era, not to confirm the king in
his conviction that, like the excuses of the faithless
Buckingham, the illness of Lord Stanley was merely
a feint to conceal his traitorous designs. This was
soon confirmed by an attempt at escape made by
the Lord Strange. He was arrested, and when in
danger of his life, confessed his guilt, and acknowledged that his uncle, Sir William Stanley, as also
Sir John Savage, and other members of his family,
were leagued with the Earl of Richmond, and intended to join him with their forces.[3] He exculpated his father, however, from all participation in
their disloyalty; pledging himself, that if his life
were spared, the Lord Stanley would prove his
fidelity by speedily joining the king. In accordance
with this compact, he sent letters to his father explaining the peril he was in, and beseeching him to
hasten to his relief.[4] He thus saved himself from
the death which his perfidious conduct had merited.
It is difficult to tell whether he spoke the truth as
regards his parent, or whether his assertion was a
mere subterfuge, arising from the desperate position
in which his treasonable practices had placed him;
certain it is that the Lord Stanley never again re-

[1] Chron. Croy., 573.   [2] Ibid.
[3] Ibid.   [4] Ibid.

turned to Richard's court to bear out the truth of his son's declaration by his subsequent conduct.

The king appears in this instance to have acted with great moderation, as although Sir William Stanley and Sir John Savage were immediately denounced as traitors at Coventry and elsewhere[1], neither the Lord Stanley nor the Lord Strange were included in the denunciation. Richard's faithful and attached partizans at York, ever foremost in testifying their love for their patron and benefactor, were not behind hand at this crisis in displaying their zeal in his cause. Immediately the citizens heard that the earl had landed, they despatched their serjeant of mace to Nottingham, to inquire of the king what aid their city should send[2]; and in obedience to his command six hundred men in harness were required in all haste to join the royal standard."[3] The councils, indeed, that were convened by the mayor, and the strong resolutions unanimously agreed to by the authorities at York[4], sufficiently evince their devotion to their sovereign, and their determination to support his prerogative. Nor does this appear to have been a solitary instance, for even the Tudor chronicler admits that immense multitudes thronged to Richard's standard, " he having continual repair of his subjects to him[5];" a fact that proves beyond all dispute that the country was not opposed to his government, although it suited the views of his political opponents to impute his downfall to that

---

[1] Chron. Croy., p. 573.
[2] Drake's Ebor., p. 120.
[3] Ibid.
[4] Ibid.
[5] Grafton, p. 215.

source rather than avow the systematic perjury and falsehood by which it was in reality effected.

Thus loyally supported, and having taken every precaution to repel the invaders, it is by no means astonishing that Richard received with pleasure[1] rather than dismay, the intelligence of Richmond having effected a landing; or that, after having been kept in a state of suspense and watchfulness for so long a period, he should express satisfaction that " the day had at length arrived, when having easily triumphed over the exiled faction, his subjects would from thenceforth enjoy undoubted peace."[2]   And he was justified in that impression, for no simultaneous rising in the southern counties took place, as was the case when the Duke of Buckingham commenced his march; no part of England betrayed symptoms of riot or insurrection; even in Wales, the land of Richmond's birth, no popular ebullition characterised his appearance. Stealthily and cautiously he pursued his course, keeping along the sea-coast, that in case of a reverse he might be within reach of his shipping[3], subject to a toilsome march in a wild and half-populated country, obliged to contest the mountain passes, and to assault many places opposed to his progress[4], while his slender band of 3000 French and 2000 Bretons was only increased by a few native chieftains, whose small addition to his foreign mercenaries might well lead Richard to despise the insignificant force and inadequate means

[1] Chron. Croy., p. 573.   [2] Ibid.
[3] Blakeway's Shrewsbury, vol. i. p. 244.   [4] Grafton, p. 211.

with which his rival was come to contest the crown. Richmond himself had ample cause to tremble for the result, many circumstances having occurred to damp his ardour before he could join his kindred. Sir Walter Herbert, on whose aid he had reckoned, remained so true to the cause of the king[1], that the messengers despatched to him with the earl's proposals for the hand of his sister dared not risk their probable apprehension by venturing within the limits of his territory.[2] The Earl of Northumberland, too, was with the king, and on reaching Shrewsbury, the place fixed upon for the insurgents to cross the Severn, they were denied access into the town.[3] Happily for Richmond the messengers whom he had prudently despatched on his route to apprise the high sheriff of Shropshire, Sir Gilbert Talbot, as also the Lord Stanley, the Countess of Richmond, and others of his supporters of his approach, and whom he had appointed to meet him at Shrewsbury[4], returned so laden with rewards, and so elated with promises[5], that their report, there can be little doubt, operated favourably with the authorities[6], and induced them after a brief delay to permit the earl to pass through, on his pledge that he would do so peaceably, and without hurt to the town. Here he was

---

[1] Grafton, p. 211.   [2] Leland's Itin., vi. p. 30.
[3] Blakeway's Shrewsbury, vol. i. p. 245.
[4] Grafton, p. 211.   [5] Ibid.
[6] The chief magistrate who first opposed and subsequently opened the gates of Shrewsbury to the rebels, was Thomas Mytton, who, when sheriff of the county, had captured and delivered up the Duke of Buckingham to King Richard.—*Blakeway*, vol. i. p. 245.

met by Sir Rice Ap-Thomas[1], one of the most
powerful of the Welsh chieftains, who under the
promise of being made governor of Wales[2], in the
event of the earl gaining the throne, betrayed the
confidence which Richard had reposed in him in
consequence of the protestations of fidelity which
he had made, and the oath[3] of allegiance he had
solemnly sworn when nominated to the command
of the royal forces in the south of Wales.[4]   At
Newport, where the rebels encamped the following
night, they were joined by Sir Gilbert Talbot,
" with the whole power of the young Earl of
Shrewsbury, then being in ward[5], which were
accounted to the number of 2000 men[6]; " and at
Stafford[7] he was met by Sir William Stanley, with
whom he had a confidential interview, and by
whose advice he proceeded direct to Lichfield,
where " he was received like a prince[8]," his father-

---

[1] Blakeway's Shrewsbury, vol. i. p. 245.   [2] Pol. Virg., p. 560.
[3] For " the oath Rice Ap-Thomas stood not upon."— See note to
Turner's Middle Ages, vol. iv. p. 33.
[4] " On his way from Cardigan, Richmond was joined by an
eminent Welshman, who had been despatched to oppose him, Sir
Rice Ap-Thomas, and having settled to meet him at Shrewsbury, Sir
Rice diverged to the eastward, and advanced through the heart of
the country by Carmarthen and Brecon, collecting on the road his
tenantry and partisans, among whom the vassals of the late Duke of
Buckingham would not be the least numerous."—*Blakeway,* vol. i.
p. 244.
[5] This incident affords a striking example of the abuse of ward-
ships at this period; for notwithstanding that the young Earl of
Shrewsbury remained true to his sovereign (see *Harl. MSS.,* No. 542.
fol. 34.) and joined King Richard's banner, yet as a minor he had
no command over his tenantry, the whole of whom were carried
over to Richmond's army by his uncle and guardian Sir Gilbert
Talbot.—*Grafton,* p. 213.
[6] Grafton, p. 213.   [7] Ibid.   [8] Ibid.

in-law, the Lord Stanley, having paved the way for his favourable reception there, although he purposely departed from the city[1] on learning the approach of the earl, that he might not sacrifice the life of his son, who had been left with the king as an hostage for his fidelity.

Richard having ascertained that the object of the Earl of Richmond was to proceed direct to London[2], resolved to intercept his progress; but so much time had been lost before he knew of his having landed, or was sufficiently well informed of his movements to regulate his own actions, that notwithstanding the precautionary measures which he had adopted in anticipation of the invasion, he found his opponent was hastening to the capital with a rapidity for which he was unprepared, and was directing his way " day and night right in his face."[3] It became necessary, therefore, to move from Nottingham in all haste, although his army was not yet fully mustered, the time not having permitted many of his most trusty commanders to reach the castle as instructed. The king's indignation was greatly kindled[4] at the defection of the Talbots, the perfidy of Ap-Thomas, and the welcome given to Richmond at Lichfield; and as his spies[5] made known to him the private interview which had taken place between Sir William Stanley

---

[1] Grafton, p. 213.   [2] Ibid.
[3] Chron. Croy., p. 573.   [4] Grafton, p. 215.
[5] " And in all haste he sent out espials to view and espy what way his enemies kept and passed. They diligently doing their duty, shortly after returned, declaring to the king that the earl was encamped at the town of Lichfield." — *Grafton,* p. 215.

and the earl, as also the departure of the Lord Stanley for Atherstone the day before the rebels had entered Lichfield, Richard resolved on removing to Leicester, to prevent if possible a junction between the earl and his father-in-law, and give battle to his rival before his forces were farther augmented.

By a contemporary letter yet extant from the Duke of Norfolk[1] it appears, that he would have departed instantly, but it was the eve of the assumption of the Virgin Mary[2], and the superstition of the age rendered Richard averse to marching on that day. This he communicated to such of his partizans as had been prevented joining him, appointing Leicester as the town to which they should direct their course; and on the day after the festival he marshalled his troops in the market-place at Nottingham[3], and separating the foot soldiers into two divisions, five abreast[4], and dividing his cavalry so as to form two wide spreading wings; he placed his ammunition and artillery in the center[5], taking up his own position in a space immediately behind it.[6] Gorgeously attired in the splendid armour for which the age was remarkable, and his helmet surmounted by the crown, King Richard riding upon a milk-white charger superbly caparisoned[7], attended by his body guards, displaying the banner of England and innumerable pennons glittering with the " silver boar," with other

---

[1] See Appendix OO. [2] Paston Letters, vol. ii. p. 334.
[3] Hutton's Bosworth, p. 46. [4] Grafton, p. 215.
[5] Ibid. [6] Ibid. [7] Ibid.

insignia of his princely race, and surrounded by a
gallant band of archers and picked men-at-arms,
wended his way on the morning of the 16th August,
1485, down the steep acclivity on which stood the
noble pile where he had so long sojourned, and
quitted the castle of Nottingham for ever! He was
about to fight his last battle, but he knew it not.
His lofty spirit was undaunted, for he dreamed not
of the perfidy that was working his ruin, and his
invincible courage led him to despise all danger
which was openly and honourably incurred in the
battle-field. His army, which was very considerable, was so imposingly arranged, that it covered
the road for three miles, and must have been
" more than an hour in marching out of Nottingham, and as long in entering Leicester."[1] He did
not reach this latter town until sunset, when so
prodigious did his force appear, and so formidable
their array, that the ecclesiastical historian states
there was found at that town " a greater number
of men than was ever before seen in England fighting on one side."[2] The castle of Leicester, the
ancient demesne of John of Gaunt, hitherto the
resting-place of royalty when sojourning in its
vicinity, had become too ruinous for occupation at
this momentous period; Richard therefore took up
his abode at the chief hostelry in the town, then
probably designated after the royal badge[3], although
better known in subsequent ages by the appellation

---

[1] Hutton, p. 47.   [2] Chron. Croy., p. 574.

[3] " The proud bragging white boar, which was his badge, was
violently rased and plucked down, from every sign and place where
it might be spied."— *Grafton*, p. 255.

of the "Blue Boar." On the 17th he marched to Hinckley, and fixed his camp at the village of Elmsthorpe; but having ascertained that Richmond had not quitted Lichfield, he altered his route and took up his station on the 18th on some rising ground at Stableton, a situation admirably adapted either for observation or contest, as no enemy could approach unseen.[1] Here it appears probable that he was joined by the Duke of Norfolk, the Earl of Surrey, and Sir Robert Brackenbury; and at this period he seems for the first time to have become alive to the treachery which was shown towards him by many, who having been enriched by his liberality, now deserted his standard for that of his rival. At Stoney Stratford, Sir Walter Hungerford and Sir Thomas Bourchier, both " esquires of the body[2]," left Brackenbury under cover of the night, to join the enemy's ranks, and Sir John Savage, Sir Simon Digby, and very many other individuals, whom gratitude alone ought to have bound to their sovereign[3], proclaimed themselves openly supporters of the rebels.

Still he was too strong to fear Richmond, unless disloyalty should farther weaken his force; but his suspicions were again painfully excited by learning that the earl had quitted Lichfield, and steadily pursued his course to Tamworth, where he arrived late on the evening of the 18th August[4], by which position not only did the troops commanded by the

---

[1] Hutton, p. 50.   [2] Harl. MSS., No. 433. pp. 16. 27. 142.

[3] For the grants bestowed on Sir John Savage, see *Harl. MSS.,* No. 433. pp. 28. 102. 131. and 141.

[4] Hutton, p. 195.

Lord Stanley and his brother Sir William separate the royal forces from the earl's army, but great facility was given by their contiguity to effect secret interviews between Richmond and his kindred. One of such interviews is known to have taken place at Atherstone[1], and of infinite importance it was. It put the earl in possession of the true sentiments and intentions of the Stanleys, and encouraged him to fall in with King Richard's design of forcing him to take the field before either of the brothers had openly joined his standard. The two following days, the 19th and 20th, appear to have been passed by all parties in collecting their utmost strength, in watching the movements of their opponents, and placing their camps as desirably as circumstances admitted, for by little and little the hostile armies had so closely approximated to each other, that an engagement had become inevitable. Richmond again following the footsteps of his father-in-law, quitted Tamworth and arrived at Atherstone shortly after the departure of the Lord Stanley, who, the better to deceive the king, had marched to within three quarters of a mile of the royal troops. The Duke of Norfolk and the Earl of Northumberland, each with his powerful body of men, were also encamped on advantageous positions, and all parties felt that the fitting time had arrived for bringing to a crisis the long threatened and much desired combat.

A broad extent of uninclosed country separated the rival forces, and the scene of action even-

---

[1] Grafton, p. 218.; Pol. Virg., p. 562.; Hall, 413.

tually fixed upon was that portion of it entitled
Redmore Plain [1], since better known as Bosworth
Field, from its near vicinity to the market-town
which bears that name. Few spots could have
been better suited for the desperate encounter that
was to immortalise it for ever. It was then a wide,
open, uncultivated tract of land [2], somewhat of an
oval form, about two miles long and one mile broad,
intersected by a thick wood, and bounded on the
south side by a small river running through a low
swampy country; on the north side partly by
rising ground and partly by a boggy flat, locally
denominated "Amyon Lays." [3] Such a field afforded
advantages seldom combined for the distribution of
hostile troops. An acclivity designated Amyon
Hill, which gently rose to the northward from the
center of the plain, not only gave unusual facility
for the disposal of an army, but, as the result proved,
its more elevated portion afforded certain opportu-
nities for observation to encampments stationed on
the high grounds which in various points overlooked
the valley, and who could thus communicate by
signal [3], without seeming to act in concert with each
other. These points were speedily occupied by
the great commanders most deeply interested in
the result, for it was soon perceived that in the

---

[1] " Redmore, or Red-moor, so named from the colour of the soil,
as the meadows in the west are called white-moors for the same
reason." — *Hutton*, p. 68.

[2] " Bosworth Field, which was one piece of uncultivated land
without hedge or timber, is now so altered with both, that nothing
remains of its former appearance but the shape of the ground." —
Ibid. p. 71.

[3] Hutton, pp. 245. 248.

plain below the battle would inevitably occur. Richard's camp consisted of two lines. It is stated to have covered about eighteen acres[1], and to have been fortified by breastworks of considerable skill and labour, 300 yards long and about 50 broad.[2] Richmond was equally indefatigable, for although seven acres sufficed for the disposition of his small band, yet the experience of the Earl of Oxford, Sir James Blount, and other renowned warriors who undertook to direct his movements, fully compensated for the insignificant force he ostensibly brought to the field. Lord Stanley and his brother had so craftily placed themselves on two of the eminences just named, the one to the extreme left a little in advance, and the other to the extreme right, but somewhat to the rear of the royal camp, that though seemingly attached to King Richard by reason of their contiguity to his forces, they were in the best position for accelerating his downfall when the fitting moment arrived for joining the enemy's ranks. During the night of the 20th[3] the celebrated interview[4] between the Earl of Richmond and the two Stanleys is said to have taken place, in which they made known to him their intentions, and also, as it would appear by the result, intimated to him the probable defection of the Earl of Northumberland. On the 21st instant at day-break, Richmond broke up his camp at Atherstone, and marching thence crossed the Tweed, the small rivulet before

---

[1] Hutton, p. 50.

[2] Hutton, in his " Battle of Bosworth " (p. 62.), states that on his first visit to the scene of this memorable conflict the vestiges of the camps were yet visible.

[3] Hutton, p. 57.   [4] Grafton, p. 218.

named, and encamped on the confines of Bosworth
Field. The same day, King Richard receiving intelligence of the earl's movements, advanced to meet
him; for although he had sent away his army, and
had well and judiciously encamped his forces, so as
to preclude Richmond's farther advance towards
London, he appears to have made Leicester his
head-quarters.

Accompanied by the Duke of Norfolk, the gallant Earl of Surrey, the Lord of Lincoln, the Lord
Lovell, and most of his personal friends, as well
as by a vast concourse of people, he rode out of
Leicester in the same royal state in which he made
his entry into that town. With his regal crown
upon his helmet, and borne on a noble war-steed of
uncommon size, whose costly trappings accorded
with the rich suit of polished steel armour worn by
its accomplished rider fourteen years before at the
battle of Tewkesbury[1], Richard presented himself
before his soldiers as became a conquering prince,
a defied and insulted monarch, omitting none of
those external attributes of royalty, for the conservation of which he was on the eve of engaging in
deadly strife — a strife which, although he knew it
not, was to effect so wondrous a change in the constitution of England, and in the habits, position,
and policy of its people. Both armies were within
view of each other the greater part of the 21st; but
it was the sabbath[2], and as if by mutual consent,
each party remained inactive until towards evening,

[1] Hutton, p. 82.
[2] " Upon Sunday they heard mass ; and to a fair field took the
way." — *Harl. MSS.*, No. 542. fol. 34.

when the king broke up his encampment, and removing to the brow of the hill overlooking Bosworth plain, there took up his position for the night, that his soldiers might be refreshed, and ready for the morning's conflict. That rest, however, which the monarch desired for his troops, and which was even more requisite for himself as their leader, was incompatible with the conflicting feelings that agitated his mind. His temperament was too sensitive not to be deeply afflicted at the faithlessness already evinced by many whom he had trusted, and from whom he had merited a more generous requital[1]; but open defalcation was more easy to be borne than the perfidy which his keen foresight and acute penetration could not help anticipating from the powerful but dissimulating Stanley. Sir William had already been proclaimed a traitor; still he had not, like many others, arrayed himself publicly under Richmond's banner; so that doubts were created as to his ultimate intention more harassing than if he had pursued a less neutral course. The Lord Stanley had been so wary in his conduct that, disposed as the king must have been to resent his contemptuous disregard of his summons, yet he could not in justice lay treason to his charge, when possibly the real cause of his mysterious conduct was a natural desire to preserve a neutrality between the conflicting claims of his son-in-law and sovereign.

He had headed his trusty band of Lancashire

---

[1] The king " was sore moved and broiled with melancholy and dolour, and cried out, asking vengeance of them that, contrary to their oath and promise, had so deceived him."—*Grafton*, p. 215.

men, and commenced his march towards the royal
forces immediately it was reported that the rebels
had crossed the Severn. He had neither avowedly
allied himself with Richmond, as did Sir Gilbert
Talbot and Sir Price-ap-Thomas, nor had his
movements implied designs that corresponded with
theirs; on the contrary, he had seemed to avoid
the earl, and scrupulously to evade a junction,
although still pleading severe illness[1] as his excuse
for not appearing at the court of his sovereign.

And now, on the eve of the battle, he had encamped near to Richard's station, and at a considerable distance from that of his opponent. Sir
William too, observing the same policy, and although ranged on the side of the field occupied by
Richard, had intentionally allowed the whole of
the royal army to separate his band from that of
his brother. Under such circumstances to have
concluded perfidy, and to have denounced these
chiefs, would, perhaps, accelerate the very evil it
was the monarch's wish to prevent. King Richard,
however, was a keen reader of human character:
he had from his very birth been nurtured in the
insidious dealings which so peculiarly characterised his era, and been inured to the stealthy proceedings that were unblushingly adopted to accelerate party views. By nature endowed with
unusual sagacity, he was, moreover, gifted with a
degree of forethought that enabled him to arrive
at a conclusion less from the actions than the probable motives of the parties prejudged. The Lord

---

[1] Harl. MSS., 542. fol. 34.

Stanley had espoused the mother of Henry of Richmond. Sir William had been admitted to be faithless even by his own nephew ! The events of the last few months had taught the king how transient was popular favour ; and those even of the last few days had brought still more painfully home to his conviction the little dependance to be placed on vows of fealty, which were as easily broken as they had been enthusiastically proffered. Perplexed, harassed, scarcely knowing whom to trust and whom to suspect, Richard became a prey to those excitable feelings — that distressing restlessness which so often results from the union of two vigorous mental powers with a corporeal frame of little bodily strength. Weak in constitution, and subject to that nervous irritability which is its invariable accompaniment [1], with so much, too, of real anxiety to distract his thoughts, so much of paramount importance to absorb the attention of a mind peculiarly susceptible and anxious, it is no marvel that, as the monarch sought repose upon his couch on the eve of the approaching contest, fearful dreams and harrowing thoughts should have interrupted a rest which, under the most favourable auspices, could scarcely have been tranquil and unbroken. He awoke, agitated, dispirited, unrefreshed, " before the chaplains were ready to officiate, or the breakfast was prepared." [2]

---

[1] That such was the fact is made apparent by Sir Thomas More, who states that " he took ill rest a-nights, lay long waking and musing, sore wearied with care and watch rather slumbered than slept, troubled with fearful dreams." — *More*, p. 134.

[2] Chron. Croy., p. 573.

Prostrated in mind and body, bemoaning the direful consequences which must result to the realm
from the approaching struggle, whichever party
might gain the victory[1], and acting under the influence of that morbid feeling which results from over-
wrought nervous excitement, he unhesitatingly communicated to his trusty attendants, who, on entering
his tent, found him agitated, pale [2], and depressed,
the simple cause of that lassitude which superstition
quickly exaggerated into the appearance of super-
natural visions, and subsequent chroniclers, with
more indulgence of their imagination than became
the simplicity of their task, recorded as a visitation
of ghastly forms, forerunners of his death, or evil
spirits sent to reproach him with curses for his
alleged crimes. [3]   The only effect which, in reality,
sleeplessness appears to have had upon the mind
or intentions of the king, judging from the statement of contemporary writers, was his determination to ascertain beyond doubt the sentiments of
the Lord Stanley, whose personal attendance at
his camp he forthwith required by a special message, sent by the trusty Brackenbury.

To this determined measure he was farther actuated by a warning which had been affixed during
the night to the Lord of Norfolk's tent; a warning ambiguously worded, but which confirmed
King Richard in his misgivings that he was indeed,
as the distich pronouced, perfidiously " bought and
sold." [4]   That the nefarious plot, although it had

[1] Chron. Croy., p. 573.   [2] Ibid.
[3] Grafton, p. 209. ; Pol. Virg., p. 562. ; Hall, p. 414.
[4] John Howard, Duke of Norfolk, was warned by divers to refrain

baffled his utmost power to penetrate, was suspected by him is clear, and that suspicion must have opened his mind to a danger greater than any that could arise from Richmond's trivial band of 7000 men, the very utmost which has ever been asserted to have been openly arrayed against his own powerful force of more than double that number. In his midnight survey of his outposts too he had found a sentinel asleep [1] (or feigning to be so); and that this was not a solitary instance of negligence was evident by the warning hand that vainly strove to shake the honour of the noble Norfolk; and was afterwards more effectually proved, from the fact of Sir Simon Digby pene-

---

from the field, insomuch that, the night before he should set forward toward the king, one wrote on his gate :

" Jocke of Norfolk, be not too bold,
    For Dickon thy master is bought and sold."

Grafton, p. 230.

There can be little doubt that what Grafton ambiguously terms " the gate ' signified the door-way or entrance to the duke's tent ; for that nobleman did not rest at his own house " the night before he should set forward toward the king," but at Bury, where, by appointment, he was joined by his entire force. (See *Paston Letters*, vol. ii. p. 334.) His encampment prior to the battle of Bosworth was far removed from that of the monarch, being on a heath considerably to the rear of the royal troops, and about midway between the camps of Lord Stanley and his brother. This fact sufficiently explains the meaning of Grafton's expression — " the night before he should set forward toward the king," which he did on the morning of the battle, and thus afforded a marked contrast to the part pursued by the two Stanleys ; it also justifies the view taken by Mr. Sharon Turner (vol. iv. p. 31.) and other writers, that the warning was fixed to the Duke of Norfolk's tent on the eve of the engagement.

[1] Issuing from his tent by twilight, he observed a sentinel asleep, and is said to have stabbed him, with this remark : " I found him asleep, and have left him as I found him." — *Hutton's Bosworth*, p. 78.

trating as a spy into the centre of the royal camp [1], and communicating to Richmond much valuable intelligence, obtained by so perilous and dangerous a step.

Fable and misrepresentation has added greatly to the horrors of Bosworth Field; but the sole point which may be relied upon is this, that on Stanley's refusal to obey the royal summons, the king commanded the immediate execution of the Lord Strange, his life having been given as a surety for his father's fidelity.[2] But the day had long dawned, both armies were on the alert, and Richard was again prevailed upon [3] to spare his illustrious captive, or at least to suspend his execution until the battle was terminated.[4] Recovering his ordinary self-possession, he arranged his forces with the military skill and precision for which he had ever been remarkable. His entire force appears to have amounted to about 16,000 men; these he spread out so as to make them appear to the greatest advantage, occupying and covering entirely the eminence which rose from the centre of the plain from its base to its summit.[5] The Earl's troops were ranged in the valley beneath, his small band being protected by the wood, and the marshy swamp which intervened between that and the rivulet.[6] The two Stanleys had so placed their companies—the one consisting of five, the other of three thousand men,—that the four bands may be considered to have formed an irregular square,

[1] Hutton, p. 79.   [2] Chron. Croy., p. 574.
[3] Grafton, p. 283.   [4] Ibid. p. 284.
[5] Hutton, pp. 87, 88.   [6] Ibid.

although those of the Stanleys ranged more immediately on the side of Richard than on that of his
rival. Both armies were drawn up in similar order
of battle, each in two lines, the archers in the front,
the bill-men in the rear, and the horse forming the
wings.[1] King Richard entrusted his front line to
his faithful friend the Duke of Norfolk, to whom
was united the aid of the chivalrous Earl of Surrey.[2]
The second line appears to have been commanded
by the Lord Ferrers, in conjunction with the Earl
of Northumberland. The centre, composed of a
dense square of " seven score of serjeants, that were
chained and locked in a row, and as many bombards
and thousands of morrispikes, harquebusses, &c.
&c.,[3] " the king commanded in person. The Earl
of Richmond's front was under the entire charge of
the Earl of Oxford, supported on his right by Sir
Gilbert Talbot, on the left by Sir John Savage,
while his second line, although ostensibly apportioned to himself, was in effect commanded by his
uncle the Earl of Pembroke, a veteran warrior of
great wisdom, experience, and skill.[4]

Disdaining the slender pretensions of " Henry
Tudor," and spurning his insignificant force—outrageous at the duplicity of the Stanleys, and still
more at the base and avowed defection of many
persons whom his former bounty had fed, —Richard
advanced to the battle with that fierce and fearless
deportment which characterised his undaunted race,
and marked his own conduct at Barnet, at Tewks-
bury, and at Berwick.

[1] Hutton, p. 81.   [2] Grafton, p. 220.
[3] Harl. MSS., 542. fol. 34.   [4] Grafton, p. 220.

Previous to the battle, according to subsequent writers, each of the princely leaders is said to have addressed an energetic and powerful oration to his forces, although no mention is made of the circumstance by either of the contemporary historians [1]; neither is it named in the manuscript detail of the battle, preserved in the Harleian Library, and which appears to have been written by some person present at the conflict. [2]

Eloquent appeals, there can be little doubt, were made on both sides to rouse those vigorous efforts which each commander felt himself called upon to require when the crown of England was at stake; and its ultimate possession was the stimulus and the reward of his own individual prowess: but the speeches [3] attributed to the rival princes are clearly

[1] The chronicler of Croyland, the historian Rous, and Fabyan the city annalist.

[2] Harl. MSS., 542. fol. 34.

[3] These speeches rest solely on the authority of Grafton and Hall; and considering that these chroniclers wrote their works many years after the battle occurred, and that they frankly admit that the lengthened addresses which they give, occupying "150 lines in folio," were " in these or like words following," there can be no doubt that they were the composition of the earlier of these writers. This is rendered clear by the circumstance that Richard is made to admit the fact of the murder of his nephews, and to have expressed contrition for the deed; a fact so important, if true, that it must have become known to his contemporaries, who have so minutely described the battle and its result. But who can believe that at such a moment Richard would have so stultified himself, and ruined his own cause? This circumstance, united to the little probability of true or faithful versions being reported of verbal addresses made on the field, together with their evident partizanship to the Tudor monarch, incontestably lead to the conclusion that they form a portion of those unauthenticated rumours fabricated for political purposes, which have so miserably defamed the character of Richard III.

the compositions of a writer long subsequent to the
period — some person ignorant of the situation and
feelings of the monarchs, and swayed by prejudices
which were confirmed by subsequent events, if they
did not originate in them.   The Earl of Richmond
occupied a less prominent position in the field than
that which King Richard apportioned to himself.
Rendered yet more conspicuous by the regal
diadem[1], which, as in the instance of the Lancastrian hero, Henry V., when he headed his troops
at Agincourt, surmounted his helmet, he led on his
army as became a monarch of England, a prince
who scornfully repelled the invader of his realm.
As Richmond's army slowly advanced the royal
archers bent their bows, and from the moment that
the trumpets sounded, and the strife of actual
conflict commenced, the most daring heroism
marked King Richard's course.   Alternately he
encouraged his troops by appeals to their fidelity,
and stimulated them by the example of his own
invincible courage.

Had he been adequately supported, Henry of
Richmond, and not Richard III., would probably
have fallen on Bosworth Field[2]: but in the heat
of the battle the Lord Stanley passed over to the
earl[3], and thus neutralized the advantage which the
devoted and magnanimous Norfolk had obtained

[1] Chron. Croy., p. 574.
[2] Where between them was fought a sharp battle, and sharper
should have been if the king's party had been fast to him.   But
many toward the field refused him, and rode unto that other party;
and some stood harrying afar off till they saw to which party the
victory fell. — *Fabyan*, p. 518.
[3] Grafton, p. 227.

over the Earl of Oxford. The monarch, still and ever undismayed, strove to counteract the ascendancy thus gained by his rival, who, invigorated by fresh troops, made a desperate attack upon the yet unbroken front of the royal forces; but the Earl of Northumberland, commanding the second line, instead of supporting his sovereign — with feelings more despicable than open revolt — stood aloof: with a stoicism past comprehension, in one who had been the chief instrument, conjointly with Buckingham, in inciting Richard to aspire to the crown, he calmly viewed the distressing position of his royal master, the personal friend who had loaded him with benefits. Richard was thus deprived of aid from the quarter on which he had most relied for support.[1] Stung to the quick by such base unmerited perfidy, and furious at witnessing the death of the valiant Norfolk, the capture of the Earl of Surrey, and the slaughter of several other trusty commanders who hastened to their rescue, Richard, in an unguarded moment, quitting the central position in which he was so well protected, rushed down the hill[2] and made towards the enemy's ranks, determined to seek out Henry of Richmond, and, by challenging him to single combat, at once to terminate the fearful strife.[3] He was followed by the Lord Lovell, Lord Ferrers, Sir Gervoise Clifton, by Brackenbury,

---

[1] Grafton, p. 251.; Hall, p. 419.

[2] " Being inflamed with ire, and vexed with outrageous malice, he put his spurs to his horse, and rode out of the side of the range of his battle, leaving the avaunt guards fighting." — *Grafton*, p. 218.

[3] Hutton, p. 108.

Ratcliffe, Catesby, and many other devoted friends, who, seeing their royal master's danger, followed him to victory or to death. As they passed a spring which intervened between them and the enemy's lines, tradition states that the king momentarily checked his steed, and slaked his thirst from that fountain, which yet retains the name of " King Richard's Well." Refreshed by the cooling draught, he re-closed his helmet, and again rushed impetuously towards the spot where Richmond had been pointed out to him, standing, but indifferently guarded.[1] He dashed into the midst of the enemy's ranks with a vehemence that nothing could withstand, followed by the chosen band who were about to seal with their lives their devotion to their sovereign, and their zeal for his cause. In spite of opposition the king made his way almost to the spot occupied by his rival before his intention even had become apparent to the earl or his supporters. By almost superhuman strength he maintained his perilous position, slaying with his own hand Sir William Brandon [2], the earl's standard-bearer, and unhorsing Sir John Cheney, one of the most powerful men of his time, who had advanced to Sir William's succour.[3] Thus carrying terror, and dealing destruction into the very heart of his enemies' ranks, the king now called upon the earl to meet him in single combat, and so stop a conflict rendered appalling by the numbers of the slain, and the desperate spirit which actuated both armies.

[1] Grafton, p. 228. [2] Ibid. p. 229.
[3] Ibid.

But Richmond's friends knew that he was no match for Richard III., the most accomplished warrior of his age; and as he advanced to meet his foe numbers interposed to separate them. They stood, however, no chance against the undaunted prowess of the defied monarch and his devoted followers. He gained so sensibly upon his opponents, and so fearfully diminished the gallant band that opposed his progress, that Richmond's flight or destruction seemed inevitable, and the success of King Richard certain. Sir William Stanley, who up to this crisis had remained neuter, observing the peril of the earl [1], and aware of the king's invincible bravery, quitted the position whence he had watched the conflict [2], and speedily joining Richmond with 3000 fresh soldiers, he surrounded the king, and enclosing him, as in a net, at once cut him off from his own army, or the possibility of flight, and thus decided the fortune of the day.

At this crisis a knight, reputed to be Catesby, who saw Stanley approaching, and comprehended the evident destruction which must follow his movement, brought the monarch a fresh steed, beseeching him to save himself by flight [3], while escape was yet practicable: but the race of York were never cravens; to them death on the field of battle was glorious—flight came not within their comprehen-

---

[1] Grafton, p. 229. [2] Hutton, p. 112.

[3] " Then to King Richard there came a knight and said, ' I hold it time for ye to fly ; yonder Stanley his dynts be so sore, gainst them may no man stand. Here is thy horse, another day ye may worship again." — *Harl. MSS.*, 542. fol. 34.

sion. " Not one foot will I fly," was his answer,
" so long as breath bides within my breast; for by
Him that shaped both sea and land, this day shall
end my battles or my life; I will die King of England."[1]

Betrayed, over-reached, vanquished by treachery
alone, Richard continued to fight with the desperation induced by his perilous situation. All his
friends, all his followers, one by one, were numbered with the dead; his standard-bearer alone
remained, and he waved the royal banner on high
until both his legs " were cut him from, yet to the
ground he would not let it go[2]" till life was quite
extinct! Still Richard remained undaunted, unsubdued, slaying all who approached within his
sword's length, and performing prodigies of valour.
At last, overpowered by numbers, weakened by loss
of blood, his strength exhausted although his courage was unabated, " in battle and not in flight,"
states the Croyland historian[3], " the said king,
stricken with many mortal wounds, fell on the field
like a courageous and most daring prince."

Thus perished Richard III.! thus terminated
the Yorkist dynasty! The death of its last monarch on Redmore plain, like that of its founder, his
noble and gallant sire at Wakefield Green, being
effected by treachery so base, by a compact so perfidious, that it was less honourable to those who
conquered than to those who fell under its ignoble
influence.

[1] Harl. MSS., 542. fol. 34.   [2] Ibid.
[3] Chron. Croy., p. 574.

King Richard died the victim of ingratitude and of hypocrisy so opposed to the English character, that happily no corresponding parallel disgraces our national annals. His death was not occasioned, as it pleased the chroniclers of his rival to insinuate in after-years, by open insurrection[1], by a revolution produced by popular feeling, arising from the reputed murder of his nephews; neither was he overcome by generous efforts to restore the sceptre to its lawful owner, or to inflict upon a tyrant that just retribution which is often resorted to by an enslaved people, to extirpate the despot whose savage deeds have driven his subjects to desperation: on the contrary, the last of the Plantagenet monarchs was accompanied to the field, as had been his predecessors, by the flower of the English chivalry; and the list of those gallant knights[2] who on the eve of the combat " swore that Richard should wear the crown," together with the affecting manner in which the intelligence of his death was entered at the time in the register of the city of York[3]—he " was piteously slain and murdered,

[1] " The nation had no share in the conflict, notwithstanding all that is said about the king's unpopularity ; it was an ambush of a few perfidious and disaffected noblemen against the crown, which succeeded by their hypocrisy : and Richard perished by one of those factions in his aristocracy from which, by taking the crown, it seemed likely that he had rescued himself."—*Sharon Turner*, vol. iv. p. 53.

[2] See Appendix PP.

[3] The sentiments expressed by the historian of York on this point are very important to King Richard, founded as they are upon the examination of contemporary municipal records, and from the convincing evidence resulting therefrom. " These sketches of history," states that learned writer, after giving copies from the original documents, " I bring to light as a taste of those times, rendered dark enough by the writers of the Lancastrian party. Here is sub-

to the great heaviness of this city[1]," would alone suffice to show that neither the nation at large, nor her nobles as a body, had rejected him from being their king.

Face to face he met his foes, proudly disdaining to shrink from the danger to which he was compelled to expose his faithful adherents. To check the carnage which was exterminating the bravest of his subjects, he challenged his rival to mortal combat, that the life of one man might suffice to stay the slaughter of thousands. Led to believe that Richmond could oppose but seven thousand men to his own gallant force of sixteen thousand, but quickly shown that five thousand more were in reserve, and only awaited, under the Lord Stanley, the fitting time for rendering the combatants of nearly equal strength, he was basely deserted by one third of his own army, which was withdrawn by the Earl of Northumberland[2] at the most critical point of the battle, and hemmed in, for the purpose of destruction, by the other member of that specious triumvirate, by whose machinations

ject for an historian to expatiate largely upon; and to such I leave it." " It is plain that Richard, represented as a monster of mankind by most, was not so esteemed in his lifetime in these northern parts. And had the Earl of Northumberland staid and raised forces here, he might have struck Henry's new acquired diadem into the hazard. Wanting that nobleman's personal appearance, our city had nothing to do but with the rest of the kingdom to submit to the conqueror. His policy taught him to show great acts of clemency at his entrance into government, though he must know that neither his title nor his family were recognised or respected in these northern parts of the kingdom." — *Drake's Ebor.*, p. 124.

[1] Drake's Ebor., p. 120.

[2] Pol. Virg. p. 563.; Grafton, p. 234.; Hall, p. 419.

alone he was vanquished[1], and numbered the chief among the mighty dead who perished on Bosworth Field.

Later ages, misled by partial statements, have given a far different colouring to the events which really led to King Richard's death; but the statement of the other contemporary historian not only corroborates the eulogium bestowed by the ecclesiastical chronicler above quoted, but most graphically paints the base manner in which, with his dying breath, the monarch proclaimed that his ruin had been accomplished. " If," says Rous[2], " I may speak the truth to his honour, although small of body and weak in strength, he most valiantly defended himself as a noble knight to his last breath, often exclaiming that he was betrayed, and saying — Treason! treason! treason!"

With these words on his lips, King Richard expired on the 22d August, 1485, in the thirty-third year of his age, and after a brief reign of two years and two months — the victim of conspirators who had vowed his destruction, and craftily watched the most favourable moment for carrying it into execution. His death establishes the truth of the degrading fact which was communicated to the faithful and noble Howard the night preceding the battle; — the sovereign of England was indeed " both bought and sold!"

[1] Pol. Virg., 563.; Grafton, p. 234.; Hall, p. 419.
[2] Rous, p. 217.

CHAP. XIX.

THE fearful struggles on Bosworth Field terminated
with King Richard's life ; for the shouts of triumph
which rent the air as he sank beneath the swords

of countless multitudes[1], quickly announced to his
own army the direful fate of their illustrious and
intrepid leader.   Terror-stricken, the royal troops
fled in all directions, and were speedily followed by
the victorious party, who, unimpeded by the dead
and the dying[2], which piled in fearful numbers[3]
formed a dreadful barrier between the hostile
armies, they pursued their adversaries with that
ferocity, that unrelenting vengeance, which forms
one of the most melancholy features of civil warfare.   For nearly two miles their route is said to
be still marked by " pits or hollows,"[4] which are
supposed to be the graves of the heaps of slain that
fell in the pursuit; and although this appalling
result to the tragic scenes enacted on the battle-
field occupied less than fifty minutes[5], it was sufficiently long to secure a complete victory to
Richmond, and utter discomfiture to the supporters
of the fallen monarch.   A steep hill served to
check alike the pursuit of the victors, and farther
carnage of the vanquished.[6]   Henry, accompanied
by the Lord Stanley, the Earl of Pembroke, the
Earl of Oxford, and others of his most renowned
commanders, paused on its summit[7], and there

---

[1] " Charged and environed with multitudes that like a storm
came on him, valiant Richard falls the sacrifice of that day under
their cruel swords." — *Buck*, lib. ii. p. 61.

[2] " And many a noble knight then lost theyr life with Richard
theyr kynge." — *Harl. MSS.*, No. 542. fol. 34.

[3] There fell in this battlé about four thousand of the vanquished.
— *Hume*, chap. xxiii. p. 273.

[4] Hutton, p. 128.   [5] Ibid. p. 129.

[6] " Then they removed to a mountayne hyghe, and with a
voyce they cried King Harry." — *Harl. MSS.*, No. 542. fol. 34.

[7] Harl. MSS., No. 542. fol. 34.

received from the hands of his father-in-law that
diadem which had cost King Richard his life, and
was to secure to himself the throne.   During the
heat of the conflict, and shortly before the monarch's death, the crown which surmounted his
helmet was cleft from it.[1] Falling to the ground,
it was picked up by a soldier[2], and concealed in a
hawthorn bush[3] in the adjoining wood.   There it
was accidentally discovered by Sir Reginald Bray,
who seizing the precious relic, the possession of
which had caused the slaughter of so many gallant
warriors, he gained the victors, and presenting it
to Lord Stanley[4], that nobleman placed it on Richmond's head[5], and hailed him monarch of England.

The eminence whereon this occurred still retains
the name of " Crown Hill," in perpetuation of the
event, and the cheers and acclamations of the
conquering hosts as they greeted their leader with
cries of " King Harry, King Harry,"[6] were wafted
across the intervening space, and echoing over
Redmore Plain, announced that the pursuit was
over, and conquest complete, there remaining

---

[1] " They hewed the crown of gold from his head with dowtfull
dents." — *Harl. MSS.*, No. 542. fol. 34.

[2] Hutton, p. 132.

[3] To commemorate his being crowned with King Richard's
diadem at Bosworth Field, found in a hawthorn bush, Henry VII.
bare the hawthorn bush with the crown in it, and these letters
K. H., with which the windows of his royal chapel at Westminster Abbey are replenished. — *Sandford's Geneal. Hist.*, book vi.
p. 434.

[4] " The crown of gold was delivered to the Lord Stanley, and
unto Kynge Henry then went he, and delyveryed it." — *Harl. MSS.*,
No. 542. fol. 34.

[5] Grafton, p. 233.   [6] Ibid.

"none against whom the victor Henry VII. might renew the fight."[1]

Bosworth Field not only chronicles the only sovereign of England, save the hero of Agincourt, who went into battle wearing the royal diadem, but it commemorates also the only British monarch who was slain in battle since the Norman conquest and since Harold II. by a similar death conferred corresponding celebrity on the field of Hastings. The analogy between these two conquests and the fate of their royal leaders[2], together with the remarkable epochs in British history which they perpetuate, have been already noticed at the opening of this memoir; but the conduct of the invaders in the fifteenth century affords a painful contrast to the generous and ennobling feeling which marked that of the Norman conqueror four centuries before, although acted in times by comparison rude and uncivilised, and characterised by a far greater degree of popular excitement. They warred with the living, and not with the dead; they fought as became men and Christians, not as ruthless savages.[3] Harold fell

---

[1] Chron. Croy., p. 574.

[2] Harold, like Richard, died the victim of stratagem, for, states the old chronicler, " as an expert general, he had ordered his men in so firm a body, that no force of the Normans could disorder their ranks, till Duke William used a stratagem, commanding his men to retire and to counterfeit flight, by which he drew the English on, upon a hollow ground covered with earth, whereunto many of them fell and perished ; and besides, into an ambush of his horsemen, which unexpectedly fell upon them and cut them in pieces." — *Baker's Chron.*, p. 23.

[3] " Richard died by the hands of a multitude, who cut his body in the most shocking and barbarous manner, while he was breathing his last." — *Nicholl's Leicester,* vol. ii. p. 298.

vanquished by the victorious bands of the Norman William; but with his death all personal rancour ceased, and the conqueror honouring the valour of his rival, however much he rejoiced at his over-throw, delivered his body to his mother[1], that he might receive the interment befitting a gallant prince, although a vanquished and defeated monarch.

Far different was the conduct pursued towards Richard III. Although his intrepidity and his heroic deeds called forth eulogiums even from the Lancastrian historians, yet neither his bravery nor his misfortunes elicited sympathy from his opponents after death had sealed his fate, and when he was no longer conscious of the insults to which his mortal remains were subjected. Not contented with winning his crown, the great incentive to the combat—not satisfied with his defeat, and his having paid the forfeit of his life by his temerity, the victors searched for his body, and having found it covered with wounds[2] among a heap of slain, with a barbarity alike discreditable to the age and to the persons directly concerned in the unrelenting deed, they stripped him of his gorgeous apparel, and in outrage of decency and common humanity placed the deceased monarch naked across his war steed, "like a hog or a calf, the head and arms

---

[1] For the body of King Harold, his mother Thyra offered a great sum to have it delivered to her ; but the duke, out of the nobleness of his mind, would take no money, but delivered it freely, and then it was buried at Waltham Abbey, which himself had begun to build, at least repair. — *Baker's Chron.*, p. 23.

[2] Buck, lib. ii. p. 62.

hanging on the one side of the horse, and the legs on the other side."[1] Thus all besprinked " with mire and blood,"[2] the inanimate victim of this un-exampled barbarity was disposed of behind his poursuivant at arms, "Blanc Sanglier " (he wearing the silver boar upon his coat[3]), and carried back to Leicester as a trophy of the morning's victory[4], to be presented in the most degrading manner[5], which the inhumanity of political malice, hatred, and revenge could suggest to the view of such of his subjects as had thronged to greet him on the day previous gallantly wending his way to battle and to death. " The dead body of King Richard was found among the slain, and conveyed with great ignominy to Leicester," certifies the Croy-land writer.[6] Yet stronger is the language of the Tudor chronicler — " The dead corpse of King Richard was as shamefully carried to the town of Leicester as he gorgeously the day before, with pomp and pride, departed out of the same town."[7]

Innumerable, indeed, are the extracts that might be made of corresponding import[8]; and this cir-cumstance alone bespeaks more perhaps than all other arguments, the vindictive and personal feel-ings of malignity which influenced the conduct of Richard's adversaries, and formed the ground-work

[1] Grafton, p. 234.   [2] Ibid.   [3] Hutton, p. 141.
[4] While in the possession of a complete victory, Richmond was totally destitute of that mercy and compassion which ennobles man. — *Nicholls' Leicestershire*, vol. ii. p. 381.
[5] Fabyan, p. 518.   [6] Chron. Croy., p. 574.   [7] Grafton, p. 234.
[8] See Fabyan, p. 518.; Pol. Virg., p. 594.; Hall, p. 419.

of those fearful accusations which henceforth were circulated freely and abundantly to brand the memory of the defeated king, and to exalt the merits of his successful opponent. Superstition lent her aid[1] to magnify the terrors of the eventful day. The head of the vanquished monarch being crushed against a projecting stone, as the poursuivant threaded his way over a narrow bridge entering Leicester, there were not wanting soothsayers to protest that his left foot had touched the same spot the preceding day, and thus led to a prognostication relative to his doom, — " even so shall his head, at his return back, hit on the same place "[2] — of which nothing would have been known, had victory, not defeat, been the result of the conflict on Redmore Plain ; for, as the local historian who perpetuates the tale ingenuously admits, " these are but reports."[3]

King Richard had left his tents standing[4], so that the spoil was immense, and amply were the foreign mercenaries, as well as the less needy English soldiers repaid by pillage for their great exertions[5], and for the discomforts of their journey

---

[1] See a pamphlet, entitled " Seven several Strange Prophecies " [London, 1643], for some curious old legends concerning the death of King Richard III.

[2] Nicholls' Leicester, vol. i. p. 298.

[3] Ibid. [4] Hutton, p. 79.

[5] Lord Bacon asserts that the " great spoils of Bosworth Field came almost wholly into the hands of Sir William Stanley, " to his infinite enriching," there being found in his Castle of Holt, at the confiscation of his property, "forty thousand marks in ready money and plate, besides jewels, household stuff, stacks upon the grounds, and other personal estate exceeding great." — *Bacon's Henry VII.*, p. 133. 135.

through Wales. " The same night however, in the evening, King Henry with great pomp came to the town of Leicester, and his whole camp removed with bag and baggage."[1] The body of King Richard, brought there at the same time, was lodged at a fortified tower[2], entitled Newark, one of the chief entrances to the town; and as it would appear by a proclamation, addressed to the citizens of York by King Henry VII. on the 25th inst., certifying to them the death of their late sovereign[3], was there " laid openly that every man might see and look upon him," and be satisfied that he was indeed deceased.

The most zealous of the late king's personal friends were slain in battle with himself[4], at the head of which stands the Duke of Norfolk, who, regarding " more his oath, his honour, and promise made to King Richard, like a gentleman and a faithful subject to his prince, absented not himself from his master; but, as he faithfully lived under

[1] Grafton, p. 234.

[2] " They brought King Richard thither that night as naked as ever he was born, and in Newark was he laid, that many a man might see." — *Harl. MSS.*, No. 542. fol. 34.

[3] " And, moreover, the king ascertaineth you that Richard Duke of Gloucester, late called King Richard, was slain at a place called Sandeford, within the shire of Leicester, and brought dead off the field into the town of Leicester, and there was laid openly that every man might see and look upon him." — *Drake's Ebor.*, p. 121.

[4] The Duke of Norfolk, Sir Richard Ratcliffe, Sir Robert Brackenbury, constable of the Tower of London ; John Kendall, secretary ; Sir Robert Percy, comptroller of the household ; Walter Devereux, Lord Ferrers, and others, chiefly north countrymen, in whom King Richard most trusted. — *Chron. Croy.*, p. 574.

him, so he manfully died with him, to his great fame
and laud."[1] " Of captains and prisoners there was a
great number."[2] The Earl of Surrey, who in yielding
up his sword to Sir Gilbert Talbot nobly exclaimed,
" Our motto is to support the crown of England,"[3]
was committed to the Tower of London, where he
long remained immured, " because his father was
chief counsellor, and he greatly familiar with King
Richard[4]; but Sir William Catesby, "learned in the
laws of the realm," and " the deceased monarch's
confidential minister," with divers other were, two
days after the battle, beheaded at Leicester.[5] At
this town King Henry remained for that brief interval, as well for the refreshing of his people as
for preparing all things for his journey to London.
This afforded time for the escape of many gallant
knights who had fled from the engagement[6], when
their royal leader, whom they would have supported unto death, no longer existed to require
their efforts towards retrieving his evil fortune.
The Lord of Lincoln and the Viscount Lovell were
amongst this number, together with the Staffords,
who took refuge in sanctuaries at Gloucester[7], and
whose zealous conduct at Bosworth, when considered with reference to their affinity to the Duke
of Buckingham, cannot fail to weaken the impu-

---

[1] Grafton, p. 230.   [2] Ibid.   [3] Hutton, p. 166.
[4] Grafton, p. 231.   [5] Ibid.
[6] " Many other nobles and gentlemen got into foreign countries and sanctuaries, obscuring themselves till the storm and
smart of that day's memory was past." — *Buck*, lib. ii. p. 64.
[7] Grafton, p. 231.

tation of undue severity having been exercised towards their kinsman.

At the expiration of the two days just named, Henry VII. with his army departed for Coventry, on his progress by easy journeys to the metropolis, carrying with him the standards won at Bosworth and other trophies of his victory there.[1] The mortal remains of the deceased king were exposed to the rude gaze of the multitude during the whole of his rival's sojourn in Leicester[2]; and even his triumphant departure from the town did not witness the termination of a spectacle sufficiently protracted to gratify revenge however deadly, and satisfy the most sceptical, as regards the monarch's decease. Such at least may be gathered from the relation of Lord Bacon[3], who states that, although King Henry gave orders for the honourable interment of his vanquished foe, his commands were neglected to be obeyed; and as if the closing scene of Richard's earthly career was destined to be as singular as had been the leading events of his extraordinary life, he, the last of the Plantagenet dynasty, the sovereign by whose decease that ancient, chivalrous, and munificent race of kings became extinct, was indebted to the compassion of the nuns of Leicester — to the pitying, charitable, humane feelings of a religious sisterhood, for the performance of the last solemn rites of burial, and for receiving at their sympathising

---

[1] Bacon, p. 8.   [2] Hutton, p. 142.

[3] " Though the king, of his nobleness, gave charge unto the friars of Leicester to see an honourable interment to be given to him, yet the religious people themselves, being not free from the humours of the vulgar, neglected it, wherein, nevertheless, they did not then incur any man's blame or censure." — *Bacon*, p. 2.

hands that decent though humble sepulchre[1] which had been awarded to the meanest of his soldiers, although denied to the mutilated remains of their intrepid commander. " King Richard III., being slain at Bosworth," remarks the county historian, " his body was begged by the nuns at Leicester, and buried in their chapel there."[2] A sense of shame however, or some compunction for the unchristian spirit which had been manifested towards the deceased king, appears at length to have influenced the conduct of his enemies, and led them, at the expiration of ten years, to bestow on him a more honourable sepulture; for the same writer who has commemorated the fact of his interment by the nuns in their chapel, also states[3], that, " after revenge and rage had satiated their barbarous cruelties upon his dead body, they gave his royal earth a bed of earth, honourably appointed by the order of King Henry the VII., in the chief church of Leicester, called St. Mary, belonging to the order and society of the Grey Friars, the king in short time after causing a fair tomb[4] of mingle

---

[1] " Commanding all the hurt and wounded persons to be cured, and the dead carcases to be delivered to the sepulture." — *Grafton*, p. 232.

[2] Nicholls' Leicester, vol. i. p. 298.   [3] Ibid.

[4] Extract from the privy purse expences of King Henry VII. September 11th, an. 1495 : —

" To James Keyley, for King Richard's tomb, 10*l*. 1*s*."

This entry is deserving of attention, as it proves the statement of some writers that Henry VII. caused a tomb to be erected to Richard the Third's memory. That prince was meanly buried in the Grey Friars' church of Leicester, where afterwards King Henry caused a monument to be erected for him, with his picture in alabaster, where it remained until the dissolution under Henry VIII., when it was pulled down and utterly defaced."—Vide *Excerpta Hist.* p. 105.

coloured marble, adorned with his statue, to be erected thereupon[1]; to which Sir George Buck affirms[2] " some grateful pen had also destined the following epitaph," which, although never fixed to his stone, he had seen " in a recorded manuscript-book," chained to a table in a chamber in the Guildhall of London : " —

EPITAPHIUM

REGIS RICHARDI TERTII,

SEPULTI AD LEICESTRIAM, JUSSU,

ET SUMPTIBUS ST[1] REGIS

HENRICI SEPTIMI.

" Hic ego, quem vario tellus sub marmore claudit,
Tertius a justâ voce Richardus eram ;
Tutor eram patriæ, patrius pro jure nepotis ;
Dirupta, tenui regna Britanna, fide.
Sexaginta dies binis duntaxat ademptis
Ætatesque, tuti tunc mea sceptra, duas.
Fortiter in bello certans desertus ab Anglis,
Rex Henrice, tibi, septime, succubui.
At sumptu, pius ipse, tuo, sic assa dicaras,
Regem olimque facis regis honore coli.

[1] The bed of earth honourably appointed by the order of Henry VII., with the tomb of many coloured marble, and the statue of King Richard by which it was surmounted, is somewhat inconsistent with the proclamation issued before his interment, in which he is simply designated as " Richard Duke of Gloucester." Still more out of character is it with the bill of attainder, which Henry procured to be passed in his first parliament (*Rot. Parl.*, vol. vi. p. 276.), in which, not only are the late king's followers proclaimed traitors, and their lands forfeited to the crown, but Richard himself is attainted on a charge of high treason, for bearing arms against Henry of Richmond ; although this latter prince was at the time a claimant only for those regal honours to which Richard had been declared duly and lawfully elected, and which he rightly and justifiably defended.

[2] Buck, lib. v. p. 147.

Quatuor exceptis jam tantum, quinq. bis annis
Acta trecenta quidem, lustra salutis erant,
Antique Septembris undena luce kalendas,
Redideram Rubræ jura petita Rosæ.
At mea, quisquis eris, propter commissa precarem
Sit minor ut precibus pœna levata tuis."

DEO O. M. TRINO ET UNO,
SIT LAUS ET GLORIA ÆTERNA.
AMEN.[1]

At the suppression of the monasteries by King
Henry VIII., Richard's tomb and the " picture of
alabaster representing his person " was utterly defaced[2]; " since when, his grave, overgrown with
nettles and weeds, is not to be found."[3]   His body

---

[1] This epitaph is also registered in a book in the College of Arms,
a literal copy from which source is given by Sandford in his " Genealogical History of the Kings of England," book v. p. 410.   It
has been thus rendered into English in Bishop Kennet's reprint of
" Buck's Life and Reign of Richard III." — See *Complete History
of England*, vol. i. p. 597.

EPITAPH OF RICHARD III., BURIED AT LEICESTER BY THE
ORDER AND EXPENSE OF KING HENRY VII.

I who am laid beneath this marble stone,
Richard the Third, possessed the British throne.
My country's guardian in my nephew's claim,
By trust betray'd, I to the kingdom came.
Two years and sixty days, save two, I reign'd,
And bravely strove in fight ; but unsustain'd
My English left me in the luckless field,
Where I to Henry's arms was forced to yield.
Yet at his cost, my corse this tomb obtains,
Who piously interred me, and ordains
That regal honours wait a king's remains.
Th' year fourteen hundred 'twas and eighty-four,
The twenty-first of August, when its power
And all its rights I did to the Red Rose restore.
Reader, whoe'er thou art, thy prayers bestow
T' atone my crimes and ease my pains below.

[2] Nicholls, vol. ii. p. 298.   [3] Ibid.

is traditionally reported to have been carried out
of the city, and to have been contemptuously thrown
over Bow Bridge[1], the spot already noticed as the
scene of the soothsayers alleged prediction ; while
the stone coffin which contained his body, " the
only memory of the monarch's greatness," is ordinarily reputed to have been given or sold to an
innkeeper, in whose possession it remained as a
drinking trough for horses[2], till the beginning of
the 18th century.[3] For the defacement of his tomb
and the sacrilegious use to which his coffin was applied[4], there may have have been and probably was
some foundation, considering the desecration to
which all royal mausoleums throughout the kingdom were subjected during that direful revolution,
which swept away many of the most ancient monu-
ments in the land ; but that the ashes of the ill-fated
monarch were so degradingly bestowed as is locally
reported, admits of great doubt, indeed positive
proof may be said to exist, and on the high author-

[1] Nicholls, vol. ii. p. 298.

[2] The reverend Samuel Carte, who published an account of
Leicester in the Bibl. Top. Brittanica, and who, as vicar of St.
Martin's, resided for many years in that town, says, in 1720, " I
know of no other evidence that the stone coffin formerly used for a
trough was King Richard's, but the constancy of the tradition.
There is a little part of it still preserved at the White Horse Inn, in
which one may observe some appearance of the hollow, fitted for retaining the head and the shoulders." The son of this learned
divine, Thomas Carte, the eminent historian, was one of King
Richard's most zealous defenders, and some very striking arguments
in refutation of his alleged crimes will be found in his account of
this monarch's reign, in his valuable History of England, published
1754, in 4 vols.

[3] Nicholls, vol. ii. p. 298.

[4] Considerable doubt, however, cannot but be entertained, whether
the remains of the coffin described by Mr. Carte was that which had
belonged to King Richard, inasmuch as stone coffins of that shape

ity of Dr. Christopher Wren[1], that his relics, however profanely disturbed, were suffered to rest finally in consecrated ground. " At the dissolution of the monastery where he was interred," states that learned antiquary, " the place of his burial happened to fall into the bounds of a citizen's garden ; which being after purchased by Mr. Robert Heyrick, some time mayor of Leicester, was by him covered with a handsome stone pillar three feet high, with this inscription, " Here lies the body of Richard III., sometime King of England." This he shewed me walking in the garden, 1612."[2]

No remains, however, of this or of any other monument now mark the place where the monarch was interred.

His name is inseparably connected with Leicester, but the precise spot where his mouldering remains were at length permitted to rest in peace is no longer known. To the circumstance, however, of his having been exposed to public view in this town so long before his burial, and under such unfavourable auspices, may, in all probability, be traced the source of those extravagant descriptions of his person, which unhappily have so long prevailed. It has been already shewn that these descriptions were not derived from contemporary writers, neither are they borne out by coeval statements, but that they had

and kind were not used so late as the time of that monarch, neither had they been for centuries before.

[1] " Christopher Wren, B. D., at that time tutor at St. John's College, Oxford, to the eldest son of Sir William Heyrick, of Beaumanor, Leicestershire, a near relative of the Mr. Robert Heyrick, who is named in the foregoing quotation.

[2] Wren's Parentalia, p. 114.

their rise in Tudor times, and were perpetuated by Tudor chroniclers. There can indeed be little doubt, that the hideous accounts which were first promulgated by them, and which have invested Richard with such injurious notoriety, originated from the statements of such of his enemies as beheld him in the agonies of death, when with his limbs distorted and his features convulsed by the desperate struggles which preceded his violent end, he was for " a season exposed to view that all men might see him."[1] Such an exhibition, it is very certain, would produce a far different effect on the beholder who so looked on their deceased sovereign for the first time, his face livid, his body mangled, and the expression of his countenance altogether disfigured by the contending passions which marked his dying hour, to those which were impressed on the memory of writers who framed their reports in the full tide of his prosperity, when he was an honoured and esteemed prince, not a calumniated and a vanquished monarch.

The physical power which Richard displayed when seeking out Henry of Richmond on Redmore Plain, must prove to every impartial mind how great a mixture of fable has been intermingled with the historical facts. A withered arm could not have slain Sir William Brandon, or unhorsed Sir John Cheyney, the most powerful man of his time; neither if it had been withered from his birth, could Richard have performed corresponding acts of heroism at

[1] Fabyan, p. 518.

Barnet, to those which have been so eulogised on Bosworth Field!

The reports, however, of his mental and bodily deformity were fully considered in an earlier portion of this work, when weighing the relative merits of contemporary writers with the historians from whom Shakespeare derived the marvellous tales which he has so graphically depicted. The subject might be pursued with advantage to the memory of the monarch, from the period of his birth up to the very moment of his decease, for there is scarcely an action connected with his memorable career that has not been reported with a political bias, and been represented as springing from motives, designs, and prejudices for which there is no other authority or foundation.

The momentous events which preceded and succeeded his elevation to the throne were in themselves so important, and necessarily exacted such minute details, and such searching examination into the origin of the erroneous impressions under which many of them have long been viewed, that to renew the subject now, in connection with Shakespeare's tragedy of Richard III., would be to repeat the arguments which were adduced when separately considering the same striking scenes, with reference to history and tradition. One of the most remarkable features in the historical plays of our immortal bard is his close adherence to the statements of those chroniclers, whose relations furnished him with the materials he dramatised; and it is by that very fidelity that Shakespeare's rich and incomparable poetry has unhappily fixed upon the traduced monarch " a gloomy celebrity as durable as his own genius."[1]

The assumption by King Richard of the office of Lord Protector, his deposition of Edward V., and his subsequent acceptance of the crown, the reported murder of the young princes in the Tower, and the charge of having poisoned his queen in order to espouse his niece, — all presented subjects of too great importance to his character to be other-wise than closely examined and tested by such con-temporary documents as helped to place the transactions themselves in the fairest and truest light. But to these documents, coeval with the monarch, the Bard of Avon had no access : he contented himself with adopting the plots presented to him through the medium of the most popular chroniclers [2] of the day ; and the romantic colour-ing which they gave to many events, in themselves unimportant, and the tragical tales which they in-corporated in their narrative, made their relation a far more winning and fitting theme for the poet and the dramatist [3] than he would have found the

[1] Sharon Turner, vol. iv. p. 60.
[2] Gents. Mag., vol. xvii. p. 498.
[3] The reign of King Richard III. has ·not only exercised the talents of our great national bard, but the conflict which commemo-rates his decease has afforded subject for the muse of many poets greatly distinguished in their day : amongst whom may be enu-merated " Michael Drayton," a native of Atherstone, born in 1563, whose " Bosworth Field " ranks amongst the best of his heroical epistles ; Sir John Beaumont, Bart., of Grace Dieu, Leicestershire, born 1582, and Judge of the Court of Common Pleas, whose most popular poem relates to the same subject, and was considered one of the best productions of the age in which he flourished ; and Charles Aleyn (1620), famed for his " Life of Henry VII.," with the " Battle of Cressy and Poictiers " in heroic verse. — *Winstanley's Lives of English Poets*, pp. 105. 145. 165.

concise and meagre details which comprise the only truthful histories of Richard III. Foremost among the embellishments thus literally transferred from Sir Thomas More's pages to Shakspeare's tragedy is the statement of Richard demanding strawberries from the Bishop of Ely, when waiting the fitting time for Lord Hastings' execution [1], and of the displaying his withered arm to convict the conspirators of witchcraft and necromancy. [2]

No allusion can be found to this latter astounding accusation in the earlier and contemporary writers; it rests, indeed, on no firmer basis than rumour: whereas Richard's dauntless courage and military prowess, which he displayed before thousands at his death, is of itself conclusive evidence that the scene, however imposing in the drama [3], has no foundation in historical truth. The oration de-

---

[1] " My lord, you have verye good strawberries in your gardayne in Holborne. I require you to let us haye a messe of them."— *More*, p. 70.

> " My lord of Ely, when I was last in Holborn,
> I saw good strawberries in your garden there ;
> I do beseech you send for some of them."
>
> *Richard III.*, act iii. sc..4.

[2] " And therewith he plucked up hys doublet sleeve to his elbow upon his left arm, where he showed a werish withered arme, and small as it was never other."—*More*, p. 74.

> " Then be your eyes the witness of their evil,
> Look how I am bewitch'd ; behold mine arm
> Is, like a blasted sapling, withered up."
>
> *Richard III.*, act iii. sc. 4.

[3] See also the following passage : —

Hastings.—" Certainly, my lord, if they have so heinously done," (alluding to the conspirators who, acting under evil influence, had withered his arm,) " they be worthy heinous punishment." " What," quod the protector, ' thou servest me, I ween, with iffes and andes. I tell thee they have so done, and that I will make good on thy body, traitor !"—*More*, p. 72.

livered before the battle partakes of the same character [1]; and very many other. examples of a similar nature might be advantageously adduced: but the most destructive scene as regards King Richard's condemnation is that wherein the ghosts of Edward of Lancaster, Henry VI., George Duke of Clarence, Rivers, Grey, and Vaughan, the Lord of Hastings, the two young princes, Queen Anne, and the Duke of Buckingham, are made to visit the doomed monarch, and to flit before him with reproaches for every crime which posthumous calumny and legendary lore has fastened upon him.[2] Here not Shakspeare's authorities, but Shakspeare's own genius, is brought to bear against the memory of the monarch: what wonder is it, then, that by this terrific scene the mind of the spectator becomes so imbued with a conviction of this monarch's horrible guilt, that it would be difficult to banish the impression, even upon after-reference to genuine records, or to be satisfied that the simple, and by no means uncommon effect of a

---

Hast. " If they have done this deed, my noble lord —
Glos. If ! . . . .
     Talk'st thou to me of ifs ?   Thou art a traitor."
                        Richard III., act iii. sc. 4.
In allusion to which scene the late lamented author of the " Commentary on the Historical Plays of Shakspeare " judiciously observes, that these " smaller incidents confirm 'the probability that More's history was derived from Bishop Morton, if not written by that prelate himself."— *Courtenay's Commen.*, vol. ii. p. 87.

[1] " And to begin with the Earl of Richmond, captain of this rebellion, he is a Welsh milksop."— *Grafton*, p. 222.
    " And who doth lead them but a paltry fellow,
    Long kept in Bretagne at our mother's cost ?
    A milksop."
                        Richard III., act v. sc. 3.

[2] Richard III., act v. sc. 3.

fearful dream, was the sole foundation for a scene " made to embody and realise conceptions [1] which had hitherto assumed no distinct shape." [2]　Justly, indeed, has it been observed of King Richard, in an admirable essay exposing the false impressions received of this monarch as he is ordinarily represented on the stage, that " nothing but his crimes, his actions are visible; they are prominent and staring; the murderer stands out, but where is the lofty genius, the man of vast capacity,— the profound, the witty, accomplished Richard?" [3]

Where, indeed! for, until within a comparatively brief period, little else was known of this monarch's proceedings than the appalling portraiture of his alleged crimes, thus powerfully delineated by the master hand of the immortal Shakspeare.　The danger of confounding moral with personal deformity has likewise been ably depicted by the above-named forcible writer [4], who most effectively portrays " this humour of mankind to deny per-

---

[1] Drayton, as well as Shakspeare, with the licence of a poet, has transformed the undefined images of the old chroniclers into the ghosts of all those individuals whose violent deaths were ascribed to the monarch :

" Both armies, well prepard, tow'rds Bosworth strongly prest,
　And on a spacious moor, lying southward from the town,
　Indifferent to them both, they set their armies down,
　Their soldiers to refresh, preparing for the fight ;
　Where to the guilty king, that black fore-running night,
　Appear the dreadful ghosts of Henry and his son,
　Of his own brother George, and his two nephews done
　Most cruelly to death ; and of his wife, and friend
　Lord Hastings, with pale hands, prepared as they would rend
　Him piece-meal."

Drayton's Bosworth Field.

[2] Lamb's Essays " On the Tragedies of Shakspeare with reference to their fitness for Stage Representation," vol. ii. p. 5.

[3] Ibid. p. 22.　　　　　　　　　[4] Ibid. p. 156.

sonal comeliness to those with whose moral attributes they are dissatisfied."

Perhaps no instance on record better demonstrates the truth of this hypothesis than the unmitigated prejudice which is universally felt with reference to the fallen monarch. Of his merits as Duke of Gloucester—of his brilliant career as a firm, faithful, and uncompromising prince, striving to retrieve his brother's evil fortune, and to sustain the royal prerogative — of his undeviating fidelity to Edward IV. amidst every reverse and amidst all temptation — of his stern resistance of the French king's bribes, and wise neutrality in the factious proceedings which distracted the English court,—of all this, and yet more, of his shining abilities, his cultivated mind, his legislative wisdom, his generosity, his clemency, and the misfortunes that led to his downfal, but little notice is taken: every bright point in his character has been carefully concealed, every manly virtue scrupulously withheld, as if by common consent; and a monster of depravity, whose very name seemed to typify deformity of the most revolting description, corporeal as well as mental, is the impression that prevailed for ages, and to a certain degree still prevails, respecting a monarch whose actions, during his brief reign alone, deserved a more just, a more faithful representation.

If a veil of mystery was thus studiously thrown over his public career, it is not to be marvelled at that still fewer records remain of his private life. That he was the last survivor of "his hearth" has been already shown, and that his short reign was characterised by the remarkable occurrence of the decease of the heir apparent to the throne, and the reigning queen, has been also related. Little else is known of his domestic history beyond the fact of his having preceded his venerable mother[1] to the grave, and of his having left two illegitimate, but not unacknowledged children—a son and a daughter, both apparently older than the young Prince of Wales, with whom they were probably brought up at Middleham[2]; as from occasional notices in the oft-quoted registry they would seem to have been educated with great care, and were recognised by the king as his offspring. The eldest, John, sometimes " surnamed of Gloucester[3]," sometimes " of Pomfret[4]," was knighted, it will be remembered, by Richard after his second coronation at York; and, shortly before the monarch's decease he appointed him Captain of Calais for

[1] Cecily Duchess of York, mother to King Richard III., as already detailed, became a nun of the Benedictine order in 1480. (See *Cott. MSS. Vitel.*, 1. fol. 17.). She survived this her youngest son for the space of ten years, as appears by the following notice in Lord Bacon's Life of King Henry VII. (p. 144.): " Thus died also this year (1495) Cecile Duchess of York, mother to King Edward IV., at her castle of Berkhampstead, being of extreme years, and who had lived to see three princes of her body crowned, and four murdered. She was buried at Foderingham, by the side of her husband." The life of this illustrious lady is perhaps unexampled for its vicissitudes ! a brief summary of which may be found in the Archælogia, vol. xiii. fol. 7. Sandford states, that on her coffin being opened, in the reign of Queen Elizabeth, " the Duchess Cecily had about her neck, hanging on a silk riband, a pardon from Rome, which, penned in a fine Roman hand, was as fair and fresh to be read as if it had been written but the day before." — *Sandford*, book v. p. 374.

[2] See Harl. MSS., 433. fol. 269.

[3] Drake's Ebor., p. 117.   [4] Harl. MSS., 433. fol. 99.

life, and governor of the fortresses of Rysbank,
Guisnes, Hammes, and all the marches of Picardy
belonging to the English crown. It would appear
from the wording of the patent[1], which conveyed
to his son this permanent provision, that the young
Plantagenet gave promise of no ordinary degree of
excellence: nothing is known, however, of his
subsequent proceedings, neither does there appear
to be preserved any other document relating to
him beyond an entry in the Harl. MSS. of a
donation from the king, of "silk clothes[2]," and
other articles of dress suitable to the position in
life which his son was about to fill, and bearing date
two days before the patent above named.

His other child, a daughter, seems to have ranked
high in her father's favour—judging, at least, from
the innumerable grants and gifts bestowed upon
her and her husband. She was early married to
William Herbert, Earl of Huntingdon, secretary to
the young Prince of Wales[3]; and in the deed of
settlement[4] which conveys the king's consent to

---

[1] 1485. 11th March, 2d Rich. III.—Patent reciting that whereas " the vivacity of wit, agility of limbs, and proneness to all good
habits (ingenii vivacitas, membranumque agilitas, et ad omnes bonos
mores pronitas), of our beloved bastard son, John of Gloucester,"
gave the king " great and undoubted hope of his future good service,
he had appointed him Captain of Calais, and of the Tower Rysbank,
and Lieutenant of the Marches of Calais, for life, with all profits
thereunto pertaining, excepting the right of appointing officers during
his minority." He was at the same time appointed Captain of the
castles of Guisnes and Hammes in Picardy.—*Fœdera,* vol. xii.
p. 265.

[2] Harl. MSS., 435. fol. 211.

[3] " To William Herbert, secretary to my lord prince, an annuity of
40 marcs, for occupying of the said office."—*Harl. MSS.,* 433. fol. 34.

[4] See Appendix QQ.

the alliance, she is styled " Dame Katherine Plantagenet, daughter to our said sovereign lord King Richard III." The king undertakes to make and bear the cost and charge of the same marriage, and to endow her with an annuity of 400 marcs. He shortly afterwards granted to William Earl of Huntingdon a confirmation of the name, state, and title of the said earldom[1]; he bestowed upon him the stewardship of many rich demesnes[2], nominated him to various important offices[3]; and in the last year of his reign further granted to " William Herbert, Earl of Huntingdon, and Katherine his wife, jointly an annuity of 152l. 10s. 10d., until the king should grant to them and their heirs lands of like annual value."[4] Tradition numbers a third child[5] with the two that are thus authenticated by history, another son bearing his father's name of " Richard," but who, for some unexplained cause, appears to have been kept in ignorance of his parentage until the eve of the battle of Bosworth, when the monarch is stated to have sent for him, and to have made known his intention of acknowledging him as his offspring if he survived the approaching conflict and gained the victory over his enemies. Prior to the engagement it is farther stated that the king placed him on an eminence, where he could watch the progress of the battle, enjoining him to instant flight, for which he fur-

---

[1] Harl. MSS., 433. fol. 66.   [2] Ibid. fol. 46.
[3] Ibid. fol. 67.   [4] Ibid. fol. 29.
[5] See " Peck's Desiderata Curiosa ;" Seymour's Top.; and Hist. Survey of Kent ; Leland's Kent ; and Gent.'s Mag., vol. xxxvii. p. 408., vol. lxii. p. 1106.

nished him with the means, in the event of his
death. When the fatal result took place, the youth,
quite a stripling, precipitately fled, and after en-
during great privations, and having no means of
subsistence, it is said that he proffered his services
to a stonemason at Eastwell in Kent, where he
lived obscurely and worked in penury to the age of
between seventy and eighty, carefully concealing
his name, until circumstances, a few years before his
death, led him to make known his history to an
ancestor of the present Earl of Winchelsea, who
suffered him to erect a cottage in his grounds, and
in whose family this tradition has been perpetuated.
Singular as this romantic tale may appear, there
are not wanting facts which throw over it an air of
credibility. The registry of the death and burial
of " Rychard Plantagenet," at Eastwell, in 1560, is
yet extant[1]; the foundation of the little dwelling
where he is traditionally reported to have lived and
died are also still visible in the park adjoining :
these realities, and a well in the same parish called
to this day by his name, furnish strong presumptive proofs, if not of the actual truth of the whole
story, at least for there being some solid ground
for a tradition[2] so curious and remarkable.   Never-

---

[1] Through the zealous kindness of the Rev. Hans Mortimer the
author has been enabled to procure a certified copy from the ancient
register of the parish of Eastwell, relative to the burial of Richard
Plantagenet.   It runs thus : —
" Anno Domini, 1560.
Rychard Plantagenet was buried the xxii daye of Decembre,
Anno di supra."
Likewise of the truth of the facts mentioned in the text relative to
his humble abode, and the well which perpetuates his name.
[2] A very interesting letter will be found in the Gentleman's

theless it is but tradition! and although in itself a
matter of no great importance, it furnishes another
example of the mystery, uncertainty, and obscurity
which pervade even the most trivial matters connected with the memoirs of Richard III.

The most ordinary incidents in other men's lives
with him seemed fated to be alternately the subjects of romance or of tragedy. Even the inn
where he abode during his brief sojourn at Leicester,
even the very bed on which he there reposed, are
not exempt from the tales of horror which are associated with the memory of this prince. On his
departure for Bosworth it appears from the result
that he must have left many articles of value, either
too cumbersome to be removed, or in themselves
ill-suited for a temporary encampment, at the house
of entertainment where he had been abiding, and
which, as being the chief hostelry in Leicester, was
distinguished by the appellation of Richard's badge[1],
" the Silvery Boar: " but on his defeat and death,
and the dispersion of his followers, the victorious
army, with the infuriated rage which in all ages
accompanies any popular excitement, compelled the
owner of the inn to pull down the emblem of the

Magazine, dated August 10. 1767, entitled " The Story of Richard
Plantagenet authenticated," from the pen of the erudite Rev.
Samuel Pegge, under his assumed signature of " T. Row." Likewise another letter of singular import, as regards the tradition, from
the rector of the parish of Eastwell, in the same year, who states, with
reference to the entry of Richard's burial, " It is also remarkable
that in the same register, whenever any of noble family was buried,
this ꙥ mark is prefixed to the name; and the same mark is put
to that of Richard Plantagenet."— *T. Parsons, Rector of Eastwell,*
1767. *July.*

   [1] Nichols, vol. ii. p. 381.

deceased king, and to substitute the blue for the white boar.[1] The apartments which the king had occupied were pillaged and ransacked, and the hangings[2] of the richly-carved bed on which he had slept during his stay in the town were torn off, and either carried away as booty with other portable articles, or were destroyed on the spot. The bed-stead, however, being large and heavy, and apparently of no great value, was suffered to remain undisturbed with the people of the house; thenceforth continuing a piece of standing furniture, and passing from tenant to tenant with the inn: for King Richard and his secretary being both slain, and all his confidential friends executed, imprisoned, or exiled, it could not be known that the weight of the bulky wooden frame-work left in his sleeping apartment arose from its being in reality the military chest of the deceased monarch.[3] It was at once his coffer and his couch. Many years, however, rolled on before this singular fact became known, and then it was only accidentally discovered, owing to the circumstance of a piece of gold dropping on the floor when the wife of the proprietor was making a bed which had been placed upon it. On closer examination a double bottom was discovered, the intermediate space between which was found to be filled with gold coin to a considerable amount.[4]

The treasure thus marvellously obtained, although carefully concealed, helped in time to ele-

[1] Nichols, vol. ii. p. 381.   [2] Ibid.
[3] Hutton, p. 48.   [4] Ibid.

vate the humble publican, " a man of low condition[1]," to the proud station of chief magistrate of
his native town.[2] But at his death the vast riches
that accrued to his widow excited the cupidity of
menials connected with her establishment; and the
wilful murder of their mistress, in 1613, led to the
execution of her female servant, and of seven men
concerned with her in the ruthless deed[3]: thus
adding another tragedy to the many of higher import which are inseparably connected with the
recollection of this unhappy prince.

The inn itself, rendered so remarkable as the
last abiding-place of the last monarch of the middle
ages, " a large, handsome, half-timber house, with
one story projecting over the other[4]," remained
for upwards of three centuries unchanged, an interesting relic alike of the architecture of its period
as of the remarkable epoch which it perpetuated.
But in the year 1836, although undecayed, unin-
jured, and defying the ravages of time, this venerable fabric was razed to the ground, to the regret
of all who hold sacred such historical memorials,
and hallow the relics which link bygone ages with
the present time. Its site, with the appellation of
an adjoining thoroughfare to which it formed an
angle, and which still retains the name of " Blue
Boar Lane," together with the description and

---

[1] Nichols, vol. i. p. 380.   [2] Ibid.
[3] The full particulars of this tragedy are given by Sir Roger
Twysden, who had it from persons of undoubted credit, who were
not only inhabitants of Leicester, but saw the murderers executed.—
Nichols' Leicestershire, vol. i. p. 380.
[4] Hutton, p. 47.

delineation of its picturesque appearance, are now all that connects King Richard with this interesting memorial of his last days at Leicester.

Not so, however, the bedstead. That appendage to the inn, although three hundred and fifty years have elapsed since it was used by the sovereign, is still in existence, and in the most perfect state of preservation. Richly and curiously carved in oak, with fleur-de-lys[1] profusely scattered over it, its panels inlaid with black, brown, and white woods, the styles consisting of Saracenic figures in high relief, it proves from the singularity of its construction the true purpose for which it was designed, every portion of it but the body being fabricated to take to pieces and put up at will; so that for travelling it speedily became transformed into a huge chest, although ingeniously framed

---

[1] During the Plantagenet era this royal emblem of France formed a conspicuous feature in the heraldic embellishments of the English crown. By reference to the frontispiece of vol. ii. of this work, it will be seen that the surcoats in which King Richard and his son are delineated by their contemporary in the Rous roll are alternately fleur-de-lys and lions. The hangings, which were torn from the bed after the monarch's decease, were in all likelihood of great value, and richly ornamented with his badge; for there was scarcely any article of domestic use more highly prized during the middle ages than beds, and their costly furniture, the embroidering of which was a frequent occupation of ladies of the highest quality and their attendant gentlewomen. John of Gaunt, at his death in 1399, bequeaths in his will his " large bed of black velvet embroidered with a circle of fetterlocks," the badge of the house of Lancaster; and the Duke of York, killed at Agincourt, bequeaths to his dear wife Philippa " my bed of feathers and leopards, also my white and red tapestry of garters, fetterlocks, and falcons." The " Testamenta Vetusta," from whence the above examples were selected, abounds in legacies of a similar nature; and very curious behests may also be found in Nichols' " Royal Wills," proving how highly this article of furniture was estimated by its owners.

for the twofold purpose which led to its preservation.[1]

This relic, insignificant in itself, is the only
known memorial connected with the personal history of Richard III.   His political career will be
for ever perpetuated by Bosworth Field.[2]   Un-

---

[1] Through the courtesy of the present owner of this valuable
relic, the Reverend Matthew Babington, the author was permitted
thoroughly to examine it, and was farther favoured with many interesting particulars connected with its preservation and the peculiarity
of its construction.   It seems, that after the murder of Mrs. Clarke,
in 1613, the bedstead still remained at the Blue Boar Inn, and continued to do so for the space of 200 years, when it came into the
possession of a person whose rooms being too low to admit of its
transit, the feet were cut off: they were two feet six inches long,
and each six inches square.   It was purchased some years after by Mr.
Drake, an alderman of Leicester, grandfather to the present proprietor, and by him held in great estimation, and very carefully
preserved.   Two of the richly-carved panels are said to represent
the Holy Sepulchre ; the tester is carved and inlaid with different-
coloured woods in various patterns ; the posts are very massive in
parts, and very taper in others, and their construction is said to be
most ingenious.   Modern feet have been added ; but in all other
respects this very remarkable piece of antique furniture remains in
its pristine state, excepting that the rich gilding mentioned by Sir
Roger Twysden was unfortunately removed by the carelessness of
the person employed by Mr. Drake to cleanse it, after it was purchased by him.

[2] Deeply it is to be lamented that no memorial has ever been
raised upon this celebrated plain ; the
    " Battle to describe, the last of that long war,
      Entitled by the name of York and Lancaster."
                                            Drayton.
Or any national monument erected that could perpetuate the era
which was to
    " Enrich the time to come with smooth-face'd peace,
      With smiling plenty, and fair prosp'rous days ! "
                                            Shakspeare.
and yet more to
    " Abate the edge of traitors,
      That would reduce these bloody days again !
      And make poor England weep in streams of blood ! "
                                            Ibid.

changed this memorable spot can scarcely be expected to have continued from so remote a period up
to the present time. But although the country has
been enclosed, hedges planted and fences have grown
up, and that the prospect generally is impeded[1],
still such is the peculiar character of Redmor
Plain, that, with the aid of the local appellations
by which the sites of the leading events of the day
are traditionally commemorated, its ancient appearance may very well be understood, even from its
modern aspect. The scene is indeed a still continuing monument of the action by which it is
rendered celebrated. The churches of Bosworth
and Atherstone in the distance, the heights of
Stapelton, where Richard first encamped his army
of observation, of Anbeam Hill, whither he removed
preparatory to the conflict, and Amyon Hill,
where the army were arranged in order of battle,
the wood, the rivulet, the marshy ground, which
protected Richmond in the disposition of his
army, the well[2] from which King Richard drank,
the eminence on which King Henry was crowned,
the alleged position of the camps of the Stanleys,
of Norfolk, and of Northumberland, and " Dickons'
Nook," the place where King Richard is stated to
have addressed his army ! — these and many other

---

[1] Introduction to Nichols' reprint of Hutton, p. 4.

[2] Owing to the learned Dr. Samuel Parr, the site of this memorable spot will be handed down to the latest posterity. Having heard
that the well was in danger of being destroyed by cattle from being
in dirty, mossy ground, and from the draining of the land, he proceeded to Bosworth Field in the year 1813, accompanied by some
gentlemen interested in the preservation of this traditional relic ; and
having discovered, by means of local information, the identical spot,

less memorable sites spread an unfading interest around a spot which notwithstanding the years that have elapsed, and the cultivation to which it has been subjected, seems by the air of solitude which yet reigns about it, the want of habitations, and the loneliness which pervades the whole district, to harmonise fitly with the tragical and touching exploits, the dark and stealthy deeds, which are inseperably interwoven with Bosworth field, and which have afforded such a fertile theme for poets.[1]

he took measures to have it preserved by means of the following inscription : —

AQVÂ EX HOC PVTEO HAVSTÂ
SITIM SEDAVIT
RICARDVS TERTIVS REX ANGLIAE
CVM HENRICO COMITE DE RICHMONDIÂ
ACERRIMÈ ATQVE INFENSISSIME PRAELIANS.
ET VITÂ PARITER AC SCEPTRO
ANTE NOCTEM CARITVRVS.
XI. KAL. SEPT. A. D. M. CCCC LXXXV.

In English thus :
With water drawn from this well,
Richard the Third, King of England,
When fighting most strenuously and intensely
With Henry Earl of Richmond,
Quenched his thirst ;
Before night about to be deprived
Alike of his life and sceptre.
11th of the Calends of September, A.D. 1485.

This inscription, deeply cut on white stone, is placed immediately over the spring, and within a small building of unhewn stone of a pyramidal form, and which, although rudely constructed, serves to mark the spot and preserve the very classical memorial by which Dr. Parr has perpetuated the tradition.

[1]   " Here valiant Oxford and fierce Norfolk meet ;
        And with their spears each other rudely greet ;
        About the air the shined pieces play,
        Then on their swords their noble hand they lay ;

These associations, however, together with many more which might be adduced, such as the chivalrous scene which ensued between the Lords of Surrey and Talbot, Sir Richard Clarendon, and Sir William Conyers [1], the desperate encounter of the faithful Brackenbury with the traitor Hungerford [2], and the romantic tale already related of the friendship which linked Sir John Byron and Sir Gervis Clifton [3], notwithstanding their political feelings — naturally as they arise when contemplating the present aspect of a site so memorable and deeply interesting, — fade into insignificance by

> And Norfolk first a blow directly guides
> To Oxford's head, which from his helmet slides
> Upon his arm, and biting through the steel
> Inflicts a wound, which Vere disdains to feel,
> But lifts his faulchion with a threat'ning grace,
> And hews the beaver off from Howard's face ;
> This being done, he, with compassion charm'd,
> Retires asham'd to strike a man disarm'd ;
> But strait a deadly shaft sent from a bow,
> (Whose master, though far off, the duke could know,)
> Untimely brought this combat to an end,
> And pierc'd the brains of Richard's constant friend.
> When Oxford saw him sink, his noble soul
> Was full of grief, which made him thus condole : —
> *Farewell, true knight, to whom no costly grave*
> *Can give due honours, would my tears could save*
> *Those streams of blood, deserving to be spilt*
> *In better service ; had not Richard's guilt*
> *Such heavy weight upon his fortune laid,*
> *Thy glorious virtues had his sins outweigh'd."*
>
> *Beaumont's Bosworth Field.*

These brave commanders had lived in friendship, and were of one family, Oxford's mother being a Howard and first cousin to the duke. Norfolk knew Oxford by the device on his ensign, a star with rays ; and he knew Norfolk by his silver lion. — *Hutton,* p. 101.

[1] Hutton, p 104.   [2] Ibid. p. 116.
[3] Ibid. p. 117.

comparison when considered with reference to the
mighty issue of that brief but decisive conflict.

The battle itself, fiercely as it raged, lasted but
two hours[1]; yet those two hours were fraught
with the most important results to England. The
downfal of King Richard proved the downfal
also of that overwhelming baronial ascendancy
which had led to his destruction. From the time
that the race of York had presided over the destinies
of the realm it had been the aim of their dynasty
to curb the inordinate power of its arrogant nobles,
and to check the undue influence of the priesthood:
but it was reserved for the calculating, the phlegmatic Richmond to bring about that great revolution
in the constitution, and to consummate that policy,
which the Yorkist monarchs, with their shining
abilities, had failed in effecting. The temporizing
Stanleys were to Richard III. what the imperious
Nevilles had been to Edward IV.; and Northumberland, wily and selfish, represented to the fallen
monarch the part pursued by the vainglorious and
ambitious Buckingham towards young Edward V.
and his kindred. The entire epoch of the Yorkist
rule was characterised by one vast and desperate
struggle between the sovereign and the aristocracy;
and none but a prince so cautious, so mistrustful,
so secret in his habits and reserved in his manners[2],
as the founder of the Tudor race[3] could have per-

---

[1] Grafton, p. 231.

[2] " A dark prince, and infinitely suspicious."—·Bacon, p. 242.

" Full of thought and secret observations, and full of notes and
memorials of his own hand, especially touching persons." — Ibid.
p. 243.

[3] " He was of an high mind, and loved his own will and his own

fected the system which had been so admirably
commenced, but unavailingly pursued, by his predecessors ; and realized their projects by means of
that very revolution which, producing their ruin
and leading to his own elevation, made him fully
alive to the danger which must accrue to every
monarch of England so long as the supreme
control of affairs rested virtually, although not ostensibly, in her turbulent barons.   Early initiated
into their deep designing schemes, and from necessity made fully acquainted with the subtle means
by which they compassed their ends, the new
monarch was well prepared to observe, and to resist,
the earliest indication of attempts similar [1] to those
in which, as the exiled Richmond, he had acted so
prominent a part ; and his execution of Sir William
Stanley within ten years of the period when, through
his aid, Richard III. had been slain, and himself
proclaimed king, affords evidence that he saw the
necessity [2] of watching his personal attendants, and
acting towards his " lord chamberlain " with a stern
resolution of purpose, which, had a similar relentless
course been pursued by the betrayed monarch to
" the high steward of his household," might have
preserved to him both his life and his throne.   It

way, as one that revered himself and would reign indeed.   Had he
been a private man he would have been termed proud ; but in a wise
prince it was but keeping of distance, which indeed he did towards
all, not admitting any near or full approach, either to his power or
to his secrets ; for he was governed by none." — *Bacon*, p. 238.

[1] Through the agency of secret spies, which he did employ both
at home and abroad, by them to discover what practices and conspiracies were against him. — *Bacon*, p. 240.

[2] See Howell's State Trials, vol. iii. p. 366.

is certain that this severe measure of King Henry struck a panic into the disaffected, that greatly induced to the safety of his throne, on the breaking out of that rebellion of which it was the precursor.

His jealousy of his nobles[1], and his undisguised dislike to all persons and matters connected with the Plantagenet rule, led him steadily but progressively to loosen the bonds which had long enslaved the humbler classes, and to encourage and protect the growing interests of that great commercial and trading body which had first been made to feel their importance by Edward IV., with the view of balancing the overgrown power of the feudal lords, and had been, from more enlarged views, the peculiar object of the legislative wisdom of their patron and benefactor King Richard III.

This monarch, by striving to suppress the hosts of military retainers, and, above all, by his prohibitory enactments[2] against the ancient custom of giving badges, liveries, and family devices to multitudes of armed followers, struck at the root of the evil, which arose from each chieftain having a standing and well-disciplined army at command, to over-awe the crown and perpetually disturb the peace of the realm. But the odium which attached to this daring measure of abridging a power so dangerous to the throne led to King Richard's ruin; while the merit of carrying out a policy

---

[1] " He kept a strict hand on his nobility, and chose rather to advance clergymen and lawyers which were more obsequious to him, but had less interest in the people, which made for his absoluteness, but not for his safety."— *Bacon*, p. 242.

[2] See Harl. MSS., 433. fol. 111. 138. 188. 230.

which Richard began, doubtless too precipitately and boldly, has been exclusively apportioned to Henry VII., who, treading in the same steps with his predecessor, although circumspectly and with caution, attained the object, and the appellation of the Father of English liberty, from the identical cause, and from pursuing the same measures which laid King Richard in the dust, and procured for him the name and the character of a tyrant!

How far he merited this epithet must depend upon his acts, and the degree of credit which is due to those who have branded him with it. Many of the greatest, wisest, and most powerful monarchs in all countries have been usurpers, or ascended the throne irregularly: and the reason is obvious; without rare talents and ability for government they could not have acquired sufficient ascendancy over their fellow-men to break the direct line of succession, and to be invested with the sovereign power. But such political changes, when brought about by the voice of the country, and without having recourse to arms, by no means imply the elevation of a tyrant, although it may denote incapacity in the monarch deposed. If Richard erred in yielding to the evil counsels [1] of those who knew that ambition was inherent in his race, and formed the predominant feature in his character, he at least proved himself, when called upon to exercise the regal power, a patriotic and enterprising monarch, distinguished for wisdom in the senate and

[1] " Let us speke of Rycharde in his dignitie, and the mysfortune that hym befell; a wicked counsell drew hym." — *Harl. MSS.*, 542. fol. 30.

for prowess in the field. His reign was signally advantageous to the realm; and he gave earnest of being disposed to make amends for any imputation of injustice that might be laid to his charge, arising from his irregular accession to the throne.

The nation were indebted to him for provident statutes of lasting good; and he was alike a firm protector of the church, and strict in the administration of justice to the laity.[1] He was a generous enemy, notwithstanding that he was an ill-requited friend : and that this his clemency and forbearance did not arise from personal fear, is evidenced by the intrepid bravery, undaunted courage, and contempt of danger, which even his enemies have perpetuated.

> " he did a stately farewell take,
> And, in his night of death, set like the sun ;
> For Richard in his West seem'd greater, than
> When Richard shined in his meridian.

> " Three years he acted ill, these two hours well
> And with unmated resolution strove :
> He fought as bravely as he justly fell.
> As did the Capitol to Manlius prove,
> So Bosworth did to him, the monument
> Both of his glory and his punishment."[2]

A close examination into the earliest records connected with his career will prove that, among all the heavy and fearful charges which are brought

---

[1] Could this king be brought off from the horrid imputation that lies upon his memory, of much bloodshed, oppression, and gross hypocrisy, to gain and keep the crown, one might judge him a good king. For in several passages of his reign, and public declarations by him made, he expressed a care of the good estate of his people. and concern to have sin and wickedness checked, and carried himself with a regard to learning and religion. — *Kennet,* p. 576.

[2] Hist of Hen. VII., by Charles Aleyn.

against him, few, if any, originate with his contemporaries, but that the dark deeds which have rendered his name so odious were first promulgated as rumour, and admitted as such by Fabyan, Polydore Virgil, and Sir Thomas More, in the reign of his successor[1]; that they were multiplied in number, and less unhesitatingly fixed upon him by Grafton, Hall, and Hollingshed, during the ensuing reign; and that towards the close of the Tudor dynasty, every modification being cast aside, they were recorded as historical truths by Lord Bacon, Sir Richard Baker, and many others, and rendered yet more appalling by the moral and personal deformity with which King Richard was by that time invested by the aid of the drama. If, however, by a retrograde movement, these calumnies are found gradually to lessen one by one, and that the progress can be traced to no more copious source than the evil fortune which overwhelmed King Richard at Bosworth, and gave the palm of victory to his rival, —if his administration, though brief, affords evidence of the sound views which influenced his conduct,— and if, apart from fear and from jealousy of the

[1] The Croyland historian, who terminated his valuable work with the death of King Richard, intimates very plainly the little probability there was of truth prevailing in subsequent narratives of that monarch. "Forasmuch as the custom of those who write histories is to be silent on the actions of the living, lest the description of their faults should produce odium, while the recital of their virtues might be attributed to the fault of adulation, the afore-named writer has determined to put an end to his labour at the death of Richard III." (*Gale*, p. 577.) This he did on the 30th April, 1486, about eight months after King Henry's accession ; a period, however, sufficiently long for him to perceive that silence was desirable with reference to his actions, and that odium would be incurred by the admission of his faults.

baronial power, he resolutely pursued that system
of domestic policy which he felt would ameliorate
the condition of his people, and contribute to the
prosperity of the country at large, then surely,
as was observed at the opening of this Memoir, it
is time that justice was done him as a monarch,
and that the strictest inquiry should be made into
the measure of his guilt as a man. Time, indeed,
as was farther remarked, may not have softened the
asperity with which a hostile faction delighted to
magnify his evil deeds; but time, and the publication
of contemporary documents, have made known many
redeeming qualities, have furnished proof of eminent
virtue, and certified to such noble exemplary deeds
as already suffice to rescue King Richard's memory
from at least a portion of the aggravated crimes
which have so long rendered his name odious, and
inspired great doubts as to the truth of other accusations which rest on no more stable authority.

If Lord Bacon[1] could panegyrise " his wholesome laws," and pronounce him " jealous for the
honour of the English nation,"[2] — if Grafton could
so far eulogise his proceedings as to admit " that if
he had continued lord protector the realm would
have prospered, and he would have been praised
and beloved,"[3] — if Polydore Virgil could speak in
commendation of his " piety and benevolence," and
laud " the good works which his sudden death alone
rendered incomplete,"[4] — if contemporary writers
testify to his noble conduct in the field, and the

---

[1] Bacon, p. 2.
[2] Ibid.
[3] Grafton, p. 235.
[4] Pol. Virg., p. 565.

treachery that worked his destruction[1], and certify that before his accession he was so " loved and praised" that many would have " jeoparded life and goods with him, "[2] — if the universities of Oxford[3] and Cambridge[4] perpetuate his love of letters, his patronage of the arts, and his munificence to these seminaries of learning, — and if the register of his public acts [5] abounds in examples of liberality to the church, of equity, charity, beneficence, and piety, surely every impartial mind, with reference to his long-imputed but unsubstantiated crimes, must respond to the sentiments of the old poet, —

> " Here leave his dust incorporate with mould:
> He was a king; that challengeth respect."[6]

True it is that from the great distance of time in which he lived some parts of his history must still rest upon reasoning and conjecture; and mystery will, probably, ever envelope many portions of his career, the destruction of original documents rendering impossible a close examination into several that rest on report alone: yet if so great an advance has already been made as the admission that the " personal monster whom More and Shakspeare exhibited has vanished, "[7] and that the restless habits resulting from a nervous temperament, and which have been made to indicate a

---

[1] Chron. Croy. p. 574.; and Rous, p. 217.
[2] Fabyan, p. 517.   [3] Gutch's Hist. Oxford, p. 639.
[4] Cooper's Annals of Cambridge, p. 228.
[5] Harl. MSS. fol. 433.   [6] Aleyn's Henry VII.
[7] D'Israeli, Amenities of Literature, vol. ii. p. 105.

Nero or Caligula [1], are shown [2] to have been, not the result of a demoniacal temper, but the usual accompaniment of those impetuous feelings, and of that vivid rapidity of thought, which, seeing all things clearly, could not brook opposition, or the unmanly subterfuge of double dealing, it is earnestly to be hoped, for the credit of our national history, for the honour of England and of her monarchs, that farther discoveries, by throwing yet more light upon the dark and difficult times in which Richard III. flourished, will add to the proofs which already exist of his innocence as regards the great catalogue of crimes so long and so unjustly laid to his charge; and that thus his moral, equally with his personal, deformity may vanish under the bright influence of that searching examination into historical truth, that firm resolution of separating fact from fiction, which peculiarly characterises the present enlightened period.

These philosophical views having already rescued his memory from one portion of the fabulous tales which have made him a bye-word and reproach to posterity, fair ground is open for belief that the day is not far distant when truth and justice will prevail over prejudice and long-received opinion, and unite in discarding mere rumour and tradition for the recognition of facts that can be fully established; so that, the character and conduct of this prince being displayed in its true light, his actions

---

[1] Pol. Virg., p. 565.
[2] Turner's Middle Ages, vol. iv. pp. 54. 84.

dispassionately considered, and the verified details of his reign balanced against the unworthy motives attributed to him on no ground but surmise, atonement, however tardy, may at length be made to a monarch who, for three centuries and upwards, has been so unsparingly reviled, so bitterly calumniated, as

RICHARD THE THIRD.

APPENDIX.

APPENDIX.

A.

GRANT TO RICHARD DUKE OF GLOUCESTER, OF THE
WARDENSHIP OF THE WEST MARCHES OF ENGLAND.

(See p. 4.)

ON the 18th Feb. 22 Edward IV. 1483, an act was passed
reciting that it had been agreed between the king and
Richard Duke of Gloucester, that the duke and the heirs
male of his body should have the wardenship of the West
Marches of England, towards Scotland; in consideration
whereof the former was to assure him by authority of parliament, certain castles, lordships, manors, &c. That the king,
the lords spiritual and temporal, and the commons, considering "that the said duke being warden of the said West
Marches, late by his manifold and diligent labours and
devoirs, hath subdued great part of the west borders of
Scotland adjoining to England by the space of thirty miles
and more, thereby at this time not inhabite with Scotts,
and hath got and achieved divers parcels thereof, to be
under the obeissance of our said sovereign lord, not only
to the great rest and ease of the inhabitants of the said
West Marches, but also to the great surety and ease of the
north parts of England, and much more thereof he intendeth
and with God's grace is like to get and subdue hereafter:
and the said West Marches the more surely to be defended
and kept against the Scotts, if the said appointments and
agreements be performed and accomplished." It was
therefore enacted that the duke and his heirs male should
have the wardenship of the West Marches of England,
towards Scotland, and for occupying the same should

have the castle, city, town, and lordship of Carlisle, the castle, manor, and lordship of Bewcastle in Cumberland, with Nicoll Forest; also the countries and ground in Scotland called Liddesdale, Eskdale, Ewsdale, Annandale, Wallopdale, Clydesdale, and the West Marches of Scotland "whereof great part is now in the Scot's hands, and all new castles, lordships, manors, lands, &c., within the same dales and borders, which he or his heirs have, or shall hereafter get or achieve;" in addition to which he was to receive 10,000 marks in ready money.

Rot. Parl. vol. vi. p. 204.

B.

THE TOWER OF LONDON, FORMERLY THE ABODE OF THE ENGLISH MONARCHS.

(See p. 39.)

For several centuries the White Tower was used as a royal residence, and continued to be occupied as such, until the reign of Queen Elizabeth. King Henry III. strengthened it as a fortress, and beautified and adorned it as a palace. It being the chief residence of himself and his court, he had the apartments fitted up with that importance and splendour which led to its being inhabited by so many of his successors; and the ancient chapel of St. John's (now occupied as a repository for records) he greatly enriched, with sculpture, tapestry, and painted glass.

The First, Second, and Third Edwards were occasional residents within its walls, and Richard II. dwelt there in his minority with his royal mother, "who was lodged in that part of the Tower Royal called the Queen's Wardrobe." During the insurrection of Wat Tyler, the court and principal nobility, to the number of six hundred, were domiciled within its precincts. Henry IV. and Henry V. are recorded as departing from "their castle of London" on many occasions of festivity and rejoicing; and to the hapless Henry VI. this regal abode was by turns a palace and a prison. Edward IV. frequently kept his court here in great magnificence, and both himself and Queen Elizabeth Wydville, the parents of the ill-fated Edward V., lodged at the Tower before the day fixed upon for their coronation; proceeding thence to Westminster, according to ancient usage, to be invested with the symbols of royalty. —See *Berner's Froissart — Hearne's Fragment — Stow's Chronicle — Bayley's History of the Tower — and Brayley's Londiniana.*

C.

CECILY, DUCHESS OF YORK, PROFESSES HERSELF A NUN OF THE BENEDICTINE ORDER.

(See p. 61.)

[Cott. MS. Vitel. L. fol. 17.]

THE fact of the Lady Cecily having enrolled herself a sister of the order of St. Benedict in the year 1480 is proved beyond dispute by the MS. details preserved in the Cottonian library, but it is equally certain from other documents, that she did not retire altogether from the world or lead a life of seclusion in any religious house belonging to the order whose vows she had embraced.

It appears from the Paston Letters (vol. iv.) that during the middle ages it was customary for persons growing in years to procure by purchase or gift a retreat in some holy society; where, abandoning worldly matters, the piously disposed might pass the remainder of their days in prayer and supplication; but this connection with religious houses did not imply always the adopting formally a conventual life or becoming an inmate of those monastic establishments in whose "merits, prayers, and good works," the new member of their fraternity shared. Margaret, Countess of Richmond and Derby, for example, mother of King Henry VII., and the contemporary of Cecily, Duchess of York, was enrolled a member of five devout societies; but although she abstained from that period, as far as was compatible with her exalted station, from all worldly pleasures and occupations, yet it is well known that she never became an inmate of any religious house. A recluse in her own dwelling she certainly was, for she never quitted the retirement she had voluntarily embraced, excepting when a sense of duty required a temporary sojourn in the metropolis; and in all likelihood the same devotional feelings, qualified by reservations insurmountable in her remarkable position, influenced the Duchess of York, when she professed herself a member of the Benedictine Sisterhood.

That she never removed from her castle at Berkhampstead excepting for brief intervals, is clear, because she expired within its walls; and the severity of her life there in declining years is made known by the rules and regulations, which have descended to this present day, and which attest that she considered Berkhampstead as her home throughout the varied changes of her troubled life, and that her occasional residence at Baynard's Castle, arose more from the necessity of the measure with reference to others, than from any reprehensible indulgence in those ambitious feelings which influenced her actions at an earlier period of life.

D.

LETTER FROM KING EDWARD V. TO OTES GILBERT, ESQ.,
COMMANDING HIM TO BE PREPARED TO RECEIVE
KNIGHTHOOD AT HIS APPROACHING CORONATION.

(See p. 67.)

[Harl. MSS. No. 433. p. 227.]

"TRUSTY and well-beloved, we greet you well; and
by the advice of our dearest uncle, the Duke of Gloucester, Protector of this our royaume during our young
age, and of the Lords of our Council, we write unto
you at this time, willing and natheless charging you to
prepare and furnish yourself to receive the noble order of
knighthood at our coronation; which, by God's grace, we
intend shall be solemnised the 22d day of this present
month at our palace of Westminster, commanding you to
be here at our Tower of London, four days before our said
coronation, to have communication with commissioners concerning that matter; not failing hereof in any wise, as you
intend to please us, and as ye will answer.

"Given, &c. &c. the 5th day of June.

"To Otes Gilbert, Squier."

Similar letters to this appear to have been sent to forty-
nine other persons; amongst whom were the Lord Ormond,
the Lord Stourtoun, the son and heir of Lord Bergavenny,
the Lord Grey of Ruthin, the son and heir of the Lord
Cobham, and Henry Colet, alderman of London.—See *Sir
Henry Ellis's Original Letters,* 2d *Series,* p. 147.

E.

LIST OF ROBES ORDERED FOR KING EDWARD V.

(See p. 67.)

" A SHORT gown, made of two yards and three quarters of crimson cloth of gold, lined with two yards and three quarters of black velvet; a long gown, made of six yards D of crimson cloth of gold, lined with six yards of green damask; a short gown, made of two yards and three quarters of purple velvet, lined with two yards and three quarters of green damask; a doublet and a stomacher, made of two yards of black satin &c.; besides two foot-cloths, a bonet of purple velvet; nine horse harness and nine saddle housings of blue velvet : gilt spurs, with many other rich articles and magnificent apparel for his hench-men and pages." (See *Hist. Doubts*, p. 64.) The ward-robe account, from whence the foregoing robing extract is taken is written on vellum and bound up with the coro-nation rolls of Henry VII. and Henry VIII.; the latter, however, are merely written on paper. It is the office account of Piers Curteis, keeper of the great wardrobe, and contains a statement of deliveries, from the day of Edward IV.'s death to the month of February in the follow-ing year, including the time of the intended coronation of Edward V., and the actual coronation of Richard III. The number and similitude of the robes delivered for each of these kings justifies the conclusion, (arrived at in conse-quence of the discussion that ensued, when public attention was directed to the above-named coronation roll,) that the robes ordered for ' Lord Edward, son of Edward IV.,' were designed for the apparel of this young prince at his own contemplated coronation, and were not, as Lord Orford was at first led to imagine, used by him to grace the procession of that of his uncle, Richard III. — See *Archæologia.*, vol. i. p. 361. and *Supplement to Hist. Doubts*, in Lord Orford's Works, vol. ii.

F.

GLOUCESTER—AN ILL-OMENED TITLE.

(See p. 71.)

In addition to the mysterious murder of Humphrey Duke of Gloucester at Bury[1], may be instanced the yet more appalling death of Thomas of Woodstock, Duke of Gloucester, uncle of Richard II., who was treacherously inveigled from his castle at Pleshy by the young monarch himself, then aged but twenty years, and by his command cruelly murdered for having opposed his wishes when a minor.[2]

Also Thomas Le Despencer, Earl of Gloucester, closely allied to the house of York, who was beheaded at Bristol by command of Henry IV., in the first year of his usurpation.[3] To this catalogue may be added the names of Richard Duke of Gloucester[4], the subject of this present memoir; Henry Duke of Gloucester, the youngest son and companion in misery of the ill-fated Charles I.[5]; and William Duke of Gloucester, only son of Queen Anne, and sole survivor of seventeen children, who, after giving promise of the most extraordinary excellence[6], expired almost suddenly in the eleventh year of his age.

[1] Hall, p. 209.
[2] Froissard, lib. iv. c. 86. 92.
[3] Heylyn, p. 330.
[4] Rous, p. 217.
[5] Sandford, lib. vii. p. 570.
[6] Burnett's Own Times, vol. iv. p. 357, 358.

G.

LETTER FROM RICHARD DUKE OF GLOUCESTER TO THE
MAYOR AND ALDERMEN OF THE CITY OF YORK.

(See p. 72.)

"THE Duke of Gloucester, brother and uncle of kings,
Protector and Defender, Great Chamberlain, Constable,
and Lord High Admiral of England.

" Right trusty and well-beloved. We greet you well.
Whereas by your letters of supplication to us delivered by
our servant John Brackenbury, we understand that by
reason of your great charge that ye have had and sustained,
as well in defence of this realm against the Scots as otherwise, your worshipful city remains greatly unpaid for, on
the which ye desire us to be good mover unto the king's
grace, for any ease of such charges as ye shall yearly bear
and pay unto his grace's highness. We let you wot, that
for such great matters and businesses as we now have to
do, for the weal and usefulness of the realm, we as yet ne
can have convenient leisure to accomplish this your business, but be assured that for your loving and kind disposition to us at all times shewed, which we never can forget,
we in all goodly haste shall so endeavour for your ease in
this behalf, as that ye shall verily understand we be your
special good and loving Lord, as our said friend shall shew
you, to whom it would like you him to give further
credence unto, and for your diligent service which he hath
done, to our singular pleasure unto us at this time, we pray
you to give unto him laud and thanks, and God keep you!

" Given under our signet at our Tower of London this
8th day of June."

" To our trusty and well-beloved the Mayor,
   Aldermen, Sheriffs and Commonalty of
   the City of York."

                              Drake's Eborac., p. 111.

H.

LETTER FROM RICHARD DUKE OF GLOUCESTER, DE-
LIVERED TO JOHN NEWTON, MAYOR OF YORK BY
RICHARD RATCLIFFE, KNIGHT, REQUIRING THE AID
OF ARMED MEN FROM THE NORTH TO PROTECT HIM
FROM GREAT PERIL.

(See p. 73.)

[15th June A°. 1 Ed. V. 1483.]

" THE Duke of Gloucester, brother and uncle of king's,
Protector and Defender, Great Chamberlain, Constable,
and Admiral of England.

" Right trusty and well-beloved, we greet you well.
And as you love the weal of us, and the weal and surety
of your own self, we heartily pray you to come unto us
in London in all the diligence ye can possible, after the
sight hereof, with as many as ye can make defensibly arrayed, there to aid and assist us against the queen, her
bloody adherents and affinity, which have entended, and do
daily entend to murder and utterly destroy us, and our
cousin the Duke of Buckingham, and the old royal blood
of this realm, and as is now openly known, by her subtle
and damnable ways forecasted the same, and also the final
destruction and disherison of you, and all other the inheritors and men of honour, as well of the north parts as other
countries that belong unto us, as our trusty servant this
bearer shall more at large shew you ; to whom we pray you
to give credence; and as ever we may do for you, in time
coming, fail not, but haste you to us.

" Given under our signet at London the 10th of June.

" To our trusty and well-beloved the Mayor,
    Aldermen, Sheriffs and Commonalty of
    the City of York."

Drake's Eboracum, p. 111. That author asserts, that both
this and the preceding letter are given, so far as it is
legible, verbatim from the original MS.

I.

INSTRUCTIONS SENT TO LORD MOUNTJOY, GOVERNOR OF
CALAIS, TO DISPOSE HIS SOLDIERS TO DEPART FROM
THEIR OATH TO KING EDWARD V. AND TO TAKE
ANOTHER TO KING RICHARD III.

(See p. 119.)

[Harl. MSS. No. 433. fol. 238.]

"THAT howbeit such oath of allegiance was made soon
upon the death of the said King Edward IV. to his son,
not only in Calais, but also in divers places in England,
by many great estates and personages being then ignorant
of the very true and sure title which our sovereign lord
that now is, King Richard III., hath and had at the same
time to the crown of England. That oath, notwithstanding, now every good true Englishman is bound, upon
knowledge had of the said very true title, to depart from
the first oath, so ignorantly given to him to whom it appertained not; and therefore to make his oath anew, and owe
his service and fidelity to him that good law, reason, and
the concord assent of the lords and commons of the realm,
have ordained to reign upon the people, which is our said
sovereign lord King Richard III., brother to the said
King Edward IV., late deceased, whom God pardon;
whose sure and true title is evidently shewed and declared in a bill of petition which the lords spiritual and
temporal and the commons of this land solemnly presented
unto the king's highness at London the 26th day of June;
whereupon, the king's said highness, notably assisted by
well near all the lords spiritual and temporal and the
commons of this realm, went the same day to his palace of
Westminster, and there, in such royal honorable robes
apparelled, within the great hall, took possession, and
declared that the same day he would begin to reign upon his
people; and from thence rode solemnly to his cathedral
church of London, and was received with procession and

with great congratulation and acclamation of all the people in every place and by the way that the king was in that day. The copy of which bill will be sent unto Calais, and there to be read and understanded together with these presents; desiring right effectually all manner of persons within these three jurisdictions, what estate, degree, or condition that they be of, and also they of Guisnes and Hammes, to make their faith and oaths to him, as their sovereign lord, like as the lords spiritual and temporal, and many other great number being in England, freely and of good heart have done the same for their parts; and that the same town of Calais and all castles and fortresses, being within the said marches, they will safely keep unto the behoof of the said sovereign lord, King Richard III., and them not to deliver to any person but by his commandment."

Similar instructions were forwarded to the governors of Guisnes and Hammes. — See *Harl. MSS.*, No. 433. fol. 239.

K.

PRECAUTIONARY MEASURES ADOPTED BY RICHARD III.
PRIOR TO HIS CORONATION.

(See p 123.)

[Rymer, Add. MSS. No. 4616. Art. 16.]

" PREVIOUSLY to the coronation of Richard III. a proclamation was issued, forbidding any person under penalty of death, on account of any old or new quarrel, to make any challenge or affray whereby the peace might be broken, or any sedition or disturbance of the peace within the city of London, or the parts thereunto adjoining; that all parties offending should be brought before the mayor of London, or the steward of the king's household, as the case might be, until the king's pleasure should be taken thereupon. It was strictly enjoined, that strangers and aliens should not be molested; it was commanded that no man, under pain of imprisonment, should take any lodging in the city or suburbs, except by appointment of the king's harbingers; every one was to be in his lodging by ten o'clock at night; and the carrying of glaives, bills, long and short swords and bucklers was prohibited."

L.

"THESE be the dukes, earls, lords and knights that were at the coronation of our sovereign lord King Richard III. and Queen Anne, the first year of his noble reign, the 6th day of July, 1483."

(See p. 124.)

[From an ancient MS. roll, printed in the Excerpta Historica, p. 384.]

Duke of Buckingham	Earl of Lincoln
Duke of Norfolk	Viscount Lisle
Duke of Suffolk	Viscount Lovell
Earl of Northumberland	Lord Stanley [1]
Earl of Arundel	Lord Audley
Earl of Kent	Lord * * * * * [2]
Earl of Surrey	Lord Ferrars of Chartley
Earl of Wiltshire	Lord Powys
Earl of Huntingdon	Lord Fitzhugh
Earl of Nottingham	Lord Scrope of Upsall
Earl of Warwick	Lord Scrope of Bolton

[1] In a MS. copy of this list in the College of Arms, the name of Lord Stanley is omitted. The following variations may also be noticed: for Sir Gilbert Dike, Sir Gilbert Debnam (in the margin of the Harleian MSS. it is written "Broke"); for Sir Terry Robsart, Sir Peter Robsart; for Sir George Wentworth, Sir Harry Wentworth; for Sir Ralph Ashton, Sir Rofe Aston; for Sir Roger Fynes, Sir Roger Ryves; for Sir James Arowsmyth, Sir James Strangewishe and for Sir Robert Everard, Sir Robert Elyard.

[2] Dacres.

Lord Grey of Codner
Lord Grey of Wilton
Lord Stourton
Lord Cobham
Lord Morley
Lord Abergavenny
Lord Zouche
Lord Ferrers of Groby
Lord Wells
Lord Lumley
Lord Maltravers
Lord Harbert
Lord Beauchamp
Sir James Tyrell
Sir William Knevett
Sir Thomas A. Brough
Sir William Stanley
Sir William A. Parro
Sir George Browne
Sir George Midleton
Sir John Heningham
Sir Michael Latimer
Sir Thomas Montgomery
Sir Thomas Sandes
Sir Gilbert Dike, or Driby
Sir Terry Robsart
Sir William Brandon
Sir John Savell
Sir George Wentworth
Sir Edward Stanley
Sir Richard St. Maur
Sir William Yonge
Sir Thomas Bowseer
Sir Henry Wingfield
Sir Thomas Wortley
Sir John Sentlow
Sir Charles Pilkington
Sir John Ashley
Sir Thomas Barkley
Sir Richard Bewchamp of the
    Carpett
Sir William Gorney, or Goney

Sir Richard Lodlow
Sir William St. Low
Sir Thomas Twayts
Sir Edward Dudley
Sir Rafe Ashton
Sir Richard Charlington
Sir Thomas Grey
Sir Phillip Barkley
Sir James Harington
Sir John Gresley
Sir John Coniers
Sir William Stoner
Sir Phillip Cortney
Sir William Eastney
Sir Richard Midleton
Sir Roger Fynes
Sir George Vere
Sir Henry Percey
Sir John Wood
Sir John A. Parr
Sir John Grey
Sir James Danby
Sir Robert Talboyse
Sir Thomas Ridid
Sir John Harynge
Sir William Stoner
Sir Richard Henderby
Sir John Barkley
Sir James Arowsmyth
Sir Rafe Tarbock
Sir Giles Daubney
Sir John Constable
Sir Robert Everard
Sir Robert Dorell
Sir John Gilford
Sir John Lewknor
Sir John Merbury
Sir Thomas Powys, or Howys
Sir John Bolayn
Sir Edward Bedingfield
Sir William Norris

These following were made Knights of the Bath at his coronation: —

Sir Edmund de la Pole, son to the Duke of Suffolk	Sir Thomas Arundell
	Sir Thomas Bulleyn
Sir John Grey, son to the Earl of Kent	Sir Edmund Bedingfield
	Sir Gervoise of Clifton
Sir William, brother to Lord Zouche	Sir William Sey
	Sir William Enderby
Sir Henry Neville, son to Lord Aberganey	Sir Thomas Lewkner
	Sir Thomas Ormond
Sir Christopher Willoby	Sir John Browne
Sir William Barkley	Sir William Barkley.
Sir Henry Barington	

See also *Harl. MSS.* 2115. fol. 152., and
Buck's Richard III. lib. 1. p. 26.

M.

ORDINANCE MADE BY KING RICHARD III. FOR THE REGULATION OF HIS HOUSEHOLD IN THE NORTH.

(See p. 144.)

" THIS is the ordinance made by the king's good grace for such number of persons as shall be in the north as the king's household, and to begin from the 24th day of July, Anno 1ᵐᵒ. 1484.

" First, that the hours of God's service, diet, going to bed and rising, and also shutting of the gates be at reasonable time, and hours convenient.

" Item, that monthly the treasurer and comptroller show the expences to one of the council or two, the which shall appoint themselves monthly, throughout the year.

" Item, that if any person offend in breaking of any of the said ordinances, or of any other made by the council, to punish or expel the offender after their discretions out of the house according to their demerits.

" Item, my Lord of Lincoln and my Lord Morley be at one breakfast; the children together at one breakfast; such as be present of the council at one breakfast; and also that the household go to dinner at the furthest by eleven of the clock on the flesh day.

" Item, the treasurer to have the keys of the gates, from the time of the dinner and supper beginning to the end of the same.

" Item, that stuff of household be purveyed and provided for a quarter of a year before the hand.

. " Item, the costs of my Lord of Lincoln, when he rideth to sessions, or any meetings appointed by the council, the treasurer to pay for meat and drink.

" Item, at all other ridings, huntings, and disports, my said lord to be at his own costs and charges.

" Item, that no liveries of bread, wine, nor ale, be had, but such as be measurable and convenient, and that no pot of livery exceed measure of a pottle, but only to my lord and the children.

" Item, that no boys be in household but such as be admitted by the council.

" Item, that every man that is at day wages be at their check, and those that be at standing wages without check.

" Item, that none servant depart without assent of the treasurer, and upon pain of losing his service.

" Item, that no breakfast be had in the house, but such as be assigned.

" Item, that convenient fare be ordained for the household servants and strangers to fare better than others."—*Harl. MSS.* No. 433. fol. 265.

N.

KING RICHARD'S VISIT TO OXFORD.

(See p. 147.)

[Anno Domini, 1483. 1 A°. Rich. III.]

" THE 22d of July this year the founder of Magdalen College came to Oxford, to the end provision might be made at his college for the reception of King Richard III. The 24th of the said month the king came from Windsor, and approaching Oxford was met by the chancellor, regents, and non-regents at the town's end, where, after they had expressed their love and duty to him, he was honorably and processionably received into Magdalen College by the founder, president, and scholars thereof, and lodged there that night. At the same time came with the king, the bishops of Durham, Worcester, St. Asaph, and Thomas Langton, the bishop elect of St. David's, the Earl of Lincoln, Lord Steward, Earl of Surrey, Lord Chamberlain, Lord Lovel, Lord Stanley, Lord Audley, Lord Beauchamp, Sir Richard Radcliffe, knight, and many other nobles — all which lodging in the college, the University gave to most of them wine and gloves. The next day being St. James's day, were at the command and desire of the king two solemn disputations performed in the common hall of the said college, viz. in Moral Philosophy by Mr. Thomas Kerver, opponent, and a certain bachelaur of the said college, respondent, which being concluded, a disputation in Divinity was made before the king by Mr. John Taylor, S. T. P., opponent, and Mr. William Grocyn, respondent, which being also finished, he rewarded the disputants very honorably, that is to say, to the doctor he gave a buck and 5l.; to the respondent, a buck and five marks; the master that opposed in Philosophy, a buck and five marks; and to the bachelaur, a buck and 40s. He gave also to the president and scholars two bucks and five marks for wine.

" The next day being St. Anne's day, he with his nobles visited several places in the University, and heard also disputations in the public schools, scattering his benevolence very liberally to all that he heard dispute or make orations to him; so that after the Muses had crowned his brows with sacred wreaths for his entertainment, he the same day went to Woodstock, the University then taking leave of him with all submission. Not long after, according to a promise made to the scholars at his reception, he confirmed the privileges of the University, granted by his predecessors; as part of an epistle from the University to him attesteth:— ' Nos vero quos concessis a primogenitoribus tuis privilegiis etiam sine pretio donasti, quantum tibi debemus.' "

Gutch's History of Oxford, Edit. 1792, p. 638.

O.

RELATION OF THE MESSAGE DECLARED BY GRANFIDIUS DE SASIOLA, ORATOR OF ISABELLA, QUEEN OF CASTILLE, TO KING RICHARD III., DRAWN UP BY HIMSELF IN LATIN.

(See p. 154.)

" ON the 8th of August 1483 [1] Geoffry de Sasiola, the orator of the Queen of Spain, stated on her behalf to the king and council at Warwick, that she wished to maintain a firm peace and to enter into a strict alliance with him; that if it were his intention to go to war with Louis, King of France, for the recovery of the possessions pertaining to the crown of England, she would open her ports to his army, and supply them with arms and provisions at a reasonable price, and would, on the same terms, lend him her ships: she also promised to raise a force of knights, men-at-arms, and foot-soldiers, well armed and in sufficient number, the king paying their wages.

"Besides these instructions given in writing by this orator, he shewed to the king's grace by mouth, that the Queen of Castille was turned in her heart in times past from England, for the unkindness which she took against the king last deceased, for his refusing of her, and taking to his wife a widow of England. For which cause also was mortal war betwixt him and the Earl of Warwick, the which took ever her part at the time of his death; and therefore she moved for these causes against her nature, the which was ever to

---

[1] Sir H. Ellis, in his Orig. Letters, 2d Series, calls this name " Granfidius " and not Geoffry, p. 152.

love and favor England, as he said she took the French king's part and made leagues and confederations with him. Now the king is dead, which shewed her this unkindness, and, as he said, the French king hath broken four principal articles appointed betwixt him and the King of Castille and her; wherefore she, now returning to her kind and natural disposition, desireth such things to be appointed betwixt the realms of England and Spain, as ye may understand by these instructions of her said orator. Another cause which moved her to depart from King Louis was, that she had a grant from the Queen of Navarre to have her daughter and heir for the Prince of Castile her son, if the consent of King Louis might thereon have been had; and forasmuch as he, by no manner would be thereto agreeable, she taketh a great displeasure with him, and desireth by all means to her possible to make these alliances and confederations with the king's good grace as be shewed in these instructions."[1]

Harl. MSS. 433. fo. 235

P.

THE ORDER WHICH RICHARD III. SENT FROM YORK ON THE LAST DAY OF AUGUST TO PIERS COURTEIS, KEEPER OF HIS WARDROBE.

(See p. 159.)

"BY THE KING.

"WE will and charge you to deliver to the bringers hereof for us the parcels following, that is to say, one doublet of purple satin lined with Holland cloth, and interlined with busk; one doublet of tawney satin lined in likewise;

[1] Sir H. Ellis, who has also copied this instrument from the Harl. MSS., adds (after the word "Instructions") "the first part of this statement is fully corroborated by the English historians, viz. Hall, Grafton, and Leland." — *Collect.* tome i. p. 500.

two short gowns of crimson cloth of gold, the one with "drippis," and the other with nets lined with green velvet; one cloak with a cape of velvet ingrained, the bow lined with black velvet; one stomacher of purple sattin, and one stomacher of tawny sattin; one gown of green velvet lined with tawny sattin; one yard and three quarters corse of silk nedled with gold and as much black corse of silk for our spurs; two yards and a half and three nails of white cloth of gold for a "crynelze" for a board; five yards of black velvet for the lining of a gown of green sattin; one placard made of part of the said two yards and one half and two nails of white cloth of gold lined with buckram; three pair of spurs, short, all gilt; two pair of spurs, long, white parcell gilt; two yards of black buckram for amending of the lining of divers trappers: one banner of sarsnet of our Lady; one banner of the Trinity; one banner of St. George; one banner of St. Edward; one of St. Cuthbert; one of our own arms all sarsenet; three coats of arms beaten with fine gold, for our own person; five coat armours for heralds, lined with buckram; forty trumpet banners of sarcenet; seven hundred and forty pencells of buckram; three hundred and fifty pencells of tartar; four standards of sarcenet with boars; thirteen thousand quinysans of fustian with boars."

Drake's Eborac. p. 117.

Q.

PARCELS OF THE CLOTHING TO BE DELIVERED BY THE
BISHOP OF ENACHDEN TO THE EARL OF DESMOND.

(See p. 171.)

[See Harl. MSS. 433. fo. 265.]

" First—A long gown of cloth of gold, lined with sattin or damask.

" Item — A long gown of velvet, lined with sattin or damask.

" Item — Two doublets, one of velvet, and another of crimson sattin.

" Item — Three shirts, and kerchiefs for the stomachers.

" Item — Three pair of hosen, one of scarlet, another of violet, and the third of black.

" Item — Three bonnets, two hats, and two tippets of velvet. A collar of gold of 20 oz. =30*l.*

The Bishop of Enachden was farther instructed to dispose the Earl of Desmond concerning the king's high pleasure and intent for the earl to renounce the wearing and usage of the Irish array, and from thenceforth to give and apply himself to use the manner of the apparel for his person after the English fashion.

R.

VAGUE AND UNCERTAIN REPORTS, RELATING TO THE DEATH OF EDWARD V. AND HIS BROTHER, IN THE LIFETIME OF SIR THOMAS MORE.

(See p. 189.)

[Supplement to *Hist. Doubts* in Lord Orford's Works, vol. ii. p. 215.]

" FROM that very scarce book called ' The Pastime of the People,' and better known by the title of ' Rastell's Chronicle,' I transcribed verbatim the following paragraphs : —

" ' But of the manner of the death of this young king, and of his brother there were divers opinions. But the most common opinion was, that they were smouldered between two feather-beds, and that in the doing, the younger brother escaped from under the feather beds, and crept under the bedstead, and there lay naked awhile till that they had smouldered the young king, so that he was surely dead. And after that, one of them took his brother from under the bedstead, and held his face down to the ground with his one hand, and with the other hand cut his throat whole asunder with a dagger. It is a marvel that any man could have so hard a heart to do so cruel a deed save only that necessity compelled them, for they were so charged by the Duke the Protector, that if they shewed not to him the bodies of both those children dead on the morrow after they were so commanded, that then they themselves should be put to death. Wherefore they that were commanded to do it were compelled to fulfill the protector's will. And after that, the bodies of these two children, as the opinion ran, were both closed in a great heavy chest, and by the means of one that was secret with the protector, they were put in a ship going to Flanders; and when the ship was in the black deeps, this man threw both those dead bodies so closed in the chest over the hatches into the sea, and yet none of the mariners, nor none in the ship, save only the said man, wist what thing it was, that was there so inclosed; which saying divers men conjectured to be true, because that the bones of the said children could never be found buried, neither in the Tower, nor in no other place.

" ' Another opinion there is, that they which had the charge to put them to death caused one to cry so suddenly *treason, treason;* wherewith the children being afraid, desired to know what was best for them to do. And then they bad them hide themselves in a great chest, that no man should find them, and if any body came into the chamber, they would say they were not there. And according as they counselled them, they crept both into the chest, which anon after they locked. And then anon they buried that chest in a great pit under a stair, which chest was after cast into the black deeps as is before said.'"

We find from Ames's Typographical Antiquities (p. 147.) that this book was printed in 1529, the 21st year of Henry VIII., and from page 141., that Rastall, the compiler and printer, married Sir Thomas More's sister. Rastall was not only his relation but printer—his very next publication being a dialogue written by More, and printed in the same year with the Chronicle.

Nor did Sir Thomas More pick up the materials for his own history after the appearance of Rastall's Chronicle, which was published but six years before Sir Thomas's death, when the persons from whom he gained his intelligence must have been dead likewise. But Sir Thomas's own words betray, not only doubts in his own breast, but thorough proof of the uncertainty of all the incidents relative to the murder. He tells us that he does not relate the murder in every way he had heard it, but according to the most probable account he could collect from the most credible witnesses.

S.

GRANTS TO ROBERT BRACKENBURY, 1 AND 2 RICH. III.
1473-4.

(See p. 195.)

[Harl. MSS. 433.]

Fol. 23^b.—Robert Brackenbury Esq. appointed Constable of the Tower, and Master of the Mint.

Fol. 56^b.—Re-appointed Constable of the Tower, with a yearly fee of 100*l.*; keeper of the king's lions in the Tower, with a fee of 12*d.* per day, and 6*d.* per day for the keep of each lion and leopard.

Fol. 57.— Appointed the king's receiver of various lordships.

Fol. 74^b.—Receiver-general of all lands being in the king's hands by attainder or forfeiture in various counties.

Fol. 75^b.—Had confirmation of various offices granted to him by Sir Thomas Montgomery.

Fol. 87. — Had an assignment made to him by writ of Privy Seal of 100*l.*

Fol. 91^b.—Appointed Constable of Tunbridge Castle with a fee of 10*l.* yearly, besides lands, &c.

T.

LETTER FROM KING RICHARD III. TO THE MAYOR OF YORK.

(See p. 263.)

[Drake's Eboracum, p. 118.]

" BY THE KING.

" TRUSTY and well-beloved: We greet you well, and let ye wit that the Duke of Buckingham traitorously has turned upon us, contrary to the duty of his allegiance, and entendeth the utter destruction of us, you, and all other our true subjects that have taken our part; whose traitorous intent we with God's grace intend briefly to resist and subdue. We desire and pray you in our hearty wise that ye will send unto us as many men defensibly arrayed on horseback as ye may goodly make to our town of Leicester the 21st day of this present month without fail, as ye will tender our honour and your own weal, and we will see you so paid for your reward and charges as ye shall hold ye well content. Giving further credence to our trusty pursuivant this bearer. Given under our signet at our city of Lincoln the 11th day of October."

" To our trusty and right well-beloved the
    Mayor, Aldermen, 'Sheriffs and Com-
    monalty of the City of York."

The entry of the above letter in the city records is preceded by the annexed memorial: —

" Mem. — 13 Oct. 1 Ric. III. 1483. John Otyr, Yeoman of the Crown, brought the following letter to the Lord Mayor, Aldermen, Sheriffs and Commonalty."

534 APPENDIX.

U.

SUMMARY OF THE PROCLAMATION ISSUED BY KING
RICHARD III. AT LEICESTER.

(See p. 265.)

23 Octr. A° 1 Rich. III. 1483. A proclamation was
issued tested by the king at Leicester, setting forth that
he, remembering the profession of mercy and justice made
by him at his coronation, had issued a generall pardon,
trusting thereby to have caused all his subjects to have
adhered to him according to their duty and allegiance;
and had in his own person visited various parts of his
realm for the indiferent administration of justice. Yet
this notwithstanding, Thomas, late Marques of Dorset,
" holding the unshamefull and mischevous woman called
Shore's wife, in adultery," Sir William Norreys, Sir
William Knevet, Sir Thomas Bourchier of Barnes, Sir
George Brown, Knights, and others with them traitorously
associated, had gathered his people by the comfort of his
great rebel and traitor, the late Duke of Buckingham and
the Bishops of Ely and Salisbury, intending not only the
destruction of his royal person, but also the maintenance
of vice and sin: promises a free pardon to such as will
withdraw from their company; offers a reward of 1000*l*. in
money or 100*l*. in land for the taking of the duke, 1000
marks in money or 100 in land for either of the bishops,
and 500 marks in money or 40*l*. in land for each of the
said knights; and forbids any one to aid or assist them with
goods, vituals, or otherwise, under the penalty attached to
treason.

Rymer's Fœdera, vol. xii. p. 204.

V.

SINGULAR PRESERVATION OF THE HEIR OF THE DUKE
OF BUCKINGHAM AFTER THE CAPTURE AND EXECU-
TION OF HIS FATHER.

(See p. 269.)

[From a copy of an old roll of paper[1] found out in the treasury at
Thornbury Castle among the evidences there — mensis Julii, anno
1575.]

" M^d the second[2] year of King Richard the Third, Duke
Henry of Buckingham came from Brecknock to Webblie,
and with him brought my lady his wife, my Lord Stafford and my Lord Henry, and there tarryed one week,
and sent for the gentlemen of the country unto him; and
when he had spoken with them departed thence. My
lord his father made him a frieze coat, and at his departing
he delivered his son and heir to Sir Richard Delabeare,
Knight, for to keep until he sent for him by a token, &c.,
viz. *et tu es Petrus O super hanc petram.*

" Item — John Amyasse, that went with my Lord
away, delivered my Lord Stafford in the Little Park
of Webbeleye to Richard Delabeare, Knight, and then
came after Sir William Knevet and Mistress Cliffe, and
so they came to Kynnardsley all together. And when
they came to Kynnardsley there were xx^{ti} of my Lord's
servants in the place.

" Item — At that time Dame Elizabeth Delabeare being
servant to Sir Richard Delabeare, Knight, took my Lord
Stafford on her lap, and bare him amongst and through
them all into a chamber of the Place of Kynnardsley, and
then went again and fetched Sir William Knevet and the

---

[1] It has been considered advisable in this as in many of the preceding extracts, to modernise the spelling, although the words themselves remain unchanged.

[2] This is an error, for the conspiracy occurred in the first, and not
the second year of King Richard III.

gentlemen, and brought them into the chamber to my
Lord Stafford.

"Item — A proclamation come to Hereford for the said
duke his son and Sir William Knevet, that whosoever
would take them, he should have for the said duke four
thousand pounds, for the Lord Stafford a thousand marks,
for my Lord Henry five hundred pounds, and for Sir
William Knevet five hundred marks, the which proclamation Sir William Knevet read himself, and prayed that
it should not miss, but be proclaimed. And then was
there great search made where this said company was
become. And so all the gentlemen of Herefordshire were
sent for by privy seal to King Richard to Salisburie, and
by that time Duke Henry of Buckingham was brought
by Sir James Tyler the third day, where he was pitifully
murdered by the said king, for raising power to bring in
King Henry the Seventh. And after the said duke was
taken, the Vaughans made great search after my Lord of
Stafford, and for the said Sir William Knevitt, which
Lord Stafford and Sir William Knevitt were in the keeping of Dame Elizabeth Delabeare and William ap Symon.
In the mean time, she shaved the said Lord Stafford's
head, and put upon him a maiden's 'raiment, and so conveyed him out of Kynnardsley to New-church. And then
came Christopher Wells bourne from Sir James Tyler to
Kynnardsley, and said his father commanded to have the
said Lord Stafford delivered. And then answered the
said Dame Elizabeth Delabeare and William ap Symon,
that there was none such Lord there 'and that shall ye well
know, for ye shall see the house searched.' And then
went he to Webbely to my Lady, and there met with
Sir John Hurlestone's brother, and fetched my Lady of
Buckingham, and brought her to the king to London.
And the said Dame Elizabeth and William ap Simon
fetched the said lord again to Kynnardsley, and the said
Sir William Knevit, and brought them into the Place
of Kynarsly, and there kept them until David Glin

Morgan came thither from King Richard, and said Mr. Delabeare was arrested, and said, there he should abide until he delivered Lord Stafford; and then said Dame Elizabeth and William ap Symon, ' that ye shall well know there is none such here, and ye shall come and see the place, and it please you,' and so in great malice he departed thence.

"Item — The night before that David Glin Morgan came to Kynnardsley, the said Dame Elizabeth and William ap Symon conveyed my Lord Stafford and Sir William Knevet to a place called Adeley in the parish of Kynnardsley, and there rested they four days, and then the said Lord Stafford and Sir William Knevet were fetched again to Kynnardsley by the said Dame Elizabeth and William ap Symon, for because they could not convey meat and drink to them aright. And they kept them there one sennight, and then there came a great cry out of Wales, and then the said Dame Elizabeth took my Lord Stafford in her lap, and went through a brook with him into the park of Kynnardsley, and there sat with him four hours, until William ap Symon came to her, and told her how the matter was that no man came nigh the place. And in the mean time Sir William Knevet went out with one William Pantwall into the fields, and left Mistress Olyffe in the place all this while. After that the Dame Elizabeth and William ap Symon took the said Lord Stafford, and went to Hereford in the midst of the day, and he riding behind William ap Glin aside upon a pillion like a gentlewoman, rode in a gentlewoman's apparel. And I wis he was the fairest gentlewoman, and the best that ever she had in her days, or ever shall have, whom she prayeth God daily to preserve from his enemies, and to send him good fortune and grace. And then the said Dame Elizabeth and William ap Symon left my Lord Stafford in a widdow's house, a friend of hers at Hereford, and Mistress Oliffe with him, and at that time Sir William Knevet departed from my Lord Stafford."

Blakeway's Hist. of Shrewsbury, vol. i. p. 241.

W.

UNWORTHY CONDUCT OF SIR THOMAS ST. LEGER, AS
SHEWN IN THE ACT OF ATTAINDER, PASSED AFTER
HIS EXECUTION.

(See p. 277.)

" In the parliament assembled at Westminster, 23d Jan.
A° 1 Ric. III. 1484, a bill was preferred, reciting that
on the 3d Nov. A° 1 Edw. IV. 1461, Henry late
Duke of Exeter was attainted of high treason, whereby
his duchy of Exeter, with his other possessions, were
forfeited; that subsequently Sir Thomas St. Leger, by
seditious means, married Anne Duchess of Exeter, late
wife of the said duke, he being then living, and of her
begot a daughter, called Anne; that the said Thomas induced the said late king that his said daughter should in-
herit the duchy of Exeter, and caused him to suffer an act
of parliament to be enacted on the 3d June, in the seventh
year of his reign, 1467, whereby the said daughter had
between the said Thomas and the said late duchess, for
default of issue of Anne, daughter of the said late duke
and duchess, which lived but short time after, might
enherit the said duchy and other hereditaments; that after
the passing of the said act, the said Anne, daughter of the
said duke and duchess, died without issue, and the said
late duchess deceased with issue of her body by the said
duke; after whose decease, by the labour of the said
Thomas by another act of parliament, 20th Jan. A° 21
Edw. IV., it was enacted, that Richard Gray, Knight,
should have and enjoy certain manors: the said acts are
hereby repealed, and the grants made by them are resumed."

Rot. Parl., vol. vi. p. 242.

X.

SUBSTANCE OF TWO WRITS ISSUED AT WINCHESTER BY
RICHARD III. 1483.

(See p. 279.)

[Harl. MSS. 433. fol. 123.]

" ART. 1563.—Warrant to Mr. John Gunthorpe, keeper
of the privy seal, to discharge Richard Bele from his
place in the office of the said prive seale, to which he
had been admitted, contrary to the old rule and due order,
by mean of giving of great gifts, and other sinister and
ungodly ways, in great discouraging of the under clerks,
which have long continued therein, to have th' experience
of the same, to see a stranger, never brought up in the
said office, to put them by of their promotion, &c.

" Yeven at Winchester, the 22d day of November,
anno primo.

" Art. 1564. — Grant to Robert Belman, of the place of
one of the clerks of the prive seale, for the good and
diligent service done by the said Robert in the said office,
and specially in this the king's great journey, and for his
experience and long continuance in the same ; declaring
that no more clerks shall be admitted in the said office
until the time the said office shall be reduced to the
number ordered and stablished in the days of King Edward
III.

" Yeven the 22d day of November, *anno primo.*"

Y.

RECAPITULATION OF KING RICHARD'S TITLE TO THE THRONE, WITH THE ACT THAT WAS PASSED FOR THE SETTLEMENT OF THE CROWN UPON HIM AND HIS HEIRS.

(See p. 289.)

[Rot. Parl. vol. vi. p. 240.]

" To the High and Myghty Prince Richard Duc of Gloucester.

" PLEASE it youre Noble Grace to understande the consideraçon, election, and petition underwritten of us the lords spiritual and temporal and commons of this reame of England, and thereunto agreably to geve your assent, to the common and public wele of this lande, to the comforte and gladnesse of all the people of the same.

" Furst, we considre how that heretofore in tyme passed this lande many years stode in great prosperite, honoure, and tranquillite, which was caused, forsomuch as the kings then reignyng used and followed the advice and counsaill of certaine lords spuelx and temporelx, and othre personnes of approved sadnesse, prudence, policie, and experience, dreading God, and havyng tendre zele and affection to indifferent ministration of justice, and to the comon and politique wele of the land ; then our Lord God was dred, luffed [loved], and honoured; then within the land was peace and tranquillite, and among neghbors concorde and charite ; then the malice of outward enemyes was myghtily repressed and resisted, and the land honorably defended with many grete and glorious victories ; then the entrecourse of merchandizes was largely used and exercised ; by which things above remembred, the land was greatly enriched, soo that as wele the merchants and artificers as other poor people, laboryng for their lyvyng in diverse occupations, had competent gayne to the sustentation of thaym and their households, livyng without miserable and intolerable

povertie. But afterward, whan that such as had the rule
and governaunce of this land, deliting in adulation and
flattery and lede by sensuality and concupiscence, fo-
lowed the counsaill of persons insolent, vicious, and of
inordinate avarice, despising the counsaill of good, ver-
tuous, and prudent personnes such as above be remembred, the prosperite of this lande dailie decreased, soo that
felicite was turned into miserie, and prosperite into adver-
site, and the ordre of polecye, and of the law of God
and man, confounded; whereby it is likely this reame to
falle into extreme miserie and desolation,—which God
defende,—without due provision of convenable remedie bee
had in this behalfe in all godly hast.

"Over this, amonges other thinges, more specially we
consider howe that the tyme of the raigne of Kyng
Edward IV., late decessed, after the ungracious pretensed
marriage, as all England hath cause so say, made betwixt
the said King Edward and Elizabeth sometyme wife to
Sir John Grey, Knight, late nameing herself and many
years heretofore Queene of England, the ordre of all poli-
teque rule was perverted, the laws of God and of Gode's
church, and also the lawes of nature and of Englond,
and also the laudable customes and liberties of the same,
wherein every Englishman is inheritor, broken, subverted,
and contempned, against all reason and justice, so that this
land was ruled by self-will and pleasure, feare and drede,
all manner of equitie and lawes layd apart and despised,
whereof ensued many inconvenients and mischiefs, as
murdres, estortions, and oppressions, namely, of poor and
impotent people, soo that no man was sure of his lif, land,
ne lyvelode, ne of his wif, doughter, ne servaunt, every
good maiden and woman standing in drede to be ravished
and defouled. And besides this, what discords, inward
battailes, effusion of Christian men's blode, and namely,
by the destruction of the noble blode of this londe, was
had and comitted within the same, it is evident and
notarie through all this reaume unto the grete sorrowe

and heavynesse of all true Englishmen. And here also
we considre howe that the said pretensed marriage, bitwixt
the above named King Edward and Elizabeth Grey, was
made of grete presumption, without the knowyng or assent
of the lords of this lond, and alsoe by sorcerie and wiche-
crafte, committed by the said Elizabeth and her moder,
Jaquett Duchess of Bedford, as the common opinion of
the people and the publique voice and fame is through
all this land; and hereafter, if and as the case shall require,
shall bee proved suffyciently in tyme and place convenient.
And here also we considre how that the said pretenced
marriage was made privatly and secretly, with edition of
banns, in a private chamber, a profane place, and not
openly in the face of church, aftre the lawe of Godd's
churche, but contrarie thereunto, and the laudable custome
of the Churche of England. And howe also, that at the
tyme of contract of the same pretensed marriage, and
bifore and longe tyme after, the said King Edw̃ was and
stoode marryed and trouth plyght to oone Dame Elianor
Butteler, doughter of the old Earl of Shrewesbury, with
whom the saide King Edward had made a precontracte of
matrimonie, longe tyme bifore he made the said pretensed
mariage with the said Elizabeth Grey in manner and
fourme aforesaide. Which premises being true, as in
veray trouth they been true, it appeareth and followeth
evidently, that the said King Edward duryng his lyfe and
the said Elizabeth lived togather sinfully and dampnably
in adultery, against the lawe of God and his church; and
therefore noe marvaile that the souverain lord and head
of this londe, being of such ungodly disposicion, and pro-
vokyng the ire and indignation of oure Lorde God, such
haynous mischiefs and inconvenients as is above remembered, were used and committed in the reame amongst
the subjects. Also it appeareth evidently and followeth
that all th' issue and children of the said king beene
bastards, and unable to inherite or to clayme anything by
inheritance, by the lawe and custome of England.

" Moreover we consider howe that aftreward, by the thre estates of this reame assembled in a parliament holden at Westminster the 17th yere of the regne of the said King Edward the iiijth, he then being in possession of coroune and roiall estate, by an acte made in the same parliament, George Duc of Clarence, brother to the said King Edward now decessed, was convicted and attainted of high treason; as in the same acte is conteigned more at large. Because and by reason whereof all the issue of the said George was and is disabled and barred of all right and clayme that in any wise they might have or challenge by enheritance to the crowne and roiall dignitie of this reame, by the auncien lawe and custome of this same reame.

" Over this we consider howe that ye be the undoubted sonne and heire of Richard late Duke of Yorke verray enheritour to the said crowne and dignitie roiall and as in ryght Kyng of Englond by way of enheritaunce and that at this time the premisses duely considered there is noon other person lyvyng but ye only, that by right may clayme the said coroune and dignitie roiall, by way of enheritaunce, and how that ye be born within this lande, by reason whereof, as we deme in our myndes, ye be more naturally enclyned to the prosperite and comen wele of the same: and all the three estates of the land have, and may have more certain knowledge of your birth and filiation above said. Wee considre also, the greate wytte, prudence, justice, princely courage, and the memorable and laudable acts in diverse battalls which we by experience knowe ye heretofore have done for the salvacion and defence of this same reame, and also the greate noblesse and excellence of your byrth and blode as of hym that is descended of the thre most royal houses in Christendom, that is to say, England, Fraunce, and Hispaine.

" Wherefore these premisses by us diligently considered, we desyring affectuously the peas, tranquilitie and wele publique of this lande, and the reducion of the same to the auncien honourable estate and prosperite, and havyng in your greate prudence, justice, princely courage and excellent virtue, singular confidence, have chosen in all that in us is and by this our wrytyng choise you, high and myghty Prynce into our Kyng and soveraine lorde &c., to whom we knowe for certayn it appartaneth of enheritaunce so to be choosen. And hereupon we humbly desire, pray, and require your said noble grace, that accordinge to this election of us the three estates of this lande, as by your true enheritaunce ye will accept and take upon you the said crowne and royall dignitie with all things thereunto annexed and apperteynyng as to you of right belongyng as well by enheritaunce as by lawfull election, and in caas ye do so we promitte to serve and to assiste your highnesse, as true and faithfull subjietz and liegemen and to lyve and dye with you in this matter and every other just quarrel. For certainly we bee determined rather to aventure and comitte us to the perill of our lyfs and jopardye of deth, than to lyve in suche thraldome and bondge as we have lyved long tyme heretofore, oppressed and injured by new extorcos and imposicons, agenst the lawes of God and man, and the liberte, old police and lawes of this reame wherein every Englishman is inherited. Oure Lorde God Kyng of all Kyngs by whose infynyte goodnesse and eternall providence all thyngs been pryncypally gouverned in this worlde lighten your soule, and graunt you grace to do, as well in this matter as in all other, all that may be accordyng to his will and pleasure, and to the comen and publique wele of this land, so that after great cloudes, troubles, stormes, and tempests, the son of justice and of grace may shyne uppon us, to the comforte and gladnesse of all true Englishmen.

"Albeit that the right, title, and estate, whiche oure souverain lorde the Kyng Richard III. hath to and in the crown and roiall dignite of this reame of England, with all thyngs thereunto annexed and apperteynyng, been juste and lawefull, as grounded upon the lawes of God and of nature, and also upon the auncien lawes and laudable customes of this said reame, and so taken and reputed by all suche personnes as ben lerned in the above-saide laws and custumes. Yet, neverthelesse, forasmoche as it is considred that the moste parte of the people of this lande is not suffisiantly lerned in the abovesaid lawes and custumes whereby the trueth and right in this behalf of liklyhode may be hyd, and not clerely knowen to all the people and thereupon put in doubt and question: And over this howe that the courte of Parliament is of suche autorite, and the people of this lande of suche nature and disposicion, as experience teacheth that manifestation and declaration of any trueth or right made by the thre estats of this reame assembled in parliament, and by auctorite of the same maketh before all other thyng, moost faith and certaintie; and quietyng men's myndes, remoweth the occasion of all doubts and seditious language:

"Therefore at the request, and by the assent of the three estates of this reame, that is to say, the lords spuelx and temporalx and comens of this lande, assembled in this present parliament by auctorite of the same, bee it pro-nounced, decreed and declared, that oure saide souveraign lorde the kinge was and is veray and undoubted kyng of this reame of Englond; with all thyngs there-unto within this same reame, and without it annexed unite and apperteynyng, as well by right of consanguinite and enheritance as by lawful election, consecration and coronacion. And over this, that at the request, and by the assent and autorite abovesaide bee it ordeigned, enacted and established that the said crowne and roiall dignite of this reame, and the inheritaunce of the same, and other thyngs thereunto within the same reame or without it annexed, unite, and now apperteigning, rest and abyde in the personne of oure said souveraign lord the kyng duryng his lyfe, and after his decesse in his heires

' of his body begotten. And in especiall, at the request and by the assent and auctorite abovesaid, bee it ordeigned, enacted, established, pronounced, decreed and declared that the high and excellent Prince Edward, sone of our said souveraign lorde the kyng, be hiire apparent of our saide souveraign lorde the kyng, to succeed to hym in the abovesayde crown and roiall dignitie, with all thyngs as is aforesaid thereunto unite annexed and apperteignyng, to have them after the decesse of our saide souveraign lorde the kyng to hym and to his heires of his body lawfully begotten."

To this bill the Commons gave their assent, and it consequently passed.

Z.

SUBSTANCE OF THE BILL OF ATTAINDER PASSED ON THE
1ST PARLIAMENT OF RICHARD III. JAN. 1484.

(See p. 290.)
[Rot. Parl. vol. vi. p. 244.]

ACT 23 Jan. 1., Ric. 3. 1484, reciting that, "Whereas in late days herebefore great troubles, commotions, assemblies of people, conspirations, insurrections and heinous treasons have been committed and made within this realm by divers persons, unnatural subjects, rebels and traitors unto our sovereign lord King Richard III. and great multitude of people by them abused to consent and be partners of the same offences and heinous treasons, whereby both the king's highness and his peace, and also the politic rule and common weal of this his realm have been greatly inquieted and troubled; they intending thereby, as much as in them was, the universal subversion and destruction of the same, and also of the king's most royal person, the which troubles, commotions, and other offences abovenamed, by God's grace, and the great and laborious vigilance of our said sovereign lord, with the assistance of his true and faithful subjects, been now repressed. Wherein howbeit that his said highness for great considerations touching the weal of this his realm, having therewith respect to the abuse and deceit of the said multitude as before is rehearsed, moved with benignity and pity, and laying apart the great rigour of the law, hath granted to divers persons culpable in the said offences his grace and pardon yet: nevertheless, such it is according to reason and all policy that such notary and heinous offences and treasons, in no wise utterly passe unpunished, which if it should so happen the example thereof might and should be a great occasion, cause, and boldness unto other hereafter to attempt and commit like offences and ' exerbitations,' whereby great inconveniences might and were like to ensue, tho' God forbid. And also to the intent that benignity and pity be not so exalted that justice be set apart, nor that justice so proceed that benignity and pity have no place, but that a due moderation and temperament be observed in every behalf as appeareth to eschew the manyfold and irreparable jeopardies and the inconveniences that else might and be like to ensue :

"Considering furthermore that those persons whose names be underwritten were great and singular movers, stirrers and doers of the said offences and heinous treasons; that is to say, *Henry late Duke of Buckingham now late days standing and being in as great favour, tender trust, and affection with the king our sovereign lord, as ever subject was with his prince and liege lord, as was notarily and openly known by all this realm*, not being content therewith, nor with the good and politique governance of his said sovereign lord, but replete with rancour and insatiable covetise; and also John Bishop of Ely, William Knyvet late of Bodenham Castle in the Shire of Norfolk, John Rush late of London, merchant, and Thomas Nandike late of Cambridge, ' Negromancier,' being with the said Duke of Brecknock in Wales the 18th Oct. A° 1483, falsely conspired the death and destruction of the king and to depose

him, and to execute their said purpose assembled at Brecknock as aforesaid with great number of people harnessed
and arrayed in manner of war to give battle to the king
and his true lords and subjects; and after various
traitorous proclamations there made, proceeded thence to
Weobley. And also the said duke on the 24th September
by his several writings and messages by him sent, procured
and moved Henry calling himself Earl of Richmond and
Jasper late Earl of Pembroke being there in Brittany, great
enemies of our said sovereign lord, to make a great navy
and bring with them an army from Brittany; by reason
whereof the said Henry and Jasper and their adherents
came from Brittany with a navy and army of strangers and
landed. And over this, George Broun late of Beckworth
co. Surrey (and others who are named), at the traitorous
procurement and stirring of the said duke, the said 18th
day of October in the year aforesaid at Maidstone as re-
bells and traitors intended &c. the king's death, and on that
day and on the 20th of the same month at Rochester, and
on the 22d at Gravesend, and on the 25th at Guildford,
assembled, harnessed and arrayed in manner of war and
made sundry proclamations against the king to execute
their said traitorous purpose: and also at the traitorous
motion of the said duke, William Noreys late of Yacken-
don co. Berks, knight, Sir William Berkeley of Beverston,
Sir Roger Tocote of Bromham, Richard Beauchamp Lord
St. Amand, William Stonor, knight (and others who are
named), on the said 18th October, at Newbury co.
Berks, and John Cheyney (and others who are named), at
Salisbury, compassed and imagined the king's death. The
parties enumerated were therefore declared to be convicted
and attainted of high treason, and their estates to be
forfeited."

A A.

TENOR OF THE OATH OF ALLEGIANCE TO RICHARD III.
ADMINISTERED BY COMMISSIONERS APPOINTED FOR
THAT PURPOSE.

(See p. 293.)

[Harl. MSS. No. 433. fo. 141.]

" I SHALL true and faithfull leigeman be, to our sovereign
lord King Richard the Third, by the grace of God King of
England and of France, and Lord of Ireland, and to him, his
heirs and successors, Kings of England, my truth and faith
shall bear during my life, nor no treason nor other thing hide
that should be hurtful to his royal person, but that I shall
open and disclose it to his highness or to some of his noble
council in all haste possible that I can, and his part utterly
take against all earthly creatures, nor no livery, badge, nor
cognisance shall take from henceforth of any person, nor
none of his rebels and traitors succour, harborer, nor favour
contrary to the duty of allegiance, but put me in my
uttermost devoir to take them. So help me God," &c.

Given at Sandwich 16th January, Aº 1 Ric. III., 1484.

B B.

PLEDGE GIVEN BY KING RICHARD III. FOR THE
SAFETY OF THE DAUGHTERS OF EDWARD IV.

(See p. 304.)

[Harl. MSS. No. 433. fo. 308.]

MEMORANDUM that I Richard by the grace of God
King of England and of France and Lord of Ireland, in
the presence of you my lords spiritual and temporal, of
you mayor and aldermen of my city of London, promise
and swear *verbo regio* and upon these Holy Evangiles of

N N 3

God by me personally touched, that if the daughters of Dame Elizabeth Gray, late calling herself Queen of England, that is to wit, Elizabeth, Cecil, Anne, Katherine, and Bridget, will come unto me out of the sanctuary of Westminster, and be guided, ruled, and demeaned after me, I shall see that they be in surety of their lives, and also not suffer any manner of hurt, by any manner person or persons to them or any of them in their bodies and persons to be done by way of ravishment or defouling contrary to their wills, nor them nor any of them imprison within the Tower of London or other prison, but that I shall put them in honest places of good name and fame, and their honestly and courteously shall see to be found and treated, and to have all things requisite and necessary for their exhibition and finding as my kinswomen. And if I shall, do marry such of them as now be marriageable to gentlemen born and every of them give in marriage lands and tenements to the yearly value of two hundred marks for term of their lives, and likewise to the other daughters when they come to lawful age of marriage if they live; and such gentlemen as shall happ to marry with them I shall straitly charge from time to time lovingly to love and intreat them as their wives and my kinswomen as they will avoid and eschew my displeasure. And over this that I shall yearly from henceforth content and pay, or cause to be contented and paid for the exhibition and finding of the said Dame Elizabeth Gray during her life, at three terms of the year, to John Neffeld, one of the esquires for my body, for his finding to attend upon her, the sum of seven hundred marks of lawful money. And moreover I promise to them that if any surmise or evil report be made to me of them by any person or persons, that then I shall not give thereunto faith nor credence, nor therefore put them to any manner of punishment, before that they or any of them so accused may be at their lawful defense and answer. In witness whereof, &c., the 1st day of March in the 1st year of my reign (1484).

C C.

BRIEF SKETCH OF THE HISTORY OF THE COLLEGE OF ARMS FROM ITS FOUNDATION BY RICHARD III. TO THE PRESENT TIME.

(See p. 310.)

COLD Harbour, the "right fair and stately house" munificently awarded to the College of Heralds by King Richard III., was anciently styled Coldeherbergh. Stow calls it Cole-herbet, Maitland and Pennant Cold Harbour. It is thus described in the letters patent that perpetuate the grant : — "one messuage with the appurtenance in London, in the parish of All Saints called Pulteney's Inn, or Cold Harbour." This house, which had long been the residence of the princes of the blood, the nobility, and the highest gentry, was built in the reign of Edward III. by Sir John Poultney, who had been Lord Mayor of London four times, whence it was called Poultney's Inn, and which name it long retained after it passed into other hands. Its last owner, John Holland Duke of Exeter, (who was the first husband of Anne, eldest sister of Edward IV. and Richard III.) lost it by attainture of parliament, so that at Richard's accession it was in the Crown, and was by him bestowed, as above narrated, on the officers of the College of Arms in the 1st year of his reign. On the death of this monarch at Bosworth field, all his acts were rendered null; he was attainted, pronounced an usurper, and all his grants were cancelled. That to the Heralds was declared void, and the Officers at Arms were ordered to remove. It was in vain that they pleaded having performed the duties enjoined them, or that Garter king-at-arms claimed it in his private capacity, the mansion was taken possession of by Henry VII., and the Heralds were compelled to quit their college. They retired to a conventual building near Charing Cross, intitled "our Lady of Ronceval," which had been a cell to the priory of Roncevaux in Navarre, and stood upon part of the site of the present Northumberland House; but having no claim to the property, they were there only upon sufferance of the Crown, and in the reign of Edward VI. the place was bestowed upon Sir Thomas Cawarden. During the previous reigns of Henry VII. and Henry VIII. the Heralds frequently and earnestly petitioned the throne for a grant of some house or place wherein to hold their assemblies, but without success. King Edward VI., however, in a charter in his third year, and by authority of parliament, endeavoured to make them some amends by exemplifying to them their ancient privileges, but it was not until the reign of Queen Mary that the Heralds were re-established in a permanent abode. This sovereign by charter bearing date the 18th July in the second year of her reign re-incorporated " the Kings, Heralds, and Poursuivants at Arms;" and their original habitation at Cold Harbour having been taken down, and a number of small tenements erected upon its site, the queen bestowed upon them " a messuage with its appurtenances called Derby House within the city of London, and in the street leading from the south door of the cathedral church of St. Paul's to a place thence called Paul's Wharf, thentofore parcel of possessions of Ed. Earl of Derby, and to be by the said corporation held in free burgage of the city of London."

In this edifice — and restored to their pristine importance — the Officers of Arms continued to dwell undisturbed during the sovereignty of Elizabeth, James I., and Charles I.; but the reign of Charles II. found them once more bereft of a house, — the great fire of London in the year 1666 having entirely consumed their college. The Heralds, however, had the great good fortune to save all their muniments and books, except one or two; and the re-building of their college, now in ruins, was, by act of parliament for re-building the city, directed to be begun within three years. On the site then of the former edifice was erected the regular quadrangular building as it now appears, and which was considered at that time one of the best designed and handsomest brick edifices in London. The hollow archway of the great gate in particular was esteemed " a singular curiosity." In November 1683, the college part of the building being finished, the rooms were divided among the Officers of Arms by their mutual agreement, and according to their degrees. This arrangement was afterwards confirmed by the Earl Marshall, consequently the apartments thus selected at the re-establishment of the collegiate body have been ever since annexed to their respective offices. — See *Edmondson's Body of Heraldry*, pp. 143. 154.; and *Noble's Colleges of Arms*, pp. 54. 56.

D D.

DECREE OF THE UNIVERSITY OF CAMBRIDGE IN RE-QUITAL OF KING RICHARD'S BENEFACTIONS.

(See p. 313.)

[Cott. MS. Faustina, ch. iii. 405.]

" To all the faithful in Christ who shall inspect these letters. The most reverend father in Christ, the Lord Thomas Rotherman, by the grace of God Archbishop of York, Primate of England, Legate of the Apostolic See, and Chancellor of the University of Cambridge, and the unanimous assembly of the Regents and Non-regents of the same University, greeting in the Saviour of all. Whereas the most renowned prince the King of England and France, and Lord of Ireland, Richard, after the Conquest, the Third, has conferred very many benefits upon this his University of Cambridge, and especially has lately, liberally, and devoutly founded exhibition for four priests in the Queen's College. And now also the most serene Queen Anne, consort of the same lord the king (that most pious king consenting and greatly favouring), has augmented and endowed the same college with great rents. Whereas also, the same most fortunate king has, with the greatest kindness, bestowed and expended not a little money for the strength and ornament of the university, both in most graciously ratifying the privileges of the university, as also with most devout intention founding and erecting the buildings of the King's College, the unparalleled ornament of all England. These, and many designs considering in our minds, we, the aforesaid chancellor and the unanimous assembly of the masters of the said university, embracing with gratitude such great and royal munificence, and desiring as far as we can to bestow spiritual recompense, decree, that for all time to come whilst the same renowned prince shall continue in this life, on the second day of May, the mass of Salus Populi shall be celebrated by the whole congregation of regents and non-regents of the aforesaid university, for the happy state of the same most renowned prince and his dearest consort Anne. And after the aforesaid most renowned King Richard shall depart this life, we appoint and decree, that when that shall first come to our knowledge, exequies for the dead, and a mass of requiem, diligently and devoutly we will perform for the soul of the same most illustrious Prince Richard, and the souls of all the progenitors of the same. And that every of the premises granted and decreed may obtain strength and virtue, these our present letters concerning them we have caused to be sealed with the common seal of our university, and also with the seal of the chancellor affixed to fortify the same.

> " Given in the year of our Lord 1483, in the 1st year of the reign of the said most renowned king, and on the 16th day of the month of March."
>
> Printed in *Cooper's Cambridge*, p. 228.

E E.

LETTER FROM JAMES THE THIRD, KING OF SCOTLAND, TO KING RICHARD THE THIRD, THE SOVEREIGN OF ENGLAND.

(See p. 359.)

[See Harl. MS. 433. fol. 246.]

By the King of Scots.

"RIGHT excellent high and mighty prince, and right trusty and well-beloved cousin, we commend us unto you in the most heartily-wise. And howbeit that oft time afore, certain ruption, break, and disturbance has been betwixt the realms of England and Scotland by the workings and means of evil-disposed persons in contrary our mind and intention, as God knows. Nevertheless, we remain in the same purpose as afore, like as we write to the right noble prince your brother, whom God assoil, to observe and keep love, peace, concord, and amity with all Christian princes, and above others, with our neighbours and realms next approaching to the borders of our realm of Scotland." — Dated 16th August, 1484.

He desires to be informed of the king's mind and intention herein.

LETTER FROM RICHARD THE THIRD TO THE KING OF SCOTLAND, DATED 16TH SEPTEMBER, WHEREIN HE ACKNOWLEDGES THE RECEIPT OF THE PRECEDING LETTER, BY THE KING OF ENGLAND.

" COUSIN, we ascertain you our mind and disposition is, and ever shall be, conformable to the will and pleasure of God our Creator, in all reasonable and convenient peace, without feigning that, should be desired of us by any nation; and if that your desire and pleasure be to send hither such personages to treat for the accomplishing thereof, we having knowledge from you of their names, shall give unto them our sure safe conduct for a reasonable number and season."

Harl. MS. 433. *fol.* 247.

F F.

COPY OF THE LETTER TO BE DELIVERED TO THOSE FROM WHOM THE COMMONS REQUESTED LOANS IN THE KING'S NAME.

(See p. 374.)

[See Harl. MS. No. 433. fol. 276.]

SIR,

" THE king's grace greeteth you well, and desireth and heartily prayeth you, that by way of loan ye will let him have such sum, as his grace hath written to you for. And ye shall truly have it again at such days as he hath shewed and promised to you in his letters. And this he desireth to be employed for the defence and surety of his royal person, and the weal of this realm. And for that intent his grace and all his lords thinking that every true Englishman will help him in that behalf, of which number his grace reputeth and taketh you for one. And that is the cause he this writeth to you before other, for the great love, confidence, and substance that his grace hath and knoweth in you which trusteth undoubtedly that ye, like a loving subject, will at this time accomplish his desire."

G G.

EXTRACTS FROM SIR HARRIS NICOLAS'S MEMOIR OF "ELIZABETH OF YORK," pp. 42—46.

(See p. 382.)

" THE question whether Richard intended to marry Elizabeth in the event of the death of his wife is important to his character; and the truth of the assertion that before

Queen Anne's decease he was not only accepted, but eagerly courted by Elizabeth, is no less material to her fame. Richard's detractors have insisted that after he discovered the intentions of the friends of Elizabeth and of the Earl of Richmond to blend their respective pretensions to the crown by their marriage, he was impressed with the policy of strengthening his own title by making her his queen; that this became apparent in the similarity of her costume to the dress of her majesty, as early as Christmas 1484, and that to promote his wishes he actually poisoned his wife."

" That it was not his [King Richard's] interest to marry the Princess Elizabeth, and consequently that the strongest testimony is necessary to prove that he intended to do so, is apparent from the following circumstances: — It was the act of the first parliament which he summoned to bastardise the children of his brother, because their legitimacy would have been an insurmountable bar to his right to the throne ' by inheritance,' which was the title he pretended to possess. In the only document which has been discovered relative to them, dated in March 1484, they are treated as illegitimate, and on the death of the Prince of Wales in April the Earl of Lincoln was declared heir to the crown. It is certain that they were still considered in the same light so late as August in that year, when, with the view of strengthening the alliance with Scotland, Richard promised his niece Anne, the daughter of the Duchess of Suffolk, to the Prince of Scotland, she being his nearest female relation whose blood was not bastardised or attainted. These acts occurred many months after he became aware of the design of marrying the Earl of Richmond to Elizabeth of York, and there seems no greater reason why he should have thought it politic to marry Elizabeth after August 1484 than previous to that time. Independent of his relationship to her, there were other obstacles to their union. His title to the crown would not have been strengthened by marrying a woman whom the law had declared a bastard; and to have repealed that declaration would be to call into existence his right to the crown, and to proclaim himself an usurper. A measure so inconsistent with his safety, so contradictory to the whole tenor of his policy, seems incredible; and can it for a moment be believed that he endeavoured to effect it by the murder of a wife who was fast hastening to the tomb with disease, and by a marriage which even the authority of the Pope could not, it is said, reconcile to the feelings and manners of his subjects?

" There is no difficulty in supposing that Richard would commit any crime which his interest might dictate, but it is not easy to imagine that he would imbrue his hands in the blood of his wife to gain an object, which, so far from promoting his interests, must have materially injured them. The worst enemies of the usurper have contented themselves with representing him as an atrocious villain, but not one of them has described him as a fool."

H H.

LETTER FROM KING RICHARD III. TO THE MAYOR AND CITIZENS OF YORK, IN ALLUSION TO THE REPORT OF HIS INTENDED MARRIAGE WITH HIS NIECE.

(See p. 405.)
[Drake's Eboracum, p. 119.]

" BY THE KING.

" TRUSTY and well-beloved, we greet you well. And where it is so that divers seditious and evil disposed persons both in our city of London and elsewhere within this our realm enforce themselves daily to sow seeds of noise and slander against our person, and against many of the lords and estates of our land, to abuse the multitude of our subjects and alter their minds from us, if they could by any mean attain to that their mischevous intent and purpose; some

by setting up of bills, some by message and sending forth
of false and abominable language and lies; some by bold
and presumptuous open speech, wherewith the innocent
people which would live in rest and peace and truly under
our obeissance as they ought to do, being greatly abused,
and oft times put in danger of their lives, lands, and goods
as oft as they follow the steps and devices of the said
seditious and mischevous persons to our heavyness and
pity. For remedy whereof, and to the intent the truth
openly declared should suppress all such false and contrived
inventions, we now of late called before us the mayor and
aldermen of our city of London, together with the most
sad and discreet persons of the same city in great number,
being present many of these lords spiritual and temporal
of our land, and the substance of all our household, to
whom we largely showed our true mind of all such things
which the said noise and disclander run upon in such
wise as we doubt not all well-disposed persons were and
be therewith right well content. Where we also at the
same time gave straitly in charge as well to the said mayor
as to all other our officers, servants, and faithful subjects
wheresoever they be, that from henceforth as oft as they
find any person speaking of us or any other lord or estate
of this our land, otherwise than is according to honour,
truth, and the peace and rightfulness of this our land, or
telling of tales and tidings whereby the people might be
stirred to commotions and unlawful assemblies, or any
strife or debate arise between lord and lord, or us, and any
of the lords and estates of this our land, they take and
arrest the same person unto the time he hath brought
forth him or them of whom he understood that that is
spoken, and so proceeding from one to other unto the time
the first author and maker of the said seditious speech and
language be taken and punished according to his deserts.
And that whosoever first find any seditious bills set up in
any place he take it down and without reading or shewing
the same to any other person bring it forthwith unto us or

some of the lords or other of our council. All which charges and commandments so by us taken and given by our mouth to our city of London we notify unto you by these our letters, to the intent that ye shew the same within all the places of your jurisdiction, and see there the due execution of the same from time to time, as ye will eschew our grievous indignation and answer to us at your extreme peril.

" Given under our signet at our city of London the 11th day of April."

To our trusty and well-beloved the Mayor
　　　and his Brethren of the City of York.

I I.

LETTER ADDRESSED BY KING RICHARD III. TO THE COMMISSIONERS OF ARRAY FOR THE COUNTY OF YORK.

(See p. 419.)

[Harl. MSS. 433. fol. 220.]

" BY THE KING.

" TRUSTY &c. And forasmuch as certain information is made unto us that our rebels and traitors associate with our ancient enemies of France, and other strangers intend hastily to invade this our realm and disheriting of all our true subjects. We therefore will and straitly command you that on all haste possible after the receipt hereof, you do put our commission heretofore directed unto you for the mustering and ordering of our subjects in new execution according to our instructions, which we send unto you at this time with these our letters. And that this be done with all diligence as ye tender our surety, the weal of yourself and of all this our realm.

" Given at Nottingham the 22nd day of June."

" To our trusty and well-beloved our Com-
    missioners of Array appointed within
    our County of York."

Like letters to all other commissioners in every shire in England.

K K.

INSTRUCTIONS SENT BY KING RICHARD III. TO THE COMMISSIONERS OF ARRAY THROUGHOUT THE KINGDOM.

(See p. 419.)

[Harl. MS. 433. fol. 220.]

" FORASMUCH as the king's good grace understandeth by the report of his commissioners and other the faithfull dis positions and readiness that his subjects be of to do him service and pleasure to the uttermost of their powers for the resisting of his rebels, traitors, and enemies, the king's highness therefore will that the said commissioners shall give on his behalf especial thanking unto his said subjects, exhorting them so to continue.

" Item, that the said commissioners in all haste possible review the soldiers late mustered before them by force of the king's commission to them late directed, and see that they be able persons well horsed and harnessed to do the king service of war, and if they be not, to put other able men in their places, &c.

" Item, that the said commissioners on the king's behalf give straitly in commandment to all knights, esquires, and gentlemen to prepare and array themselves in their proper persons to do the king service upon an hour's warning, when they shall be thereunto commanded by proclamation or otherwise. And that they fail not so to do upon peril of losing of their lives, lands, and goods. And that they be attending and waiting upon such captain or captains as the king's good grace shall appoint to have the rule and leading of them, and upon none other.

" Item, that the commissioners make proclamation that all men be ready to do the king service within an hour's warning whenever they be commanded by proclamation or otherwise.

" Also to shew to all lords, noblemen, captains, and other, that the king's noble pleasure and commandment is that they truly and honorably all manner quarrels, grudges, rancours, and unkindness, lay apart and every of them to be loving and assisting to other on the king's quarrel and cause, shewing them plainly that whosoever attempt the contrary, the king's grace will so punish him that all other shall take example by him."

L L.

TENOR OF THE LETTERS DIRECTED TO ALL SHERIFFS THROUGHOUT ENGLAND AND WALES, BY COMMAND OF KING RICHARD III.

(See p. 422.)

[Harl. MS. 433. fol. 221.]

" TRUSTY and well-beloved, we greet you well. And forasmuch as we have commanded our commissioner of array within our counties of Nottingham and Derby to put our commission to them heretofore directed for mustering and ordering our subjects in new execution according to our instructions to them directed. We therefore will and straitly command you that incontinently upon the receipt hereof ye fully dispose you to make your continual abode within the shire town of your office or your deputy for you, to the intent that it may be openly known where you or he shall be surely found for the performing and fulfilling of such things as on our behalf or by our said commissioners ye shall be commanded to do, &c."

" Given, &c., at Nottingham the 22nd day of June."

M M.

PROCLAMATION OF RICHARD III. MADE TO EVERY SHIRE UNDER THE GREAT SEAL OF ENGLAND BY A WARRANT UNDER THE SIGNET, CALLING UPON HIS SUBJECTS TO RESIST HENRY TUDOR, AS A TRAITOR.

(See p. 422.)

[See Paston Letters, vol. ii. p. 319.; also Harl. MS. 433. fol. 221.]

Ric. Rex.

" FORASMUCH as the king our sovereign lord hath certain knowledge that Piers Bishop of Exeter, Jasper Tydder [Tudor], son of Owen Tydder, calling himself Earl of Pembroke, John late Earl of Oxon, and Sir Edward Wodeville, with other divers his rebels and traitors disabled and attainted by the authority of the high court of parliament, of whom many be known for open murders, advoutres [adulterers], and extortioners contrary to the pleasure of God, and against all truth, honor, and nature, have forsaken their natural country, taking them first to be under th' obeisance of the Duke of Bretagne, and to him promised certain things which by him and his counsell were thought things greatly unnatural and abominable for them to grant, observe, keep, and perform, and therefore the same utterly refused.

" The said traitors, seeing the said duke and his council would not aid nor succour them nor follow their ways, privily departed out of his country into France, and there

taking them to be under the obeissance of the king's ancient enemy Charles calling himself King of France, and
to abuse and blind the commons of this said realm, the
said rebels and traitors have chosen to be their captain
one Henry Tydder, son of Edmund Tydder, son of Owen
Tydder, which of his ambitiousness and insatiable covet-
ius encroacheth and usurpeth upon him the name and
title of royal estate of this realm of England, where unto
he hath no manner, interest, right, or colour, as every man
well knoweth, for he is descended of bastard blood, both
of father's side and of mother's side; for the said Owen, the
grandfather, was bastard born, and his mother was daughter
unto John Duke of Somerset, son unto John Earl of
Somerset, son unto Dame Katherine Swynford, and of their
indouble avoutry [1] gotten, whereby it evidently appeareth
that no title can nor may in him which fully entendeth
to enter this realm proposing a conquest; and if he should
achieve his false intent and purpose, every man's livelihood
and goods shall be in his hands, liberty and disposition,
whereby should ensue the disheriting and destruction of all
the noble and worshipful blood of this realm, for ever, and
to the resistance and withstanding whereof every true and
natural Englishman born must lay to his hands for his own
surety and weal. And to the intent that the said Henry
Tydder might the rather achieve his false intent and
purpose by the aid, support, and assistance of the king's
said ancient enemy of France, hath covenanted and bar-
gained with him and all the counsell of France to give up
and release in perpetuity all the right, title, and claim that
the king of England have had, and ought to have to the
crown and realm of France, together with the duchies of
Normandy, Anjou, and Maine, Gascoign and Guyne
Cascell [Castle] and towns of Calais, Guynes, Hammes,
with the marches appertaining to the same, and dissever
and exclude the arms of France out of the arms of England
for ever.

[1] Double, or perhaps indubitable adultery.

" And in more proof and shewing of his said purpose of conquest, the said Henry Tydder hath given as well to divers of the said king's enemies as to his said rebels and traitors, archbishopricks, bishopricks, and other dignities spirituel, and also the duchies, erledomes, baronies, and other possessions and inheritances of knights, squires, gentlemen, and other the king's true subjects within the realm, and intendeth also to change and subvert the laws of the same, and to induce and establish new laws and ordinances amongst the king's said subjects, and over this, and besides the alienations of all the premises into the possession of the king's said ancient enemies, to the greatest anyntishments, shame, and rebuke, that ever might fall to this said land, the said Henry Tydder and others, the king's rebels and traitors aforesaid, have extended at their coming, if they may be of power, to do the most cruel murders, slaughters, and robberies, and disherisons, that ever were seen in any Christian realm. For the which and other inestimable dangers to be eschewed, and to the intent that the king's said rebels, traitors, and enemies may be utterly put from their said malicious and false purpose, and soon discomforted, if they enforce to land, the king our sovereign lord willeth, chargeth, and commandeth all and every of the natural and true subjects of this his realm to call the premises to their minds, and, like good and true Englishmen, to endower themselves with all their powers for the defence of them, their wives, children, and goods, and heriditaments ayenst the said malicious purposes and conspiracions which the said ancient enemies have made with the king's said rebels and traitors for the final destruction of this land as is aforesaid.

" And our said sovereign lord, as a well willed, diligent, and courageous prince will put his most royal person to all labour and pain necessary in this behalf for the resistance and subduing of his said enemies, rebels, and traitors, to the most comfort, weal, and surety of all his true and faithful liege men and subjects.

" And over this our said sovereign lord willeth and commandeth all his said subjects to be ready in their most defensible array to do his highness service of war, when they by open proclamation, or otherwise shall be commanded so to do, for resistence of the king's said rebels, traitors, and enemies. Witness myself at Westminster, the 22d day of June, in the second year of our reign."

N N.

LETTER FROM HENRY EARL OF RICHMOND, BEFORE HE WAS KING, TO HIS FRIENDS HERE IN ENGLAND FROM BEYOND THE SEAS.

(See p. 424.)

[Harl. MS. 787. fol. 2.]

"RIGHT trusty, worshipfull, and honourable good friends, and our allies, I greet you well. Being given to understand your good devoir and intent to advance me to the furtherance of my rightful claim due and lineal inheritance of the crown, and for the just depriving of that homicide and unnaturall tyrant which now unjustly bears dominion over you, I give you to understand that no christian heart can be more full of joy and gladness than the heart of me your poor exiled friend, who will, upon the instance of your sure advertise what powers ye will make ready and what captains and leaders you get to conduct, be prepared to pass over the sea with such forces as my friends here are preparing for me. And if I have such good speed and success as I wish, according to your desire, I shall ever be most forward to remember and wholly to requite this your great and most loving kindness in my just quarrel.

" Given under our signet.   " H. R.

" I pray you give credence to the messenger of that he shall impart to you."

O O.

LETTER FROM THE DUKE OF NORFOLK TO JOHN
PASTON, ESQ., WRITTEN A FEW DAYS PREVIOUS TO
THE BATTLE OF BOSWORTH.

(See p. 441.)

[Paston Letters, vol. ii. p. 334.]

" WELL beloved friend, I commend me to you, letting
you to understand that the king's enemies be a land, and
that the king would have set forth as upon Monday, but
only for our Lady day[1], but for certain he goeth forward
as upon Tuesday, for a servant of mine brought to me the
certainty.

" Wherefore I pray you that ye meet with me at Bury,
for by the grace of God I purpose to lie at Bury as upon
Tuesday night, and that ye bring with you such company
of tall men, as ye may goodly make at my cost and charge,
besides that ye have promised the king, and I pray you
ordain them jackets of my livery, and I shall content you
at your meeting with me,

" Your lover,

" J. NORFOLK.

" To my well-beloved friend
 John Paston be this bill
 delivered in haste."

---

[1] The Assumption of the Virgin.

P P.

"Part of their names shall you hear that came to Kynge Richard."

(See p. 461.)

[See Harl. MS. No. 542. fol. 34.]

The Duke of Norfolk
The Earl of Surrey, his heir
The Earl of Kent
The Earl of Shrewsbury
The Earl of Northumberland
The Earl of Westmoreland
Robbert Ryddysh
Sir Robert Owlrege
Sir John Huntyngdon
Sir John Wilynn
Sir John Smally
Sir Bryan of Stapleton
Sir William, his cousin
The Lord Bartley
The heirs of Bartley
The Lord Fryn, so gray,
The Lord Lovell, chamberlain of
England
The Lord Hugh, his cousin
The Lord Scroop of Upsall
The Lord Scroop of Bolton
The Lord Dacres, raised the
North Country
The Lord Ogle
The Lord Bower
The Lord Graystoke, he brought
a mighty many;
Sir John Blekynson
Sir Raffe Harbottle
Sir William Ward
Sir Archibald, with the good
Ridley;
Sir Nicholas Nabogay was not
away;
Sir Oliver of Chaston
Sir Henry de hynd Horsay

Sir John de Grey
Sir Thomas de Mingumbre
Sir Roger Standfort
Sir Robert Brackenbury
Sir Harry Landringham
Sir Richard Chorwelton
Sir Raffe Rolle
Sir Thomas Marcomfeld
Sir Roger Sandyll
Sir Christopher Ward
Sir William Beckford
Sir John Cowburne
Sir Robert Plumpton
Sir William Gascoye
Sir Marmaduke Constable
Sir William Conyers
Sir Martin of the Fee
Sir Robert Gilbard
Sir Richard Heaton
Sir John Lothes
Sir William Ratcliffe
Sir Thomas, his brother
Sir William, their brother
Sir Christopher de Mallyre
Sir John Norton
Sir Thomas de Malleveray
Sir Raffe Dacres of the North
Sir Christopher the Morys
Sir William Musgrave
Sir Alexander Haymor
Sir George Martynfield
Sir Thomas Broughton
Sir Christopher Awayne
Sir Richard Tempest out of the
Dale
Sir William, his cousin

Sir Raffe of Ashton   Sir John Adlyngton
Sir Roger Long in Arpenye   Sir Roger Heron
Sir John Pudsey   Sir James Harryngton
Sir Robert of Middleton   Sir Robert, his brother
Sir Thomas Strickland   Sir Thomas Pilkington.
Sir John Nevill of Bloodfallhye

" All these sware that King Richard should wear the crown."

[From an ancient contemporary manuscript preserved in the Harleian Library, supposed to have been written by a follower of Lord Stanley, and entitled, " Narrative borrowed of Henry Savyll."]

Q Q.

CONTRACT FOR THE MARRIAGE OF DAME KATHERINE PLANTAGENET, DAUGHTER OF KING RICHARD THE THIRD.

(See p. 487.)

[Harl. MS. 258. fol. 11ᵇ.]

" This endenture, made at London the last day of Februare, the first yere of the raigne of our souverain lord King Richard Third, betwene oure said souverain lord on the oon partie, and the right noble Lord William Erle of Huntingdon on the other partie, witnesseth, that the said erle promiseth and graunteth to our said souverain lord, that before the fast of St. Michael next commying by God's grace he shall take to wiff Dame Katerine Plantagenet, doughter to oure saide souverain lord, and before the day of their marriage to make or cause to be made to his behouff a sure, sufficient, and lawfull estate of certain his manoirs, lordships, lands, and tenements in England to the yerely valeue of ccᵗⁱ over all charges, to have and hold to him and the said Dame Katerine, and to their heires of their two bodies lawfully begotten remayndre to the right heires of the said erle, for the whiche oure saide souverain lord graunteth to the said erle and to the said Dame Katerine to make or cause to be made to theim before the said day of mariege a sure, suffisaunt, and lawfull estate of manoirs, lordships, lands, and tenements of the yerely value of a M. marc over all reprises to have to theim and to theire heires masles of their two bodyes lawfully begotten in maner and fourme folowinge, that is to wit, lordships, manoirs, lands, and tenements in possession at that day to the yerely value of vj^c. marc, and manoirs, lordships, lands, and tenements in reversion after the decesse of Thomas Stanley Knight, Lord Stanley, to the yerely value of iiij^c. marc; and in the mean season oure said souverain lord grauntith to the said erle and Dame Katerine an annuite of iiij^c. marc yerely to be had and perceyved to theim from Michelmasse last past during the lif of the said Lord Stanley of the revenues of the lordships of Newport, Brekenok, and Hay in Wales by the hands of the receyvours of theim for the time being, and overe this oure said souverain lord granteth to make and bere the cost and charge of the said mariage at the day of the solemnizing therof.

" In witnesse whereof oure said souverain lord to that oon partie of these endentures remaynyng with the said erle hath set his signet, and to that other partie remaynyng with oure said souverain lord the said erle hath set his seal the day and yere abovesaid."

THE END.

RICHARD III AS DUKE OF GLOUCESTER AND KING OF ENGLAND

by Caroline A. Halsted. In two volumes.

INDEX, compiled by Linda Miller.

Entries under characters (excepting the chroniclers and historians) are arranged in the chronological order of their lives rather than the order in which the events occur in the text. 1 = volume 1; 2 - volume 2.

Badges, family: meaning and description of: 1:346-7, 2:234; as represented on inn signs: 1:452-3

Baker, Sir Richard: 2:503

Ballad, rhyming the children of the Duke of York and Cicely Neville: 1:31, 47-8, 408-9

Banastre, see, Bannister

Bannister, Humphrey (or Ralph): gives Duke of Buckingham into custody at the collapse of the latter's rebellion: 2:269-71, 281-2

Barking, Church of Our Lady at: 2:356

Barnard Castle: description of: 1:342-6; boar badge at: 1:345-6, college founded at: 349, associations with Sir Robert Brackenbury: 1:353, 354, 355

Barnet, Battle of: 1:177-81, 453

Bath, Dr. Stillington, Bishop of, see, Stillington, Dr. Bishop of Bath

Bayley, John: 'History and Antiquities of the Tower of London': Sir Thomas More's prejudice against Richard III 1:106, 2:194; deaths of Montagu and Warwick: 1:181-2; sources for his work: 2:194; Sir James Tyrrel: 2:197 Royalty's residence at the Tower: 2:213; description of the buildings of the Tower: 2:193 Richard III's additions to the Tower: 2:356

Baynard's Castle: in possession of Duke of York: 1:58-9, 75, Edward IV becomes King there: 1:85-6; home of Cicely Duchess of York: 1:360, 2:60, 514; Richard III leaves for Bishopsgate: 2:66; nobility beg Richard III to assume the throne at: 2.100, 104; Chancellor receives seals at: 2:116; church at: 2:172; Richard III supposedly swears oath concerning the safety of the Princes in the Tower at: 2:193; Richard III's additions to: 2:356

Beauchamp, Sir John: 2:362

Bauchhamp, Lord: at Oxford with Richard III, 1483: 2:147, 526

Beauchamp, Richard, Earl of Warwick, see, Warwick, Richard Beauchamp, Earl of

Beaufort family: legitimacy and the succession: 1:32-3, 2:242, 252, 254, as maintainers of Lancastrian dynasty: 2:239

Beaufort, Cardinal: 2:149

Beaufort, Edmund, Duke of Somerset, see, Somerset, Edmund Beaufort, Duke of

Beaufort, Joan, wife of Ralph Neville, Earl of Westmorland, see, Westmorland, Joan, Countess of

Beaufort, John, Duke of Somerset, see, Somerset, John Beaufort, Duke of

Beaufort, Margaret, mother of Henry VII: early life: 2:252-3; at funeral of Duke of York at Fotheringhay: 1:432; at coronation of Richard III: 2:130, 131, 137, 239, 243, implicated in rebellion of Duke of Buckingham against Richard III: 2:239-40, 254; suggests to Elizabeth Woodville the marriage of Henry Tudor and Elizabeth of York: 2:247, 248, 304, estates forfeited following collapse of Buckingham's rebellion: 2:290-1; retirement from public life following accession of Henry VII: 2:514

other mentions: 1:12, 365

Beaumont, Sir John: 'Bosworth Field' (poem): 2:481, 496-7

Bedord, George, Duke of. son of Edward IV: 1:385

Bedford, Jacquetta Woodville, Duchess of: and marriage of Edward IV to Elizabeth Woodville: 1:140, 2:299, 542

Bele, Richard: 2:539

Belman, Robert: 2:539

Belts, Sir Quinton: 2:203

Benevolences: as levied by Edward IV, Richard III, and Henry VII: 1:370-2, 2:152

Bergavenny, Lord: 2:515

Berkhamstead, castle of: residence of Cicely, Duchess of York: 1:53, 2:514, part of the inheritance of the house of York: 1:420, 421

Bernall, Lord Richard, governor of Edward, son of Richard III: 1:368

Berwick, siege of, 1482: 1:372-5

Berkely, Sir William: 2:548

Beverley, William, Recotr of Middleham: foundation of Richard III's college at Middleham: 1:337-8, 341

Bisham Priory: 1:182

Bishopsgate Street, situation of Crosby Place: 2:102, 104

Blount, Sir James: transfers allegiance to Henry Tudor immediately before Battle of Bosworth; 2:417; at Bosworth: 2:446

Boar Badge: description and illustration of: 1:346-7; used by Richard III: 1:348, 2:442

Bodleian Library, foundation of: 1:446

Borthwick, Earl of: 1:373

Bosworth Field: description of the battlefield area: 2:445-6, 466, 495-6; see also, King Richard's Well

Bosworth, Battle of: 2:453-66; list of Richard III's supporters at the battle: 2:568-9

Bothe, Sir Philip: 2:367

Bourchier, Henry, Earl of Essex: see, Essex, Henry Bourchier, Earl of

Bourchier, Sir Thomas: transfers allegiance to Henry Tudor prior to battle of Bosworth: 2:443, 534

Bourchier, Thomas, Archbishop of Canterbury: associate of Richard III during Protectorate: 2:64; attempts to persuade Elizabeth Woodville to release Richard Duke of York from sanctuary: 2:86, 87; at coronation of Richard

III: 2:128, 131; character of: 2:132-3; pledge of safety given concerning safety of the Princes in the Tower: 2:87, 296

Bourchier, William, Earl of Essex, see, Essex, William Bourchier, Earl of

Brackenbury, John: in the service of Richard III: 2:196, 518

Brackenbury, Sir Robert: friendship with Richard III: 1:345; and Barnard Castle: 1:353-5; grants from Richard III 2:144, 284-5, 532-3; More's account of his connection with the Princes in the Tower: 2:190-1, 192, More's account examined 2:193-7, 200, 201, 214, 217; and Battle of Bosworth: 2:434, 443, 451, 457, 497

Brackenbury, Thomas: in the service of Richard III: 2:72, 196

Bramburgh, John: 2:293

Brandon, Sir William: standard-bearer to Henry Tudor at Battle of Bosworth: 2:458, 479

Brandone, William: 2:216

Bray, Reginald: his part in Buckingham's rebellion: 2:247; waits for Henry Tudor's invasion: 2:428; discovers the crown after Battle of Bosworth: 2:466

Brecknock castle, and Buckingham's rebellion against Richard III: 2:238, 245, 248, 266, 268, 547, 548

Bretagne: 1:309

Bridenorth: 2:239

Bridget, Princess, daughter of Edward IV: birth: 1:385; in sanctuary with Elizabeth Woodville: 2:550

Bristol: 2:517

British Museum library, foundation of: 1:445-7

Brittany, Henry Tudor takes refuge at, in early life: 2:239-40, 248, 253; he sails from during Buckingham's rebellion: 2:274; other rebels escape to: 2:277, 316, 332, 548; Henry Tudor en route to France: 2:334; Charles VIII discourages him from returning to: 2:335

Brittany, Francis, Duke of: Henry Tudor a state prisoner of: 2:253; Henry's escape and return: 2:255-6; treaty with Richard III: 2:256-7, 259, promise extracted from to recapture Henry Tudor: 2:333-4; helps Henry Tudor following his flight from Brittany: 2:335-6, 426, 427, 563; further treaty with Richard III, 1484: 2:361

Brown, Sir George: implicated in Buckingham's rebellion against Richard III: 2:534, 548

Buck, Sir George: 'Life of Richard III': first defender of Richard III and his sources authority: 1:94-5, 187, 219-20, 235; appearance of Richard III: 1:97; his character: 1:130, 131, 2:358, death of Edward of Lancaster: 1:187, 276; character of Anne Neville: 1:231, Richard III's wardenship of the west marches: 2:4; Richard III as Lord Protector: 2:7, 52; gifts from Louis XI to English nobles: 2:57; Edward IV's marriage to Eleanor Butler: 2:90, 91, 104; on Dr. Shaw's sermon: 2:97-8, 101; Richard III becomes King: 2:110; Richard III and Gloucester: 2:150-1, fate of the Princes in the Tower: 2:201-2, 212-3, 225, 228; on Perkin Warbeck: 2:203, 204 Elizabeth Woodville's first husband: 301; Richard III's ecclesiastical foundations: 2:356; Scottish embassy to Richard III: 2:357-8; Anne De La Pole: 2:360; Anne Neville's grief at the death of her son: 2:375-6; on Richard III's rumoured marriage with Elizabeth of York: 2:378-9, Richard III's affection for Anne Neville: 2:394, 397; Elizabeth of York sent to Sherriff Hutton, 1485: 2:406; Richard III's death at Bosworth: 2:465; his tomb at Leicester: 2:475

Buckby, Manor of: 2:314

Buckingham, Anne, Duchess of, sister of Cicely, Duchess of York: given custody of the latter, 1459: 1:73-4, 75; becomes a nun, 1480: 2:60

Buckingham, Katherine, Duchess of (wife of Henry Stafford): marriage to Duke of Buckingham: 2:28, 137, 183; Richard III grants an annuity to following Buckingham's rebellion: 2:283; her son escapes after the rebellion: 2:535, 536

Buckingham, Henry Stafford, Duke of:
Stafford badge: 2:234; appointed Lord High Steward: 1:324; children of: 2:268, supports Richard III against Woodvilles following death of Edward IV: 2:12, 16, 71, 183; successfully attempts to secure Edward V: 2:18-19, 22-3, 26, 28, 35, 36 suggests Edward V be lodged at the Tower: 38: appointments and grants during Protectorate of Richard III: 2:45-6, 64: Hastings plots against, and the aftermath of this: 2:73-4, 77, 83, 116, 121; encourages Richard III's claim to the throne: 2:101-2, 104; at Richard's coronation: 2:129, 131, 137: grants from Richard III following coronation: 2:143-4, 215, 235-6, 244-5: rebellion against Richard III, and Buckingham's possible connection with the Princes in the Tower: 1:393, 2:179-80, 181-3, 184, 189-90, 233-50, 254, 256, 257-68; attainder (text): 2:547-8; capture and death: 2:269-75, 277-8, 286; preservation of his heir following Buckingham's execution: 2:535-8 character: 2:183-4, 235
other mentions: 1:451, 2:11, 55, 63, 286, 288, 322, 342, 421, 435, 437. 457, 472, 498

Burford, Baron of: 1:51

Burgundy: Duke of Clarence and Richard III escape to, 1461: 1:82, 83; return to England from: 87; other mentions: 1:61, 309, 378

Burgundy, Charles, Duke of: marriage to Margaret, sister of Richard III: 1:142,

Tewkesbury: 1:222, 246-8; dispute over Richard III's attempts to marry her: 1:247-54, 255, 259-60, 275, 309; and Countess of Warwick's release from sanctuary: 1:305-6; invasion of France 1475 and subsequent settlement: 1:310, 313; death of his wife: 1:318, 2:376-7; proposal to marry Mary of Burgundy: 1:319-20, 334; imprisonment, attainder, and death: 1:320-2, 326, 328-9, 337, 339-40, 448-9, 2:61, 62, 103, 324, 543: other mentions: 1:225, 308, 338, 342, 359, 363, 2:13

Clarence, Isabel Neville, Duchess of: marriage to Duke of Clarence: 1:142-3, 145-8, 233-4, 236-8, 244-5, 254-5, 257, 259; given custody of Anne Neville after battle of Tewkesbury: 1:247; inheritance from Earl of Warwick: 1:444 death: 1:318, 319, 334, 366, 2:376-7
   other mentions: 1:231, 232, 233, 248, 365

Clarence, Lionel, Duke of: created Duke of Clarence: 1:407, 423; death: 1:408; descendants: 1:18, 19 (table)

Clerenceux King-at-arms: 1:423

Clarendon, Sir Richard: 2:497

Clarke, Mrs. proprietress of 'Blue Boar' inn at Leicester: and story of King Richard's bed': 2:492, 494

Cleck, John: 1:456

Cleret, Peter, and Treaty of Picquigny: 1:447-8

Clifford family: attainder: 1:250, 434

Clifford, Lord Henry (Shepherd Lord): escape following Battle of Wakefield and subsequent career: 1:39, 413-5, 2:269

Clifford, Lord John, father of the above: after Battle of Wakefield: 1:35, 38, 39, 283, 413

Clifford, Lady, Baroness Vesci: and her son the 'Shepherd Lord': 1:413-4

Clifford, Robert, pardon granted to (as recorded in Harleian MSS 433): 2:216; death: 2:366

Clifton, Sir Gervase: devotion to Richard III: 2:421-2; at Battle of Bosworth 2:457, 497

Clofer, Manor of: 2:337

Cobham, Lord: 2:515

Cold Harbour: residence of College of Arms: 2:309-10; history of: 2:551, 552

Colet, Henry: 2:515

Collingham, John: 2:293

Colyngbourne, William: execution: 2:337-9, 340

Commines, Philippe de: his personal observation of Edward IV: 1:92-3, 357, 436; on Edward's policy in battle: 1:128; Louis XI's gifts to English nobility: 2:57; Richard III's celebration of Christmas, 1483: 2:285, French aid to Henry Tudor: 2:426

Coningsburgh: 1:423

Coningsburgh, Richard, see, Cambridge, Richard, Earl of

Conway, Hugh: 2:248

Conyers, Sir William: 2:497

Corbet: 2:203

Corfe Castle: Richard III granted lordship of: 1:88, 432

Cornwall, Sir Edward: 1:51

Coronations, Plantagenet: described: 2:162-3

Cotton, Sir Robert: his collection of MSS described: 1:287, 446

Courtenay family: and Buckingham's rebellion: 2:267, 278

Courtenay, Sir Edward: and Buckingham's rebellion: 2:264; captured: 2:277; outlawed: 2:278

Courtenay, Lord: 2:209

Courtenay, Peregrine: 'Commentaries on Shakespeare's historical plays': deaths of Edward of Lancaster and Henry VI: 1:195, 216; Shakespeare's innacuracy as a historian: 1:270, 271, 294; Elizabeth I's reaction to Shakespeare's 'Richard III': 1:293

Courtenay, Piers, Bishop of Exeter: at coronation of Richard III: 2:131; and Buckingham's rebellion: 2:264, 563; his flight to Brittany: 2:277, 278; pardoned by Richard III: 2:291

Courtenay, William, Earl of Devon, see, Devon, William Courtenay, Earl of

Coventry: 1:435

Coverham: Richard III's gifts towards repair of church at: 1:301, 356

Covesgrave, Manor of: 2:314

Crofte, Richard, tutor of Edward IV: Edward IV's attachment to: 1:54-5, 56; his devotion to the house of York: 1:196

Crosby, Sir John: 1:362

Crosby, Place: description of: 1:362-3; residence of Richard III immediately prior to his accession: 2:67, 102, 104

'Crown Hill', see, Bosworth Field

Croyland Chronicle: contemporary with Richard III: 1:5, 206, 289, 2:24-5; Battle of Wakefield: 1:40; appearance of Richard III: 1:97; Warwick's break with Edward IV: 1:142; Battle of Tewkesbury: 1:192; death and funeral of Henry VI: 1:209-10, 274; Clarence conceals Anne Neville: 1:248-249; her marriage to Richard III 1:253-5; death of Duke of Clarence: 1:321, 322, 330; recounts the supposed fate of the Princes in the Tower: 1:392, 2:178-9, 180, 182, 184, 259, Edward IV as Warwick's prisoner: 1:435; Richard III

created Earl of Salisbury: 1:434; proposed marriage to daughter of Duke of Buckingham: 2:77; household at Middleham following accession of Richard III: 2:144-5, 146, 157-8; absence from coronation of Richard III: 2:138, 157; created Lieutenant of Ireland: 2:142; proposed marriage to daughter of Ferdinand and Isabella of Spain: 2:154; invested at York as Prince of Wales and Parliament creates heir-apparent: 2:157-8, 160-2, 289, 546; nobility swear oath of allegiance to: 2:305-6; proposed marriage to Elizabeth of York: 2:385-6; death: 2:318-20, 322, 349, 557

other mentions: 1:121, 2:282, 486

Edward VI: 2:552

Elizabeth, sister of Richard III, see, Suffolk, Elizabeth, Duchess of

Elizabeth of York, Princess, daughter of Edward IV: birth: 1:139-40, 385, 442, 2:382 at marriage of Richard Duke of York: 1:450; Edward IV offers her in marriage to Henry Tudor: 2:255, proposed marriage to Edward, son of Richard III: 2:385-6; Henry Tudor's vow to marry: 2:241, 247-8, 256, 292, 302-3; proposed heiress to throne: 2:258-9; at the court of Richard III, and rumour of proposed marriage to him following the death of Anne Neville: 2:379-92, 400-6, 550, 556-8; sent to Sherriff Hutton castle prior to Battle of Bosworth 2:406-7, death at Tower of London, 1502: 2:39

other mentions: 2:360

Elizabeth I, Queen: her reaction to Shakespeare's 'Richard III': 1:293; survey of the Tower taken by her orders: 2:221; other mentions: 2:229, 552

Elmsthorpe: 2:443

Elrington, Sir John: treasurer to Edward IV: 1:373; and war with Scotland, 1482 1:456, 457, preparations for coronation of Edward V: 2:68, 299

Eltham: 1:78

Ely, John Morton, Bishop of, see, Morton, John Bishop of Ely

Enachden, Bishop of: receives allegiance of Earl of Desmond to Richard III: 1:71, 2:171; delivers clothing to the Earl: 2:529-30

Erber, the (King's palace): description and history: 1:361-2; improvements undertaken by Richard III: 2:356

Essex, Ann Plantagenet, Countess of: 2:132

Essex, Henry Bourchier, Earl of: marriage to Isabel, sister of Duke of York: 1:24, 2:132

Exeter: Richard III at, following collapse of Buckingham's rebellion: 2:275, 278, 280

Exeter, Ann, Duchess of, sister of Richard III: birth, and first husband: 1:45, 60, 409, 2:551; character: 1:60, 64; devotion to house of York: 1:78; mediates in disputes between Duke of Clarence and Edward IV: 1:171-2; second marriage to Sir Thomas St. Leger: 2:277, 538; death: 1:367

Exeter, Piers Courtenay, Bishop of, see, Courtenay, Piers, Bishop of Exeter

Exeter, Henry Holland, Duke of: allegiance to Henry VI: 1:60, 78; marriage: 1:82, 164, 2:551; and Cold Harbour: 2:551, attainder: 2:277, 538

Everingham, Sir Thomas: 2:321

Fabyan, Robert: 'New Chronicles of England and France':
death of Edward of Lancaster: 1:193-4; death of Henry VI: 1:216-7; death of Duke of Clarence: 1:323; confinement of the Princes in the Tower: 1:390 Coronation of Henry VI: 2:68; Hastings conspiracy: 2:80, 82-3; Elizabeth Woodville in sanctuary: 2:87; on Dr. Shaw's sermon, 1483: 2:95-6, 99-100, 101-2; date of accession of Richard III: 2:108-9; citizens of York's support for Richard III: 2:117-8, 141; on Richard's accession: 2:125; describes public opinion towards Richard III: 2:179; on the Princes in the Tower: 2:185, 211; on Perkin Warbeck: 2:204; Buckingham's rebellion: 2:269, 276; on Richard's return from London following collapse of rebellion: 2:362 execution of Sir Robert Clifford: 2:366; Richard III borrows money from citizens of London: 2:373; lack of comment on rumour of marriage between Richard III and Elizabeth of York: 2:387; Battle of Bosworth: 2:456; on crimes attributed to Richard III: 2:503

Fakenham, Abbey of: 2:297

Falconbridge, Thomas, Bastard of: attack on London following Battle of Tewkesbury: 1:198-201; attempt to release Henry VI from the Tower: 1:203-4 treaty with Edward IV: 1:225

Ferrars, Walter Devereux, Lord: and Buckingham's rebellion against Richard III: 2:266; at Battle of Bosworth: 2:454, 457

Ferrier, Sergeant: 2:209

Fisher, John, Bishop of Rochester: at coronation of Richard III: 2:128; beheaded by Henry VIII: 2:295-6

Fitzalan, Thomas, Earl of Arundel, see, Arundel, Thomas Fitzalan, Earl of

Fitzwater, Lord: 2:203

Flanders: 2:369, see also, Burgundy

Fleetwood Chronicle, see, History of the Arrival of Edward IV in England

Forest, Miles: and ballad of 'Babes in the Wood': 1:391, 392, More's account of as one of the supposed murderers of the Princes in the Tower: 2:181, 200, servant of Cecily, Duchess of York, and death: 2:205, 215-6

Fortescue, Sir John: 2:417

Fotheringhay: Richard III born at: 1:42, 46, 48; other children of Duke of York born at: 1:45, 46; college founded at, following funeral of Duke of

Katherine, Princess, daughter of Edward IV: betrothal to Infanta of Spain: 1:357; marriage to Earl of Devon: 1:385; in sanctuary with Elizabeth Woodville: 2:550

Katherine, illegitimate daughter of Richard III, see, Plantagenet, Katherine

Kempe, Dr., Bishop of London: Edward V stays with on entry into London, 1483: 2:37; Jane Shore delivered to: 2:94

Kendall, John, secretary to Richard III: grants from Richard II: 2:144, 215; letter to citizens of York prior to York coronation of Richard III: 2:156, 157, 158, 159, 165-6, appointed Keeper of the Prince's Wardrobe in London: 2:285

Kenilworth: 2:418

Kent, Earl of: at coronation of Richard III: 2:128, 137

Kent, Joan of: 1:445

Kerver, Thomas: 2:526

Keyley, James: 2:474

Kildare, Earl of: appointed Deputy Leiutenant of Ireland: 2:142, 170

King Richard's Diary, see, Harleian MSS 433

King Richard's Well, Bosworth Field: traditionally used by Richard III during the Battle of Bosworth: 2:458; inscription places, 1813: 2:495-6

King's Mews, Charing Cross: 2:362

King's Wardroke, London: 2:362

Kinnardsley: heir of Duke of Buckingham hidden here following collapse of Buckingham's rebellion: 2:535-7

Knighthood, in the fifteenth century: 1:101, 109-112, 426-7

Knights Banneret: 2:198

Knyvet, William: and Buckingham's rebellion: 2:534; ensures flight and safety of Buckingham's heir following rebellion: 2:535-7; other mentions: 2:547

Kydwelly, Morgan: attorney to Richard III: 2:214; grants from Richard III; 2:275; intelligence activities on behalf of Henry Tudor: 2:428-9, 431-2

Lacon: 2 269

Lamb, Charles: essay on Richard III. 2:484-5

Lancaster, House of: emblem (red rose): 1:22, 453

Lancaster, Earls of: Earldom of Leicester and Pontefract castle: 1:265-6

Lancaster, Edmund, Earl of, son of Henry III: comparison with Richard III: 1:102-3

Landois, Pierre, Treasurer to Francis, Duke of Brittany: negotiations with Richard III over Henry Tudor: 2:333-5, 336

Langley, Edmund, Duke of York, see, York, Edmund Langley, Duke of

Langton, Thomas, Bishop of St. David's: at Oxford with Richard III, 1483: 2:147, 526; does homage to Pope for Richard III; 2:297

Latimer, Lady Elizabeth: 1:364

Latimer, Lord George: 1:425

Latimer, Lord John: 1:24

Leicester: Richard III on Progress at, 1483: 2:155, 156; York troops requested to meet him at, 1483: 2:263; Richard III at, prior to Buckingham's rebellion 2:264; offers reward for capture of the rebels at: 2:265, 534; leaves for Coventry: 2:266; Richard III at immediately before Battle of Bosworth: 2:441; stays at 'Blue Boar' Inn: 2:442-3; Richard's body taken to Leicester following his death in the battle: 2:469; Catesby and Earl of Surrey executed at 2:472; tomb of Richard III at: 2:473-9

Leicester, 'Blue Boar Inn': and supposed bed of Richard III: 2:442-3, 490-4

Leicester, St. Mary's Church: scene of burial of Richard III: 2:473-6

Leicester, Earldom of: 1.265-6

Leland, John: 'Collecteana': death of Henry VI: 1:211; compiliation of 'Collecteana and Itinerary': 1:231

Lewis, Dr: conveys to Elizabeth Woodville Henry Tudor's offer to marry Elizabeth of York: 2 247, 248, 302

Lichfield: Henry Tudor at, prior to Battle of Bosworth: 2:439, 440, 441, 443

Lincoln: Richard III at, following news of Buckingham's rebellion: 2:260, 261, 262; proclamation issued from: 2:263

Lincoln, John De La Pole, Earl of: descent: 1:367; at coronation of Richard III 2:128 grants from Richard III: 2:144, 285; as Lord of the North: 2:145, 524, 525, on Progress with Richard III, 1483: 2:147, 526; appointed Lieutenant of Ireland: 2:170; Richard III nominates as his heir: 2:328-9, 359, 557, and Battle of Bosworth: 2:447, 472; death at Battle of Stoke: 2:108, 246

Lincoln, John Russell, Bishop of, see, Russell, John, Bishop of Lincoln

Lisle, Edward Grey, Lord: at funeral of Edward IV: 2:8; flight following Hastings conspiracy: 2:85; transfers allegiance to Richard III: 2:116; at coronation of Richard III: 2:129

Lisle, Lord (of Scotland): 2:358

Lock, William: 2:352

London, city and corporation of: in 1472: 1:401 relations with Edward IV: 2:350, victory celebrations following 1483 war with Scotland: 1:377-8; attitude to accession of Richard III, and relations with him: 2:92-3, 100, 102, 117-8, 123, 135, 361-2, 404; coronation preparations, 1483: 2:521-2; during the absence of Richard III following his coronation: 2:350-2, encouraged to

325; treachery of Louis XI: 1:379; Duchess of York's opposition to the marriage of Edward IV and Elizabeth Woodville: 2:13; Richard III assumes Protectorate and Edward V's reaction: 2:16, 20, 21, 23, 30, 32-3, 34, 42, 43, 54, 62, 66-7, 69, 71; Hastings conspiracy: 2:76, 77, 78, 79, 83, 482; Richard Duke of York removed from sanctuary to Tower of London: 2:84, 87, 133; Dr. Shaw and Dr. Penker: 2:94, 344; Richard III assumes the throne: 2:100; administers justice: 2:119 character of Earl of Warwick: 2:154; Archbishop of York's reaction to deposition of Edward V: 2:161; character of John Morton: 2:182-3; first printing of 'History of King Richard III: 2:200; character of Duke of Buckingham: 2:235, 243; Buckingham's rebellion: 2:236; Richard's demeanour before Battle of Bosworth: 2:450

Morgan, David Glyn: 2:537
Morley, Lord: 2:524
Mortimer, Anne, Countess of Cambridge, see, Cambridge, Anne Mortimer, Countess of
Mortimer, Edmund, Earl of March, see, March, Edmund Mortimer, Earl of
Mortimer, Edward, Earl of March, see, March, Edward Mortimer, Earl of
Mortimer, Sir Hugh: 1:51
Mortimer, Lady: governess to the children of the Duke of York: 1:51
Mortimer, Roger, Earl of March, see, March, Roger Mortimer, Earl of
Mortimer's Cross, Battle of: 1:284, 347

Morton, John, Bishop of Ely: gifts from Louis XI: 2:57; member of the Council during the Protectorate of Richard III: 2:64; Richard III imprisons following Hastings conspiracy, releases and commits to custody of Duke of Buckingham: 2:80, 83-4, 121; and rebellion of Duke of Buckingham against Richard III: 2 182-3, 238, 245-9, 256, 321, 334, 417, 534; attainted, and possessions distributed by Richard III: 2:281, 291, 547; and Henry Tudor's attempts to gain the throne: 2:257; attitude towards Richard III, and his version of the fate of the Princes in the Tower: 1:107, 108-9, 2:187-90, 237-8; and Sir Thomas More 1:408, 427-9, 2:187

Mountfort, Sir Simon: 2:203
Mountjoy, Walter Blount, Lord: 1:72; governor of Guisnes: 2:370; instructions from Richard III regarding garrison's oath: 2:520-1
Mowbray, Anne, Duchess of Norfolk, see, Norfolk, Anne Mowbray, Duchess of
Mowbray, John, Duke of Norfolk, see, Norfolk, John Mowbray, Duke of
Multon, Margaret: 2:361
Mytton, Sir Thomas: captures Duke of Buckingham following collapse of rebellion: 2:271, 438; grants from Richard III following this: 2:281
Nandike, Thomas: 2:547
Neffield, John: appointed Captain of the Guard over Westminster Abbey, 1483: 2:202; attendant upon Elizabeth Woodville: 2:550
Nesfield, John: 2:321
Neville family: relations with Edward IV: 1:140, 2:498; inheritance of Sherriff Hutton: 2:330, 331; grants from Richard III: 2:331
Neville, Anne wife of Richard III:
Early life at Middleham, and early relationship with Richard III: 1:117-8, 230-4, 236, 263-4 betrothal to Edward of Lancaster: 1:160, 230, 239-45, 263-4, 442-3; Clarence obtains custody of following Battle of Tewkesbury: 1:246-254, 274-5; marriage to Richard III and inheritance of Earl of Warwick: 1:256-7, 433, 444; retires to Middleham after marriage, and birth of her son: 1:263-7, 299-300; ill health: 1:366 children of: 1:366-7, 2:146; in London during Protectorate: 2:69; her coronation: 2:122, 127-32, 134-8; joins Richard III on Progress at Warwick, 1483: 2:153, 155, 324; second coronation at York: 2 158, 160-1, 165; founds Margaret College, Cambridge: 2:314, 553-4; death of Edward Prince of Wales: 2:318, 322, 375-6; relationship with Edward Earl of Warwick: 2:323-4; relationship with Elizabeth of York: 2:305, 384-7; last illness and death: 2:376-9, 383, 392-7, 556-7
as represented in Shakespeare's 'Richard III': 1:273-7, 279, 282, 2:483 other mentions 1:331, 364, 452, 2:282
Neville, Cicely, see, York, Cicely, Duchess of
Neville, Elinor, sister of the above: 2:63
Neville, George, Archbishop of York: as Archbishop of York: 1:147; installation as Archbishop: 1:231-2, 233; helps to take Edward IV prisoner, 1469: 1:435
Neville, George, Baron Abergavenny, see, Abergavenny, George Neville, Baron
Neville, Henry: 2:63
Neville, Isabel, Duchess of Clarence, see, Clarence, Isabel Neville, Duchess of
Neville, John, Marquis of Montagu, later Earl of Northumberland, see, Montagu, John Neville, Marquis of
Neville, Lord: letter from Richard III for support (June 1483): 2:74, grants from Richard III: 2:144, 215
Neville, Richard, Earl of Salisbury, see, Salisbury, Richard Neville, Earl of
Neville, Richard, Earl of Warwick, see, Warwick, Richard Neville, Earl of
Newbury: 2:548
Newton, Manor of: 2:314
Newton, John, Mayor of York: letter from Richard III: 2:519
Norfolk, Anne Mowbray, Duchess of: marriage to Richard Duke of York: 1:332-4, 449-451; death: 2:109

Worcester, Dr. Alcock, Bishop of, see, Alcock, Dr., Bishop of Worcester
Worcester, William of: on Earl of Rutland: 1:38; contemporary chronicler: 1:48
Wren, Christopher: 2:478
Wyatt, Sir Thomas: 1554 rebellion: 1:4
Wydville, see, Woodville
Wyndham, Sir William: 2:109
Wrycester, William of, see, Worcester, William of
York, City of: supports Richard III against Woodvilles: 2:16-18, 88, 118; re-
    lations with Richard III: 2:72-3, 280, 519; at accession of Richard III: 2:72-3,
    280; scene of Richard III's second coronation: 2:156, 158-67, 175, 179,
    249; supports Richard against Duke of Buckingham: 2:263, 518; Richard III
    based at, 1484: 2:322, 326, 327, 336; letter from Richard III concerning
    rumour of marriage to Elizabeth of York: 2:406, appeals from Richard for
    support in 1485 invasion: 2:419, 436-7
    other mentions: 1:292, 435, 2:357
York, House of: its badge (white rose): 1:22, 453, description of the badges of
    its individual members: 1:404-5; inheritance of: 1:420-4
York, Palace of: used by the Kings of England: 2:161; Richard III makes extensions
    to: 2:361
York, George Neville, Archbishop of, see, Neville, George, Archbishop of York
York, Thomas Rotherham, Archbishop of, see, Rotheram, Thomas, Archbishop
    of York
York, Cicely, Duchess of:
    early life and character: 1:42-4, 60-4, 152-5, 409; brothers and sisters listed:
    1:424-5; children of: 1:45-8, 50; listed in ballad: 1:408-9; household routine
    described: 1:52-8, 417-9; relations with her children: 1:68-9, 156-7; imprison-
    ment (1459) and attainder: 1:71, 72-4 return to London, and Battle of
    Wakefield: 1:75, 76, 78, 80, 82, 83-5; retires to Berkhampsted: 1:86-7, 2:513-
    4; annuities granted by Edward IV: 1:87-8; marriage of Edward IV to Elizabeth
    Woodville, and knowledge of its invalidity: 1:155-6, 2:13, 91; and rebellion
    of 1469 and Woodville influence over Edward IV: 2:12-13, 61-2; her life
    during the reign of Edward IV, and the death of the Duke of Clarence: 1:329-30,
    2:60-2, will of Edward IV: 2:60-1; and Protectorate of Richard III: 2:12-14,
    62-3; character impugned in sermon urging Richard III to assume the throne:
    2:96, 98-9, 103-4, 105; relationship with, and letter from Richard III: 2:239-
    40 death and burial: 1:421, 2:99, 486
    other mentions: 1:40, 112, 135, 140, 234, 283, 356, 360, 450, 2:11, 100
York, Edmund Langley, Duke of: marriage: 1:20; death of heir: 1:22; and
    Fotheringhay: 1:46, 421
York, Edward, second Duke of (son of Lionel of Clarence): succeeds as Duke of
    York, and death at Battle of Agincourt: 1:22, 125; Richard, son of the Earl
    of Cambridge his heir: 1:23; founds Fotheringhay collegiate church: 1:421
York, Richard, Duke of:
    Badges: 1:404-5; inheritance: 1:408, 420-4; early life and character: 1:20-28,
    61, 415-6; marriage to Cicely Neville: 1:44-5, 2:82; as heir to the throne:
    1:34, 67, 68; flight to Ireland, and attainder: 1:70-71, 2:171 return to
    London and created Prince of Wales: 1:78-80, 2:106; Battle of Wakefield,
    and death: 1:36-38, 80-81, 116, 410-412; funeral at Fotheringhay: 1:125-6,
    421, 430-2
    other mentions: 1:338, 356, 2:103, 254
York, Richard, Duke of, son of Edward IV:
    Birth: 1:385; marriage to Anne Mowbray: 1:332-4, 358, 449-51, 2:109;
    temperament at accession of Edward V: 2:33, moved to Tower of London to
    join Edward V after deposition: 2:84-5; absence from coronation of Richard
    III: 2:138
    see also, Princes in the Tower.

SUBSCRIBERS TO THE 1977 EDITION

1. David L. Colbourne, 4 Upperwood Road, Darfield, Barnsley, South Yorkshire
2. Mrs. M. Walker, 21 Carrhill Road, Mossley, Ashton-under-Lyne, Lancashire
3. Miss Valerie L. Young, 12 Norwood Avenue, Heaton, Newcastle-upon-tyne
4. Miss L. Miller, 44 Lansdowne Terrace, North Shields, Tyne & Wear
5. Mrs. Laura Barker, 19 Deal Court, White Acre, London
6. Margaret McBride, 46 Brookland Street, Lisburn Road, Belfast
7. Mrs. Glynis Edwina Berridge, 19 Underwood Crescent, Sapcote, Leicester
8. Mr. W. Mendelsson, 57 Leeside Crescent, London
9. Miss Lynn Roberts, 4 Freda Close, Broadstairs, Kent
10. Mr. H. Savery, 1 Beechwood Court, Carshalton, Surrey
11. Mr. D. A. Page, 75 Kilbury Drive, Worcester
12. Mrs. V.D. Crapnell, 3 Penpol Vean, Hayle, Cornwall
13. Mrs. Janis Castle, 14 Hawthorn Crescent, Marton in Cleveland, Middlesbrough
14. Miss Louise M. Ward, M.T. Section, R.A.F. Brampton, Huntingdon, Cambridgeshire
15. Kenneth A. Hillier, Conaree, Elcot Lane, Marlborough, Wiltshire
16. Miss Christine Keen, 16 Moss Bank Road, Moss Bank, St. Helens, Merseyside
17. Mrs. Jean Dyson, 43 Cleehill Drive, Preston Grange, North Shields, Tyne & Wear
18. Sheila Hadden, 22 Campdale Road, Tufnell Park, London
19. Rosemary Jane Fish, 5 Wiseholme Road, Skellingthorpe, Lincoln
20. Miss Christine Leonard, 181 Valley Drive, Gravesend, Kent
21. Mrs. Joan Macaulay, The Grove, Weston-under-Penyard, Ross-on-Wye, Herefordshire
22. J. Bullock, 4 Sandon Court, Goodmayes Lane, Ilford, Essex
23. Dorothy Ramsden, 1 Canford Crescent, Canford Cliffs, Poole, Dorset
24. Peter Gargett, 10 Linsdale Gardens, Arnold Lane, Gedling, Nottingham
25. Miss Carol Smith, 25 Connaught Avenue, East Sheen, London
26. Francis Long, 160 Old Shoreham Road, Hove, Sussex
27. Peter James Corbett, 61 Peveril Crescent, Long Eaton, Nottinghamshire
28. Niki B. Theodorou, 62 Nevern Square, London
29. Mrs. Sybil S. Ashe, 229 South Street, Medfield, Massachusetts, U.S.A.
30. Mrs. Fay Hughes, Clandara, Churchdown, Gloucestershire
31. Mrs. Valerie Ray, 24 Woodvale Avenue, South Norwood, London
32. Juanita Louise, Knapp, 38A Church Trees, Swinegate, Grantham, Lincolnshire
33. Andrew P. Kearley, 149 Fairlands Avenue, Thornton Heath, Surrey
34. Claire A. Greenbury, 50 Elsworthy Road, London
35. P. Comley, 21H Kingwood Road, Fulham, London
36. Mr. R.G. Hayton, 21 Spring Gardens, Anlaby Common, Hull, East Yorkshire
37. Mrs. I.P. Watts, Cobblers, 34 High Street, Navenby, Lincoln
38. K. J. Holden, 40 St. Mary's Road, Benfleet, Essex
39. Mr. W.G. Bird, 134 Scotland Green Road, Ponders End, Enfield, Middlesex

40 Miss Sara Downing, 12 Shelton Road, Merton Park, London
41 John F. Kendrick, 100 Alfall Road, Coventry
42 Richard A.C. Barnard, 41 Manorway, Bush Hill Park, Enfield
43 Mrs. P. Homfray, Hawthorne Cottage, Great Doward, Whitchurch, Herefordshire
44 Miss Christine Dalton, 55 High Street, Clayhanger, Brownhills, West Midlands
45 Mrs. P. Benstead, 37 Bosworth Avenue, Sunnyhill, Derby
46 Mrs. A.L. Chamberlain, Beneah, Littleworth Lane, Belton, Oakham, Leicestershire
47 James T. Herbert, 24 Lyndon Mead, Sandridge, St. Albans
48 Audrey Williamson, 29 Turner House, Erasmus Street, London
49 Ms. C.A. James, 249 Henwick Road, Worcester
50 Mr. Edward Coles, 101 St. James Crescent, Brixton, London
51 Dr. P. Stone, Queen Mary's Hospital, Roehampton, London
52 Ralph Taylor, 20 High Park Crescent, Bradford, Yorkshire
53 Mr. David Farmer, 26 Lichfield Road, Liverpool
54 R.C. Winnard, 55 Lon-y-Celyn, Whitchurch, Cardiff
55 J.C.P. Trevett, 17 Well Lane, Enmore Green, Shaftesbury, Dorset
56 Miss D.K. Strong, 59 Worton Way, Isleworth, Middlesex
57 Michael W. Powell, Sherwood, Blackmoor Road, Abbots Leigh, Bristol
58 P.A. Bates, 63 Omar Road, Copeswood, Coventry
59 C.J.S. Guthrie, 18 North Vale Road, Timperley, Altrincham, Cheshire
60 Mr. & Mrs. P.S. Colclough, Cherry Trees, 40 Andrew Lane, High Lane, Cheshire
61 Mr. J.F.E. Holmes, 33 Grange Hill, Edgware, Middlesex
62 Ms. Eirene Webb, 132 Greenway, Hayes, Middlesex
63 David Spurr, Blanc Sanglier, 34 Haldane Crescent, Pinders Heath, Wakefield
64 Mrs. Molly Jessop, Mill House, Nailstone Road, Carlton, Nr. Nuneaton
65 Mrs. Lesley A. Sands, 4 Sudbrooke Road, Scothern, Lincoln
66 D. Seaton-Reid, Villa Carita, Los Chaparros 9, El Castillo, Fuengirola, Spain
67 Kaj Engholm, 28 Skovbrynet, 2800 KGS, Lyngby, Denmark
68 Mr. L. Robottom, 124 Lewisham Road, Smethwick, Warley, West Midlands
69 Miss D. Gooderson, 2 Masons Place, Newport, Shropshire
70 Mrs. Anne Macdonald, 13 Laverockbank Grove, Edinburgh
71 Mr. H. Ruddick-Bracken, 10 Ancroft Avenue, North Shields, Tyne & Wear
72 Vivienne Chandler
73 W.F. Butler, 1 London Road, Sleaford, Lincolnshire
74 Mr. A.V. Denton, 13 Wendron Close, Bromsgrove, Worcestershire
75 Richard III Society, Barton Library, London
76 Peter W. Hammond, 3 Campden Terrace, Linden Gardens, London
77 Z.J. Mugaseth, 7 Ivere Drive, Barnet
78 Douglas D. McBee, IS Division, SHAPE, BFPO 26
79 Miss R.M. Carty, 33 Gladys Avenue, North End, Portsmouth
80 S.M. Maude, 8 Olicana Park, Ilkley, Yorkshire
81 Michael Matthews, 4 Cadogan Gate, London
82 I. Scott Small, 10 Meadowood Drive, Stoughton, MA, U.S.A.
83 Julie S. Lord, 650 Bement Avenue, Staten Island, New York, U.S.A.
84 Karen Snyder, 33 Waverly Place, Baldwin, Long Island, New York, U.S.A.
85 Barbara Brandes, 5233 McKinley Parkway, Hamburg, New York, U.S.A.

86 Miss Maude D. French, Box 214, Hanover, New Hampshire, U.S.A.
87 Terry Elizabeth Deer, 1107 Richmond Road, Apt. C. Williamsburg, Virginia, U.S.A.
88 Curtis L. Taub, 11990 Duncan Street, San Jose, California, U.S.A.
89 Janice Patterson, P.O. Box 16132, Phoenix, Arizona, U.S.A.
90 Jean G. Howe, 89 Westmorland Road, Urmston, Manchester
91 M.J. McMullen, 407 Highland Avenue, Grove City, PA, U.S.A.
92 John J. Murphy, 11 Warmington Street, Paddington, Queensland, Australia
93 Robert Du Rard, 126 Clark Drive, San Mateo, California, U.S.A.
94 Ernest B. Holmwood, 32659 Simpson Lane, Fort Bragg, California, U.S.A.
95 Dr. Joanne Simpson, P.O. Drawer 5508, Charlottesville, Virginia, U.S.A.
96 Richard III Society, Melbourne, Australia Branch
97 Susan Pashaian, 45-39 171 Place, Flushing, New York, U.S.A.
98 G.H. Bailey, 90 Cambridge Gardens, London
99 Mrs. Janet Reynolds, 58 Coronation Way, Comberton, Kidderminster, Worcestershire
100 Mrs. L.M. Phillips, 9 Trafalgar Avenue, Poynton, Cheshire
101 Peter J. Ong, 19 Sturges Field, Chislehurst, Kent
102 Susan Douglas, 239 Edgwarebury Lane, Edgware, Middlesex
103 Robert & Susan Fitter, Rake Villa, Rake Lane, Hawarden, Deeside, Clwyd
104 Lynne M. Galpin, 13 St. Mary's Close, Bottesford, Nottingham
105 Miss S.J. Empson, 12 Lichfield Road, Northwood, Middlesex
106 Mr. R.G. Doughty, 7 Church Croft, Bramshall, Uttoxeter, Staffordshire
107 Mrs. M.R. Talbot, 73 Lechmere Avenue, Woodford Green, Essex
108 Lorraine Freeman, 33 Alconbury Road, Clapton, London
109 Mr. S.F.J. Brooks, 50 Goodhart Way, West Wickahm, Kent
110 Revd. Thomas C.H. Clare, Saxelbye Rectory, Melton Mowbray, Leicestershire
111 Patrick J. Sharpe, West End, Harlaxton, Grantham, Lincolnshire
112 Joanne Claire Stone, 10 Thorn Park, Mannamead, Plymouth
113 June Frances Galley, 15 Lune Way, Ditton, Widnes, Cheshire
114 Janet M. Stonestreet, Greengates, Turkey Hall Lane, Bacton, Nr. Stowmarket, Suffolk
115 Mrs. Shirley Castle, 26 Heather Close, Copthorne, Crawley, Sussex
116 Ms. Lois M. Ray, 22 Cresswell Road, S. Norwood, London
117 Mrs. I.E. Pross, Iona, 124 Wellsway, Bath, Avon
118 Mrs. A.J. Puddy, 57 Wash Road, Hutton, Brentwood, Essex
119 Mrs. John De Gaynesford, Snail Hall, Polstead, Colchester, Essex
120 G.M.A. Sells, Pump Cottage, Wyaston, Nr. Ashbourne, Derbyshire
121 Claire Turnill, 14 The Oak, London Road, Bracknell, Berkshire
122 Mrs. Ruth Richmond, 76 Harrow Road, West Bridgford, Nottingham
123 Mrs. Mary Boyd, Pensione Crocini, Corso Italia, Firenze, Italy
124 Myra Morales, P.O. Box 1215, Poughkeepsie, New York, U.S.A.
125 Daphne M. Williams, 8 The Heights, 165 Mountview Road, London
126 Frede Solve, B.A., 59 Jagive, 5000 Odense C., Denmark
127 G.J. Honig, 32 Hooestraat, Koog a/d Zaan, Netherlands
128 Bruce R. Galloway, 14 Briers Gardens, Hastings
129 Karl Michael Eising, Freiherr vom Stein-Str.1, 425 Bottrop, West Germany
130 Joy Elizabeth Barrowclough, 26 Kingsley Drive, Adel, Leeds
131 Jeremy Potter, 41 Woodsford Square, London
132 Robert Downes, 14 New House Farm Lane, Wood Street, Guildford, Surrey

DATE DUE
